T0159132

# PRAISE FOR *MCB*
## from
## The World's Leading Authority on Natural Bond Orbitals

**From:** weinhold@chem.wisc.edu
**Subject:** **MOLECULES and the Chemical Bond**
**Date:** August 1, 2013 3:29:09 PM EDT
**To:** henry.abent@gmail.com

Dear Henry,

Thanks indeed for the completed *MCB* volume and your (too) many
kind references to NBO theory. The species chosen for discussion
are fascinating. I would love to think of working through the
NBOs of all your examples, sitting side by side with you to search
for the possible connections with your conceptual VB formulations.
Realistically, life is probably too short, and other obligations
too demanding, for this to be possible. But I hope there can be
further opportunities (similar to Roald's dimer hunt) where
the messiness of full NBO analysis can be compared with the
elegance of your insights[*] for mutually constructive resonances.
With best regards from Madison,

Frank

Frank A. Weinhold                    e-mail: weinhold@chem.wisc.edu
Department of Chemistry         voice: (608)262-0263
University of Wisconsin            fax: (608)262-9918
Madison, Wisconsin 53706      office: Room 8305H, Chemistry

* Based on examination of Valence Sphere Models of Molecules.

# More Praise for *MCB*

An excellent treatise on Conceptual Valence Bond Theory.

—PROFESSOR TERRY COLLINS, *Carnegie Mellon University*

The author's contributions to the field have been and continue to be monumental.

—PROFESSOR DIANE BUNCE, *The Catholic University of America*

A delightful collection of essays, philosophy, and wisdom. I enjoyed the forward by the author's daughter. I, too, grew up with a chemist father and eventually ended up in the same discipline.

—PROFESSOR CHERYL FRECH, *Central Oklahoma University*

Bent's discourse is fascinating and thorough. There is almost a narrative feel to it. Interested readers will be enthralled by its short paragraphs and diagrams. A great supplement for college students going through their chemistry courses. Anyone with an ounce of interest in valence theory will find this a must have book.

THE US REVIEW OF BOOKS

The "Best of Bent". A collection of Henry's wonderful explanations and musings from the 60's and 70's, and beyond. Look up Bent's rule on the web and you'll see the deep expertise of this author in this area. Much more than just bonding, including the philosophy of induction and invention. A true FUN read and page-turner, covering the collective wisdom of an amazing career. VERY reader friendly.

From reviews of the five major specialty titles on the subject of chemical bonds most frequently purchased by university and graduate libraries, May 24, 2013

# MOLECULES
## and
# The Chemical Bond

## An Introduction to Conceptual Valence Bond Theory
### An Exclusive Orbital Model of Semi-Localized Electrons
*The Shortest and Simplest Route to Electron Density Profiles*

*A Chemical Mechanics of Close Confederations
of Atomic Cores and Wave-Like Fermions*

$$\Psi(1, 2, \ldots) = -\Psi(2, 1, \ldots)$$
$$\rightarrow$$
$$\Psi(1, 1, \ldots) = 0$$

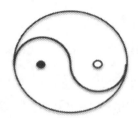

Dots to Domains
*New Life for Lewis Structures*

How Far One Can Go from an
Exclusive Orbital Perspective

*A Conceptual Companion to
Computational Valence Theory*

## Volume II
Fourth Edition

# Henry A. Bent

Order this book online at www.trafford.com
or email orders@trafford.com

Most Trafford titles are also available at major online book retailers.

© Copyright 2013 Henry A. Bent.
All rights reserved. No part of this publication may be reproduced, stored in a retrieval system, or transmitted, in any form or by
any means, electronic, mechanical, photocopying, recording, or otherwise, without the written prior permission of the author.

Print information available on the last page.

ISBN: 978-1-4907-1394-6 (sc)
ISBN: 978-1-4907-1407-3 (e)

Library of Congress Control Number: 2013917259

Because of the dynamic nature of the Internet, any web addresses or links contained in this book may have changed
since publication and may no longer be valid. The views expressed in this work are solely those of the author and do
not necessarily reflect the views of the publisher, and the publisher hereby disclaims any responsibility for them.

Any people depicted in stock imagery provided by Thinkstock are models,
and such images are being used for illustrative purposes only.
Certain stock imagery © Thinkstock.

*Trafford rev. 02/11/2015*

**Trafford** PUBLISHING®   www.trafford.com

**North America & international**
toll-free: 1 888 232 4444 (USA & Canada)
fax: 812 355 4082

# ALTERNATIVE TITLES

*The hardest thing to do is to convey the sense of a great idea* [in a few words].

POINCARE [augmented]

Exclusive Orbital Theory
Old Wine in New Bottles
Electron Density Profiles
Semi-Localized Electrons
The Genius of G. N. Lewis
Valence Theory Simplified
Valence Theory in a New Key
Bonding across the Periodic Table
The Organic Chemists Were Right!
Frontier Orbital Theory at a Glance
An Electride Ion Model of Molecules
Criticisms of Conceptual MO Theory
New Life for Classical Bond Diagrams
Ionic Models of Covalent Compounds
Exclusive Orbital Models of Molecules
Valence Theories' Oracles and Editors
A Greening of Classical Valence Theory
Making Sense of Schrödinger's Equation
Valence Theory without Atomic Orbitals
From Electron Dots to Electron Domains
Fitting Bond Diagrams to Experimental Data
Geometrical Methods in Valence Bond Theory
Simple Models of Localized Molecular Orbitals
Chemical Bonding from a Unified Point of View
A Chemical Mechanics of the Exclusion Principle
Chemical Implications of Matter's Impenetrability
Simple Models of Molecular Electron Density Profiles
Models of Localized Bonding and Antibonding Orbitals
The Theory of the Valence Stroke and the Valence Sphere
Valency and Bonding from an Exclusive Orbital Perspective
Theory and Uses of Molecular Models of Unrivaled Simplicity
Chemical Bonding and Molecular Geometry Simply Explained
Covalent, Ionic, and Metallic Bonding from a Unified Point of View
Valence Stroke Diagrams and Valence Sphere Models of Molecules
Stereochemical Implications of Exclusive Orbital Models of Molecules
Lewis' Zero-Dimensional Dots Inflated to Three-Dimensional Domains
An Introduction to the Inductions of Conceptual Valence Bond Theory
Implications of the Antisymmmetric Character of $\Psi$ for Valence Theory
Zero-, One-, and Three-dimensional Models of Localized Molecular Orbitals
Valence Theory for Newcomers to Chemical Thought and Its Connoisseurs
A Self-Help Book for Acquiring an Intuitive Understanding of Valence Theory
The Saturation and Directional Character of Chemical Affinity Simply Explained
The Endless Stereochemical Possibilities of Valence Sphere Models of Molecules
An Introduction to the Theory and Uses of Exclusive Orbital Models of Molecules
The Role of the Indistinguishability of Electrons in Conceptual Valence Bond Theory

*[W]e have no other evidence of universal Impenetrability
besides a large Experience without an experimental Exception.*

NEWTON

*Above all I love my analogies.*

KEPLER

*The real glory of science is that we can find ways
of thinking such that its laws seem self-evident.*

*Sometimes it's useful to see how little theoretical
machinery one needs to obtain a given result.*

RICHARD FEYNMAN

*If I have had any success in theoretical physics,
it has been by avoiding mathematical difficulties.*

J. WILLARD GIBBS

*When you get hold of the right end of the stick,
nice things tend to happen.*

WM. BRAGG

*To achieve successful innovations in science,
change as little as possible.* HEISENBERG

*Change dots to domains and
valence strokes to valence spheres.* KIMBALL

*But whether electrons occupy exclusive domains or not,
this much is certain, granting that that be so, molecules
would appear much as they now do.*

DALTON, slightly paraphrased

Some quotations are from memory.

Dedicated to Gilbert N. Lewis, for taking the first step in the valence-stroke's journey to a valence sphere, and to George Kimball, for taking the last step (in asking: What's the simplest quantum mechanical model of molecules?),

and to students, teachers, and professionals in the pure and applied sciences who might welcome accounts of molecular structure that, in Einstein's words, are as simple as possible but [it's believed] no simpler and that provide, thereby, in Gibbs' words, points of view from which its topics appears in their greatest simplicity.

The accounts concern the central concern of the central science. After one has settled with Dalton issues regarding existence of atoms, the next question is: What is the nature of the chemical bond between them in molecules?

# "It can't be that simple!"

A remark overheard following a physical chemistry seminar at the University of Minnesota, 1962, on "Tangent Sphere Models of Molecules".

Expressed is the belief that the models violate Einstein's second admonition regarding simplicity. Illustrated is a need for an account of the models that champions their unrivaled simplicity and their extraordinary explanatory power, expressed in a nutshell by one word: *coordination*, of anionic, exclusive, localized, valence shell electron domains of *finite size* by smaller cationic atomic cores located in interstices of surrounding close-packed electron domains.

Seen at a glance, without recourse to atomic orbitals and associated complexities of Schrödinger's equation (the only source of atomic orbitals), are simple, spatial reasons for chemical affinities' chief features: its saturation and its directional character.

Created is a stereochemical mechanics based on a fundamental Principle of Electronic Spatial Exclusion. Featured, for easy, visual analysis of inter- and intra-molecular electron-pair donor-acceptor interactions is, with this volume's companion volume, the world's largest library of drawings of three-dimensional models of molecular electron density profiles generated by simply replacing noncrossing valence strokes of classical bond diagrams of organic chemistry by mutually impenetrable valence spheres analogous to the monatomic anions of ion-packing models of structural inorganic chemistry.

Produced is a geometrical expression of the physical fact that electrons of like spin tend to avoid each other.

*"This effect is most powerful,"* wrote a famous quantum mechanician over half a century ago, *"much more powerful than that of electrostatic forces. It does more to determine the shapes and properties of molecules than any other single factor. It is the exclusion principle which plays the dominant role in chemistry* [and this book]. *Its all-pervading influence does not seem hitherto to have been fully realized by chemists, but it is safe to say that ultimately it will be regarded as the most important property to be learned by those concerned with molecular structure."* J. Lennard-Jones, Adv. Sci. *11*, 136 (1954).

A case in point: A textbook for a course in inorganic chemistry taken by one of the author's grandsons as a senior chemistry major at a well-known liberal arts college features a huge dose of molecular orbital theory without mention, *anywhere*, of the Exclusion Principle! A flower may have its greatest flowering, it's said, shortly before it dies.

Owing to the role of the exclusion principle in this book, beginning with its front cover, it's believed that the book's account of molecular structure is, broadly speaking, destined to stand the test of time for so long as it is the case that methane molecules are tetrahedral, their valence shells are occupied by four pairs of electrons, and for so long as, owing to Nature's nature, the arrangement of four close-packed spheres is tetrahedral.

# THE BACK STORY
## *Evolution of the Electride Ion*

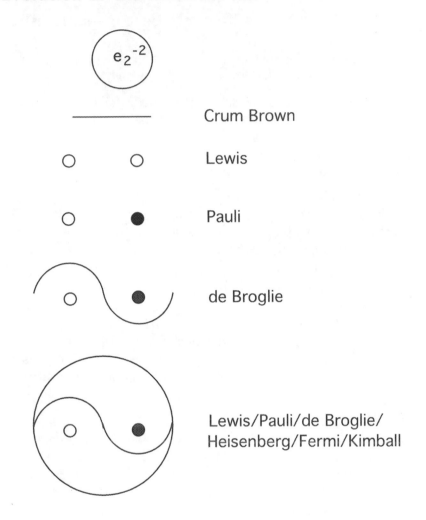

$e_2^{-2}$

——————— Crum Brown

○　　　○ Lewis

○　　　● Pauli

○　　　● de Broglie

○　　　● Lewis/Pauli/de Broglie/
Heisenberg/Fermi/Kimball

**Crum Brown:** Mutual saturation of atoms' combining capacities can be represented by valence strokes.

**Lewis:** A valence-stroke represents two particle-like, countable electrons.

**Pauli:** Electrons have a "classically indescribable two-valuedness", called "spin".

**de Broglie:** Electrons have a wave-like character.

**Lewis/Pauli/de Broglie/Heisenberg/Fermi/Kimball:** Electrons obey a Principle of Spatial Exclusion. Two electrons of the same spin cannot be at the same place — nor even, for practical purposes, suggest the facts of chemistry, in the same general region of space — at the same time.

## SYNOPSIS
# The Versatile Valence Sphere

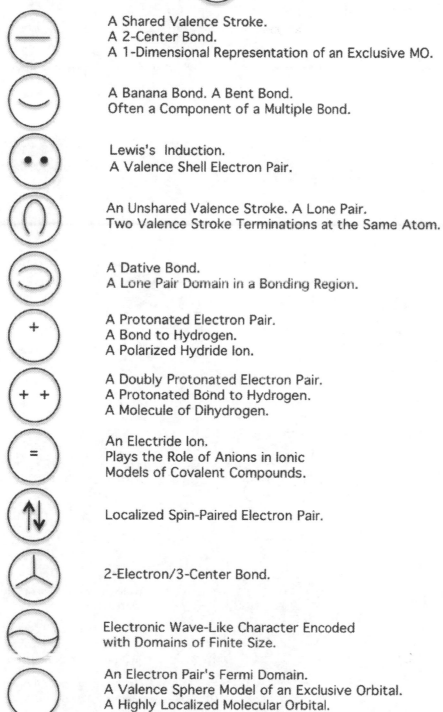

A Shared Valence Stroke.
A 2-Center Bond.
A 1-Dimensional Representation of an Exclusive MO.

A Banana Bond. A Bent Bond.
Often a Component of a Multiple Bond.

Lewis's Induction.
A Valence Shell Electron Pair.

An Unshared Valence Stroke. A Lone Pair.
Two Valence Stroke Terminations at the Same Atom.

A Dative Bond.
A Lone Pair Domain in a Bonding Region.

A Protonated Electron Pair.
A Bond to Hydrogen.
A Polarized Hydride Ion.

A Doubly Protonated Electron Pair.
A Protonated Bond to Hydrogen.
A Molecule of Dihydrogen.

An Electride Ion.
Plays the Role of Anions in Ionic
Models of Covalent Compounds.

Localized Spin-Paired Electron Pair.

2-Electron/3-Center Bond.

Electronic Wave-Like Character Encoded
with Domains of Finite Size.

An Electron Pair's Fermi Domain.
A Valence Sphere Model of an Exclusive Orbital.
A Highly Localized Molecular Orbital.
A "Loge" (Daudel).

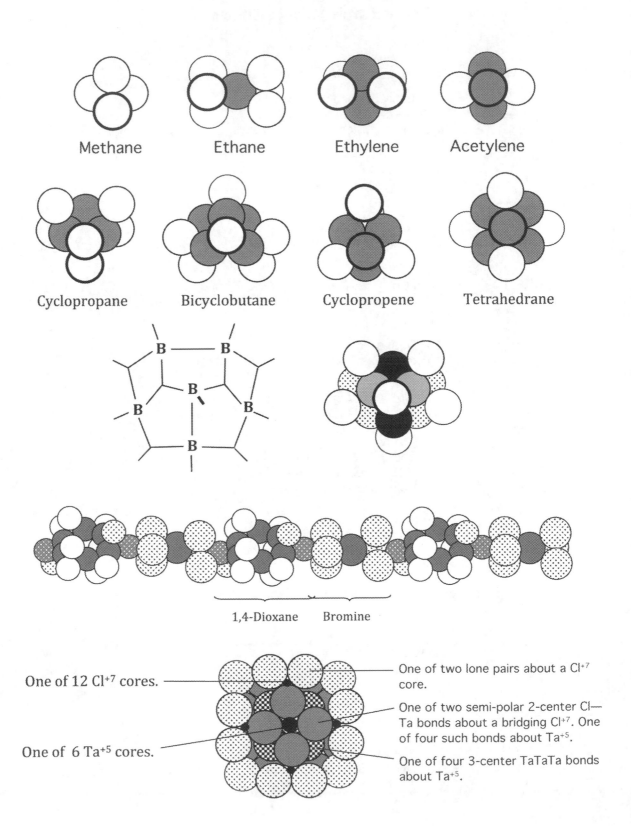

Methane

Ethane

Ethylene

Acetylene

Cyclopropane

Bicyclobutane

Cyclopropene

Tetrahedrane

1,4-Dioxane    Bromine

One of 12 Cl$^{+7}$ cores.

One of 6 Ta$^{+5}$ cores.

One of two lone pairs about a Cl$^{+7}$ core.

One of two semi-polar 2-center Cl—Ta bonds about a bridging Cl$^{+7}$. One of four such bonds about Ta$^{+5}$.

One of four 3-center TaTaTa bonds about Ta$^{+5}$.

# FOREWORD

## Excerpts from *Valency and Bonding* by Weinhold and Landis

Chemistry is, in large part, the science of molecular profiles: their nucleophilic bumps and electrophilic dimples. Two methods exist for creating pictures of those profiles: Computational Valence Theory, using Schrödinger's expression of electrons' wave-like character ($H\Psi = E\Psi$) in conjunction with Heisenberg's expression of electrons' indistinguishability [$\Psi(1, 2, . . .) = - \Psi(2, 1, , . . .)$], followed by an electron localization procedure; and Conceptual Valence Bond Theory, using at the outset exclusive orbital models of molecules derived from classical bond diagrams by substitution of three-dimensional spheres for one-dimensional valence strokes. Remarks regarding the computational method, by Weinhold and Landis in their book *Valency and Bonding: A Natural Bond Orbital Donor-Acceptor Perspective* (Cambridge, 2005), serve, virtually word for word, as a foreword for the present nonmathematical companion to their book, which serves as a bridge between quantitative and qualitative aspects of Valence Theory.

- Our principle goal has been to translate the deepest truths of the Schrödinger equation into a visualizable, intuitive form that "makes sense" even for beginning students.

- The emphasis is on orbital diagrams and "doing quantum mechanics with pictures".

- The book contains a considerable amount of previously unpublished material that we believe to be of broad pedagogical interest.

- We hope to sharpen, revitalize, and enhance the usefulness of qualitative bonding concepts.

- The book reflects the influence of a "donor-acceptor" perspective.

- Emphasis is placed on individual chemical species that hold special fascination for students of bonding theory.

- In the present work we generally restrict attention to molecular ground states.

- In practice the chemist seldom requires numerically exact answers to chemical questions. [Usually required are qualitative, topological diagrams.]

- One must recognize the two possible orientations of the intrinsic "spin" angular momentum of each electron.

- Furthermore we must insure that the total electronic wave function is antisymmetric as required by the *Pauli exclusion principle*.

- The primary goal of a [quantitative] theory of valency and bonding is to find the model Hamiltonian that most simply describes the broad panorama of chemical bonding phenomena.

- The fundamental starting point for a rational theory of valency and bonding is the Lewis-structure representations of the shared and unshared electrons in each atomic valence configuration.

- Our viewpoint is deeply tied to traditional bonding concepts. It takes advantage of a model Hamiltonian that describes localized electron-pairs.

- The change from a "countable" to a "continuous" picture of electron distribution is one of the most paradoxical (but necessary) conceptual steps to take in visualizing chemical phenomena in orbital terms.

- Vacant orbitals [the dimples of exclusive orbital models] represent an atom's *capacity for change*.

- Becoming familiar with the shapes [and locations] of vacant orbitals is an essential key to understanding the give and take of chemical bonding .

- It is a quite remarkable feature of quantum-mechanical superposition that a low-lying filled orbital [an exposed exclusive orbital] can further lower its energy by mixing with a *higher*-energy [dimple or] unoccupied orbital.

- The general capacity of atomic and molecular species to make judicious use of available filled and unfilled orbitals [through electron-pair donor-acceptor interactions] is a fundamental guiding principle of chemical valency and bonding.

- Natural bond orbitals can be used to represent exactly any property of a system on localized terms

- "Lewis-type" Natural Bond Orbitals of highest occupancy can be directly associated with the localized electron pairs of the chemist's *Lewis-structure* diagram.

- The set of Lewis-type NBOs [Natural Bond Orbitals] typically include a one center core and a valence lone pair as well as two-center bond orbitals.

- NBO-based models provide a framework for analyzing chemical phenomena in terms of familiar Lewis-structural concept.

- Attractive donor-acceptor interactions between Lewis-type (filled) and Lewis-type (vacant) valence NBOs provide a unifying *leitmotif* that governs many valency and bonding phenomena.


Occupied Lewis-type NBOs correspond to valence sphere models' exclusive, localized, electron-pair *domains*. Vacant NBOs correspond to the models' *dimples*.

Electron pair donor-acceptor interactions correspond to occupancy of dimples by exposed domains of ring domains of small ring species: namely, lone pairs, of one-member rings; and bonding pairs, of two-member rings, of multiple bonds; and occasionally ring bonds of three-member rings.

# A Daughter's Foreword
## for
## *Molecules and the Chemical Bond, Volume I*

This book is the culmination of my Father's insights into the molecules he has literally breathed, consumed, and digested, for the past 84 years. It is his intimate knowledge about the elements, learned from a lifetime of reading, experimenting, and teaching that makes this book different. Dad truly loves (and believes in!) molecules, and that single tenet comes across on every page. Flat valence stroke diagrams are inflated to three dimensional valence sphere models whose geometries correlate with observations and calculations and provide, with ease, explanations for reaction mechanisms, multicenter bonds, and molecular geometries considered "exceptions" or "unexpected". Describing molecules as "electron deficient" or "hypervalent" suggests something abnormal or unnatural, and is misleading since "nature is always natural". Concepts, principles, models, and rules are presented from historical perspectives with logical rigor, eliminating inconsistencies that bug you as a chemistry student, but you can't really put your finger on why. From the correct placement of helium above beryllium in the periodic table, to pointing out the problems with omitting nucleus-electron attractions in the popular Valence Shell Electron Pair Repulsion theory (where "correct conclusions regarding molecular shapes support an incorrect conceptual model"), this book challenges many of the generally accepted concepts taught in chemistry courses, shaking up the establishment, and demanding rigor in the presentation of the subject.

Teaching has been HAB's life. Children learn their mother tongues from mothers and other linguists who point and tell; likewise, pointing and telling should be the way to introduce students to chemistry's new terms for new concepts. Dad practiced this philosophy by teaching from demonstration-experiments in his teaching at the University of Connecticut, University of Minnesota, North Carolina State University, University of Pittsburgh, and, most recently, in exposing thousands of young students to chemical demonstrations taken to schools in "van programs". During these van visits, he and the students were most excited when things didn't go as expected, and together they had to figure out why. Rave reviews came in from jazzed kids, their parents, and teachers (even after shutting down a school from a powerful explosion of a balloon filled with a hydrogen and oxygen mixture, sending years of accumulated soot from Pittsburgh's steel-making days off gym rafters, at which point "you couldn't see your hand in front of your face").

HAB's interest in chemistry comes naturally. His Father loved the subject, and never tired of posing questions: will the candle in this lantern extinguish if we drop the lantern into free-fall? (This question was the focal point of many discussions and experiments one summer at our family-built log cabin in northern Minnesota, and was subsequently incorporated into Dad's class curriculum.) Chemists from my Grandfather's era blew their own glassware and ran experiments without high tech instrumentation. Their hands-on experiments gave them a chance to get to know the elements and marvel at their properties. This sense of awe and wonder and exploration was passed along to his son, and is what seems to get lost in the hurry to teach all the "required" concepts in chemistry texts and classes today. My Grandfather wisely recognized that a love of the subject is the most important thing. When young Henry came home from school, excited that his teacher had taken something to absolute zero, his Father did not correct the teacher's obvious blunder, but recognized that the important thing was that Henry was excited about it! This philosophy was passed along as Dad's own son, my brother, Brian, came home from high school saying they couldn't run an experiment because the teacher couldn't find the required 1-inch test tubes (apparently searching for 1-inch long test tubes). The teacher was not a chemistry ace, but wisely assigned his students the job of teaching fellow students, and Brian went on to teach chemistry at Columbia University and to love the subject as much as his Father and Grandfather did.

You can't be around HAB long before his enthusiasm for some chemistry topic tumbles out. When I was in high school taking my first chemistry class, Dad often used our 5-mile before-school runs as a dry "run" for his own chemistry class lectures. One morning, tired and exasperated that I couldn't follow the day's lecture, I ran up the hills particularly hard so he would have to stop talking for a few minutes. Alas, with all the training he did with my brother, he was in far better shape than I, and never missed a beat in his "lecture". Dad went on to run a sub 3-hour marathon while in his middle 50's.

Widely read (always making notes in the margins), there is no topic in which Dad will not enthusiastically engage, offering insights and asking questions. Family, running, canoeing, hiking, sports, music, the list of interests goes on, but ultimately, it comes back to his love of chemistry, his love for the atoms and molecules that make up every thing, and his desire to pass along new insights into this fascinating atomic world to the rest of us.

Libby Weberg
East Aurora, NY
March 2011

# AUTHOR'S PREFACE

*MOLECULES and the Chemical Bond* follows in the footsteps of the fathers of *visual thinking in chemistry*, beginning with Dalton's atomic hypothesis, followed by Archibald Couper and Crum Brown's efforts to account from a unitary point of view (as in *MCB*) for the greatest number of facts in the simplest possible manner, with bond diagrams, and continuing with Kekule and van't Hoff's easily grasped physical models of molecules, which make many chemical facts clear, even obvious.

George Polya's classic *How to Solve It* has influenced *MCB's* content. Polya ends his suggestions on how to solve mathematical problems with a question: *Can you see the solution at a glance?* It's the inspiration for two of *MCB's* leading features: line drawings, scannable at a glance, and many short, often one-page, single-topic essays, *easily scannable*. Continuity of thought arises from repeated use of a small number of Primary and Secondary Structural Principles of Modern Conceptual Valence Bond Theory.

The book's novel outlook challenges conventional wisdom and may change how chemists and chemical educators think about chemistry. It leads to simple explanations of unusual molecular geometries and to unique critiques of conceptual MO Theory, VSEPR Theory, and the concept of "antiaromaticity". By focusing on fundamental physical principles and avoiding use of atomic orbitals and attendant mathematical difficulties arising from Schrödinger's equation (the only source of atomic orbitals), it yields scientifically sound, student-friendly discussions of modern valence theory.

The adjective "Modern" in the phrase "Modern Conceptual Valence Bond Theory" refers to frequent use of a Generalized Bond Number Equation, a Valence Stroke Termination Rule, Electron-Pair Donor-Acceptor Interactions, Different Structures for Different Spin Sets, the s-Character Rule, a new notation for Dative Bonds, Multicenter Bonds, and Valence Sphere Models of Molecules. The adjective "Conceptual" refers to the emphasis on concepts over numerical calculations and, accordingly, on the role of imagination in the formation of an inductive science's inductions.

*Modern Conceptual Valence Bond Theory endows classical valence theory with new life.* By substituting valence spheres for the valence strokes of classical valence stroke diagrams and for the dots of Lewis dot diagrams, it makes the new (valence sphere models) familiar and the familiar (bond diagrams and Lewis structures) new, as first steps in creation of models of *molecular electron density profiles* for understanding at a glance the saturation and directional character of primary and secondary chemical affinities and, accordingly, for understanding molecular geometries, locations within molecules of leading nucleophilic and electrophilic sites and, consequently, for understanding inter- and intra-molecular electron-pair donor-acceptor interactions, and reaction mechanisms. *Conceptual Valence Bond Theory stands alone, it's believed, as chemistry's only truly stand-alone, **qualitative** theory of molecular structure.*

# Author's Preface for the Third Edition of *MCB II*

Science changes. It's a work in progress. Books about it often appear in multiple editions. This third edition of the second volume of *Molecules and the Chemical Bond* extends previous reports of the explanatory power of molecular electron density profiles produced by replacing valence strokes of valence stroke diagrams by space-filling valence spheres, in the belief that the greater the volume and variety of a theory's successful applications, the greater confidence in the theory.

For the convenience of readers who may be familiar with previous editions of this book, new material is located in one place, near the end (pages 261 – 293). Were the book's contents arranged throughout logically, rather than, finally, chronologically, it might begin with these essays from its additional set:

*A Thesis, Antithesis, and Synthesis 261*
*Induction of Wave Functions' Antisymmetric Property 262*
*Leading Evidence for Exclusive Orbital Models of Electron Density Profiles 263*
*Electron Localization: by Induction and Deduction 264*
*Organic Stereochemistry: The Story on One Page! 265*
*Exclusive Orbital and Molecular Orbital Models of $CH_4$, $NH_3$, $H_2O$, and HF 266*
*Geometrical Models of Primary and Secondary Chemical Affinities 267*
*BEYOND HYDROGEN: An Explanatory Note 268*

The book's discussion of its central theme (localized exclusive orbital models of molecules in their ground states) leads naturally to critiques of its alleged competition: delocalized, non-exclusive orbital models of molecules, a.k.a. "Conceptual MO Theory". That theory is deemed to be an incomplete theory of molecular structure, in that, in and of itself, it has no way of indicating where the orbitals of its method of construction of molecular orbitals, from linear combinations of atomic orbitals, *are!* (except by execution of a complete calculation using the Variation Theorem, starting from scratch with no knowledge whatsoever of where the atoms are, which, for most multi-atomic systems, is generally deemed to be impractical). Also, in its initial formation of its orbitals, Conceptual MO Theory takes no account whatsoever of the Exclusion Principle. And moreover -

From the standpoint of Exclusive Orbital Theory, *Conceptual MO Theory is paradoxical.* For it seems illogical to hold in mind the idea that –

(1) Electrons are *indistinguishable fermions* with, accordingly, antisymmetric wave functions that, therefore, vanish if two electrons of the same spin are at the same place at the same time, which would seem to indicate that electronic wave functions have *to some degree* exclusive orbital character; but then, *simultaneously,* to hold in mind (to repeat) a picture of electronic structure in which –

(2) Individual fermions reside in *delocalized* orbitals *spread out over entire molecules!*

True, approximate orbital exclusivity may be, in a purely mathematical sense, slight: yet, perhaps, significant? There's a way to find out. *Experiment!* Try replacing non-intersecting valence strokes of classical valence stroke diagrams with mutually exclusive valence spheres. The result? This book.

# Author's Preface for this Fourth Edition of *MCB II*

In 1905 Einstein published three famous papers: one on his Theory of Relativity, for which he became famous world wide; one on his interpretation of the photoelectric effect, for which he received a Nobel Prize, in 1921; and one on his prediction of a phenomenon called "Brownian motion", his most often-cited paper, of which he said:

> *"My major aim was to find facts which would guarantee as much as possible the existence of atoms of finite size."*

Similarly -

> *The major aim of MCB has been to marshal facts which guarantee as much as possible the existence in molecular ground states of exclusive molecular electron pair domains of finite size.*

The chief fact in support of a theory of exclusive molecular electron pair domains is the ultimate justification for any physical theory.

> *It works!*

With a "Starter Kit" of two spheres and two pre-assembled trigonal sphere-sets, one can exhibit, almost magically, in a few moments, so simply that, in words of a poet (Szymborska), a smile would do to describe a viewers response to the charming creation of approximate electron density profiles for methane (3+1), ethane (3+1+3), ethene (3+3), ethyne (1+3+1), and species isoelectronic with those molecules. Additional features of the stereochemistry of the chemically active elements of the first row of the *p*-block of periodic tables (B, C, N, O, and F) are largely logical extensions of the locations of substituents about the single, double, and triple bonds of those molecules (page 1).

Seldom in science has so much been achieved so simply.

The physical basis of those results is expressed perhaps most directly by the fact that dhydrogen gas has a finite molar volume, however high the pressure, which suggests that *two electrons can occupy the same region of space at the same time* (as, e.g., in a molecule of dihydrogen, H—H) *but not three electrons. Consequently,* <u>*two electron pairs*</u> *cannot be at the same place at the same time.*

As in Huckel Theory, simplicity arrives on setting certain molecular orbital overlap integrals equal to zero. That's indefensible, of course, save for the fact that the results it gives are surprisingly good.

One result, distinctive of this fourth edition of *MCB II,* is a set of refined proposals for graphic representation of the prototypical dative bond, between boron and nitrogen in the molecular complex $H_3B \cdot NH_3$ (page 288). Other new material includes: Lennard-Jones' remarks regarding the primacy in valence theory of the Exclusion Principle (page viii), Einstein's remark regarding the aim of his paper on Brownian motion (this page), Planck's remarks regarding reception of new ideas (pages xxi and 252), the Role of the Tetrahedron in Chemical Thought (page xxiii), A Simple Resolution of an embarrassment of Riches (294), Complementary Features of Computational and Conceptual Valence Theory (295), and the book's concluding essays: Errors of Omission and Commission in Chemical Thought (311-313), 3-Electron Bonds (314), Epilogue (315), and the Triangle of Valence Theory (329).

Comments welcomed.

Henry.ABent@gmail.com
Pittsburgh, PA

# INTRODUCTION

## "Riveting"*

I was going home to dinner, past a shallow pool, which was green with springing grass, . . . when it occurred to me that I heard the dream of the toad. It rang through and filled all the air, though I had not heard it once. And I turned my companion's attention to it, but he did not appear to perceive it as a new sound in the air. Loud and prevailing as it is, most men do not notice it at all. It is to them sort of a simmering and seething of all nature. That afternoon the dream of the toad rang through the elms of Little River and affected the thoughts of men, though they were not conscious that they heard it. How watchful we must be to keep the crystal well that we are made, clear!

THOREAU

A "dream of the toad" rings through chemical journals and fills their pages. Most readers do not notice it at all. It is to them sort of a simmering and seething of Nature's chemical nature. It affects their thoughts, though they may not be conscious that -

> Valence strokes of valence stroke diagrams
> represent occupancy by electron pairs
> of exclusive localized molecular orbitals
> whose profiles, suggest molecular structures,
> are often approximately spherical.

Produced is a chemical mechanics of close confederations of atomic cores and space-filling Fermions that yields at once leading features of chemical thought, particularly the saturation and directional character chemical affinity.

"How watchful we must be," adds Thoreau, "to keep the crystal well that we are made, clear!"

* Joel Liebman. Not to be taken to mean that Liebman believes that the entire document is "riveting". It's not. Some of its longer essays may, indeed, be a bit boring. They're included to illustrate, in some instances, the detail regarding reaction mechanisms that valence sphere models may provide.

# Memorandum

**To:**      Chemistry Students and their Teachers
**Subject:** The Planck Phenomenon Regarding Reception of New Ideas

**Planck's Lament.** In his *Scientific Autobiography*, Planck wrote: *"It was one of the most painful experiences of my entire scientific life that I have but seldom—in fact, I might say, never—succeeded in gaining universal recognition for a new result, the truth of which I could demonstrate by a conclusive albeit only theoretical proof. . . All my sound arguments fell on deaf ears. It was simply impossible to be heard against the authority of men like Ostwald, Helm, and Mach."*

**Likewise:** *Gaining universal recognition for the usefulness of electron density <u>profiles</u> created by replacement of valence strokes of conventional valence stroke diagrams by valence spheres has failed for over half a century. Arguments for use of **exclusive** orbitals,*
such as, e.g., the fact that -

- $\psi(x_1, x_2, . . .) = - \psi(x_2, x_1, . . .)$ implies, with mathematical rigor, that two electrons of the <u>same spin</u> cannot be at the same place at the same time, and, thus, that molecular wave functions have to some degree exclusive orbital character; and the fact that -

- $H_2$, He, and LiH have **finite molar volumes**, however high the pressure, which implies that two electron pairs cannot be at the same place at the same time; and, additionally, -

- Lewis's identification of the noncrossing valence strokes of classical structural theory as electron pairs implies, yet again, a Principle of Mutual Exclusion for electron pairs; and the fact that -

- use of exclusive localized electron pair domains creates a deep analogy in valence theory, in which cations of ionic compounds stand to their coordinated anions as atomic cores in covalent compounds stand to their coordinated electron pair domains

*have fallen on deaf ears. It has been simply impossible to be heard against the authority of Mulliken and other experts on the theory of **nonexclusive, delocalized** molecular orbitals.*

**Planck's Enlightenment.** *"My experience,"* said Planck, *"gave me an opportunity to learn a fact—a remarkable one, in my opinion: A new scientific truth does not triumph by convincing its opponents and making them see the light, but rather because its opponents eventually die, and a new generation grows up that is familiar with it."*

> Linus Pauling's response to "Tangent Sphere Models of Molecules" illustrated Planck's "new scientific truth". The author of "Pauing's Rules of Crystal Chemistry" would welcome, it was thought, naively, the deep consilience between Pauling's Rules regarding arrangements in crystals of cations and anions and arrangements in molecules of atomic cores and electron pairs (pages 15-17). Not so! "Henry," said Pauling to a mutual friend, "should stick to his work in the laboratory."

**Henry Hopes** "a new generation" will discover in the following pages what Professor William Jensen said in a Foreword for the first volume of *MCB* that he discovered as a student "with great enthusiasm", namely (emphasis added): *"a simple, easily visualizable, and physically understandable way of inflating flat topological Lewis diagrams into 3D structures with endless stereochemical consequences."*

For teachers, Professor Jensen remarks that "One may not always agree with what [Henry] says, but careful readers will always find it stimulating and exciting, if for no other reason than it will force them to think why they disagree."

# Dual Aspects of Valence Theory

It's often alleged that there are two Valence Theories, deemed to be rivals: computational Molecular Orbital Theory (MOT) featuring quantum physics and use of atomic orbitals, delocalized molecular orbitals, Schrödinger's Partial Differential Equation, and complex computer-based numerical computations of physical quantities derived from calculated molecular electron density distributions; and conceptual Valence Bond Theory (VBT) featuring chemical ideology and use of localized molecular orbitals, Langmuir's Algebraic Bond Number Equation, and elementary back-of-the-envelope topological formulations of valence stroke diagrams isomorphic with valence sphere models of molecular electron density profiles.

## VALENCE THEORIES

| MO Theory | VB Theory |
|---|---|
| Delocalized Molecular Orbitals | Localized Molecular Orbitals |
| Computational | Conceptual |
| Numerical | Topological |
| Based on Quantum Mechanics | Based on Chemical Ideology |
| Use of Schrödinger's Equation | Use of Langmuir's Equation |
| Wave Functions | Bond Diagrams |
| Atomic Orbitals | Valence Strokes |
| Electron Density *Distributions* | Electron Density *Profiles* |

The cited features of the two "theories" have, *jointly*, a noteworthy feature. They are, in a manner of speaking, *orthogonal* to each other. A feature possessed by one of them is not possessed by the other one. The two "Theories" are, in a word, *complementary*. A more descriptive caption for the tabulation is -

## VALENCE *THEORY*

| Numerical *Aspect* | Topological *Aspect* |
|---|---|

Jointly the two aspects yield a comprehensive *Theory*. Its numerical aspect has a feature — not mentioned above — that makes possible the deduction that the two aspects are, indeed, different aspects of the same thing. That feature is –

### The Indeterminacy of Slater Determinants

Columns or rows of a Slater determinantal wave function can be added to each other without changing the value of the determinant.

Accordingly, the delocalized orbitals of Valence Theory's numerical aspect can be transformed into the localized, Lewis-type, atomic core, bonding pairs, and lone pairs featured in Valence Theory's topological aspect, and in this document. *The computationally convenient delocalized molecular orbitals of textbooks' truncated versions of computational Valence Theory, in which wave functions are not subjected to operation of the Variation Theorem, are deemed to be without physical significance.*

# SHORT TABLE OF CONTENTS

Front Material

## ANALYSIS

Leading Visual Features of Conceptual Valence Bond Theory  1
Additional Conceptual Features of Valence Bond Theory  37
Critiques of Conceptual MO Theory and VSEPR Theory  54
Concluding General Remarks Regarding Conceptual VB Theory  74

## SYNTHESIS

Examples of the Explanatory Power of Conceptual Valence Bond Theory

### Organic Systems

Molecules, Radicals, or Ions Containing 1–4 Carbon Atoms  97
1,3-Butadiene  116
Two Nonexistent C-O Species  123
Cyclic Systems  129
Aromatic Systems  136

### Inorganic Systems

Compounds of Elements of the p-Block's First Row  160
Compounds of Elements of the p-Block's Second Row  207
Valence Sphere Model of a Metal  221
Alkaline Earth Metal Dihalides  224
Species with Weak Bonds Involving Hydrogen  230

## ADDITIONAL ESSAYS  261
(Third Edition)

## A SINGLE-FIGURE SUMMARY OF THIS VOLUME'S CONTENTS

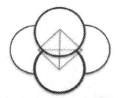

**A Tetrahedral Arrangement of Four Close-Packed Spheres**
(The inscribed polyhedron whose edges connect the spheres' centers has *four* faces.)

The Tetrahedron is the Leading Figure of Modern Conceptual Valence Bond Theory.
(It graces the cover of the first volume of *MCB*.)

The tetrahedral arrangement of electron pair domains is an arrangement for many occasions. It accounts for the saturation and directional character of the chemical affinities of the small atomic cores $B^{+3}$, $C^{+4}$, $N^{+5}$, and $O^{+6}$ and for molecules that obey the Octet Rule it generates directly an approximate profile of the electron density distribution about those cores, whether they are engaged in single, double, or triple bonds. Seldom, it seems, has so much stereochemistry been expressed so simply.

For chemically informed eyes a tetrahedral arrangement of close-packed spheres is truly one of Nature's most beautiful arrangements.

# CONTENTS

Alternative Titles vi

Dedication viii

"It Can't Be that Simple!" (and Lennard-Jones on the Exclusion Principle) ix

The Back Story x

Synopsis: The Versatile Valence Sphere xi

A Glance Ahead: a Brief Sample of Valence Sphere Models xii

Foreword (Chiefly Excerpts from Weinhold and Landis: *Valency and Bonding*) xiii

A Daughter's Foreword xv

Author's Preface xvii

Author's Preface to the Third Edition of *MCB II* xviii

Author's Preface to this Fourth Edition of *MCB II* (and Einstein's goal for his paper on Brownian Motion) xix

Introduction (and Thoreau on the Song of the Toad) xx

Memorandum to Students and Teachers (and Planck's Lament regarding slow acceptance of new ideas) xxi

Dual Aspects of Valence Theory xxii

Short Table of Contents xxiii

A Tetrahedral Arrangement of Four Close-Packed Spheres xxiii

## *Summarizing Statements*

Old Wine (Valence Stroke Diagrams) in New Bottles (Valence Sphere Models) 1

A Correspondence between Structural Organic and Structural Inorganic Chemistry 15

Converging Lines of Evidence in Support of Exclusive Orbital Models of Molecules 90

Leading Accomplishments of Conceptual Valence Bond Theory 241

VSD: Valence Stroke Diagram      VSM: Valence Sphere Model

VB: Valence Bond      MO: Molecular Orbital      EO: Exclusive Orbital

VSTR: Valence Stroke Termination Rule      VSEPR: Valence Shell Electron Pair Repulsion

MCVBT: Modern Conceptual Valence Bond Theory

## *ANALYSIS*

"[A]lthough the arguing from Experiments and Observations by Induction be no Demonstration of general Conclusions, yet it is the best way of arguing that the Nature of Things admits of. This is the Method of Analysis."      NEWTON, *OPTICKS*, Book Three, Part I

### *Leading Visual Features of Conceptual Valence Bond Theory*

Seeing is believing. ANON.

The eye comprehends in a sweep. RUDOLPH ARNHEIM

The soul never thinks without an image. ARISTOTLE

When finally we understand something we say, "Oh, I see." NORBERT HANSEN

My task which I am trying to achieve is, by the power of the written word to make you hear, to make you feel—it is before all to make you *see*. That—and no more, and it is everything.

JOSEPH CONRAD, Preface
*The Nigger of the Narcissus*

**Old Wine** (Valence Stroke Diagrams) **in New Bottles** (Valence Sphere Models)
*Organic Stereochemistry in a Nutshell* 1

**The Tetrahedron, the Cube, and the Tetrahedral Angle**
*Chemistry's Leading Geometrical Figures* 2

**The Tetrahedron's Back Story**
*Leading Inductions from Two Familiar Facts and Number of Isomers of $CH_2Cl_2$* 3

The Nature of the Double Bond
*Hybrid Atomic Orbitals and the Bent Bond Model 5*

Frontier Orbitals: *A Localized Electron Domain Perspective*
*Locations of Leading Exposures of Electron Domains and Atomic Cores 8*

Mental Images of Atoms: *From Newton to Modern Times*
*Contributions of Rutherford, Bohr, Lewis, Linnett, and Kimball 10*

Inter- and Intra-molecular Electron Pair Interactions
*FNO and the Trimethyl Ammine-Diiodine Charge-Transfer Complex 11*

$I_2(g)$, $I_2(c)$, & $I_2(soln)$
*Donor-Acceptor Interactions in Crystalline Diiodine and Solution 12*

Structure of Carbon Dioxide's van der Waals' Dimer $(CO_2)_2$
*Implications of a Valence Sphere Model Confirmed 13*

Valence Sphere Model of an $S_N2$ Reaction
*An Electron Cloud as a Frame of Reference 14*

Correspondence between Structural Organic and Inorganic Chemistry
*Coordination Compounds' Anions may be Electron Pairs and Cations Atomic Cores 15*

Consilience between Computational and Conceptual Valence Theories
*A Test of the Theory in Which It Occurs. 18*

Visual "Puns": Different Ways of Looking at the Same Thing
*The Octahedron and Face-Centered Cube 19*

Space-Filling with a Complement of s-, p-, and d-Electrons
*Uses of a Cube's Corners, Edges, and Faces to Locate Orbitals' Lobes 22*

The Valence Stroke *Termination* Rule
*Valence stroke diagrams san elements' symbols determine locations of atomic cores 23*

Valence Strokes, Lines of Force, Chemical Bonds, and Electron Clouds
*Chemistry's Valence Strokes are Like Faraday's Lines of Force in Four Ways 24*

Lines of Force, Gauss's Law, and Valence Stroke Diagrams
*Valence Strokes' Leading Properties Are Analogous to those of Faraday's Lines of Force 25*

The Logic of the Rabbit-Ear Representation of Lone Pairs
*Graphic Resolution of the Issue of "Variable Valence" 26*

Valence Stroke Arrangements that Satisfy the VSTR for $S^{+6}$
*Sulfur Core Environment for Electron Pair Coordination Numbers of 4, 5, and 6  27*

Expanded Octets about $S^{+6}$ Continued
*Instances Where Expanded Octets Are Favored over Octet-Rule Structures 28*

Large C—H Models
*Electron-Pair Domains Aren't All the Same Size 29*

Charges and Relative Sizes of Atomic Cores of *p*-Block Elements
*Atomic Cores Aren't All the Same Size 30*

Model of the Extraordinary Stability of $SF_6$
*Classical Radius-Ratio Rules Yield a Good Account of $SF_6$'s Structure and Properties 31*

Bond Types
*Core Sizes Account for Two Types of Elements and Three Types of Bonds 32*

Exposed and Frustrated Electrophilic and Nucleophilic Sites
*From Gaseous $BeH_2$ to Steric Effects in Reactions of Dihydrogen  33*

### *Additional Conceptual Features of Valence Bond Theory*

**Density Functional Theory**
*Excerpts from Walter Kohn's Nobel Lecture of 1999 37*

**Density Functional Theory and the Valence Stroke Termination Rule**
*Fractional Rates of Change of Electron Densities at Nuclei's Sites Yield Nuclei's Zs 38*

**The Bond Number Equation: $\sum(n-1)B_n = \sum(EPCN)_i - V$**
*Illustrative Application: $Al_2(CH_3)_6$ 39*

**Valence Bond Systematics**
*Construction of a Bond Diagram for NOF 40*
Square-Planar Uncomplexed Cyclobutadiene
*An Unconventional Explanation for its Nonexistence 41*

**Oracles and Editors of Computational and Conceptual Valence Theories**
*"The finest things in life include having a clear grasp of correlations." EINSTEIN 42*

**Application of VB Theory's Oracle and Editor to the Formula $B_4H_4$**
*Poor Valence Stroke Diagrams Have Poor Valence Sphere Models 43*

**Test of Valence Bond Theory with $B_5H_{11}$**
*Satisfactory VB Diagrams May, Nonetheless, Not Correspond to Known Molecules 44*

**Orbitals, Wavefunctions, and the Variation Theorem**
*Conceptual Garbage in May Not Be Numerical Garbage Out 45*

**"Where Are Your Equations?"**
*Valence Spheres Encode Geometrically Computational Chemistry's Leading Equations 46*

**A Conventional Bond Diagram for "Hypervalent" XeNOF**
*As Terminal Atoms of 0 F.C., N, O, and F Are Bound by Single, Double, and Triple Bonds 48*

**Bond Angle Theorem**
*The More Electron Domains an Atom C Shares with Atoms A and B, the Larger <ACB 49*

**"Bond Lengths"**
*A Union with Chemical Theory of Interatomic Distances from Experiment or Calculation 50*

**Regions of Zero Electron Density?!**
*Doesn't Close Packing of Exclusive Orbitals Yield Interstices of Zero Electron Density? 52*

**Missing in Action**
*The Exclusion Principle Plays No Role in Formation of Canonical Molecular Orbitals 53*

### *Critiques of Conceptual MO Theory and VSEPR Theory*

**Grounds for X-Rating Conceptual MO Theory in General Chemistry**
*It's Overwhelming, Unnecessary, Incomplete, and Misleading 54*

**Z-Matrices**
*Input to Computational Valence Theory from Conceptual VB Theory 55*

**General Remarks Regarding Two Aspects of Modern Valence Theory**
*Numbers and Concepts, Jointly, Comprise the Whole of Modern Valence Theory 56*

**A Comparison of Conceptual VB and MO Theories**
*When we finally understand something we say, "Oh, I see." 57*

**The Leading Induction of Modern Conceptual Valence Bond Theory**
*Fermi Holes + The Facts of Chemistry ---> Fermi Domains 60*

**Toward an Explanation of Hund's Rules?**
*Use of DODS to Account for $O_2$'s Paramagnetism Suggests an Explanation for Hund's Rule 61*

**"A" or "The" Molecular Orbital Theory?**
*Our Language Reveals Deep-Seated Assumptions Regarding Nature's Nature 62*

**Mullikan's Willful Departure from "Chemical Ideology"**
*A Wrong Turn? 63*

**Why Are Methane Molecules Tetrahedral?**
*An Appraisal of Computational MO Theory 64*

**A Check on the Electride-Ion Model of Matter**
*We do calculations to see if our pictures are plausible. SCHRÖDINGER 66*

**VSEPR Theory and $CH_4$**
*Planar or Tetrahedral? 70*

**An Appraisal of VSEPR Theory**
*Right Answers for Wrong Reasons 71*

### Concluding General Remarks Regarding Conceptual VB Theory

**Atomic Orbitals Irrelevance for Conceptual Valence Bond Theory**
*Interpretative Chemistry Requires Electron Density's Profiles, Not Its Inner Contours 74*

**Chemically Modified "Atomic Orbitals"**
*Solutions of Schrödinger's Equation for the Hydrogen Atom Lack Chemistry's Directionality 75*

**Primary and Secondary Principles of Conceptual Valence Bond Theory**
*An Overview 77*

**$B_2H_6$, the Isoelectronic Principle, and Double Bonds**
*Implications of the Structure of $B_2H_6$'s Protonated Double Bond for the Structure of $C_2H_4$ 78*

**Four Routes to a Bent Bond Model of Double Bonds**
*Two Former and Two New Routes 79*

**Conceptual Valence Bond Theory and Fundamental Physical Forces:**
*Nuclear-Electron Attraction, Nuclear-Nuclear Repulsion, and Electron-Electron Repulsion 80*

**Effects of Nuclear-Nuclear Repulsion on Bond Angles and Bond Lengths**
*Physical Explanation of the s-Character Rule and Ethylene's Geometry 81*

**Brief Summary of Evidence for a Principle of Exclusion**
*All Lines of Evidence Lead to the Same "Rome" 74*

**A Brief History of Localized Molecular Orbitals**
*From Valence Strokes Through Lewis' Dot Diagrams to 3D Exclusive Orbitals 83*

**Shapes of Exclusive Orbitals**
*A Sphere Is the Simplest Shape for a 3-Dimensional Exclusive Orbital 84*

**Exposures of Small Rings' Bent Bonds**
*The Smaller a Ring the More Bent Its Bonds and the Greater Their Exposure 86*

**A Teachable Topic**
*An Early Introduction to Valence Sphere Models 87*

**A Pedagogically Attractive Feature of Conceptual Valence Bond Theory**
*Suggestions for a Multi-Year Curriculum for a Central Topic of the Central Science 88*

**Conceptual Valence Bond Theory's Correspondence Principles**
*A Development from Disparate Points of View Yields a Variety of Analogies and Correlations 89*

Converging Lines of Evidence in Support of Exclusive Orbital Models of Molecules
*A Recapitulation and Extension of Previous Remarks 90*
William Whewell on "The Fundamental Antithesis of Science"
*Fact-Binding Inductions' Usefulness Is Demonstrated by their Applications to Other Facts, in What Newton Called "Synthesis" 95*

## *SYNTHESIS*

*"Synthesis consists in assuming the Causes discover'd and establish'd as Principles, and by them explaining the phenomena proceeding from them."*     NEWTON, *OPTICKS*, Book Three, Part I

*Examples of the Explanatory Power of Conceptual Valence Bond Theory*

## Organic Systems

*Molecules, Radicals, or Ions Containing 1-4 Carbon Atoms*

Unsaturation and Hydrogenation
*Reactions with Dihydrogen of Ethylene, Ethane, and Methylene 97*

Cyclopropane Formation from Ethylene and Methylene
*A Localized  Orbital Perspective 98*

Planar Methane
*Conceptual Valence Bond Theory's Point of View of 102*

Additional Remarks Regarding Exotic Structures for Methane
*Three Center Bonding in Pyramidal Methane 103*

HCO
*To be Explained: a Short CO Bond and a Long (and Weak) CH Bond 104*

An Explanation for Formaldehyde's Low Bond Dissociation Energies
*$H_2CO$'s CH BDE's Are Anomalous from the Point of View of the s-Character Rule 105*

Toward a Bond Diagram for $C_2$
*The Bond's Length Suggests a Double Bond with Some Triple Bond Character 106*

$C_3$
*A Candidate for Two Three-Center Donor-Acceptor Interaction 107*

Acetylenes
*A Sweet Spot for Organic Chemists: Energy Rich Yet Kinetically Persistent (HOFFMANN) 108*

Acetylene's First Excited State
*A Trans-Bent Structure with a Carbon-Carbon Bond Longer than a Normal Double Bond 109*

Structure of the Dication $C_2H_4^{+2}$
*A Candidate for a Diprotonated Triple-Bonded Structure 111*

The Cyclopropenyl Cation $C_3H_3^+$
*Illustrated Are Several  Unique Features of Conceptual Valence Bond Theory 112*

Electronic Structures of Cyclobutadiene Dianions of the Carbon Group
*Cores of Different Sizes Account for Different Structures of Dianions of C, Si, and Ge 113*

*1,3-Butadiene*

Bond Angles, Bond Lengths, and Energies of Rotamers of 1,3-Butadiene
*Manifestations of Nuclear Displacements Owing to Nuclear-Nuclear Repulsion 116*

trans, gauche, and cis Confomers of 1,3-Butadiene

Existence of a cis Confomer as a Potential Energy Minimum is Problematical 119

Stereochemistry of Reduction of Butadiene with Sodium in Liquid Ammonia
Implications of Classical $S_N2$-type Rearrangements 120

## Two Nonexistent C-O Species

Nonexistence of Oxirene
Elusiveness from Adjacency of Nucleophilic and Electrophilic Sites 123

Stability and Instability of OCCO and Related Species
A Concordance between Computational and Conceptual Valence Theory 126

## Cyclic Systems

Unusual Acidity of Cycopropene
An Acidity-Lowering trans-Annular Interaction 129

Paradoxical Stabilities of Cyclopentadienyl Anion and Cation
Loss of $H^+$ and $H^-$ Yield the Same Number of Resonance Structures But Opposite Stabilities 130

Stabilities of Cyclopentadiene and Cycloheptatriene's Ions
Alternatives to "Antiaromaticity" 133

Tricycopentane
Extraordinary Strain and Extraordinary Bonding? 134

Bicyclic Pentalene
Another Instance of Anti-"Antiaromaticity"? 135

## Aromatic Systems

Beware of Tidings of Delocalization
By the Virial Theorem E(total) = - (Kinetic Energy), Which Declines with Delocalization 136

Aromaticity's 4n + 2 Rule
Each Aromatic Ring Added to Benzene's 6 π Electrons Adds to the System 4 π Electrons 137

An Interpretation of Naphthalene's Bond Lengths
Recent Data Require a Reinterpretation of Napthalene's Resonance Structures 138

Calculated Ring Currents for Cyclic Conjugated Hydrocarbons
A Surprise: An Instance in which Resonance Diminishes Aromatic Character 141

## Inorganic Systems

### Compounds of Element of the s-Block

The Alkali Metals
Exclusive Orbital Models of the Atoms, Gaseous Dimers, and bcc Solids 142

Valence Sphere Models of Lithiated Boron Hydrides
Another Extension of the Domain of Applicability of Valence Sphere Models 144

Structure of the Carbenoids $LiCH_2F$
Support for an Exclusive Orbital Model of Valence Shell Electron Density Profiles 146

Distances to a Tetrahedron's Center from Its Corners, Edges, and Faces
Calculations Preparatory to an Application of a Valence Sphere Model 149

Calculated and Observed Lithium-Oxygen Distances in $Li_2O(s)$
Evidence for Anticoincidence of Oxide Ions' Spin Sets in $Li_2O(s)$ 150

$LiCO^+$ and $COLi^+$
Evidence of the Irrelevance in Understanding Chemical Bonding of Dipole Moments 151

**Electron Domain Model of Dilithium Methane**
*A Common Misinterpretation of Molecular Geometry 152*

**Localized Electron Domain Models of the Lithium Methyl Tetramer**
*A Lithiated Methide Ion Has Both Nucleophilic and Electrophilic Sites 154*

**The Alkali Halide Paradox**
*Forty Percent of the Alkali Halides' Structures Violate the Radius Ratio Rules 156*

**Significance of Anomalous Crystal Structures of LiCl, LiBr, and LiI**
*Evidence of Charge Leakage from Anions to Cations 157*

**Remarks Regarding the Charge-Leakage Model of the Lithium Halides**
*Charge Leakage Decreases Formal Charges and Increases Cations' Sizes 158*

**Dimerization of (Hypothetical) $Be_2$**
*Formation of Four 3-Center Bonds Yields a Tetrahedral Structure for $Be_4$ 159*

## Compounds of Elements of the p-Block's First Row
### B   C   N   O   F

**Valence Sphere Model of $Be_4B_4H_8$**
*An Octa-Capped Octahedron Has Sites for 8 Octet-Rule-Satisfying Cores 160*

**Bond Diagram for HBCBH**
*2-Center Bonds Acting as Donors in D-A Interaction Become 3-Center Bonds 161*

**Multicenter Bonding in Boron Hydrides**
*Bond Diagrams for $B_4H_{10}$, $B_5H_9$, and $B_5H_{11}$ 163*

**Bond Diagram for the Borane Carbonyl $B_2(CO)_2$**
*Diboron Dicarbonyl is Isoelectronic with Triacetylene and $NCC_2CN$ 165*

**Borazine**
*Ring Bonds Are All the Same Length, Yet the Molecule Is not Significantly Aromatic 166*

**Local Orbital Models for the Δ-hedral Closo-Boranes $B_nH_n^{-2}$ (n = 6-12)**
*And Reasons Why Some Boron Hydrides Do Not Exist 167*

**Why $B_4Cl_4$ Exists but Not $B_4H_4$**
*A Tetracapped Tetrahedron is Congested with the Equivalent of Four Triple Bonds 175*

**Bent $Ph_3P=C=PPh_3$**
*In a Linear Structure the Phosphorus Cores Are Coordinatively Unsaturated 177*

**Bond Angles and Bond Lengths in the $NH_n$ Species, n = 1, 2, and 3**
*$NH_2$'s Bond Angle of 103 Degrees Seems at First Sight Unusually Small 179*

**Ammonium Ion's Unusual Bond Lengths**
*The Ion Seems to Violate, at First Sight, the s-Character Rule 181*

**Bond Diagrams for Nitric Oxide**
*For Odd-Electron Species their Two Spin Sets Cannot Have the Same Structure 182*

**Molecular Modeling of the Gas Phase Hydration of $NO^+$**
*Many Reported Features of the Reaction Fit Nicely Its Valence Sphere Model 183*

**Nitrogen Dioxide**
*Double Spin Set Theory Provides a Way of Rationalizing the Molecule's Bond Angle 192*

**Structure and Reactivity of Nitrous Oxide**
*The Molecule, Overall, Is Unusually Short 194*

**Explanations of Selected Properties of $N_2F_2$**
*Illustrations of Several of the Resources of Conceptual VB Theory 196*

Valence Stroke Diagrams for $H_2O^+$
*A Response to a Common Incorrect Criticism of Valence Bond Theory 200*

Structures of FOF, HOF, and HOH
*Effects of Nuclear-Nuclear Repulsion and Donor-Acceptor Interactions 202*

Electronic Structures and Molecular Geometries of $O_2$, $O_2^-$, and $O_3^-$
*Additional Illustrations of the Explanatory Power of Conceptual Valence Bond Theory 203*

Geometrical Structure and Valence Stroke Diagram for $O_4^-$
*The Molecule Appears to Have a Planar Rectangular Structure 206*

### Compounds of Elements of the p-Block's Second Row
### Al  Si  P  S

Exclusive Orbital Models for the Dianion $Al_4^{-2}$
*Is a Model Designed for Organic Molecules Applicable to a Species Such as $Al_4^{-2}$? 207*

Calculated Structure of the Chain-like Dianion $Si(C_4)_2^{-2}$
*SiCC Bond Angles Are Less Than 180° 210*

Non-Planar $Si_2H_4$ and Non-Linear $Si_2H_2$
*$Si_2H_2$'s Doubly Protonated Triple Bond Provides 2 Lone Pairs to Solvate the Large $Si^{+4}$ Cores 212*

Bond Lengths of the Phosphorus Pentahalides
*Axial-Equatorial Differences Suggest Occurrence of Nonspherical Anticoincident $P^{+5}$ Cores 213*

Fluxional Phosphorus Pentafluoride
*A Stretched-Rubber-Band Model Models Elegantly the Pseudo-Rotation 215*

The Double Bond of $OPF_3$
*An Anticoincident Spin-Set Model Has Bond Angles Close to Those Observed 216*

Tetrasulfur Tetranitride
*A Valence Sphere Model Fits Remarkably Well This "Poorly Understood Species" 217*

Orbital Descriptions of Bonding in $SF_6$
*Have "Hypervalent" Species "Expanded Octets"? 220*

### Valence Sphere Model of a Metal 221

### Alkaline Earth Metal Dihalides

Crystal and Gas Phase Models
*Some Gaseous $MX_2(g)$ Molecules Are, As Expected, Linear, but Some Are Bent 224*

Valence Sphere Models of Gaseous Alkaline Earth Dihalides
*Bent Species Imply the Presence Non-spherical $M^{+2}$ Cores 226*

An Arithmetical Model of the Shapes of Gaseous $MX_2$ Species
*The larger $M^{+2}$ and the Smaller $X^-$ the Greater the Tendency for $MX_2(g)$ to Be Bent 227*

Length of the BeF Bonds in Gaseous Beryllium Difluoride
*Calculated Lengths and Models Suggest Bond Orders of ca. 2.5 for $BeF_2(g)$'s BeF Bonds 228*

$Ta_6Cl_{12}^{+2}$: A Test of the Bond Number Equation
*The Valence Sphere Model Has 8 3-Center TaTaTa Bonds and 24 2-Center Ta—Cl Bonds 229*

*Species with Weak Bonds Involving Hydrogen*

**Dihydrogen Complexes with Metal Coordination Compounds**
*$H_2$ and Coordinatively Unsaturated Metal Ions Are Weak Nucleophiles and Electrophiles 230*

**Geometries and Electronic Profiles of Halide Ion Monohydrates**
*Monohydrates of $F^-$ and $I^-$ Have Different Geometries 231*

**Bonds to Hydrogen and Hydrogen Bonds**
*An Exclusive Orbital Model of Electron Density about $H^+$ During a Proton Transfer 232*

**Unusual Hydrogen Bond between Water and Methane**
*The Proton-(Donor Heavy-Atom) Distance Does Not Steadily Increase 234*

**Probing Nucleophilic Sites with Brönsted Acids and a Lewis Acid**
*Rotational Spectroscopy Yields Many Structural Details 235*

SUMMARY
Leading Accomplishments of Conceptual Valence Bond Theory *241*
That's It *243*

APPENDICES
*Mistakes Happen 244*

**Regularities in the Periodic System Contingent on Location of He above Be**
*The System Is about Atoms (Such As He $1s^2$), Not Simple Substance (Such As Inert Gases) 245*

**Two Heliums**
*Names, Noted John Locke, Come To Have Different Significations 246*

**A Striking Atomanalogy**
*He : Be :: H : Li*

**Criticisms and Refutations**
*A Dialogue Concerning Two Valence Systems 247*

**Full Disclosure**
*Comments, Pro and Con, by a Famous Physical Chemist 253*

**Disclosures Continued**
*Evidence for Existence in Western Civilization of "Two Cultures" 254*

**Suggestions for Teaching General Chemistry from Demonstration-Experiments**
*Seeing Is Believing 256*

**Thermodynamics**
*"It's not difficult if you can just keep track of what you are talking about." 260*

## ADDITIONAL ESSAYS FOR A THIRD EDITION OF *MCB* II

Thank you very much for sending me the documents with Brian's name in it.
I truly appreciate it. I am delighted to see that you are still active scientifically
and encourage you not to stop.                    GABOR SOMORJAI, UC - Berkeley

**Introduction.** *MOLECULES and the Chemical Bond* is about an induction: Exclusive Orbital Theory.  No formal proof for it, by deduction, exists. The most powerful case for it is, simply: *It* *works*. Its bond diagrams are chemistry's lingua franca. The theory's many applications provide, accordingly, no place "to stop" an account of its many uses and unrivaled simplicity.

## ANALYSIS

**A Thesis, Antithesis, and Synthesis** *261*
Bohr (Dynamic Electrons) + Lewis (Static Electrons) = Kimball (Dynamic Electrons in Static Domains)

**Induction of Wave Functions' Antisymmetric Property** *262*
A Response to the Question: *Where Are Your Predictions?*

**Leading Evidence for Exclusive Orbital Models of Electron Density Profiles** *263*
*Four Kinds of Evidence Support Replacement of Valence Strokes by Valence Spheres*

**Electron Localization** *264*
*By Induction, from Chemical Evidence, and by Deduction, from Schrödinger's Equation*

**Organic Stereochemistry** *265*
*The Story on One Page!*

**Exclusive Orbital and Molecular Orbital Models of $CH_4$, $NH_3$, $H_2O$, and HF** *266*
*The Hydrocarbon Story Extended to Compounds of Nitrogen, Oxygen, and Fluorine by Means of the Phenomenon of Isoelectronicity*

**Geometrical Models of Primary and Secondary Chemical Affinities** *267*
*Electron Pair Coordination Numbers 5 and 6*

**BEYOND HYDROGEN: An Explanatory Note** *268*
*Much of Conceptual Valence Theory Is Absent in a Mathematical Analysis of Dihydrogen*

**"Electrocyclic Reactions"** *269*
*A Geometrical Model of p-Orbitals' Positive and Negative Lobes and Completion of Curly Arrow Circuits by Catalytic Hydrogen-Bonding Solvents, and Metals*

**Catalysis of a Walden Inversion by Proton Donors and Acceptors** *270*
*Curly Arrow Circuit-Completion by Way of Proton Transfers*

**As Bohr Liked to Say . . .** *271*
*The Opposite of a Profound Statement May Be a Profound Statement*

**Letter to Hoffmann Regarding Critiques of Valence Theories** *273*
*Static Domains Populated by Dynamic Electrons Bridge the Gap Between Physical and Chemical Models of the Electronic Structure of Matter*

**Scientific Phrases Related to the Concept of a Chemical Bond** *274*
*Banishing the Word "Bond" Would Impoverish the Language of Chemistry*

**Once More: MO Theory's Orbital Placement Problem** *275*
*Why is methane tetrahedral?*

**Unexpected Critiques of Conceptual MO Theory** *276*
*Conceptual Valence Bond Theory Stands Alone as a Working Theory of Valence*

**An Explanation for Bent's Rule** *277*
*Use of the Isoelectronic Principle and the Hellman-Feynman Theorem*

## SYNTHESIS

**Tetrahedane** *278*
*Postulated Mechanism of Decomposition*

The Methyl Radical: Planar or Pyramidal? *279*
*An Application of Bent's Rule.*

Small Molecules with Incomplete Octets *280*
*Challenges for Exclusive Orbital Theory*

Qualitative Valence Bond Theory of Small Hydrocarbon Dications *282*
*A Comparison with Quantitative Molecular Orbital Theory Conceptual VB Theory of Boron-*

Boron Bond Lengths in $B_2Cl_4$ and $H_2B_2O$ *284*
*Uses of the Valence Stroke Termination Rule and CVBT's "R Equation"*

$NO_3F$ *285*
*A Molecule Isoelectronic with 1,1-Difluoro- and 1,1-Dimethyl Cyclopropane*

s-trans-Nitrosyl O-Hydroxide: HO—ON *286*
*The Longest Known Oxygen-Oxygen Bond*

The Enigma of the Nonexistence of Pentazole *287*
*Possession of a Unique Route to Decomposition*

$H_3B \cdot NH_3$ *288*
*Bond Diagrams for the Borane-Ammonia Complex*

Structure of the Donor-Acceptor Complex $C_2H_4 \cdots BrCl$ *289*
*An Intermolecular Donor-Acceptor Interaction with the Donor an Electron Pair of a Double Bond*

CONCLUDING REMARKS

Linus Pauling's 1954 Nobel Lecture Abridged [and Slightly Annotated] *290*
*A Brief History of Valence Bond Theory by Its Leading 20th Century Advocate*

Principal Take Away Messages? *292*
*A Summary of Leading Ideas*

Philosophical Postscript *293*
*Different Schools of Thought Regarding the Principle Character of an Inductive Science*

A Simple Resolution of an Embarrassment of Riches *294*
*Two Strikingly Different Versions of Valence Theory Viewed as Teammates*

Complementary Features of Computational and Conceptual Valence Theories *295*
*A Tabulation of Leading Features of Different Versions of Valence Theory*

ACKNOWLEDGMENTS *296*
GLOSSARY *297*
Related Publications by Bent *308*
The Author *309*
Sketch of a Scientific Autobiography *311*
3-Electron and 5-Electron Bonds *314*
Epilogue *315*
INDEX *316*
List of Drawings of Molecular Electron Density Profiles *327*
List of Bond Diagrams *328*
Exercises Involving Chemistry's Leading Icons *329*

# The Valence Stroke and the Valence Sphere
## One- and Three-Dimensional Models of Localized Molecular Orbitals

This book is about old wine (valence stroke diagrams) in new bottles (valence sphere models).

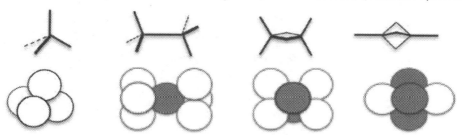

Strokes and spheres represent *localized **molecular orbitals***, in the sense that, divorced from their diagrams and models they have no significance. The essence of organic stereochemistry lies in locations of substituents off single, double, and triple bonds.

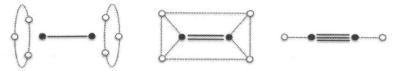

Valence Sphere Models generate those locations *almost magically*. Illustrated is an observation made many years ago, in the 19th century, by Thomson and Tait, in the preface to their classic *Elements of Natural Philosophy*. "It is particularly interesting to note how many theorems, even among those not ordinarily attacked without the help of the Differential Calculus [and, today, in valence theory, with quantum mechanics and computers], have here been found to *yield easily* **to geometrical methods** of the most elementary character" [emphasis added].

Both representations above — stroke and sphere — place a tetrahedral arrangement of electron pairs about sites of atomic cores (not shown in the valence sphere models), whether the cores are involved in single, double, or triple bonds; or with lone pairs.

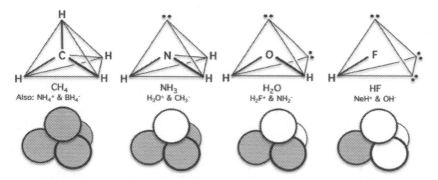

*One arrangement* (the tetrahedral arrangement) *fits all* (atomic cores that obey the Octet Rule: usually $B^{+3}$, $C^{+4}$, $N^{+5}$, $O^{+6}$, and $F^{+7}$). The arrangement may be generated, easily, in two ways: by occupancy of alternate corners of a cube, with the atomic core in question at the cube's center; and by the centers of four close-packed spheres, with the atomic core in question in the spheres' interstice, called in packing of, e.g., oxide ions about smaller cations in crystalline oxides a "tetrahedral interstice". A tetrahedral arrangement of electron pair domains accounts for a large part of organic stereochemistry.

## The Tetrahedron, the Cube, and the Tetrahedral Angle

A tetrahedron's corners occupy alternate corners of a circumscribed cube.

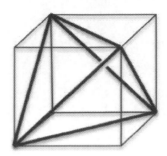

The tetrahedron's faces face the cube's other corners.
A face lies opposite a tetrahedron's corner.
(Those facts, we shall see, have enormous consequences for reaction mechanisms.)

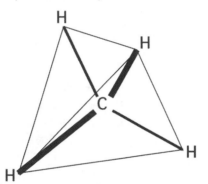
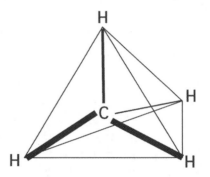

The symbol "C" stands for the atomic core $C^{+4}$. In attack by reagents that have protruding electron domains, the $C^{+4}$ core moves outward, thereby lengthening its bond that lies opposite the attacked face.

Chemistry's most famous bond angle is "the tetrahedral angle": 109.47°

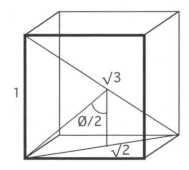

$$\sin(ø/2) = (\sqrt{2}/2)/(\sqrt{3}/2)$$
$$\rightarrow$$
$$ø/2 = 54.736°$$
$$\rightarrow$$
$$ø = 109.47°$$

Bond angles HCH, HNH, and HOH of $CH_4$, $NH_3$, and $H_2O$ are 109.47°, 107.1°, and 104.5°.

PERSONAL NOTE: The author's interest in molecular structure was initially ignited on reading about those cited bond angles in an article by R. S. Mulliken, in 1952.

# The Tetrahedron's Back Story

Chemistry has but one noteworthy theory and but one set of hypothetical ideas, the theory of the combination of atoms into molecules with its fundamental idea of valence. It is a most beautiful theory, surpassed by none other in the intellectual satisfaction it affords. NORMAN CAMPBELL

The tetrahedron's back story in chemistry, presented here for newcomers to chemistry, illustrates the nature of the evolution of thought in an inductive science. The story begins with two familiar facts and ends with one of the leading inductions in the history of chemistry (along with John Dalton's Atomic Hypothesis and G. N. Lewis's conjecture regarding electron pairs), by van't Hoff, chemistry's first Nobel Laureate, in 1901.

TWO FAMILIAR FACTS. Molecules of water and carbon dioxide have the chemical formulas $H_2O$ and $CO_2$.

A FACT ABOUT HYDROGEN ATOMS. No molecules have chemical formulas of the type $HX_n$ for n > 1. ($HN_3$ — "hydrazoic acid" — is an exception.)

AN INFERENCE ABOUT HYDROGEN ATOMS. Hydrogen atoms are never attached by chemical bonds to more than one atom. ($HN_3$'s order of atomic attachments is HNNN.)

AN INDUCTION REGARDING $H_2O$. $H_2O$'s order of atomic attachments is HOH (not HHO).

A LINGUISTIC CONVENTION REGARDING H. Chemists assign hydrogen atoms a "combining capacity" or "valence" of 1. Hydrogen, they say, is *monovalent*.

A DEDUCTION REGARDING OXYGEN ATOMS. Chemists deduce — from their linguistic convention for hydrogen; from the reason for that convention; and from the formula for water molecules — that oxygen atoms are *divalent*.

FACTS ABOUT COMPOUNDS OF CARBON AND OXYGEN. COO designates a peroxide, not thermodynamically stable carbon dioxide.

A CONCLUSION REGARDING CARBON DIOXIDE. Both atoms of oxygen of a molecule of carbon dioxide are attached to the carbon atom.

A DEDUCTION REGARDING CARBON ATOMS. Carbon atoms are *tetravalent; or quadrivalent*.

GRAPHIC EXPRESSIONS OF VALENCE ASSIGNMENTS. Chemists represent valence assignments by "valence strokes": 1 for H, 2 for O, 4 for C.

$$H\!\!- \qquad -O- \qquad -\overset{\displaystyle |}{\underset{\displaystyle |}{C}}-$$

BOND FORMATION. To generate models of molecules, chemist indicate the "mutual saturation of chemical affinities" by pointing at each other valence strokes of two different moieties. Generated with hydrogen atoms are the figures -

$$H\!\!- \;+\; -\!\!H \;=\; H\!\!-\!\!-\!\!H \;=\; H\!-\!H$$

Molecular hydrogen is, indeed, diatomic, molecular formula $H_2$. Illustrated is -

THE RULE OF NO DANGLING VALENCE STROKES. Molecular hydrogen, for instance, is not H—.

Produced by the Rule are correct atomic linkages and molecular formulas for molecules of dihydrogen (H—H), water (H—O—H), and hydrogen peroxide (H—O—O—H). Not accounted for, however, by the drawing —O—, is -

A FACT ABOUT OXYGEN MOLECULES. They're diatomic!

AN INFERENCE REGARDING OXYGEN ATOMS. As for adjacent valence strokes of polyvalent carbon atoms, the pair of directed valence strokes of an oxygen atom are not collinear.

> In an oxygen atom's "valence shell", together with its two valence strokes that represent shared electron pairs (discussed later; and illustrated on p1) are two pairs of unshared electrons.

For molecules of dioxygen and water, valence assignments together with "the mutual saturation of chemical affinities" procedure, the Rule regarding dangling affinities, and the angular inference regarding oxygen's affinities yield these valence stroke diagrams:

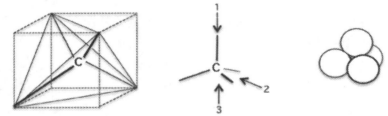

$H_2O$ is, indeed, a bent molecule (<HOH = 104.5°).
(OO bonds of $O_2$, whose valence strokes don't point at each other, are called "bent bonds".)

A FACT ABOUT HYDROGEN CHLORIDE. Its molecular formula is HCl.

AN INFERENCE REGARDING CHLORINE ATOMS. They're monovalent, in HCl.

A DEDUCTION REGARDING COMPOUNDS OF C, H, AND Cl THAT CONTAIN ONE CARBON ATOM. Their molecular formulas are $CH_4$, $CH_3Cl$, $CH_2Cl_2$, $CHCl_3$, and $CCl_4$.

A FACT ABOUT $CH_2Cl_2$. Only one substance with the molecular formula $CH_2Cl_2$ exists!

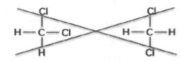

CONCLUSION: *Carbon's four valence strokes,* suggested van't Hoff, *are directed toward the corners of a tetrahedron.*

For $CH_3Cl$ all three C—H bonds are (therefore, by supposition) equivalent to each other. In passing to $CH_2Cl_2$ from $CH_3Cl$ it makes no difference which H atom of $CH_3Cl$ is replaced by a Cl atom.

Mutual saturation by two carbon atoms of 1, 2, and 3 of their combining capacities yields carbon-carbon single, double, and triple bonds (p1). The remainder of organic stereochemistry is in large measure different combinations of those possibilities. A quadruple bond between two carbon atoms, according to the tetrahedral model, is impossible — and unknown.

The tetrahedral arrangement of valence strokes (left and middle figures above) introduced into chemistry *the third dimension.* That advance was continued (right figure), over half a century later, by replacement of the one-dimensional valence strokes of valence stroke diagrams (in which the strokes never cross each other) by three-dimensional domains (for wave-like electrons, only two of which — postulated Lewis — can be at the same place at the same time.

# The Nature of the Double Bond

This story of the double bond begins with organic chemistry's leading idea.

### The Tetrahedral Tetravalent Carbon Atom

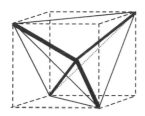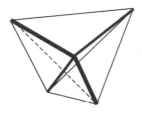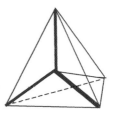

The idea accounts for the formula and structure of $CH_4$, H monovalent. To save the idea for $C_2H_6$, Kekule introduced the idea of a carbon-carbon *single bond*. For $C_2H_4$ he postulated "some denser arrangement", later called a *double bond*.

### Bent and Banana Bond Representations of a Carbon-Carbon Double Bond

Lewis's identification of a valence-stroke as a pair of *electrons* led to the idea of describing bond directions in molecules in terms of atomic orbitals for electrons.

For carbon's valence-shell the available orbitals are (from atomic spectroscopy) 2s and $2p_{+1}$, $2p_0$, and $2p_{-1}$ orbitals. They haven't, however, the desired directional character. The s-orbital is spherically symmetric. The $p_{\pm 1}$ orbitals are doughnut-shaped. Linear combinations of them yield dumbbell-shaped orbitals $2p_x$ and $2p_y$ that, with $2p_z$, point along the x, y, and z directions. It's more directionality than none at all, but not the directionality of tetrahedrally directed affinities. Slater and Pauling continued with the idea of linear combinations of atomic orbitals. The vector sum, so to speak, of $p_x$, $p_y$, and $p_z$ points toward the upper right rear corner of the cube above, the sum $-p_x - p_y + p_z$ to the upper left front corner, &c.

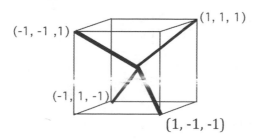

Mixing in the s-orbital, in order to achieve four linearly independent orbitals that point in the tetrahedral directions, yields the tetrahedral $sp^3$ "hybrid orbitals", te. They're *descriptions*, not explanations, of carbon's directional affinities.

$$te_1 \quad s + p_x + p_y + p_z$$
$$te_2 \quad s - p_x - p_y + p_z$$
$$te_3 \quad s + p_x - p_y - p_z$$
$$te_4 \quad s - p_x + p_y - p_z$$

To account for the HCH bond angles of ethylene, thought, initially (and incorrectly) to be 120°, and linear acetylene's 180° HCC bond angles, investigators introduced the hybrid orbitals $sp^2$ and sp.

*s/p Hybrid Orbitals, their Fractional  s-Character, and Inter-Orbital Angles*

| $sp^3$ | $sp^3$ | $sp^3$ | $sp^3$ |
|---|---|---|---|
| 1/4 | 1/4 | 1/4 | 1/4 |
| | 109.5° | | |
| $sp^2$ | $sp^2$ | $sp^5$ | $sp^5$ |
| 1/3 | 1/3 | 1/6 | 1/6 |
| | 120° | | |
| $sp^2$ | $sp^2$ | $sp^2$ | p |
| 1/3 | 1/3 | 1/3 | 0 |
| | 120° | | |
| sp | sp | p | p |
| 1/2 | 1/2 | 0 | 0 |
| | 180° | | |

Two descriptions of double bonds between small-core atoms emerged: a Molecular Orbital "sigma-pi" description (below, on the left) designed, initially, for use with double-bonded species in electronically excited states, and, following in the footsteps of organic chemistry's classical structural theory of molecules in their ground electronic states, a Valence Bond "bent bond" or "banana bond" equivalent orbital description.

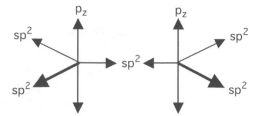  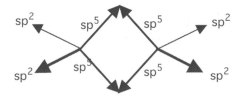

MO Description of a Double Bond          VB Description of a Double Bond

Which description is most useful? For whom? Students? Or computational chemists? And for what purpose? Description of molecules' ground states? Or molecules' electronically excited states?

It's like asking: Which mathematical coordinates are most useful: rectangular coordinates or polar coordinates? It depends on the situation. Whatever the situation, however, when viewed properly, in the light of the *indistinguishability of electrons* and the consequent *antisymmetric character of electronic wave functions*, the two descriptions of a double bond are seen to be _mathematically equivalent to each other_.

Consider a bent-bond description of a double bond between two carbon atoms A and B. Four hybrid orbitals are involved: two from atom A, two from atom B. (In the expressions below the bond axis lies along the x coordinate, with the z-axis in the plane of the page, also.)

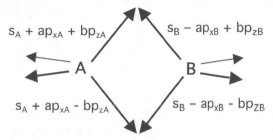

$s_A + ap_{xA} + bp_{zA}$ $\qquad$ $s_B - ap_{xB} + bp_{zB}$

$s_A + ap_{xA} - bp_{zA}$ $\qquad$ $s_B - ap_{xB} - bp_{zB}$

The two bent-bond components of the double bond are represented by the sums of the two top hybrids and the two bottom hybrids. Addition of those two partial sums yields, on division by 2, the following expression for the sigma component of a sigma-pi description of the double bond (as the overlap of two s/p hybrids of the form $s + ap_x$).

$$(s_A + ap_{xA}) + (s_B - ap_{xB})$$

Subtraction of the lower hybrid partial sum from the upper one yields, on division by 2b, the following expression for the pi component of a sigma-pi description of the double bond (as the overlap of two $p_z$ orbitals on adjacent atoms).

$$p_{zA} + p_{zB}$$

Since the system's full wave function may be expressed, in the orbital approximation, as a *determinant* whose columns' or rows' terms represent electron occupancy of individual orbitals, and since addition or subtraction of a determinant's rows or columns to or from each other does not change its numerical value, it's a matter of indifference from a purely mathematical point of view which orbitals one uses for expression of the wave function of double bonds: those of MO Theory or those of VB Theory.

On the other hand, if one thinks of a double bond solely in terms of its individual orbitals, rather than in terms of its full wave function, and if one then estimates, from the shapes of the individual orbitals, what the most likely distribution of electrons in a double bond is, then the difference between the MO and VB descriptions of the bond is, it's been said, "like the difference between night and day".

To judge the most likely distribution of indistinguishable electrons for a system from the system's orbital shapes, it is easiest to use orbitals that overlap each other as little as possible. The limiting case is the case of *exclusive orbitals*. Then the configuration of maximum probability has each electron located at an orbital's centroid of charge. For two spin-parallel electrons of a double bond the orbitals in question are those of a bent- or banana-bond VB description of the bond, with one electron located above the center of the bond and the other one located an equal distance below the center of the bond.

# Frontier Orbitals
## *A Localized Electron Domain Perspective*

The two traditional theories of the chemical bond, Valence Bond Theory and Molecular Orbital Theory, are jointly, in a way, paradoxical, from the point of view of electron-pair donor-acceptor interactions. What VB Theory lacks MO Theory has, for chemical purposes, a surfeit of: namely, orbital lobes for the description of electrophilic sites. Neither imperfection seems to have attracted much, if any, attention.

Description of valence-strokes of valence-stroke diagrams in terms of *hybrid atomic orbitals* provides Valence Bond Theory with a localized orbital account of its occupied electron domains. Symmetry adapted linear combinations of those localized orbitals generate the delocalized orbitals of Molecular Orbital Theory and, accordingly, provide an orbital account of systems' highest occupied molecular orbitals. Missing from valence stroke diagrams, however, is an account of molecules' lowest unoccupied orbitals. It is true, on the other hand, that the "pockets", "hollows", or "dimples" of valence *sphere* models of valence-stroke diagrams correspond to empty electrophilic sites, indicated in one instance below by the short arrow.

Conventional valence bond theory provides for such sites, however, no description in terms of hybrid atomic orbitals. Molecular orbital theory, on the other hand, provides, in addition to a lobe for a sigma bond A—B, from the sum of overlapping hybrid orbitals of A and B, *two* lobes from their algebraic difference: one off one end of the bond, the other off the other end. In "attack" on a molecule by a photon (in, e.g., a lone-pair/sigma* electronic transition), both lobes are occupied, simultaneously. In backside attack by nucleophilic reagents, however, only one lobe of a sigma antibonding molecular orbital is occupied. The other lobe at the other end of the bond is superfluous.

Valence Stick Theory, in summary, generates no lobes and Molecular Orbital Theory generates two lobes where only one lobe is needed in orbital descriptions of inter- and intra-molecular electron-pair donor-acceptor interactions. Description in orbital language of the pockets, hollows, or dimples of the "bumps and hollows" of valence-*sphere* models of molecules' valence-stroke diagrams requires directional, localized orbitals that for Octet-Rule-satisfying atomic cores point, as indicated in the following figure by the dashed arrows (of antibonding te* orbitals), in the opposite directions of the cores' conventional tetrahedral orbitals (te).

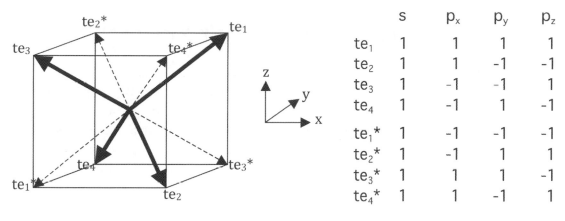

|        | s | $p_x$ | $p_y$ | $p_z$ |
|--------|---|-------|-------|-------|
| $te_1$ | 1 | 1  | 1  | 1  |
| $te_2$ | 1 | 1  | -1 | -1 |
| $te_3$ | 1 | -1 | -1 | 1  |
| $te_4$ | 1 | -1 | 1  | -1 |
| $te_1^*$ | 1 | -1 | -1 | -1 |
| $te_2^*$ | 1 | -1 | 1  | 1  |
| $te_3^*$ | 1 | 1  | 1  | -1 |
| $te_4^*$ | 1 | 1  | -1 | 1  |

$$te_1 = (1/2)(s + p_x + p_y + p_z), \text{ etc.}$$

In the case of double bonds, MO theory's pi antibonding orbitals have four lobes. Chemical attack by a nucleophilic reagent occurs, however, as indicated below by the arrow on the right, at the site of a *single* electrophilic site opposite one of the four hybrid atomic orbitals that comprise a double bond in its bent- or banana-bond formulation (at the left).

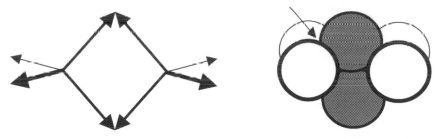

Pictured on the right is the usual electron domain model of ethylene. Domains of the C=C double bond are grey. White domains represent protonated pairs of C—H bonds.

The electron domain model of ethylene (above, on the right) illustrates reaction chemistry's two types of frontier orbitals: the highest occupied localized molecular orbitals of nucleophilic reagents (the dark domains) and the lowest unoccupied localized molecular orbitals of electrophilic reagents (indicated in one instance by the arrow). Nucleophilic sites are usually exposed, non-protonated electron-pairs of small-ring compounds, particularly 2-membered rings (double bonds) and, more often, 1-membered rings (lone pairs). Electrophilic sites are sites where atomic cores have — or can achieve most easily — their greatest, sterically accessible exposure, usually at external faces or "pockets" formed by three domains of their coordinated polyhedra of electron pairs. Those electrophilic sites correspond to the main lobes of outward-pointing, unoccupied, anti-bonding hybrid atomic orbitals complementary to inward-pointing hybrid atomic orbitals of chemical bonds.

# Mental Images of Atoms
## *From Newton to Modern Times*

Atomic Theory holds that all matter is made of atoms, and nothing else. To account for matter's mass and for the fact that two things cannot be at the same place at the same time, Newton postulated "hard massy" atoms. Rutherford localized most of their mass in tiny nuclei, to which Bohr added J. J. Thomson's corpuscular "electrons" in orbital motion, later replaced by "clouds" of G. P. Thomson's wave-like electrons.

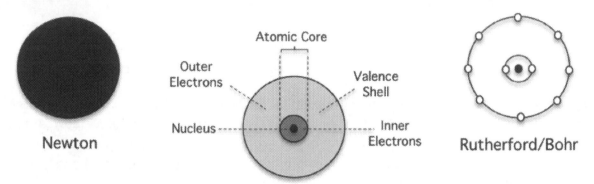

Lewis added the idea of "*electronic* structure", Linnett the idea of different structures for electrons of different spin ("up" or "down"), and Kimball the idea of exclusive charge clouds for electrons of the same spin.

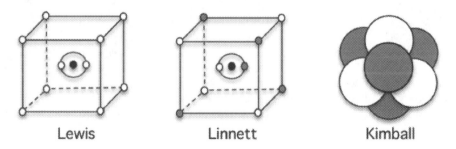

The last four figures are drawings of models of the ten-electron neon atom. Not shown in the last figure on the right are the two inner electrons of neon's atomic core, nestled out of sight in the interstice formed by the domains of its eight outer electrons.

The orientation of a free neon atom is arbitrary. Its electron cloud is a superposition of all possible orientations of its configuration of maximum probability, shown above.

The Rutherford/Bohr/Lewis/Linnett/Kimball model of the atom accounts, as mentioned, for matter's mass and for the fact that two things cannot be at the same place at the same time because two atoms cannot be at the same place at the same time because, it's postulated, the charge cloud domains of two electrons of the same spin seldom occupy the same space at the same time.

# Inter- and Intra-molecular Electron Pair Interactions

## *FNO and the Trimethyl Ammine-Diiodine Charge-Transfer Complex*

Valence sphere models have two conspicuous features: their *bumps*, of exposed domains of bonds to hydrogen and the one-member rings of lone pairs and the two-member rings of multiple bonds; and their *dimples*, where three domains meet and atomic cores are somewhat exposed. Dimples are, accordingly, electrophilic sites. Exposed electron domains are nucleophilic sites, except when protonated and in the valence shells of small, highly charged atomic cores (of electronegative atoms). The two types of sites may be so oriented as to interact with each other, in intramolecular electron pair donor-acceptor interactions, as, e.g., in FNO.

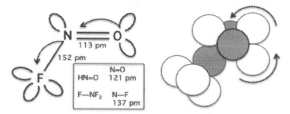

As the two oxygen lone pairs rotate counter-clockwise against the double bond's domains, with the $O^{+6}$ core following the tetrahedral interstice, thereby shortening the N=O bond, the $N^{+5}$ core moves outward toward the approaching electron domain, thereby lengthening the N—F bond.

Bump/dimple donor-acceptor interactions may occur between two molecules, forming thereby a molecular complex, as in the case of trimethyl ammine and iodine.

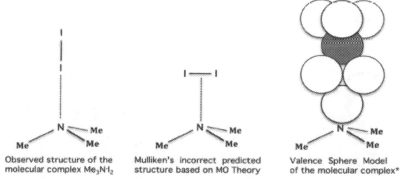

Observed structure of the molecular complex $Me_3N \cdot I_2$

Mulliken's incorrect predicted structure based on MO Theory

Valence Sphere Model of the molecular complex*

\* Constructed prior to personal knowledge by Bent of the existence of the molecular complex.

*Seldom in the history of science has so much explanatory power been achieved so simply. Valence Theory, as Newton said of geometry, "is proud of being able to achieve so much while taking so little from extraneous sources."* Prior to G. N. Lewis's electron-pair hypothesis of 1916, Valence Theory was a purely chemical theory with no connections with physics.

Such are the facts. Their interpretation? According to Valence Bond Theory, following Lewis, each domain of a valence sphere model is occupied by electron density that integrates out for the domain to two electrons (of opposite spin). Total electron counts are correct.

How is electron density distributed within domains? Uniformly (Kimball), Gaussian (Frost), as in lobes of hybrid atomic orbitals (Slater and Pauling) and in lobes of Natural Hybrid Orbitals (Weinhold and coworkers). For many chemical situations, however, *it doesn't matter!* As illustrated above for the ammine-iodine molecular complex, what's important in donor-acceptor interactions are, as shown, electron density *profiles*, not electron densities near nuclei.

# $I_2(g)$, $I_2(c)$, & $I_2(soln)$

Packing of iodine molecules in crystalline iodine is an instance of intermolecular donor-acceptor interactions.

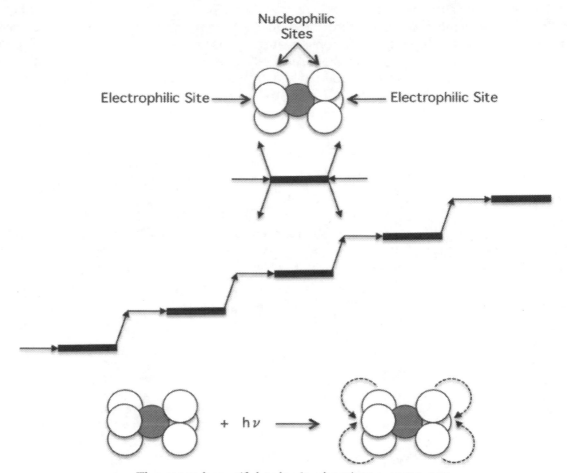

The most beautiful color in chemistry, some say.

Interaction of iodine molecules with visible light illustrates another feature of "Frontier Orbital Theory". An absorbed photon promotes electron density from the molecules' highest occupied, nucleophilic, electron-donor sites (its six lone pairs) to its lowest vacant, electrophilic, electron-acceptor sites (its two dimples opposite the I—I bond).

$I_2$(gas) and $I_2$(solute in nonpolar solvents, such as hexane and carbon tetrachloride), is a beautiful violet color. In polar, electron-pair-donor solvents, such as ammines, alcohols, aldehydes, ketones, and esters, in which its electrophilic sites are at least partially occupied, owing to intermolecular exposed-pair/external-dimple interactions, the $I_2$·solvent complex is a brown color.

$I_2$'s internal dimples, opposite its lone pairs, are electrophilic sites, in accordance with Mulliken's model of the ammine-Iodine complex, but, as the models show, they are *not sterically accessible* to external nucleophiles, owing to the presence of $I_2$'s lone pairs.

# Structure of Carbon Dioxide's van der Waals' Dimer $(CO_2)_2$

Carbon dioxide's van der Waals' dimer has a "skewed parallel structure" (1), as might have been anticipated from its valence sphere model.

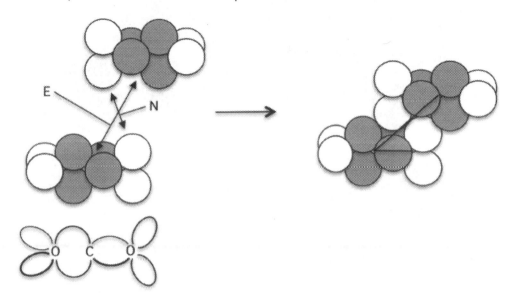

**Left:** Valence sphere and valence stroke models of $CO_2$. White circles represent domains of lone-pair nucleophilic sites (N). Gray circles represent domains of carbon-oxygen bonds. Dimples formed by three gray domains represent electrophilic sites (E). **Right:** Anticipated "bumps-and-dimples" model of the van der Waals' dimer of carbon dioxide.

The dimer's O—C—C angle, pictured on the right, is found from direct measurement with a protractor on the drawing of the equal-sphere-size model to be 54°, the smallest such angle permitted by the models. A less snug dimer would have a larger O—C—C angle. According to source (1), the skewed parallel structure [was] qualitatively predicted [by a "distributed multipole analysis" (DMA), plus short-range atomic repulsions represented by hard spheres] to have a [calculated] C—C—O angle of about 70°. The experimental value (determined sometime thereafter) was found to be 58.2°", close to the minimum value of 54° permitted by an equal-sphere-size model of $CO_2$.

For carbon dioxide a valence sphere model derived from a classical valence stroke diagram appears to yield a useful approximation to the molecule's electron density profile, as regards its "nonchemical" interaction with another carbon dioxide molecule.

[In the absence of a second molecule, $CO_2$'s electron density profile would be represented — by way of a superposition of structures (a.k.a. "resonance") — as cylindrically symmetrical.]

(1) "Current Themes in Microwave and Infrared Spectroscopy of Weakly Bound Complexes," K. R. Leopold, G. T. Fraser, S. E. Novick, and W. Klemperer, *Chem. Rev.* **1994**, *94*, 1807-1827.

# Valence Sphere Model of an $S_n2$ Reaction

Valence sphere models provide, as *frames of reference, **electron clouds,*** alternatives to arrangements of atomic nuclei. Instead of speaking, for instance, of an "inversion of configuration" in an $S_n2$ reaction, one speaks of passage of an atomic core through a trigonal interstice in an array of electron domains (Figures A to E).

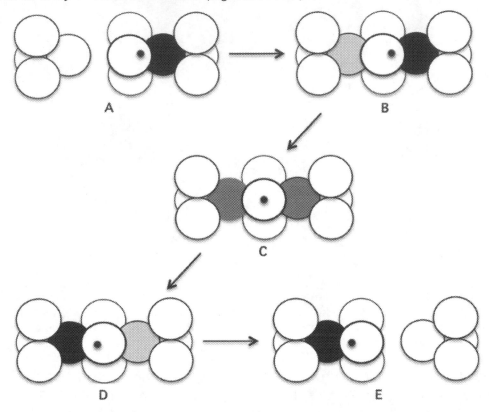

A   Reactants: e.g., a hydroxide ion and a molecule of methyl chloride. The small black circle represents, accordingly, a carbon core $C^{+4}$ (normally hidden in a drawing of a valence sphere model in a tetrahedral interstice). The large black circle represents the domain of the C—Cl bond. Not shown are the atomic cores $O^{+6}$ and $Cl^{+7}$, imagined to be in the tetrahedral interstices on the far left and the far right, respectively.

B   An electron-pair donor-acceptor/bump-and-dimple molecular complex. The structure is analogous to the iodine-trimethylammmine molecular complex. The migrating $C^{+4}$ core is beginning to establish an electrostatic hold on the gray domain of the hydroxide ion, initially a lone pair. The C—Cl bond is slightly stretched. The electron cloud is a fragment of an ABCBA close-packed array of exclusive electron-pair domains.

C   The reaction's transition state. The $C^{+4}$ core's electrostatic interaction with the adjacent electron-pair domain in the hydroxide ion has continued to increase at the expense of its hold on the electron pair of the C—Cl bond.

D   Donor-acceptor complex involving the reaction's products.

E   Reaction products: methanol and a chloride ion.

# A Correspondence between Structural Organic and Inorganic Chemistry

*Understanding is seeing that the same thing said different ways is the same thing.*

WITTGENSTEIN, slightly paraphrased

The correspondence between valence sphere models of covalent compounds and ionic models of metal oxides is extensive.

| Ionic, Heteropolar Compounds<br>Inorganic Chemistry | Covalent, Homopolar Compounds<br>Organic Chemistry |
|---|---|
| **Cations**<br>Relatively large atomic cores.<br>Their sizes and shapes are approximately independent of their chemical environment. | **Atomic Cores**<br>Nearly invariant parts of atoms.<br>Relatively small, highly charged cations. |
| **Anions**<br>Negatively charge species.<br>Usually larger and more polarizable than cations. | **Electride Ions**<br>Valence shell electron pairs.<br>Usually larger and more polarizable than anions.<br>Charge -2 if not protonated, -1 if protonated. |
| **Ionic Radius**<br>An approximate characterization of an ion's domain of influence. | **Electride Ion's Radius**<br>An approximate characterization of an electride ion's domain of influence. |
| **Crystal**<br>Large, periodic lattice of cations and anions. | **Molecule**<br>Small, aperiodic lattice of atomic cores and electride ions. |
| **Isomorphic Crystals**<br>Close analogy in chemical formulas and structures. | **Isoelectronic Molecules**<br>Same valence sphere models.<br>Same numbers of atomic cores and electride ions. |
| **Basic Oxide**<br>Oxide ion donor.<br>Relative large cations. | **Reducing Agent**<br>Electride ion donor.<br>Relatively large atomic cores. |
| **Acidic Oxide**<br>Oxide ion acceptor.<br>Relatively small cations. | **Oxidizing Agent**<br>Electride ion acceptor.<br>Relatively small atomic cores. |
| **Coordination Compound**<br>Close confederation of cations and anions. | **Covalent Compound**<br>Close confederation of small atomic cores and electride ions. |
| **Coordination Site**<br>A region of space about a cation that may be occupied by an anion. | **Exclusive Orbital**<br>A region of space about an atomic core that may be occupied by an electride ion. |
| **Pauling's First Rule of Crystal Chemistry**<br>Each cation is surrounded by a number of anions. | **The Couper/Crum Brown cum Lewis Convention**<br>Each chemical symbol is surrounded by a number of valence strokes cum electride ions. |
| **Coordination Polyhedron**<br>A description of a cation's anionic environment. | **Sextet, Octet, . . .**<br>A description of an atomic core's electride ion environment. |

15

| Ionic, Heteropolar Compounds | Covalent, Homopolar Compounds |
| --- | --- |
| **Common Cation Coordination Numbers**<br>4, 6, or 8. | **Octet Rule**<br>4 is a common atomic core coordination number. |
| **Augmented Cation Valence Shell**<br>A cation with more than its usual number<br>of coordinated anions. | **Expanded Octet**<br>An atomic core with more than four coordinated<br>electride ions. |
| **First Coordination Shell**<br>Spherical sheath about a cation.<br>Usually well-occupied by anions. | **Valence Shell**<br>Spherical sheath about an atomic core.<br>Usually well-occupied by electride ions. |
| **Second Coordination Shell**<br>Anions coordinated at faces of a cation's<br>first coordination shell. | **A Valence Shell's Valence Shell**<br>Electride Ion's coordinated at faces of an atomic<br>core's first coordination shell. |
| **Coordinatively Saturated**<br>Primary valence shell fully occupied by anions. | **Valence Rules Satisfied**<br>Primary valence shell fully occupied by electride<br>ions. |
| **Anion Deficient**<br>Insufficient anions to complete cations'<br>valence shells without sharing anions. | **Electron Deficient**<br>Insufficient electride ions to complete atomic<br>cores' valence shells without sharing. |
| **Shared Corner**<br>Two cation coordination polyhedra sharing<br>a single anion. | **Single Bond**<br>Two atomic core coordination polyhedra sharing<br>sharing a single electride ion. |
| **Shared Edge**<br>Two cation coordination polyhedra sharing<br>two anions. | **Double Bond**<br>Two atomic core coordination polyhedra sharing<br>two electride ions. |
| **Shared Face**<br>Two cation coordination polyhedra sharing<br>three anions. | **Triple Bond**<br>Two atomic core coordination polyhedra sharing<br>sharing three electride ions. |
| **Effects of Sharing on Interatomic Distances**<br>The more anions two cations share<br>the less the distance between the cations. | **Effects of Bond Orders on Bond Lengths**<br>Triple bonds are shorter than the double<br>bonds, which are shorter than single bonds. |
| **Pauling's Third Rule**<br>Shared edges and particularly shared faces<br>destabilize a structure, owing to the cation-<br>cation Coulomb term. | **Baeyer's Strain Energy**<br>Double bonds and particularly triple bonds<br>destabilize a structure, owing to the core-<br>core Coulomb term. |
| **Pauling's Fourth Rule**<br>Cations with large charges tend not to share<br>anions with each other, owing to the cation-<br>cation Coulomb term. | **Latimer's Rule**<br>Atomic cores with large charges tend not to share<br>electride ions with each other, owing to the core-<br>core Coulomb term. |
| **Irregular Polyhedra**<br>Coordination polyhedra whose anions are not<br>shared alike will usually be distorted. | **Irregular Valence Angles**<br>Electride ion polyhedra whose ions are not shared<br>alike will usually be distorted. |

| Ionic, Heteropolar Compounds | Covalent, Homopolar Compounds |
|---|---|

**Pauling's Fifth Rule**
Mutual repulsion between cations that share edges or faces of their coordination polyhedra may displace the cations from the centers of their polyhedra, with expected effects on internuclear distances and angles.

**Effects of Multiple Bonds on Molecular Structure**
Mutual repulsion between atomic cores that share two or three electride ions may displace the cores from the centers of their polyhedra, with expected effect on bond angles and lengths.

**Simple Bridging Anion**
An anion shared by two cations

**Ordinary Bonding Pair**
An electride ion shared by two atomic cores.

**Non-bridging Anion**
An anion in the coordination shell of only one cation.

**Lone Pair**
An electride ion in the valence shell of only one atomic core.

**Multiply-bridging Anion**
An anion shared by three or more cations.

**Multicenter Bond**
An electride ion shared by three or more atomic cores.

**An Empirical Rule**
Unshared anions occupy slightly more space in cations' coordination shells than do corresponding shared anions.

**The Gillespie-Nyholm Rule**
Unshared electride ions occupy angularly more space in atomic cores' valence shells than do shared electride ions.

**The Bragg-West Rule**
The size of an anion appears to be larger the larger the smallest cation to which it is coordinated.

**An Empirical Rule**
The size of an electride ion, $R$, appears to be larger the larger the smallest atomic core, $r$, to which it is coordinated: $R \approx 0.6\ \text{Å} + 0.4\ r$

**Anion Lattice**
Often the key to the simple description of an ionic compound. Often close-packed.

**Bond Diagram**
The key to the simple description of covalent compounds. Often the spheres of an isomorphic valence sphere model are a fragment of a close-packed array electride ion domains.

**Principle of Local Electrical Neutrality**
Charges in ionic crystals are usually neutralized locally, without a need for long lines of force.

**Valence Stroke Termination Rule**
Charges in molecules are usually neutralized locally (formal charges zero), without a need for long valence strokes.

Much of what has been said above is summarized in the following figure. Its top row is redrawn from a figure in Pauling's chapter on ionic crystals in his book *The Nature of the Chemical Bond*, showing "sharing of a corner, an edge, and a face by a pair of tetrahedra" [of anions].

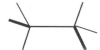  

# A Consilience between Computational and Conceptual Valence Theories

> The Consilience of Inductions takes place when an Induction obtained from one class of facts coincides with inductions obtained from another different class of facts. This Consilience is a test of the theory in which it occurs. WILLIAM WHEWELL

Valence Theory has four major Consiliences: one between Valence Stroke Diagrams and Valence Sphere Models; one between structural organic and structural inorganic chemistry; one between the Valence Stroke Termination Rule of Conceptual Valence Bond Theory and the Hohenberg-Kohn Theorem of Density Functional Theory; and one between Computational Valence Theory and Conceptual Valence Bond Theory.

---

| Computational Valence Theory | Conceptual Valence Theory |
| --- | --- |

---

| Computational Valence Theory | Conceptual Valence Theory |
| --- | --- |
| **Rooted in Planck's Quantum Theory of Black Body Radiation** | **Rooted in Lewis's Localized Electron-Pair Theory of the Chemical Bond** |
| **Born-Oppenheimer Approximation** | **Bond Diagram** |
| A molecular structure consists of two parts:<br>An electron cloud<br>Atomic nuclei | A bond diagram consists of two parts:<br>Valence strokes<br>Symbols of the elements |
| They may be considered independently. | They may be considered independently. |
| For a given nuclear geometry,<br>an electron cloud can be calculated<br>using - | For a given number of heavy atoms,<br>valence stroke diagrams can be constructed<br>using - |
| **Schrödinger's Equation** | **A Bond Number Equation** |
| **Solutions to Schrödinger's Equation** | **Isoelectronic Systems** |
| **Indistinguishability of Electrons**<br>$\Psi(1,2,...) = -\Psi(2,1,...) \rightarrow \Psi(1,1,...) = 0.$<br>Wavefunctions have, to some degree,<br>exclusive orbital character. | **Principle of Spatial Exclusion**<br>Valence strokes of valence stroke diagrams<br>never cross each other. Two electron pairs<br>cannot be at the same place at the same time. |
| **Electron Cloud** | **Array of Occupied Exclusive Orbitals** |
| **Pseudopotential**<br>Only valence electrons are dealt with explicitly.<br>Characterized by two parameters:<br>Nuclear charge<br>Cutoff radius | **Atomic Cores**<br>Only valence electrons are dealt with explicitly.<br>Characterized by two parameters:<br>Core charge<br>Core size |
| **Hohenberg-Kohn Theorem**<br>An electron density distribution determines<br>locations of atomic nuclei and their charges. | **Valence Stroke Termination Theorem**<br>A valence stroke diagram determines<br>locations of atomic cores and their charges. |
| **Ritz Variation Procedure**<br>Purpose: energy minimization.<br>Varied:<br>Electron clouds and<br>Nuclear locations | **Donor-Acceptor Interactions**<br>Purpose: energy minimization.<br>Varied:<br>Positions of electron domains and<br>Locations of atomic cores |

| Computational Valence Theory | Conceptual Valence Theory |
|---|---|
| **Virial Theorem** | **Virial Theorem** |
| Satisfied in E-minimized systems governed by Coulombic potentials: $E = -T = V/2$. | Satisfied in E-minimization of Kimball's Model, governed by Coulombic potentials: $E = -T = V/2$. |
| **Hellman-Feynman Theorem** | **Explanation of Ammonia's Bond Angle** |
| For E a minimum, forces on atomic nuclei vanish. | On passage from $CH_4$ to isoelectronic $NH_3$ the heavy atom core moves toward the lone pair. |
| **Nuclear-Electron Attraction** | **Atomic-Core/Valence-Shell Attraction** |
| The only term in the quantum mechanical Hamiltonian that leads to molecule-formation. | The term of first importance in Conceptual VB Theory, highlighted by the Octet Rule. |
| **Nuclear-Nuclear Repulsion** | **Core-Core Repulsion** |
| Tends to keep atomic cores of large charge, such as $F^{+7}$, as far apart as possible. | Accounts for the anti-s-seeking character of of electronegative substituents. |
| **Electron-Electron Repulsion** | **Mutual Repulsion of Valence Shell Electrons** |
| Of two types: between electrons of the same spin, kept apart by "Pauli Forces", and between electrons of opposite spin, kept apart by Coulombic forces, and giving rise to use of DODS: Different Orbitals for Different Spins. | Of two types: between electrons of the same spin, located in different exclusive orbitals and between electrons of opposite spin, kept apart by Coulombic forces, and giving rise to use of DSDSS: Different Structures for Different Spin Sets. |
| **Electronic Kinetic Energy** | **Electronic Kinetic Energy** |
| Responsible for the form of Schrödinger's generalization of de Broglie's relation, $\lambda = h/p$, as a second order partial differential equation: $H\Psi = E\Psi$. | Responsible for the *finite size* of Conceptual Valence Bond Theory's Exclusive Orbitals. Accounts, at a glance, for the saturation and directional character of chemical affinity. |
| **Superposition Principle** | **Resonance** |
| One of the leading principles of quantum physics. | One of the leading features of valence bond theory. |
| **Numerical Accounts of Molecules and the Chemical Bond** | **Conceptual Accounts of Molecules and the Chemical Bond** |
| **The Physical Basis of Valence Theory** | **The Chemical Significance of the Physical Basis of Valence Theory** |

The Consilience joins two of the leading achievements of scientific thought.

# Visual "Puns" with Tangent Spheres
## *Different Ways of Looking at the Same Thing*

Tangent spheres, invested with physical significance, yield *linguistic* "puns" involving the languages of structural organic and inorganic chemistry. Divorced of physical significance, they yield *visual* "puns".

## The Octahedron

Formed by gluing together three close-packed spheres is a triangular arrangement, the start of a close-packed layer, say "A". Nesting one such arrangement on top of another one, as closely as possible, yields the arrangement pictured in Figure 1.

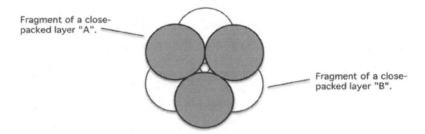

Fragment of a close-packed layer "A".

Fragment of a close-packed layer "B".

**Fig. 1.** Top view of a close-packed arrangement of two 3-membered fragments of close-packed layers, A and B.

Tilting the close packed layers, held horizontal with one member of the top layer pointing toward oneself, slightly away from oneself until the top sphere is seen to be nestled against a square-planar arrangement of four spheres, yields the orientation of the arrangement pictured twice in Figure 2.

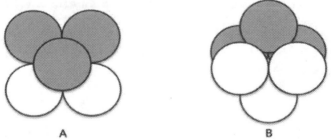

A          B

**Fig. 2.** Two views of a bicapped square-planar "octahedral" (meaning eight sides or faces) arrangement of spherical electron pair domains. A: Top view. B: Side view.

Bicapped triangles, squares, and pentagons, consisting of, respectively, 5, 6, and 7 spheres, are the trigonal, tetragonal, and pentagonal bipyramidal arrangements of electron pair domains in the valence shells of the central atoms of $PF_5$, $SF_6$, and $IF_7$.

The interstice created by an octahedral arrangement of six domains is nearly twice the size of the one created by a tetrahedral arrangement of four domains of the same size; hence existence for the large-core elements of the second and later rows of periodic tables' p-blocks of "expanded octets" with 5, 6, 7, or more valence shell electron pairs.

# The Face Centered Cube

Formed by capping the three edges of three close-packed spheres, on a flat surface, is a triangular arrangements of six spheres three spheres on a side. Nesting together two such arrangements, held horizontal, one on top of the other one, and staggered, so as to form an inner octahedron, yields the arrangement pictured in Figure 3 after adding single spheres, centered, top and bottom. Produced is a fragment of an ABCA close-packed arrangement of fourteen spheres arranged in layers of 1 6 6 1 spheres.

Fig. 3. Top view of a close-packed arrangement of fragments of four close-packed layers ABCA with, respectively, 1 6 6 1 members. (Not shown is the second "1", at the bottom of the stack, directly beneath the top sphere.)

Tilting the arrangement, with its layers initially horizontal and its second layer down from the top pointing away from oneself, until a face-centered square planar arrangement becomes visible, yields, with a slight rotation clockwise, and a backward tilt, the orientation of the arrangement pictured at the left in Figure 4.

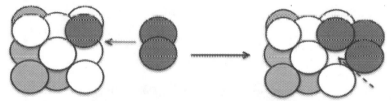

Fig. 4. Far Left: A view that shows why close packing of spheres in layers ABCA is called "face centered cubic" (fcc) close packing. It contains two types of interstices: 8 tetrahedrally surrounded interstices per unit cell, one inside each corner sphere, in a simple cubic arrangement; and octahedrally surrounded interstices centered on each of the unit cell's edge-centers, with one at the cell's center. Thus, per unit cell, the number of octahedral interstices is 1 + 12/4 = 4 themselves in a fcc arrangement (seen on translating the cell's origin at the location of a sphere to the location of an octahedral interstice). The dashed arrow on the right points to the center of an octahedral interstice. The horizontal left-pointing arrow on the left indicates partial completion of an octahedral interstice. The number of close packed spheres per unit cell is 8 x 1/8, for those at a cell's corners, plus 6 x 1/2, for those at its faces, for a total of 4 per unit cell, the same number as the number of octahedral interstices.

Location of chloride ions at the sphere's locations and occupancy of the octahedral interstices by sodium ions yields the structure of sodium chloride. Like the arrangement of cations in NaCl, the arrangement of atoms, and their atomic cores, in a number of metals is fcc. Calcium is an example. Locating its valence shell electron pairs in a fcc arrangement with calcium ions occupying the "electride" ions' octahedral interstices yields a model of the electronic structure of calcium metal that fits its structure and chemical properties, such as the metal's reaction with water, by way of proton transfers from molecules of water to powerful Brönsted bases: the electride ions, $e_2^{-2}$, of "calcium electride".

$$Ca^{+2}(e_2^{-2})(c) + 2\ HOH(l) = Ca(OH)_2(c) + H_2(g) + Heat!$$

CAUTION! A few calcium turnings in a test tube of water may bring the water to a boil.

# Space-Filling with a Complement of s-, p-, and d-Electrons
## *Uses of a cube's corners, edges, and faces to locate orbitals' lobes*

A cube's corners correspond to the principle lobes of two anticoincident sets of tetrahedrally arranged $sp^3$ hybrid orbitals. Edges correspond schematically to locations of lobes of three ($t_{2g}$) d-orbitals, and faces to lobes of two additional ($e_g$) d-orbitals.

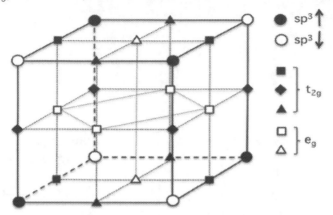

Edge-centered and face-centered lobes of d-orbitals occupy nooks and crannies created by lobes of corner-centered tetrahedral orbitals; and vice-versa. Jointly the two sets of orbitals occupy the available space about atomic cores (with still more complex chink-filling occurring for higher atomic numbers and f-type nooks and crannies).

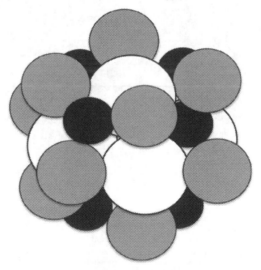

Extension of the exclusive orbital philosophy that works so well for compounds of elements of the s- and p-blocks of periodic tables to compounds of the tables' d-bock elements may, accordingly, entail, for the most part, adoption of conventional descriptions of the compounds' electronic structures, inasmuch as chemists' d-orbitals, in being functions of r times the angular functions xy, xz, yz, $x^2 - y^2$, and $z^2$, can, like p-orbitals, be mixed with s-orbitals to yield localized orbitals of desired directionality.

# The Valence Stroke Termination Rule

If lone pairs in a valence stroke diagram are represented by rabbit-ear valence strokes, both ends of which terminate at the same atomic core site, then –

*The number of valence stroke terminations at the symbol of an element of zero formal charge is equal to its core's charge.*

$C^{+4}$     $N^{+5}$     $O^{+6}$     $F^{+7}$

Valence stroke environments for local electrical neutrality of the four atomic cores of elements of the first row of periodic tables' p-blocks noted for obeying the Octet Rule.

If lone pairs and bonding pairs are treated alike, the ten valence stroke environments pictured above are isoelectronic with each other and may be represented by a single valence sphere model.

Species that have the same valence sphere models are said to be isoelectronic.

The Valence Stroke Termination Rule (VSTR) is equivalent to saying that for zero formal charges -

*Valence stroke diagrams sans symbols of the elements determine locations of atomic cores.*

The Hohenberg-Kohn Theorem of Density Functional Theory says, similarly, that -

*Electron density distributions determine locations of atomic nuclei.*

# Valence Strokes, Lines of Force, Chemical Bonds, and Electron Clouds

Chemistry's valence strokes are like Faraday's lines of force in four ways.

- They never cross each other.
- They act as though they repel each other.
- They are anchored at both ends by electrical charges.
- They satisfy Gauss' Law; i.e.: the number that enter or emerge from a region of space is proportional to the net charge within that region of space.

In one way, however, valence strokes and lines of force are not like each other.

Lines of force have a *vector character*. Tangents to them indicate directions of movement of test charges. Valence strokes haven't that character: or, rather, they have it twice over, Figure 1.

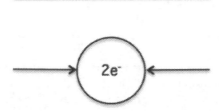

**Fig. 1.** The valence stroke (top line) after (bottom line) Lewis, Faraday, and Gauss.

The Lewis/Faraday/Gauss model of a valence stroke shows at a glance what a chemical bond is.

> *A chemical bond is two atomic cores attracted*
> *to the same intervening electrical charge.*

As an inter-core distance in a chemical system decreases, the system's energy, owing to core/bonding-charge interaction, becomes more negative.

A lone pair is a valence shell electron pair not involved in a chemical bond. A dative bond is a lone pair in a bonding region, Figure 2.

**Fig. 2.** Lewis/Faraday/Gauss models of, left, a lone pair and, right, a dative bond.

Since atomic cores' positive charges are quantized, and localized, existence of discrete lines of force between those charges and portions of an electron clouds' negative charge suggests that electron clouds consist of localized charge distributions charged with negative charges equal in magnitude to those of one or two protons.

# Lines of Force, Gauss's Law, and Valence Stroke Diagrams

Faraday's lines of force, as said (previous essay), like valence strokes, never cross each other and stay as far apart as possible while remaining anchored at electrical charges. Called to mind by the Valence Stroke Termination Rule is –

### Gauss's Law Regarding Lines of Force and Electrical Charges

*The number of lines of force* (indicative of directions of motion of a free test charge) *that enter or emerge from a region of space is proportional to the net charge within that region of space.*

Suppose that valence strokes correspond in some manner to Faraday lines of force. Take the constant of proportionality in Gauss's Law to be 1. Then, by the Valence Stroke Termination Rule and Gauss's Law, associated with the symbols H, C, N, O, and F are electrical charges of magnitude 1, 4, 5, 6, and 7, respectively. The sum of those numbers for the molecules $CH_4$, $NH_3$, $H_2O$, and HF is 8, say +8. In the electrically neutral molecules that charge sum must be balanced by charges of the opposite sign associated, presumably, with the molecules' four valence strokes.

*Associated with a valence stroke is an electrical charge of –2.*

G. N. Lewis, traveling a different route, arrived at same conclusion. The following figure illustrates Gauss's Law for a molecule of formaldehyde, $H_2CO$.

*Faraday-Gauss Diagram for $H_2CO$*

Dashed lines represent Faraday lines of force (directed, if arrows were attached to them, from positive to negative charges). The number of terminations of lines of force at circles equals the magnitude of the charges within the circles. The large dashed circle indicates a region of local electrical neutrality, consistent with the absence of any long lines of force.

# The Logic of the Rabbit-Ear Representation of Lone Pairs

*Sometimes the pencil is more powerful than the mind.*

Sulfur in its dihydride, $H_2S$, is said to be "divalent". In its hexafluoride, $SF_6$. however, it's often said, in theoretical circles, to be "hypervalent". Suppose, however, that history is altered and that we start with $SF_6$, with sulfur "hexavalent". Would we then say that in its dihydride sulfur is "hypovalent"?

Alternatively, one might address the issue of sulfur's "variable valence" by supposing that Nature is natural and neither "hyper-" nor "hypo-"something-or-other. To clarify the relation between sulfur in $SF_6$ and sulfur in $SF_2$, strip four fluorine atoms from $SF_6$.

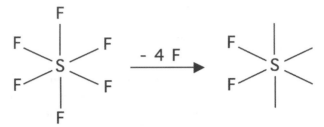

Then, with a pencil, apply a convention employed previously for encoding information in chemical formulas, viz, the Convention of No Dangling Valence Strokes. I.e., assume that *pairs of adjacent dangling affinities, represented by valence strokes, "self-saturate".*

In the words of Edward Franklin (1866), one of the fathers of valence theory:

> "These remarkable facts [regarding the phenomenon of "variable valence"] can be explained by a very simple and obvious assumption, *viz*, that one or more pairs of *bonds belonging to one and the same atom can unite, and, having saturated each other, become, as it were, latent.*"

Sulfur's maximum affinity (6) is the sum of its active and latent affinities. (The corresponding statement does not hold for oxygen and other small-core elements of the first row of the p-block, which, unlike sulfur, do not expand their octets.)

In the Lewis interpretation of bond diagrams, rabbit-ear valence strokes represent unshared valence shell electron pairs.

Unexpected arrival, with the Rabbit-Ear Convention regarding lone pairs, is a bonus, in the form of Conceptual Valence Bond Theory's *Valence Stroke Termination Rule.* If one started with that Rule, as a Lemma of the Hohenberg-Kohn Theorem of Electron Density Theory, the Rabbit-Ear Convention regarding lone pairs would emerge as a logical deduction.

The present results support the view that it's useful to suppose that sulfur in $SF_6$ is "hexavalent", where "valent" refers to numbers of active affinities, each one represented by a single valence stroke termination at the symbol "S" in $SF_6$'s valence stroke diagram and representing, physically, a valence-shell electron pair. How best to *describe* $SF_6$'s valence strokes and corresponding valence shell electron pairs *in the language of atomic orbitals* is, however, at the present time, a moot point. It's sidestepped in Conceptual Valence Bond Theory, since it does not use atomic orbitals.

# Valence Stroke Arrangements that Satisfy the VSTR for S⁺⁶

VSCN = Valence-Stroke Coordination Number of S⁺⁶

For all arrangements the central atom cores, S⁺⁶ (not shown),
have a valence shell termination number of 6.

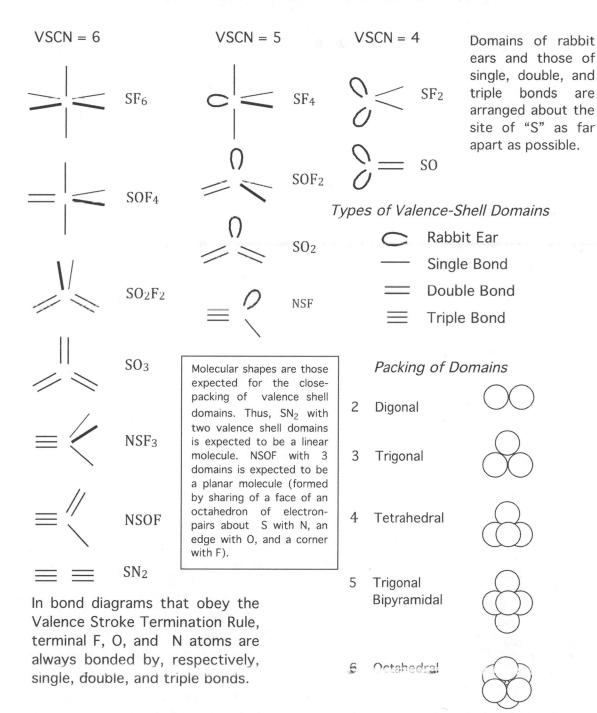

VSCN = 6

SF₆

SOF₄

SO₂F₂

SO₃

NSF₃

NSOF

SN₂

VSCN = 5

SF₄

SOF₂

SO₂

NSF

VSCN = 4

SF₂

SO

Domains of rabbit ears and those of single, double, and triple bonds are arranged about the site of "S" as far apart as possible.

*Types of Valence-Shell Domains*

⊂  Rabbit Ear
—  Single Bond
=  Double Bond
≡  Triple Bond

*Packing of Domains*

2  Digonal

3  Trigonal

4  Tetrahedral

5  Trigonal Bipyramidal

6  Octahedral

Molecular shapes are those expected for the close-packing of valence shell domains. Thus, SN₂ with two valence shell domains is expected to be a linear molecule. NSOF with 3 domains is expected to be a planar molecule (formed by sharing of a face of an octahedron of electron-pairs about S with N, an edge with O, and a corner with F).

In bond diagrams that obey the Valence Stroke Termination Rule, terminal F, O, and N atoms are always bonded by, respectively, single, double, and triple bonds.

# Expanded Octets about S⁺⁶ Continued

To judge solely from bond lengths, the sulfur oxides $SO_{1,2,3}$ and fluorides $SF_{2,4,6}$ may be formulated as follows (E represents an electron pair; bond lengths are in pm):

$$SE_2(=O) \quad SE(=O)_2 \quad S(=O)_3 \quad and \quad S(E_2)(-F)_2 \quad SE(-F)_4 \quad S(-F)_6$$

$$149 \qquad\quad 143 \qquad\quad 142 \qquad\qquad\qquad 159 \qquad\quad 155\text{-}165 \qquad 156$$

Less stable, Octet-Rule structures for those species, *absent formal charges*, are (sans lone pairs):

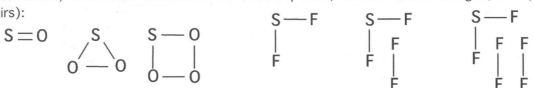

Octet-Rule, zero-formal-charge structures for SNF, SNF₃, and $S_2N_2$ are -

Observed structures, suggested by short sulfur-nitrogen bonds, are -

In each instance observed structures place more electrons in bonding regions than do the corresponding Octet-Rule structures, thereby expanding sulfur's valence shell, from eight to ten or twelve electrons. Another example of an "expanded" valence shell for S⁺⁶ is $S_3N_2O_2$.

Octet-Rule Structure          Observed Structure

Yet another example is $SO_2F_2$.

Octet-Rule Structure          Observed Structure

Formulating $SO_2F_2$ with single S—O bonds places on sulfur an unrealistic formal charge of +2 and does not account in so simple a fashion for its observed bond lengths and for Nature's preference for the observed structures over the corresponding octet structure, FOSOF.

The S⁺⁶ core (radius 29 pm) is slightly over three times larger than an octet-rule-obeying O⁺⁶ core (radius 9 pm), which, unlike S⁺⁶, would "rattle" (i.e. not fill) an octahedral interstice formed by three oxygen or six fluorine ligands (radii of bonding domains ≈ 65 pm).

# Large C—H Models

Except for ease of construction of valence sphere models, there's no reason why domains of C—H bonds should be considered to be the same size as domains of C—C single bonds. And, indeed, to fit with valence sphere models ratios of intra- to inter-molecular distances in crystalline paraffins, one must suppose that their C—H domains are some fifty percent larger than their C—C domains.

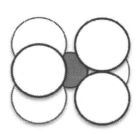 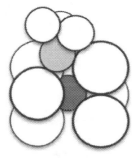

**Left:** large C—H model of ethane. **Right:** schematic representation of steric hindrance in an abortive attack on ethane's carbon-carbon bond by a hydronium ion.

Evident is the reason why ethane is a "par-affins". Its intrinsically reactive carbon-carbon bond (the dark gray domain) is protected from attack by electrophilic reagents, such as hydronium ions, by, in L. P. Hammett's words, "electronic armor" consisting of protonated electron pairs in the valence shells of $C^{+4}$ atomic cores (not shown above).

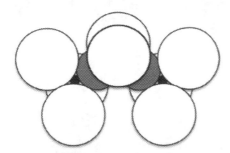

**Above:** large C—H model of propane. Small black domains represent $C^{+4}$ atomic cores. Relative sizes of domains: white 100, gray 67, black 16.

Illustrated is the fact that in ionic models of matter, whether consisting of conventional anions coordinated by conventional cations or consisting of electron pairs — and protonated pairs — coordinated by atomic cores, one size does not fit all situations.

# Charges and Relative Sizes of Atomic Cores of p-Block Elements
## Octet-Rule-Satisfying Elements

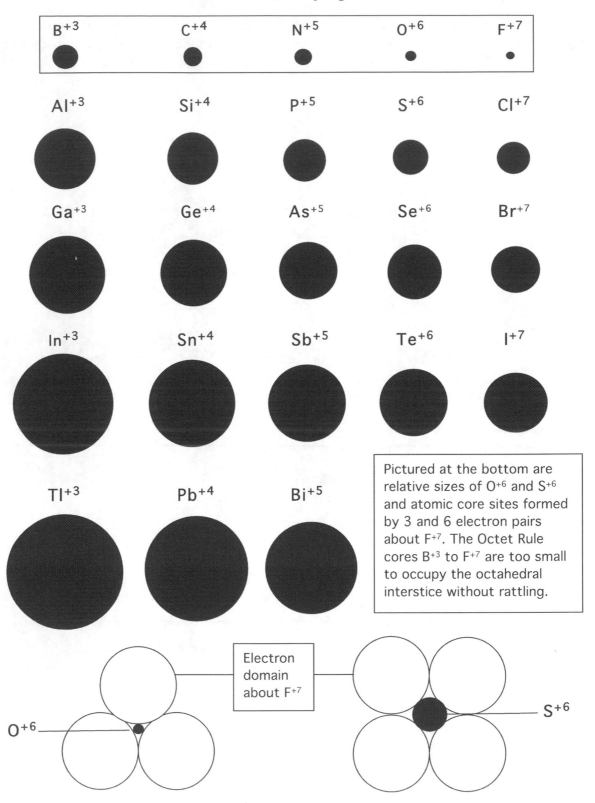

Pictured at the bottom are relative sizes of $O^{+6}$ and $S^{+6}$ and atomic core sites formed by 3 and 6 electron pairs about $F^{+7}$. The Octet Rule cores $B^{+3}$ to $F^{+7}$ are too small to occupy the octahedral interstice without rattling.

# Valence-Sphere/Atomic-Core Model of the Extraordinary Kinetic Stability of $SF_6$

"Sulfur hexafluoride is unique in its stability and chemical inertness," write Greenwood and Earnshaw (*Chemistry of the Elements*, p813): "it is a colorless, odorless, tasteless, unreactive, non-flammable, non-toxic, insoluble gas prepared by burning sulfur in an atmosphere of fluorine."

"Because of its extraordinary stability, and excellent dielectric properties," continue Greenwood and Earnshaw, "it is extensively used as an insulating gas for high-voltage generators and switch gear: at a pressure of 2-3 bars it withstands 1.0-1.4 MV across electrodes 50 mm apart without breaking down, and at 10 bars it is used for high-power underground electrical transmission systems at 400 V and above. $SF_6$ can be heated to 500 degrees without decomposition, and is unattacked by most metals, P, As, etc., even when heated. It is also uncreative toward high-pressure steam presumably as a result of kinetic factors since the gas phase reaction $SF_6 + 3H_2O \rightarrow SO_3 + 6HF$ should release 460 kJ mol$^{-1}$... Hot HCl and molten KOH are also without effect."

Pictured below are two views of an explanation for sulfur hexafluoride's extraordinary kinetic stability, in the form of drawings of a valence-sphere/atomic-core model of a molecule of $SF_6$.

**Black Sphere:** Domain of $S^{+6}$: r = 29 pm (Pauling, *Nature of the Chemical Bond*, 3$^{rd}$ edition, p514).
**Gray Spheres:** Domains of S—F bonds: R/pm = 60 + 0.4r($F^{+7}$)/pm = 60 + 0.4x7 = 63.
**White Spheres:** Domains of fluorines' valence shell lone pairs, taken to be the same size as the atoms' bonding domains. More realistically, they might be a shade larger. The drawing on the left shows only four of $SF_6$'s six fluorine ligands.

According to the model, sulfur hexafluoride's $S^{+6}$ core is extraordinarily well shielded from attack by nucleophilic reagents, by two layers of electronic armor: an outer layer of eighteen approximately close-packed fluorine lone pair domains; and an inner layer of six more closely close-packed bonding domains. If a nucleophile managed to penetrate the first layer of defense, it would face an even larger barrier in the second layer of defense.

# Bond Types

Atomic cores are, broadly speaking, of two types: large (metals) or small (nonmetals). (The large/small divide occurs at about 50 pm.) About domains of shared, bonding electrons atomic cores may be, accordingly: all small; some small, some large; or all large, corresponding to three types of chemical bonds:

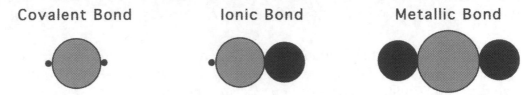

| Covalent Bond | Ionic Bond | Metallic Bond |

Below are schematic drawings in 2-dimensional flatland of valence-circle models, downward, of covalent dichlorine, ionic sodium chloride, and metallic calcium.

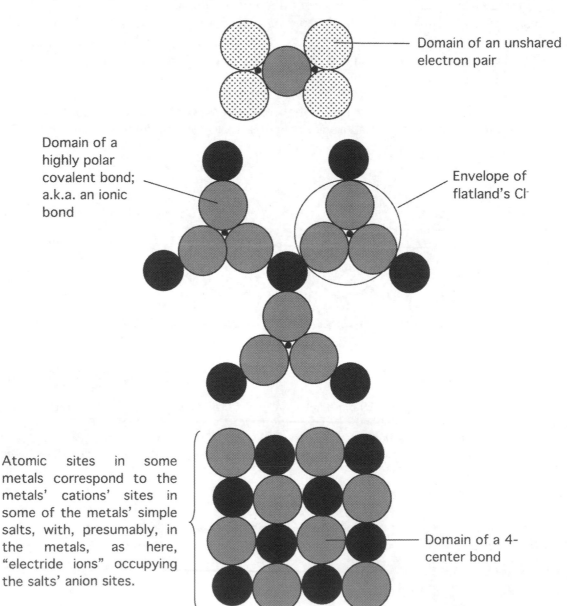

Domain of an unshared electron pair

Domain of a highly polar covalent bond; a.k.a. an ionic bond

Envelope of flatland's Cl⁻

Atomic sites in some metals correspond to the metals' cations' sites in some of the metals' simple salts, with, presumably, in the metals, as here, "electride ions" occupying the salts' anion sites.

Domain of a 4-center bond

# Screened and Exposed Electrophilic and Nucleophilic Sites

Electrophilic sites attractive to nucleophilic reagents arise from positively charged atomic nuclei that are screened from nucleophilic reagents by, first, *inner-shell electrons*, yielding atomic cores (such as $C^{+4}$, $N^{+5}$, $O^{+6}$, and $F^{+7}$) and, further, by *valence shell electrons,* yielding different degrees of residual electrophilic character, Figure 1.

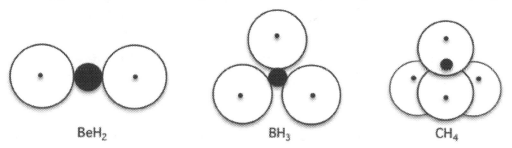

**Fig. 1.** Schematic drawings of valence sphere models of, left to right, three hydrides of increasing screening and diminishing atomic core exposure. Smallest black spheres represent protons of heavy-atom/hydrogen bonds. Larger black spheres represent the atomic cores $Be^{+2}$ (of $BeH_2$), $B^{+3}$ (of $BH_3$), and $C^{+4}$ (of $CH_4$). Largest spheres, white, represent domains of heavy-atom/hydrogen bonding electrons; i.e., with their protons, they correspond to polarized hydride ions, $H^-$.

Most exposed nucleophilic sites are those of the 1- and 2-membered rings of lone pairs and double bonds, Figure 2.

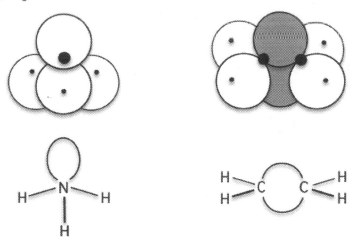

**Fig. 2.** Valence sphere models (top row) and corresponding valence stroke diagrams (bottom row) of (left) the 1-member exposed ring of the lone pair of a molecule of ammonia and (right) the 2-member, somewhat less exposed ring of the equivalent electron pair domains (shaded gray) of the double bond of a molecule of ethylene.

Exposed electrophilic atomic cores, such as $B^{+3}$ of $BH_3$ (Figure 1), form with exposed nucleophilic electron domains, such as the lone pairs of $NH_3$ (Figure 2), dative bonds of a Lewis acid-base adduct, Figure 3.

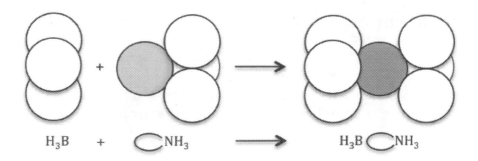

$H_3B$ + $\bigcirc NH_3$ → $H_3B \bigcirc NH_3$

**Fig. 3.** Valence sphere model of dative bond formation in the reaction of $BH_3$ with $NH_3$. The light gray sphere on the left represents the domain of ammonia's lone pair. The darker gray sphere on the right represents the  domain of the dative bond of the Lewis acid-base adduct $H_3B{:}NH_3$.

$H_3B{:}NH_3$ is isoelectronic with $H_3C{-}CH_3$. Domains of the latter molecule's carbon-hydrogen bonds are, to judge by inter- and intramolecular interatomic distances in crystalline $H_3C{-}CH_3$, some fifty percent larger than the domain of the C—C single bond, Figure 4.

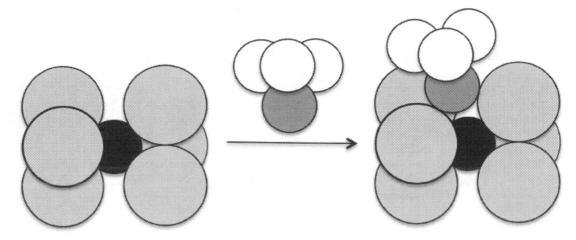

**Fig. 4. Left:** Large CH model (again) of ethane, $C_2H_6$. The domain of its carbon-carbon bond is represented by the back sphere. **Center:** Model of HF. **Right:** Protonation of the electron pair domain of the carbon-carbon bond of $C_2H_6$ frustrated by steric hindrance from $C_2H_6$'s large C—H domains.

C—H domains are neither strongly nucleophilic nor strongly electrophilic. Molecules whose surfaces are composed solely of the protonated electron pair domains of C—H bonds (the saturated hydrocarbons, $C_nH_{2n+2}$) are commonly called, accordingly, "paraffins"; for, for the most part, at room temperature, they have relatively little chemical affinity for other molecules, including themselves. Their boiling points, e.g., like those of hydrogen and helium, are relatively low, Figure 5.

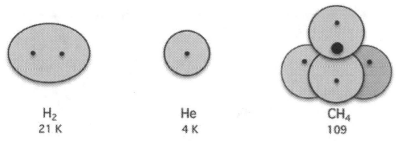

H₂
21 K

He
4 K

CH₄
109

Fig. 5. Boiling points of three well-shielded sets of atomic nuclei.

Falling in degrees of exposure between the domains of carbon-carbon bonds of paraffins, such as ethane (Figure 4), and carbon-carbon double bonds, such as ethylene (Figure 2), lie the domains of the carbon-carbon bonds of 3-membered rings, such as those of cyclopropane, Figure 5.

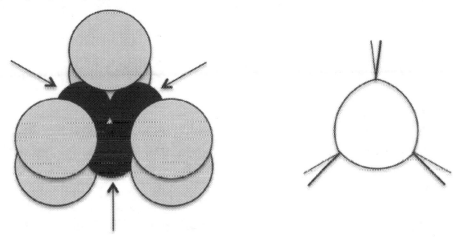

Fig. 5. Valence sphere and valence stroke models of cyclopropane, $C_3H_6$. Arrows point to the partially exposed domains of the electron pairs of the molecule's carbon-carbon bonds, somewhat less bent, as pictured explicitly at the right, than those of the 2-membered rings of $C_2H_4$ (Figure 2), and still less bent than a rabbit-ear representation of a lone pair (Figure 2).

Exposure of positively charged, electrophilic atomic cores, as in $BH_3$ (Figure 1), and, in the same chemical species, exposure of negatively charged, nucleophilic, hydride-like domains may yield dimers, Figure 6.

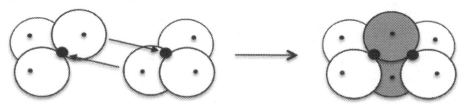

Fig. 6. Valence sphere model of the dimerization of $BH_3$ to $B_2H_6$. Gray domains represent 3-center BHB bonds.

Dimerization of the trimethyl derivative of $BH_3$, $B(CH_3)_3$, through formation of bridging BCB 3-center bonds, as in $Al_2(CH_3)_6$, is frustrated in the case of $B(CH_3)_3$, owing to shielding of the $B^{+3}$ cores by the 18 C—H domains of the 6 bulky methyl groups, **Fig. 7.**

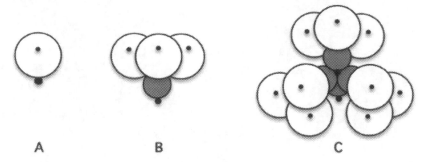

**Fig. 7.** Valence sphere models of: (**A**) a C—H bond (showing, moving upward: $C^{+4}$; the domain of the bond's electron pair; and the hydrogen atom's proton); (**B**) a methyl group; and (**C**) the nine C—H bonds of a bulky t-butyl group, which has approximately the same arrangement of methyl groups as non-dimerizing $B(CH_3)_3$.

Bulky $B(CH_3)_3$ with its shielded electrophilic $B^{+3}$ site not only does not dimerize, it also does not form an adduct with 2,6-lutidine (the center species below), whereas less hindered $BF_3$ does do so.

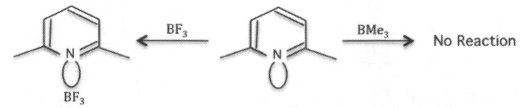

Sterically demanding Lewis acids and bases that react neither with each other nor, separately, with dihydrogen may, jointly, yield cleavage of the sterically undemanding dihydrogen molecule, heterolytically, Figure 8.

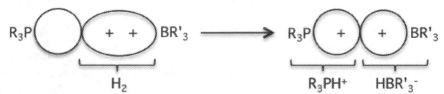

**Fig. 8.** Heterolytic cleavage of $H_2$ via a proton transfer and hydride ion coordination by a sterically hindered, frustrated Lewis acid-base pair $BR'_3$ and $R_3P$, where R = t-butyl (Figure 7C) and R' = $C_6F_5$.

Dihydrogen is also cleaved under mild conditions by sterically hindered carbenes and, analogously, by oxidative addition to coordinately unsaturated transition metal ions.

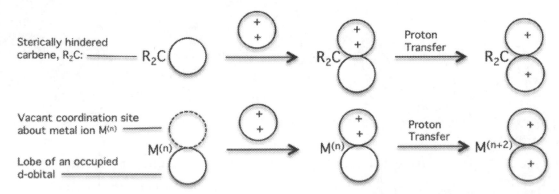

# Density Functional Theory

## Excerpts from Walter Kohn's Nobel Lecture of 1999

### [slightly annotated]

For relating bond diagrams of chemistry's classical structural theory to fundamental physical principles, Natural Bond Orbitals (NBOs) are one of the most useful developments in interpretative chemistry since G. N. Lewis' electron pair hypothesis of 1916. For obtaining the NBOs, themselves, from wavefunctions, Weinhold and coworkers use density functional theory, introduced by Hohenberg and Kohn in 1964, a year after the first paper on "Tangent-Sphere Models" of molecules' electron density profiles appeared.

### *Electronic Structure of Matter — Wave Functions and Density Functionals*

"Density Functional Theory (DFT) [like, on the conceptual side, Valence Sphere Models] is an alternative approach to the theory of electronic structure, in which the electron density distribution, rather than the many electron wavefunction, plays the central role. *All properties derivable from Schrödinger's equation are implicit in the ground state electron density distribution* [emphasis added].

"In my view DFT contributes to a fundamental *understanding* of electronic structure. Theoretical chemists and physicists, following the path of the Schrödinger equation, have become accustomed to think of *single particle orbitals*. However, when **high** accuracy is required, so many Slater determinants are required (in some calculations up to $\approx 10^{9}$!) that *comprehension* becomes difficult [and even incorrect, if accurate numerical output of a highly refined wavefunction is taken as confirming the form of the initial input]. DFT provides a complementary perspective. It focuses [as does Conceptual Valence Bond Theory] on the real 3-dimensional electron density $n(r)$ of the ground state.

"A very crude theory of electronic energy in terms of $n(r)$, the Thomas-Fermi (TF) theory, has existed since the 1920s. Although it does not lead to any chemical binding, it raised in my mind a general question: Is a *complete, exact* description of ground state electronic structure in terms of $n(r)$ possible in principle? Does the electron density $n(r)$ *completely characterize a system?*

"The Basic Lemma of Hohenberg and Kohn. **The ground state density $n(r)$ of a bound system of interacting electrons in some external potential $v(r)$** [due, e.g., to atomic nuclei] **determines this potential uniquely** [by determining, e.g., locations and charges of a system's nuclei]. The proof [by contradiction] is very simple.

"Assume there exist for a given $n(r)$ two "external potentials" that differ from each other by more than an arbitrary constant with, correspondingly, two different wavefunctions with energies $E_1$ and $E_2$. Apply the Rayleigh-Ritz energy minimum principle to both wavefunctions. Produced is the contradiction $E_1 + E_2 < E_2 + E_1$. We conclude by *reductio ad absurdum* that the assumption of the existence of a second potential [due, e.g., to the atomic nuclei] that give rise to the same $n(r)$ must be wrong.

"Density Functional Theory transforms the formidable problem of finding an energy minimum in 3N-dimensional space into the problem of finding an energy minimum with respect to the 3-dimensional space of an *electron density distribution* $n(r)$."

An electron density distribution corresponding to an energy minimum is further transformed by electron localization procedures into, e.g., Natural Bond Orbitals whose electron density profiles are similar to those of Valence Sphere Models.

# Density Functional Theory and the Valence Stroke Termination Rule

Cusps of an electron density distribution, $n(r)$, determine locations of atomic nuclei. Fractional rates of change of $n(r)$ at nuclei's sites determine the nuclei's atomic numbers, Z. Integration of $n(r)$ over the space occupied by molecules' electron clouds yields total numbers of electrons.

Similarly, valence stroke diagrams' valence strokes' junctures at elements' symbols in valence stroke diagrams and valence sphere models' interstices indicate locations of atomic cores. Numbers of valence stroke terminations at cores' sites equal cores' charges (in the absence of formal charges). And counts of diagrams' total numbers of valence strokes and the corresponding models' total number of valence spheres yield numbers of valence shell electron pairs.

Outer contours of Natural Bond Orbitals, calculated with the aid of Density Functional Theory, correspond to profiles of Conceptual Valence Bond Theory's Valence Sphere Models of Molecules.

The atomic number theorem has a simple proof. At the site of an atomic nucleus -

$$n(r) = 2 \ (1s)^2 = Ce^{(-2Zr/a_o)}$$
$$\rightarrow$$
$$d\ln[n(r)]/dr = -2Z/a_o$$
$$\rightarrow$$
$$Z = -[a_o/2n(r)])d[(n(r)]/dn$$

This essay's opening statements concerning cusps of electron density express the content of the fundamental Hohenberg-Kohn Theorem of Density Functional Theory. They correspond to Conceptual Valence Bond Theory's Valence Stroke Termination Rule.

Published accounts of Density Functional Theory and Valence Sphere Models first appear at nearly the same time, in 1964 and 1963, respectively. Chemists more or less ignored DFT for some thirty years, it's been said, and have ignored VSMs for half a century — a surprise and disappointment, initially, but later appreciated for providing an opportunity to work with the models for nearly fifty years without fear of being scooped.

# The Bond Number Equation

In drawing bond diagrams it's useful to know at the outset how many bonds connect heavy atoms (ones other than hydrogen) to each other. Suppose that a molecule contains N heavy atoms, V valence shell electron pairs, and B ordinary 2-electron/2-center bonds, and suppose, further, that each of the N atoms satisfies the Octet Rule. Given N and V, what's B?

Consider counting the number of valence shell electron pairs as follows: Each heavy atom core reports that it has in its valence shell 4 pairs for, altogether, 4N reports. Each of the B bonding pairs is, however, reported twice in the product 4N. Hence –

$$V = 4N - B \quad \rightarrow \quad B = 4N - V$$

The number of pairs shared by octets (B) is the difference between the number of pairs needed for the Octet Rule without sharing (4N) and the number on hand (V).

For instance, for the molecule $C_3H_4$, N = 3, V = 8, and B = 4x3 – 8 = 4. The molecule's excess connectivity in its heavy atom skeleton is 4 – 2(the minimum number of bonds necessary to bond 3 atoms together) = 2. The bond diagram contains, accordingly, 2 double bonds (allene), a triple bond (methyl acetylene), or a double bond and a 3-member ring (cyclopropene).

To generalize: Consider a molecule for which the Electron Pair Coordination Number (EPCN) of atomic core i is $(EPCN)_i$. The product 4N becomes $\sum(EPCN)_i$. And suppose there are $B_1$ lone pairs and bonds to hydrogen, $B_2$ 2-center bonds between octets, $B_3$ 3-center bonds, and so forth. The term B in the expression B = 4N - V becomes $\sum(n-1)B_n$. Accordingly, -

$$\sum(n-1)B_n = \sum(EPCN)_i - V$$
$$\text{with}$$
$$B_1 = V - (B_2 + B_3 + \dots)$$

For instance, for the molecule $Al_2(CH_3)_6$, N = 8. If each of the 8 heavy atoms satisfies the Octet Rule, $\sum(EPCN)_i = 4x8 = 32$. Also, V = 24. Hence $\sum(EPCN)_i - V = 32 - 24 = 8$. Thus, if bonds are either 2- or 3-center bonds, the Bond Number Equation yields -

| $B_2 + 2B_3 = 8$ | | $B_1 = 24 - (B_2 + B_3)$ |
|---|---|---|
| 8 | 0 | 16 |
| 6 | 1 | 17 |
| 4 | 2 | 18 |

Only $B_2 = 4$ and, consequently, $B_3 = 2$ yields for $B_1$ the chemically reasonable value of 18.

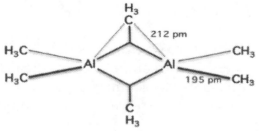

Calculated for the terminal Al—C bonds is a length of: 50 pm, for the radius of $Al^3$; plus, for the Al—C bonding pair, 2R, where R = 60 pm + 0.4r($C^{+4}$), with r($C^{+4}$) = 15 pm; plus 15 pm for the $C^{+4}$ core, yielding d(Al—$C_{terminal}$) = (50 + 132 + 15) pm = 197 pm. The greater length of the bridging Al—C bonds is presumed to arise, in part, from steric crowding of the voluminous C—H bonds (the analogous boron compound does not exist) and repulsion between bridging $C^{+4}$ cores and the $Al^{+3}$ cores. <AlCAl = 76°.

# Valence Bond Systematics
## *Construction of a Bond Diagram for NOF*

For NOF, N = 3, V = 9, and, hence, B (= 4N – V) = 3. The structure's excess connectivity is 3 - 2 = 1. The bond diagram contains a 3-member ring or a double bond.

Completion of valence shells with lone pairs yields three sites for Octet-Rule-satisfying atomic cores.

Application of the Valence Stroke Termination Rule to structures A and B yields the following assignments for core charges that yield local electrical neutrality and formal charges of zero.

The integer 5 corresponds to $N^{+5}$, 6 to $O^{+6}$, and 7 to $F^{+7}$, usually abbreviated, in valence stroke diagrams, "N", "O", and "F". Structure A is, accordingly, a bond diagram for a cyclic isomer of ozone (formation of which might account for ozone's unpredictable explosive decomposition in ozonizers). Structure B is a bond diagram for FNO, a known molecule: nitrosyl fluoride.

# Square-Planar Uncomplexed Cyclobutadiene

## An Unconventional Explanation for its Nonexistence

Synthesis of square-planar, uncomplexed cyclobutadiene has eluded investigators for many years, although the hypothetical conjugated species has, like benzene, two Kekule-like resonance structures. Its valence-sphere model has, however, a fatal flaw.

*Bond Diagram for one of two Resonance Structures for Cyclo-$C_4H_4$ Superimposed on a Drawing of a Corresponding Equal-Sphere-Size Valence-Sphere Model*

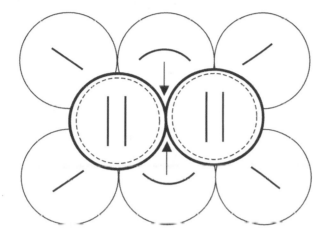

Arrows in the drawing indicate regions of *severe steric congestion*. At those locations two pairs of double-bond domains violate -

### *The Cardinal Rule of Valence-Sphere Models*

*Mutual contact between two electron-pair domains occurs only if the domains are in the valence-shell of the same atom.*

Illustrated is a companion to the theorem that molecules that have satisfactory valence stroke diagrams have satisfactory valence sphere models.

*Unsatisfactory valence sphere models correspond to nonexistent molecules.*

Not needed is the postulate that the molecule's nonexistence stems from a special phenomenon of "antiaromaticity", owing to the presence of 4n π electrons, n = 1.

In using the explanatory power of valence sphere models to account for the nonexistence of square planar uncomplexed cyclobutadiene, one attributes the nonexistence to the wave-like character of electrons in union with operation of the Heisenberg Exclusion Principle and the agency of powerful electrostatic forces that yield spatially demanding, and, sometimes, about atomic cores, mutually exclusive octets.

Behavior of close confederations of electrically charged wave-like Fermions is always the result of the joint operation of nuclear-electron attraction, nuclear-nuclear and electron-electron repulsion, and electronic kinetic energy, operating under the auspices of a Principle of Spatial Exclusion. In view of the vast library of known molecules and the theorem that corresponding satisfactory valence sphere models exist, the *joint nonexistence* for cyclobutadiene of the molecule and the model seems noteworthy.

# Oracles and Editors of Computational and Conceptual Valence Theories

The finest things in life include having a clear grasp of correlations.

EINSTEIN

A list of leading relations of Computational Valence Theory begins with Schrödinger's equation $H\psi = E\psi$ — "the ultimate oracle of chemical knowledge"* — and includes the equation's editor, so to speak, $\psi(1, 2, \ldots) = -\psi(2, 1, \ldots)$, which edits out solutions of Schrödinger's equation that, owing to the indistinguishability of electrons, haven't physical significance.

Similarly, a list of leading relations of Conceptual Valence Bond Theory begins with the Bond Number Equation $\sum(n-1)B_n = \sum(EPCN)_i - V$ ["considered to be a source of wise council" (*The American Heritage Dictionary*)] and includes the equation's editor: Valence Sphere Models, which edit out (as in the case of square planar cyclobutadiene) solutions of the Bond Number Equation that haven't chemical significance.

The list of –

*Important Relations in Computational and Conceptual Valence Theories*

Schrödinger's Equation
$\psi(1, 2, \ldots) = -\psi(2, 1, \ldots)$

Bond Number Equation
Valence Sphere Models (VSM)

may be punctuated -

$[\psi(1, 2, \ldots) = -\psi(2, 1, \ldots)]$ : $H\psi = E\psi$ :: VSM : $[\sum(n-1)B_n = \sum(EPCN)_i - V]$

and tabulated this way:

|  | Oracle | Editor |
|---|---|---|
| **Computational Valence Theory** | $H\psi = E\psi$ | $\psi(1,2,\ldots) = -\psi(2,1,\ldots)$ |
| **Conceptual Valence Theory** | Bond Number Eqn. | Valence Sphere Models |

The Oracles are oracular regarding the content of valence theory. The Editors do their editing through operation of mathematical and physical models of an Exclusion Principle.

Computational and Conceptual Valence Theory are mutually illuminating. We make calculations, said Schrödinger, to see if our insights are right. We make models to see if we can express our insights *visually*, at a *glance*. Understand is saying: "Oh, I *see*."

The Oracle/Editor analogy is one of Valence Theory's Correspondence Principles, along with the correspondence between: Valence Stroke Diagrams and Valence Sphere Models; Structural Principles of Ionic and of Covalent Compounds; the Valence Stroke Termination Rule and the Electron-Density/Atomic Nuclei Theorem of Density Functional Theory; and a Consilience between Conceptual and Computational Valence Theories.

The two theories are complementary, too, in the sense that Conceptual Valence Theory is too useful, its been said, to be true, whereas exact solutions of Schrödinger's equation are too true to be useful. Betwixt the two iies a blend of theory and calculation.

* Weinhold and Landis, *Valency and Bonding*, Cambridge University Press, p1

42

# Application of Valence Bond Theory's Oracle and Editor
## to the Formula $B_4H_4$

For $B_4H_4$ $N = 4$ and $V = 8 \rightarrow 4N - V = 8$. Ten ways exist for selecting the integers $B_2$, $B_3$, and $B_4$ such that the sum $B_2 + 2B_3 + 3B_4$ equals 8. Six of the corresponding bond diagrams are pictured below.

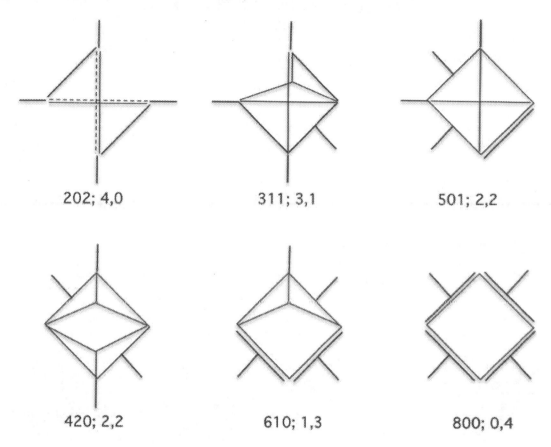

| 202; 4,0 | 311; 3,1 | 501; 2,2 |
|---|---|---|
| 420; 2,2 | 610; 1,3 | 800; 0,4 |

Shown are bond diagrams for six of ten ways to satisfy the Octet Rule for four atoms with eight pairs of electrons using 1-, 2-, 3-, and/or 4-centered bonds. Identifying strings of integers stand for $B_2B_3B_4$; $B_1$,BHB (= number of 3-center BHB bonds). $B_1$ is the number of B—H bonds, $B_2$ the number of ordinary 2-center BB bonds.

None of the displayed bond diagrams correspond to known molecules, as one might surmise from occurrence in all but the first diagram of one or more quaternary bridgehead atoms. Correspondingly, it is not possible to construct satisfactory valence sphere models for the displayed diagrams.

$B_2 + 2B_3 + 3B_4$ equals 8 for one structure for which a valence sphere model can be made, with $B_2 = B_4 = 0$, $B_3 = 4$, and, accordingly, with $B_1$ (= number of B—H bonds = V $- B_3$) = 4. It's a tetra-capped tetrahedron, in which the four $B^{+3}$ cores are crowded unusually close to each other.

# Test of the Existence Theorem for $B_5H_{11}$

A molecular formula raises several questions for Valence Stroke Theory. How many valence strokes are involved in bonds? Of what type? Arranged how? And why are alternative structures — ones that satisfy the Octet Rule, e.g.— not realized in practice? Below is an Oracle and Editor's answers to those questions for the molecule $B_5H_{11}$.

$$N = 5 \quad V = 13 \quad \rightarrow \quad 4N - V = 7$$

$$B_2 + 2B_3 = 4N - V = 7 \quad B_1 = V - (B_2 + B_3) \quad PB(\text{protonated bonds}) = 11 - B_1$$

| $B_2$ | $B_3$ | $B_1$ | PB |
|---|---|---|---|
| 1 | 3 | 9 | 2 |
| 3 | 2 | 8 | 3 |
| 5 | 1 | 7 | 4 |
| 7 | 0 | 6 | 5 |

*Valence Stroke and Valence Sphere Models for $B_5H_{11}$*

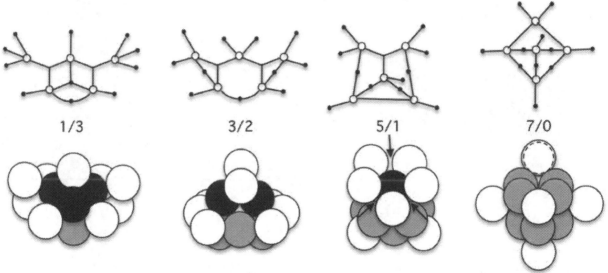

1/3      3/2      5/1      7/0

Structures $B_2/B_3 = 3/2$ and 7/0 correspond to known molecules, 1/3 and 5/1 do not, the former, presumably, because it protonates a 3-center BBB bond, not a good site for a proton, owing to the adjacency of three proton-repelling $B^{+3}$ atomic cores; and the latter owing to steric hindrance, indicated by the three arrows.

7/0, which contains no 3-center BBB bonds, corresponds to a hydrocarbon $C_5H_6$, excess connectivity 3, in the form of two 3-member rings and one 4-member ring. Other boranes that have no 3-center BBB bonds are $B_2H_6$ and cyclo-$B_3H_7$, $B_3H_7$, and $B_4H_{10}$ with, respectively, 2-, 3-, and 4-member rings of protonated BB bonds.

# Orbitals, Wavefunctions, and the Variation Theorem

Valence Theory comes in two versions: Molecular Orbital Theory, which assigns electrons to delocalized orbitals, and Valence Bond Theory, which assigns electrons to semi-localized orbitals. Each version has two aspects: computational and conceptual. From a purely mathematical point of view, computational outputs of the two versions are, in principle, equivalent to each other. Six considerations contribute to that result.

(1) Electrons are *indistinguishable*.

(2) Probabilities of configurations of electrons and nuclei are proportional to the *squares* of the configurations' wavefunctions.

(3) Electrons have a classically indescribable two-valuedness called *"spin"*.

(4) Valence strokes of valence stroke diagrams represent *pairs of spin-paired electrons*.

(5) Valence strokes in properly drawn diagrams *never cross* each other. *The probability that two electrons of the same spin are at the same place at the same time is zero.*

(6) According to the *Variation Theorem*, wavefunctions' energies improve with improvements in the wavefunctions' forms. Best possible wavefunctions are obtained by varying their forms until their computed energies are a minimum.

By (1) and (2):
$$\psi^2(1, 2, \ldots) = \psi^2(2, 1, \ldots)$$
$$\rightarrow$$
$$\psi(1, 2, \ldots) = \pm\, \psi(2, 1, \ldots)$$

Arguments "1" and "2" stand for spin and space coordinates of electrons 1 and 2.

To obtain agreement with (5) choose the minus sign.

$$\psi(1, 2, \ldots) = -\, \psi(2, 1, \ldots)$$

For then if two electrons (say 1 and 2) of the same spin are at the same place (same space and spin coordinates: "1" = "2" = x, say) -

$$\psi(x, x, \ldots) = -\, \psi(x, x, \ldots)$$
$$\rightarrow$$
$$\psi(x, x, \ldots) = 0$$

Wavefunctions are, in a word, *antisymmetric*, as are determinants. E.g.:

$$\begin{vmatrix} a_1 & a_2 \\ b_1 & b_2 \end{vmatrix} = a_1 b_2 - a_2 b_1 = - \begin{vmatrix} a_2 & a_1 \\ b_2 & b_1 \end{vmatrix}$$

Also, a determinant's columns (or rows) may be added to each other without altering the value of the determinant. E.g.:

$$\begin{vmatrix} a_1 + a_2 & a_2 \\ b_1 + b_2 & b_2 \end{vmatrix} = a_1 b_2 - a_2 b_1$$

A wavefunction formed from products of delocalized orbitals can be transformed, accordingly, via linear combinations of its orbitals, into a mathematically equivalent wavefunction formed, if one likes, from more localized orbitals, and vice-versa. Wavefunctions based on full use of the Variation Theorem yield, in principle, as said, the same *numerical* results, whatever one's initial choice of orbitals may have been. Numerical agreement between theory and experiment does not guarantee, therefore, that a *physical picture* based on a choice of orbitals *before* product antisymmetrization and *before* variations of form to minimize energy has any physical significance whatsoever! <u>With full use of the Variation Theorem, and the speeds of modern computers, conceptual garbage in does not necessarily mean numerical garbage out.</u>

## "Where Are Your Equations?"

### A *computational* chemist's question concerning *Conceptual* Valence Bond Theory

> The reason Dick's [Richard Feynman's] physics was so hard for ordinary physicists to grasp was that he did not use equations. The usual way theoretical physics was done since the time of Newton was to begin by writing down some equations and then to work hard calculating solutions to the equations. This was the way Hans [Bethe] and Oppy [Oppenheimer] and Julian Schwinger did physics. Dick just wrote down the solutions out of his head without ever writing down equations. *He had a physical picture of the way things happen, and the picture gave him the solutions directly with a minimum of calculation.* No wonder people who had spent their lives solving equations were baffled by him. Their minds were analytical; his was pictorial.
>
> FREEMAN DYSON (emphas added)

Computational Valence Theory is about *mathematical* models of molecular electron *densities*. Conceptual Valence Bond Theory is about *physical* models of molecular electron density *profiles*. Computational Valence Theory has two leading equations:

$$H\Psi = E\Psi \qquad \Psi(1, 2, \dots) = -\Psi(2, 1, \dots)$$

Which is the most important is as impossible as unnecessary to say. Each equation plays a distinctive role in determining the character of molecular wave functions. Conceptual Valence Bond Theory represents both equations, implicitly, with its exclusive orbital models of molecular electron density profiles, as indicated by the following figure.

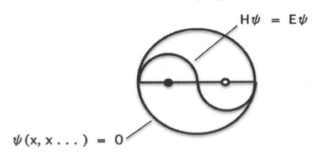

The figure's horizontal line (a valence stroke) represents two spin-paired electrons that have both countable, particle-like character (the two small circles) and space-filling, wave-like character (the Yin and Yang symbols), corresponding to the wave equation $H\Psi = E\Psi$. The large *circle* represents two things: minimum energy

$$E = H\Psi/\Psi$$

through minimum-maximum-curvature of $\Psi$; and an electron pair's van der Waals-like domain of influence, a manifestation of the operation of the principle of spatial exclusion implied by Heisenberg's equation $\Psi(1, 2, \dots) = -\Psi(2, 1, \dots)$. For if (as said several times) space-and-spin coordinates 1 and 2 are the same (1 = 2 = X, say), then (for 2 ≠ 0), $\Psi(X, X, \dots) = 0$.

Owing to $\Psi$'s continuity, if two electrons of parallel spin are at *nearly* the same place ($X_1 \approx X_2$), then the "Fermi holes" defined rigorously by the expression $\Psi(X, X, \dots) = 0$ become "Fermi *domains*": $\Psi(X_1 \approx X_2) \approx 0$, on the way to representing, in effect, "exclusive, semi-localized orbitals". The facts of structual chemistry suggest, indeed, as a testable induction, that molecular "Fermi domains" occupy, in effect, virtually all of the space occupied by molecular electron clouds, in the form of approximately exclusive orbitals of finite size with often approximately spherical profiles, yielding valence sphere models of molecules' electron density profiles.

Exclusive orbital models of molecules express implicitly, through mechanical forms, operation of both of quantum valence theory's leading equations: Schrödinger's equation $H\Psi = E\Psi$ and Heisenberg's equation $\Psi(1, 2, \ldots) = -\Psi(2, 1, \ldots)$. In addition, Conceptual Valence Bond Theory has, associated with its distinctive valence stroke diagrams two –

### Molecular Bond Number Equations

$$\sum(n-1)B_n = \sum(EPCN)_i - V \qquad B_1 = V - \sum B_n, \; n > 1$$

where:

$B_n$ = number of n-center bonds

$(EPCN)_i$ = Electron Pair Coordination Number of core i

$V$ = number of valence shell electron pairs

One is led to ask our computational chemist: Where in its output does MO Theory, with its mutually overlapping orbitals spread out almost everywhere, provide, sans localization procedures, mental images of the operation of Heisenberg's Principle of Spatial Exclusion?

In addition to its two Bond Number Equations, Conceptual Valence Bond Theory has, for atomic cores that satisfy two conditions, (1) the Electron Pair Quartet Rule, through use of 2-center bonds, and that, in addition, satisfy, for local electrical neutrality, (2) the Valence Stroke Termination Rule, — for such atomic cores Conceptual Valence Bond Theory has two additional equations. The second pair of equations below follow from the first pair of equations solved, simultaneously, as two equations in two unknowns: bp (number of bonding pairs) and lp (number of lone pairs).

### Bond-Pair and Lone-Pair Equations for Octet-Rule-Satisfying Atomic Cores

$$(1) \quad bp + lp = 4 \qquad lp = Z - 4$$

$$\rightarrow$$

$$(2) \quad bp + 2\,lp = Z \qquad bp = 8 - Z$$

where:  bp = number of bonding pairs

lp = number of lone pairs

Z = atomic core's charge

| core | $C^{+4}$ | $N^{+5}$ | $O^{+6}$ | $F^{+7}$ | $Ne^{+8}$ |
|------|------|------|------|------|------|
| Z | 4 | 5 | 6 | 7 | 8 |
| bp | 4 | 3 | 2 | 1 | 0 |
| lp* | 0 | 1 | 2 | 3 | 4 |

\* A dative bond counts for its donor as a lone pair and for its acceptor as no bond.

Conceptual Valence Bond Theory substitutes algebraic equations for Computational Valence Theory's partial differential equation $H\Psi = E\Psi$.

One notes, by inspection of the table, and by algebra, from the equations for bp and lp, that $bp + Z = 8$ and $lp + 4 = Z$.

# A Conventional Bond Diagram for "Hypervalent" XeNOF

Atoms N, O, and F bound in molecules as terminal atoms of zero formal charges are bound, respectively, by triple, double, and single bonds.

N≡ O= F—

Binding them in that fashion to an atom of xenon yields the following figure.

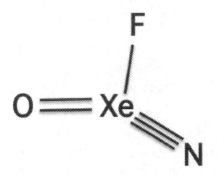

To satisfy the Valence Stroke Termination Rule for xenon, core charge +8, add to the symbol Xe a lone pair.

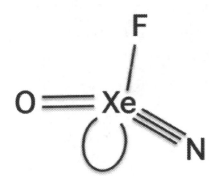

Now the number of valence stroke terminations at the symbol Xe is 8.

About the symbol Xe (standing for $Xe^{+8}$) are, altogether, four domains: those of the lone pair and the single, double, and triple bonds, arranged, accordingly, approximately tetrahedrally. The molecule is expected to be, accordingly, pyramidal, analogous to ammonia, $:NH_3$. With seven electron pairs in the valence shell of $Xe^{+8}$, hypothetical XeNOF is expected to be fluxional.

Bond angles have been drawn in accodance with a Bond Angle Theorem further illustrated in the following essay. Here we note that the sum of bond orders for the bond angles OXeF, FXeN, and OXeN are, respectively, 3, 4, and 5. For hypothetical $XeN_2$, with, again, a xenon lone pair, the bond order sum for the NXeN bond angle is 6.

# Bond Angle Theorem

*The more electron-pair domains two atoms A and B share with a third atom C
the larger tends to be the bond angle ACB.**

In other words: The larger SBO (Sum of Bond Orders) of bonds AC and BC of bond angle ACB, the larger <ACB. If, e.g., C is an Octet-Rule-satisfying atom, the well-known bond angle formed by two single bonds to C (SBO = 2) is about $110°$; for a single and a double bond (SBO = 3) about $(360 - 110)/2 = 125°$; and for two double bonds or a triple bond and a single bond (SBO = 4) $180°$. A similar pattern holds for expanded octets.

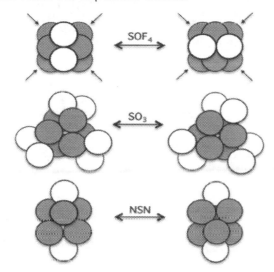

Shown above are valence sphere models for three hexavalent sulfur species. Single-headed arrows in the $SOF_4$ model point to domains of SF bonds. The molecules' electron density profiles are considered to be quantum mechanical superpositions of, in each instance, two electron domain arrangements, one for each spin set. SBO values and angles, top down, are: $2, \approx 90°$; $4, 120°$; and $6, 180°$.

Bond angles may suggest, by the Theorem, what individual bond orders should be. In, e.g., $SO_2F_2$, are the sulfur-oxygen bonds single or double bonds?

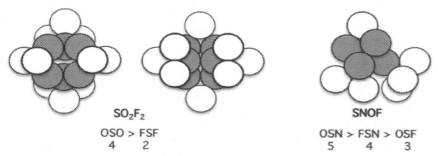

Shown above are valence sphere models for two S(VI) species and their SBO-values, on the assumption that terminally bound F, O, and N atoms are bound by, respectively, single, double, and triple bonds with, accordingly, 1, 2, and 3 lone pairs (the white domains, useful for indicating approximate locations of the atomic cores $F^{+7}$, $O^{+6}$, and $N^{+5}$). On the left for $SO_2F_2$ the view is into the OSO angle, $124°$, on the right into the FSF angle, $96°$. Visual inspection of the model for hypothetical SNOF reveals that its bond angles fall in the same order as their SBO-values: <OSN > <FSN > <OSF.

* A trigonal bipyramidal structure, $MX_5$, is an exception, since it has two sets of bond angles, $90°$ and $120°$, both with the same bond-order sum: 2.

## "Bond Lengths"

Computational Valence Theory and physical methods of molecular structure determination yield *interatomic distances*. Conceptual Valence Bond Theory yields *bond orders*. Union of distances, from experiment or calculation, with bond orders, from chemical theory, yields "bond lengths", for "single", "double", and "triple" bonds.

Bond lengths depend primarily on bond orders and identities of bonded atoms. Only secondarily do they depend on bound atoms' substituents. They are somewhat, in a word, *transferable*. Transferability of bond properties is often cited in support of local orbital models of molecules. Lengths cited below — and their differences — are in pm.

| X | Y | X——Y | | X═══Y | | X≡≡≡Y | Size of Range |
|---|---|---|---|---|---|---|---|
| C | C | 153 | 19 | 134 | 14 | 120 | 33 |
|   |   | -7 |   | -6 |   | -5 |   |
| C | N | 147 | 19 | (128) | 13 | 115 | 32 |
|   |   | -4 |   | -7 |   | -3 |   |
| C | O | 143 | 22 | 121 | 9 | 112 | 31 |
|   |   | +2 |   | +4 |   | -2 |   |
| N | N | 145 | 20 | 125 | 15 | 110 | 35 |
|   |   | -7 |   | -4 |   | -4 |   |
| N | O | 138 | 17 | 121 | 15 | 106 | 32 |
|   |   | +10 |   | 0 |   |   |   |
| O | O | 148 | 27 | 121 |   |   |   |

Highlighted (by underlining) are, at first sight, five anomalous diffences.

- -2 (triple bond column). Going from CO to NN leads to a slight increase in bond length in the single and double bond columns. In the triple bond column, however, it leads to a slight decrease, suggesting (among other possibilities) that perhaps the CO triple bond is unusually long, by about 5 pm.

- 9 (double/triple bond difference column). Compared to the other differences in its column, "9" seems too small, by about 5-6 pm, owing, again, perhaps, to an unusually long CO triple bond.

*An Octet-Rule-satisfying bond diagram of no formal charges for CO has a triple bond with one-third bond-lengthening dative bond character, rather than 100% covalent character, as in dinitrogen.*

<u>0</u> (bottom of double bond column). Four times in the table the change from N to O leads to a decrease in bond length of (top down, left to right) -4, -7, -4, and -4 pm. Yet in going from HN=O to O=O, the double bond's length, instead of decreasing, say by ca. 4 pm, remains constant, at 121 pm.

*Paramagnetic dioxygen's 12 valence shell electrons are split 5 of one spin, in a triple bond arrangement, and 7 of the other spin, in a single bond arrangement. Superposition of the two configurations is expected to yield a bond that departs from the length of a normal double bond more toward the single bond length than toward the triple bond length, for two reasons:*

1. *There are more electrons in the single bond arrangement than there are in the triple bond arrangement.*

2. *A single bond arrangement departs more from a double bond arrangement, in length, than does a triple bond arrangement.*

<u>10</u> (bottom of single bond column). In going from a C—N bond to a C—O bond, bond length normally decreases by some 4 pm, yet in going from an N—O bond to an O—O bond, by the same substitution, bond length normally increases by some 10 pm, an anomaly of ca. 14 pm in the length of an O—O bond!

<u>27</u> (bottom of first difference column). With allowance for the fact that dioxygen's double bond is some 4 pm longer than expected, the "corrected" single-bond/double-bond difference for X = Y = O is ca. (27 + 4) pm = 31 pm, rather than, say, approximately 17 pm, yielding an anomaly in length of an O—O bond of ca. (31 – 17) pm = 14 pm (again).

*The abnormally long oxygen-oxygen bond of hydrogen peroxide can be understood as an instance of "predissociation" of the molecule on its way to two free radicals whose spin sets, being anchored at only two sites ($O^{+6}$ and $H^+$), are anticoincident to a larger degree than they are in their parent molecule.*

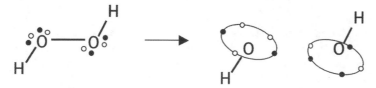

*Anti-Coincidence-Assisted Dissociation of HOOH*

Utilized in this essay on understanding "bond lengths" are two of Conceptual Valence Bond Theory's Secondary Principles: Dative Bonding and Different Structures for Different Spin Sets.

# Regions of Zero Electron Density?!

"Exclusive domain models can't possibly be right," it's said. For its electron domains have *rounded* profiles (the better to keep electronic kinetic energies low). Thus, *close-packing of exclusive domains about atomic cores appears at first glance to introduce regions of zero electron density deep within valence shells of atomic cores*, Figure 1.

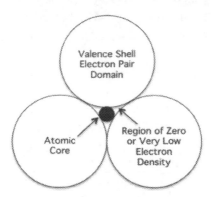

**Fig. 1.** Model in 2-dimensional Flatland of a coordinatively saturated atomic core according to Exclusive Orbital Theory's Primary Principle: close-packing of electron domains about atomic cores.

Exclusive Orbital Theory is, however, chiefly about molecular electron density's *profiles,* not electron densities near nuclei, where, according to the Theory's principal Principle (domain close-packing) an electron cloud seems, admittedly, to be infested, in a manner of speaking, with "fleas" in the form, as pictured in Figure 1, of unphysical regions of vanishing electron density. "Flea powder" formulated from Exclusive Orbital Theory's Secondary Principle of Different Structures for Different Spin Sets eliminates the "fleas", to some extent, Figure 2.

**Fig. 2.** Gray circles represent domains of, say, "alpha" electrons of one spin, dashed circles domains of "beta" electrons of the opposite spin. Absent are regions of zero electron density. Resonance is presumed to equalize density distributions' of alpha and beta spins.

Valence sphere models may be less unphysical than they may appear to be at first sight.

Another instance of "fleas" is the valence sphere, equivalent orbital model of a double bond. Along the bond axis it has a point of domain tangency — removed, in thought, however, by resonance among spin-set structures, some of which locate electron density on the bond axis.

# Missing in Action

The Exclusion Principle is the single most important principle in valence theory, it's been said. Yet Computational MO Theory gives it slight notice, at the outset.

### Steps in Computational MO Theory

1. Selection of chemically modified (p75) atomic orbitals.
2. Formation of MOs from linear combination of chemically modified atomic orbitals.
3. Assignment of up to two electrons per MO.
4. Formation of a product of MOs.
5. Antisymmetrization of the MO product.
6. Construction a Z-Matrix for use with the Variation Theorem.
7. Application of the Variation Theorem.
8. Application, for interpretative purposes, of an electron localization procedure.

Introduction in Step 5 of Heisenberg's relation

$$\Psi(1, 2, \ldots) = -\Psi(2, 1, \ldots)$$

almost seems to be an afterthought. Yet, with Schrödinger's equation, it is the only fully correct statement that can be made about wave functions.

The Principle of *Spatial Exclusion* plays no role, however, in Steps 1, 2, 3, and 4; nor in steps 6 and 7. It makes a cameo appearance in Step 5, but otherwise is missing in action.

*In formation of canonical molecular orbitals the Exclusion Principle plays no role whatsoever*, in stark contrast to its central role in formation of exclusive molecular orbitals.

The index of a recent 600-page *Introduction to Computational Chemistry* contains no entries titled "Exclusion Principle" or "Pauli Principle".

Exhaustive applications of the Variation Theorem in Step 7 corrects, computationally, for the absence of any influence of the Principle of Spatial Exclusion in Step 2, without, however, correcting, *conceptually*, for misleading mental images formed in Step 2.

Output of MO Theory's Step 7 may be entirely different than the output of its Step 2. Step 8 is essential for formation of physically meaningful mental images of molecular orbitals. It often yields, in its NBO form, Lewis-like structures.

# Grounds for X-Rating MO Theory in General Chemistry

*MO Theory is not in itself an oracle of molecular structure.*

MO Theory is a candidate for being x-rated in courses for newcomers to chemical thought for four reasons: It's *over-whelming, unnecessary, incomplete,* and *misleading.*

**Overwhelming.** MO Theory (in its use of the LCAO method of forming molecular orbitals) uses (as just mentioned) atomic orbitals, whose only source (from solutions of Schrödinger's equation for the hydrogen atom) cannot be explained to beginners (from the ground up). *Goodbye understanding! Hello massive memorization!*

**Unnecessary.** MO Theory was introduced into a valence theory of molecules in their ground states to account for, especially, dioxygen's paramagnetism and the HCH bond angle in ethylene, mistakenly thought at one time to be *exactly* 120°, in accordance with sp² hybridization of a sigma bond skeleton, plus a π-bond. It is now known, however, that bond angles opposite double bonds are, on the average, closer to the classical tetrahedral angle of 109.5° than to 120° and that Valence Bond Theory can, in fact, account for dioxygen's paramagnetism, through use of different spin-set structures for different spin sets.

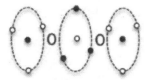

Accordingly, *it is no longer necessary to use MO Theory to account for the phenomena that were used at the outset to justify use of MO Theory,* for molecular ground states.

> MO Theory is sometimes hailed as necessary for understanding ionization energies of, e.g., methane. Proper use of Valence Bond Theory accounts, however, for the same phenomena (p65).

**Incomplete.** MO Theory's distinctive feature is its use of *delocalized* molecular orbitals. *Formed how from what?* Linear combinations of orbitals of atoms. *Located where?* MO Theory does not say! For that information, one relies on classical Valence Bond Theory.

*MO Theory is an <u>incomplete</u> theory of molecular structure.*

**Misleading.** MO Theory pictures electrons as being in orbitals that embrace entire molecules. Although the orbitals are orthogonal to each other, *they share the same regions of space.* That picture, as it stands, is at complete variance with Valence Bond Theory's picture of electrons in *localized* orbitals, as suggested, e.g., by the fundamental statement that *electrons are indistinguishable.* Hence, as said several times: $\Psi(1, 2, \ldots) = -\Psi(2, 1, \ldots)$, which implies that $\Psi(x, x, \ldots) = 0$. Electrons that have the same spin cannot be at the same place at the same time. Thus, to repeat:

*Electronic wave functions have, <u>to some degree</u>, **exclusive orbital character.***

*"The MO imagery of orbitals sprawling over one another 'almost everywhere' is profoundly illusory and physically meaningless."*

FRANK WEINHOLD, personal communication, July 3, 2011

# Z-MATRICES

*All calculations need as input a molecular geometry* [!].
*If you can draw the molecule you can do the calculation.*

*Required input is the output of Conceptual Valence Bond Theory.*

Jensen lets the cat out of the bag, so to speak. Even Computational MO Theory is not, in practice, in and of itself, a complete theory of molecular structure. It needs assistance, in the form of a trial structure, from Conceptual Valence Bond Theory, for two reasons:

- Formation of molecular orbitals from linear combinations of atomic orbitals requires knowledge of where the atoms are.

- Creation of variations of molecular geometry in applications of the Variation Theorem requires in practice an initial geometry, since beginning an application of the Theorem with no information whatsoever regarding atomic coordinates is said to be prohibitively expensive for molecules of more than a few atoms (1).

"One widely used method [of generating approximate internal molecular coordinates] is the *Z-matrix* where each atom is specified in terms of distance, angle, and torsional angle to other atoms," continues Jensen. "If the molecular geometry is optimized by the program then only rough estimates of the parameters are necessarily. In terms of internal coordinates this is fairly easy. Some typical bond lengths (Å) and angles are given below. . ." (1).

*Typical  Z-Matrix Parameters*

A — H:  A = C: 1.10; A = O,N: 1.00; A = P,S: 1.40
A — B:  A,B = C,O,N: 1.40-1.50
A ≡ B:  A,B = C,O,N: 1.20-1.30
A ≡ B:  A,B = C,N: 1.20
A — B:  A = C, B = P,S: 1.80

Angles about $sp^3$-hybridized atoms: 110°
Angles about $sp^2$-hybridized atoms: 120°
Angles about sp-hybridized atoms: 180°

Use of Z-matrices in computational MO Theory shows that -

- MO Theory requires, in practice, empirical input, regarding bond lengths and bond angles. And together with that empirical input -

- Computational chemistry requires conceptual input from classical Valence Bond Theory in order to decide in its use of the parameters available from a Z-matrix whether a selected length for a bond should be that of a single, double, or triple bond.

(1) Frank Jensen, *Introduction to Computational Chemistry* (John Wiley & Sons Ltd., 2006)

# General Remarks Regarding Modern Valence Theory
## A Summary and Review

- Modern Valence Theory has two aspects: numerical and conceptual.

- Neither aspect is a replacement for the other one.

- A round peg (Conceptual Valence Theory) does not fit a square hole (a need for, e.g., exact bond lengths and bond angles).

- Neither does a square hole (exact bond lengths and bond angles) fit a round hole (a desire for understanding bond lengths and bond angles).

- Numbers are not substitutes for concepts, nor concepts for numbers.

- Numbers and concepts represent what William Whewell called The Fundamental Antithesis of Science, between things and thought, facts and ideas, evidence and inductions, numbers (from Nature) and concepts (from Man added to Nature).

- Both aspects of Valence Theory contribute to the complete picture.

- VB and MO Theories, pursued, computationally, to the limits of their latent accuracies, yield the same numbers.

- Conceptually, however, the difference between VB and MO Theory has been likened to the difference between day and night.

- VB Theory's orbitals are semi-localized. MO Theory's orbitals are completely delocalized.

- Often delocalized orbitals can be transformed, mathematically, into localized orbitals; and vice-versa.

- Mathematically, if not conceptually, speaking, the two sets of orbitals are equivalent to each other.

- In numerical calculations, MO Theory's delocalized orbitals, expressed as linear combinations of chemically modified atomic orbitals, have been the orbitals of choice. However -

- Conceptually speaking VB Theory's localized orbitals, represented by the valence strokes of valence stroke diagrams, have been — overwhelmingly, in journal articles, monographs, and textbooks — the orbitals of choice.

- Lewis's dots may be viewed as maximally localized molecular orbitals.

- Replacement of valence dots and valence strokes of valence-dot and valence-stroke diagrams by valence spheres yields approximate electron density profiles.

- Conceptual Valence Bond Theory's output, annotated with standard bond lengths and bond angles, is Computational Valence Theory's input, in the form of Z-matrices.

# A Comparison of Conceptual VB and MO Theories for Dioxygen

Seeing is believing. ANON.
Give me pictures, not numbers. COULSON
The soul never thinks without an image. ARISTOTLE
When we finally understand something, we say, "Oh, I see." NORBERT HANSEN

REVIEW. Each of modern valence theory's two aspects, conceptual and computational, has, as said, two versions: valence bond theory and molecular orbital theory. The computational sides create numbers: bond angles, bond lengths, bond strengths, and such. With highspeed computers, sophisticated computer programs, and full use of the Variation Theorem, the two theories yield, whatever their wave functions' initial forms may be, essentially the same numerical results. On the conceptual side, however, the two theories present very different images, as illustrated below by their explanations for why dioxygen has a paramagnetic, triplet ground state, its 12 valence shell electrons split 7 of one spin and 5 of the other spin, Figure 1.

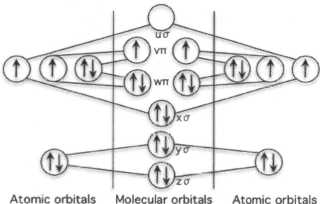

Atomic orbitals    Molecular orbitals    Atomic orbitals

**Fig. 1.** Conceptual MO theory's representation of paramagnetic dioxygen (from Coulson's book *Valence*). Orbital energy increases upward. Molecular orbitals whose energies lie *below* the energies of the corresponding atomic orbitals (zσ, xσ, and wπ; a.k.a. σ2s, σ2p, and π2p), are bonding orbitals. Their energies decrease with decreasing internuclear distance. Molecular orbitals whose energies lie *above* the energies of the corresponding atomic orbitals (yσ, vπ, and uσ, a.k.a. σ*2s, π*2p, and σ*2p) are antibonding orbitals. Their energies increase with decreasing internuclear distance.

Net number of bonding electrons in Figure 1 is *not immediately obvious*. Inspection of the Figure yields the result [4x2 – (2 + 2x1 =) 4.

"It was one of the earliest triumphs of the m.o. theory," writes Coulson, "that it accounted for this somewhat unusual situation [the paramagnetism of $O_2$] so very neatly." The account is based, in Coulson's words [emphasis added below], on "a reasonable deduction" and an "appeal" to a higher authority:

"[I]t is a reasonable deduction [essential for MO theory's explanation for dioxygen's paramagnetism] from [our] **Fig. 8** [schematic sketches of formation of molecular orbitals from atomic orbitals] [that] the overlap of the components of a.o.'s in a π-type m.o. is less than that of a σ-type m.o."

"So [in order to account for the placement of dioxygen's last two electrons] *we appeal to Hund's rule,* indicating that these two electrons [will go into different orbitals with] parallel spins."

Regarding Hund's rules, a modern authority, Robert D. Cowan, writes (in *The Theory of Atomic Structure and Spectra,* University of California Press, Berkeley, 1981, p124) that "they are now known to be misleading more often than not".

Coulson's "appeal to Hund's rule" that yields a "reasonable deduction" (dioxygen's paramagnetism) is on shaky grounds, as it is based on a rule that, according to Cowan, is "known to be misleading more often than not."

Modern Conceptual Valence Bond Theory treats the "unusual situation" regarding dioxygen through an appeal to a –

Quartet Rule

*Coordinated about atomic cores of elements of the first row of the p-block*
*in stable species are four electrons of each spin, in tetrahedral arrangements.*

Thus, if a compound of B, C, N, O, and/or F has N heavy (nonhydrogen) atoms and V electrons of a given spin, the number of electrons of that spin shared in two-center bonds, B, is equal to 4N (the number of electrons required for a spin-set's tetrahedra, without sharing) minus B (the number of electrons counted twice in the product 4N). I.e., B = 4N – V. For dioxygen's 5- and 7-membered spin sets B is equal, respectively, to 3 and 1, Figure 2.

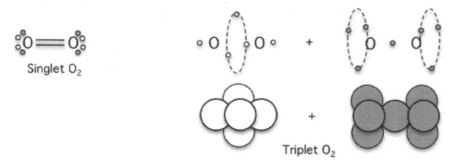

**Fig. 2.** Valence bond theory's images of the bonding in $O_2$. **Left:** Oxygen's low-lying, diamagnetic, first excited state. **Right, top line:** Lewis electron dot representation of Linnett's "double quartet" model of the ground state of triplet $O_2$. The spin set depicted on the far right shares a corner (as in a single bond), the other spin set a face (as in a triple bond) of a tetrahedral arrangement of spins about the $O^{+6}$ atomic cores ("O"). The number of electrons in the bonding region is 4, as in a double bond. **Right, bottom line:** Valence sphere models of triplet $O_2$.

Many students of chemistry are not familiar with such models. Shown in the 1960s the valence sphere model for triplet $O_2$, Linnett himself said, "Oh, I'd never thought of it in that way." And following a seminar about the models by the author at about the same time at Iowa State University, a distinguished quantum mechanician said to one of the speaker's friends in the audience, "All Henry has is pictures." Exactly! It's what *conceptual* valence bond theory has always been about: "creation of low end, inexpensive models that enable scientists to apply easy-to-use visualizations in order to understand their data through creative, human based, interpretative methods characteristic of the inductive sciences" [*SCIENCE*, **331**, 705 (2011), slightly paraphrased].

"The low end, inexpensive" valence sphere model of triplet $O_2$ (Figure 2 bottom right) offers, at a glance, a physical explanation, in terms of Coulomb's Law, for $O_2$'s triplet character. For where one of its spin sets has a trigonal arrangement of spins the other spin set has a single electron. Diminished, thereby, through partial anticoincidence of the molecule's two spin sets, is electron-electron repulsion between electrons of opposite spin. The model leads to the prediction that the paramagnetic dioxygen molecule has positive spin densities in annular, doughnut-shaped regions off its ends and along the OO axis between the atomic cores, and negative spin densities in the complementary regions of space.

Also, the unusual degree of anticoincidence of triplet $O_2$'s spin-sets permits wave-function contraction without the usual increase in electron-electron repulsion between electrons of opposite spin, thereby leading to enhanced nuclear-electron attraction, an increase in electronic kinetic energy (in accordance with the Virial Theorem), and a shortened bond: 1.2074 Å in ground state of triplet $O_2$ compared to 1.2155 Å in $O_2$'s first excited states' singlet, with two double-bond/double-bond spin-sets that are somewhat anticoincident, albeit not as much so as triplet $O_2$'s single-bond/triple-bond spin-sets.

The interatomic distance in dioxygen's molecule-ion, $O_2^+$, is 1.1227 Å, shorter than the interatomic distance of triplet $O_2$ by 1.2074 Å – 1.112 Å = 0.0847 Å. That decrease in bond length is consistent with the fact that $O_2^+$ has only 6 rather than triplet $O_2$'s 7 electrons in its most populated spin-set and, accordingly, for that spin-set, has 2 bonding electrons, in a double bond arrangement, rather than merely 1 electron, in a single bond arrangement, and, therefore, has in its bonding region a total of 2 + 3 = 5 electrons, instead of 4 (for triplet $O_2$).

The decrease of 0.0847 Å in going from triplet $O_2$ to $O_2^+$ is, however, less than half the decrease in going from a carbon-carbon single bond of 1.54 Å to a carbon-carbon double bond of 1.34 Å: (1.54 Å – 1.34 Å)/2 = 0.10 Å. The difference 0.10 Å – 0.08 Å = 0.02 Å may be attributed, in part, to the supposition that $O_2^+$'s 5- and 6-member triple-bond/double-bond spin-sets, although having fewer electrons than triplet $O_2$'s 5- and 7-membered triple-bond/single-bond spin-sets, are, nonetheless, less anticoincident than triplet $O_2$'s spin-sets and, consequently, slightly less contracted.

Conceptual MO Theory and Conceptual Valence Bond Theory are, in summary, strikingly different in their methods and in the mental images that they generate (Figures 1 and 2). Whereas Conceptual MO Theory pictures electrons in molecules as delocalized in canonical molecular orbitals *spread out over entire molecules* (Figure 1), Conceptual Valence Bond Theory pictures the electrons in exactly an opposite manner, as *localized in chemical orbitals* (Figure 2) that correspond to the valence strokes of classical valence bond theory and the dots of Lewis diagrams.

The night-and-day difference between the methods and images of the two theories stems from how they encode what has been said to be (to repeat an earlier remark) valence theory's most important physical principle: The Exclusion Principle.

Conceptual Valence Bond Theory introduces Heisenber's Principle of Spatial Exclusion *at the outset*, in a *strong form*, through use of *exclusive "chemical orbitals"* for electrons of a given spin. Conceptual MO Theory introduces Pauli's weaker physical Principle during a Bohr Aufbau Process of assigning no more than one electron of a given spin to an orbital. That procedure, since its orbitals are spread out over entire molecules, allows one to suppose — absent formation of an antisymmetrical wave function subjected to the Variation Theorem — that electrons of the same spin share the same regions of space, namely the entire space of a molecule's electron cloud.

IN SUMMARY. Conceptual MO Theory's "picture" of dioxygen is Figure 1, with an appeal at Hund's Rule. It is a physicist's account of $O_2$. Conceptual VB Theory's "picture" of dioxygen is Figure 2, with an appeal to Coulomb's Law. It is a chemist's account of $O_2$.

*Lewis Dots to Kimball Domains*

# The Leading Induction of Modern Conceptual Valence Bond Theory

The glory of science is to imagine [by induction] more than we can prove. FREEMAN DYSON

Modern Conceptual Valence Bond Theory is based, historically, on three major inductions: van't Hoff's Tetrahedral Atom, G. N. Lewis's Electron Pair, and George Kimball's Valence Sphere. Since Kimball's Sphere embraces the other two inductions, it is, in a sense, THE Induction of Conceptual Valence Bond Theory. Each Kimball domain represents a Lewis electron pair. Four close-packed Kimball domains yield a van't Hoff tetrahedral arrangement of electron pairs about the site of an atomic core that satisfies the Octet Rule. The remainder of organic stereochemistry is, in large part, episodes based on the van't Hoff/Lewis/Kimball inductions.

A physical route to the same result begins, as has been said, with Heisenberg's statement of a Principle of Spatial Exclusion for Fermions, such as electrons. Since wave functions for Fermions are antisymmetric, $\Psi(1, 2, \ldots) = -\Psi(2, 1, \ldots)$, it follows that $\Psi(x, x, \ldots) = 0$. Electronic wave functions vanish if two electrons of the same spin are at the same place at the same time.

*About electrons of a given spin are infinitesimal "Fermi holes" into which electrons of the same spin do not penetrate.*

*Electronic wave functions have to some degree exclusive orbital character. The question is: In effect, in chemical situations, how much?*

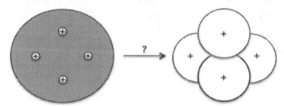

Schematic representations of methane's valence shell. **Left:** Most likely locations of four Fermi holes, enlarged, at positions of methane's protons. Each Fermi hole is a hole for each spin set. **Right:** The four Fermi holes at the left enlarged until they become electron domains of an exclusive orbital model of methane's electron cloud.

The model on the right contradicts a remark by the philosopher Morritz Schlick, echoing a view once held by many quantum physicists, that "micro-processes conceived in a visualizable manner and the method of representation by models have been abandoned". Clearly, however, that's not been the case in chemistry. The chemical model arises from *an extra-quantum mechanical principle,* of spatial exclusion, for Fermions, which the quantum physicists and Schlick may not have had in mind when dismissing the possibility of visualizing "micro-processes".

THE QUESTION: Is the induction in passing from infinitesimal Fermi holes to electron-cloud-filling "Fermi domains" scientifically significant? That question can be addressed in science's usual way. Compare with experiment stereochemical implications of electron domain models of molecules. The result? Half a century of comparisons has led in at least one instance to an affirmative answer to the question: Is one encouraged to continue?

# Toward an Explanation of Hund's Rules

*HUND'S RULES*

1. *The atomic state with the largest value of S is the most stable.*
2. *For states with the same S-value, the one with the largest value of L is the most stable.*

Hund's First Rule played an important role in the adoption by chemists of MO Theory, owing to the Theory's simple account, using the Rule, of dioxygen's paramagnetism, long a puzzle from the standpoint of classical valence bond theory.

Both Rules make sense from the standpoint of elementary considerations regarding electron-electron repulsion. Consider first the Second Rule.

Electrons circulating about the nucleus of an atom come near each other — thereby elevating electron-electron repulsion — least often if they circulate in the *same* direction. Hence Hund's Second Rule.

To account for Hund's First Rule, consider coordination, for simplicity in two dimensions, of electrons of different spins by an atomic core whose two spin sets, owing to repulsion between electrons of opposite spin, are radially partially anticoincident, per Hylleraas' model of the helium atom, one spin-set being more contracted than the other spin-set, as indicated, schematically, below, in Figure A.

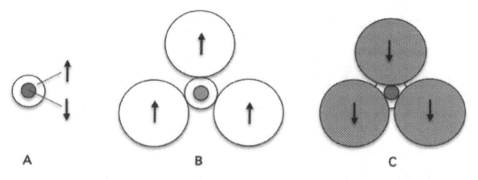

A: Profiles of two spin sets of an atomic core. B: Spin configuration for coordination by the core of valence shell domains of spins parallel to those of the core's outermost spin set: C. Spin configuration for coordination by the core of the valence shell domains of spins parallel to those of the core's innermost spin set. $E_C < E_B$.

The atomic core, A, is prepared, so to speak, to coordinate domains of electrons of spin "down", as in C, rather than domains of electrons of spin "up", as in B.

Illustrated is a difference in the roles that Hund's First Rule plays in Conceptual MO Theory and Conceptual VB Theory. Conceptual MO Theory *uses* Hund's empirical First Rule to account for dioxygen's paramagnetism. Conceptual VB Theory uses its Principle of Different Structures for Different Spin-Sets to *account* for Hund's Rule — and, accordingly, dioxygen's paramagnetism.

# "A" or "The" Molecular Orbital Theory?

In the English language the definite and indefinite articles "the" and "a" signal nouns or noun phrases — and ideological views regarding them.

The phrase "*The* Molecular Orbital Theory" — often rendered simply "Molecular Orbital Theory" — designates for an adherent of delocalized molecular orbitals not only the outstanding molecular orbital theory but, indeed, the one and only truly "*molecular orbital theory*".

On the other hand, the phrase "*A* Molecular Orbital Theory" designates for an adherent of localized molecular orbitals one member of a class of molecular orbital theories.

In both instances the "orbitals" in question are *molecular* orbitals, in that, divorced from molecules, and molecules' atomic cores, the "orbitals" have no physical significance.

Appropriation of the phrase "MO Theory" to mean "*THE* Theory of Molecular Orbitals" signals a narrow view of the field of molecular orbitals, which includes both delocalized molecular orbitals and localized molecular orbitals — and, for the latter, schematic representations using Crum Brown's strokes, Lewis's dots, and Kimball's domains.

A broad view of molecular orbitals embraces all their forms and representations, localized or delocalized, mathematical or symbolic, stroke, stick, dot, or sphere, so that one speaks, accordingly, of "a" molecular orbital theory.

"Valence Bond Theory" is a theory of semi-localized molecular orbitals.
"Molecular Orbital Theory" is a theory of highly delocalized molecular orbitals.

# Mulliken's Willful Departure from "Chemical Ideology"
## A Wrong Turn?

In 1935 R. S. Mulliken, Nobel Laureate in 1966 "for fundamental work concerning chemical bonds and the electronic structure of molecules by the molecular orbital method", published remarks in the *Journal of Chemical Physics* [volume 3, p375; reprinted in *J. Chem. Ed.*, **44**, 156 (1967)] that help one understand why chemists have today two theories of molecular structure: valence bond theory and molecular orbital theory. Mulliken wrote that:

> "Methods of assigning molecular electronic configurations may be divided into two types. In one of these atomic orbitals are used exclusively; in the other molecular orbitals of some sort are used for shared electrons. The first method follows the ideology of chemistry . . .
>
> "**Departing from chemical ideology** [emphasis added], the second method treats each molecule as a unit . . . [as, indeed, does "the ideology of chemistry", in spades, with its *bond diagrams* and *Bond Number Equation,* probably not known to Mulliken] . . . One may use exclusively two-centered ("localized") orbitals . . . or one may use many-center ("nonlocalized") orbitals *(present method). . .*
>
> "It is the writer's belief that . . . the present method may be the best adapted to the construction of an <u>exploratory *conceptual scheme*</u> [emphasis added] within whose framework may be fitted both chemical knowledge and data on electron levels from molecular spectra  . . ."

Mulliken's "departing from chemical ideology" brings to mind a remark that the author's father, Henry E. Bent, passed on to him. The remark was made by the noted physicist David M. Dennison. Dennison's doctoral thesis, in 1924, was on "The Molecular Structure and Infra-Red Spectrum of Methane". He remarked to H. E. Bent — a physical chemist — that whenever he (Dennison) and organic chemists disagreed about something concerning organic molecules [perhaps the molecular structure of methane?], it usually turned out that "The organic chemists were right".

Mulliken's personal views regarding the electronic structure of molecules, backed by his Nobel Prize, had a huge impact on chemical thought. Textbooks that for many years had used the van't Hoff bent-bond model of double bonds adopted, wholesale, without notice or apology, Mulliken's sigma-pi description, seemingly supported by a report (that turned out to be incorrect) of an HCH bond angle in ethylene of exactly 120°, exactly what Mulliken needed for a $sp^2$ sigma bond framework plus a pi bond. Mulliken's departure from classical "chemical ideology" violated chemical intuition, in removing olefins from the class of small ring compounds. Linus Pauling, ardent proponent of "chemical ideology", and Mulliken's adversary in the valence theory business, vigorously held that "bent bonds are best." The Mulliken school considered that Pauling's popularization of valence bond theory setback valence theory by several decades.

# Why Are Methane Molecules Tetrahedral?
## An Appraisal of Conceptual MO Theory

Hand-waving, conceptual MO Theory — the common textbook version of MO Theory (and rival of Conceptual Valence Bond Theory) — is a *truncated version* of Computational MO Theory. It forms molecular orbitals by the LCAO method: Linear Combinations of Atomic Orbitals. *And stops!* It doesn't form products of MOs; then trial wavefunctions (from antisymmetrized products); and, finally, energy-minimized wavefunctions (through use of the Variation Theorem). How, then, does Conceptual MO Theory show that methane molecules are tetrahedral? A recent monograph by a leading proponent of MO Theory, referred to hereafter as CW (for Conventional Wisdom), proceeds as follows *[with added remarks in italics, sometimes bracketed].*

CW starts with a discussion of a system far removed from chemical experience.

> **The $H_4$ 'Molecule'**. There are many ways of arranging four hydrogen atoms, but we shall limit ourselves to tetrahedral, since we shall be using these orbitals later."

> *The answer to the question Why is $CH_4$ tetrahedral? is assumed at the outset!*
> *The discussion postulates what it professes to explain!*
> *Its answer is more mysterious than the question!*

> "We combine them in pairs, to create two hydrogen molecules, and then ask what happens to the energy when the two hydrogen molecules are held within bonding distance, one at right angles to the other *[the tetrahedral arrangement].*

> "We meet an important rule: we are only allowed to combine those orbitals that have the same symmetry with respect to all the *[assumed!]* symmetry elements in the structure of the product *[CH4].*"

CW continues with a conventional molecular orbital diagram for hypothetical tetrahedral $H_4$. Its four molecular orbitals, constructed from four hydrogen 1s orbitals arranged tetrahedrally, have the symmetries of an s orbital and three p orbitals: $p_x$, $p_y$, and $p_z$

> **"The Atomic Orbitals of a Carbon Atom."**

> *Here lies a major pedagogical problem for orbital theories. Newcomers to physical thought have no choice but to accept statements about orbitals on FAITH! CW's discussion of $CH_4$ yields, consequently, for newcomers, a <u>description</u> of methane's molecular orbitals, not an <u>explanation</u> for why methane is a tetrahedral molecule.*

> **"Methane**. In methane we can begin by combining two hydrogen molecules into a composite $H_4$ unit and then combine the orbitals of that species with the orbitals of the carbon atom. It is not perhaps obvious where in space to put the four hydrogen atoms. They will repel each other and the furthest apart they can get is a tetrahedral arrangement."

> *Mutual repulsion of hydrogen atoms is as close as CW comes to a physical explanation for why $CH_4$ is a tetrahedral molecule. Not mentioned, explicitly, are the three fundamental forces operative in molecules (nuclear-electron attraction and nuclear-nuclear and electron-electron repulsion), and the Principle of Spatial Exclusion.*

> **"Hybridization.** One difficulty with these pictures *[of MOs for]* explaining the bonding in methane, is that there is no single orbital that we can associate with the C—H bond. To avoid this *inconvenience [emphasis added]* chemists often use Pauling's idea of hybridization; that is, they mix together

atomic orbitals of the carbon atom, adding the s and p orbitals together in various proportions, to produce a set of hybrids, before using them to make the molecular orbitals.

"This picture has the advantage that the C—H bonds do have a direct relationship with the lines drawn in the conventional *[valence stroke]* structure. The two descriptions of the *overall [antisymmetric]* wave function are in fact *identical*."

> The s/p hybrid orbitals can be solved for the individual s and p orbitals, which may then be combined to form the molecular orbitals, and vice-versa: the molecular orbitals may be solved for the individual s and p orbitals, which may then be combined to form the hybrid orbitals.

CW concludes his discussion of hybridization with several critical remarks regarding Valence Bond Theory.

"For many purposes it is wise to avoid localizing the electrons in the bonds, and to use pictures *[of molecular orbitals]*. They are, in most respects, a more realistic model [sic!!!]."

"Measurements of ionization potentials, for example, show that there are *[in methane]* two energy levels from which electrons may be removed; this is immediately easy to understand in the picture of the molecular orbitals, where there are filled orbitals of different energy, but the picture of four identical bonds hides this information *[for naïve users of the 'identical bond' model]*."

> Removal of an electron from one of a molecule's two spin sets causes the remaining electrons of that spin set to reorganize. That reorganization can occur in at least two ways, yielding for the cation two different electronic states with different energies corresponding to two ionization energies. One state for $CH_4^+$ in its valence bond representation is a vacancy in a hybrid C—H orbital resonating among all four C—H bonds. It corresponds to removal of an electron from the molecule's lowest molecular orbital, formed by superposition of the carbon 2s orbital and four in-phase hydrogen 1s orbitals. The second electronic state for $CH_4^+$ corresponds to adoption by the three-membered spin set of a trigonal arrangement of spins, two in two C—H bonds, with a larger than normal HCH bond angle, and one in a domain midway between the protons of the other two C—H bonds, with a smaller than normal HCH bond angle. Removal of an electron from no single canonical molecular orbital of $CH_4$ describes that state.

"For other purposes, however, it is undoubtedly helpful to take advantage of the simple picture provided by the hybridization model, but *it is a good practice to avoid it whenever possible[!]*."

So why are methane molecules tetrahedral?

Truth be told, *chemistry is an inductive science* (or, as chemists like to say: "Chemistry is an *experimental* science.") Chemists were led to say, in the first instance (from experiments) that methane molecules are tetrahedral, *not by rigorous deduction* from, e.g., Schrödinger's equation but, rather, *by imaginative induction* from the fact, e.g., that dichloromethane has only one isomer. But that was then. Today "the simple picture provided by the hybridization model" rests by deduction on a firm theoretical foundation based on Schrödinger's equation (admittedly, initially an induction), through the method of, e.g., Natural Bond Orbital analysis, in either its rigorous, relatively vigorous, analytical form or its geometrical, exclusive orbital form. *It seems like a good practice to use it whenever possible!*

# A Check on the Electride-Ion Model of Matter

Calculated and Observed Values of the Energy of Complete Heterolytic Dissociation of Methane
*Viewed as an Ion-Compound*

$$C^{+4}(H^-)_4$$

## A Preliminary

*The Hydrogen-Hydrogen Nonbonded Distance in CH₄*

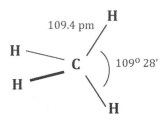

$$\sin(1/2)(109° \, 28') = (1/2)(HH \text{ distance})/(CH \text{ distance})$$
$$\rightarrow$$
$$HH \text{ distance} = 2(CH \text{ distance}) \sin(54° \, 44')$$
$$= 178.6 \text{ pm}$$

## A Check

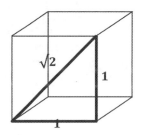
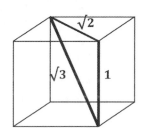
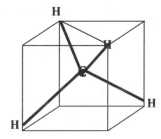

HH is to twice CH as the $\sqrt{2}$ is to the $\sqrt{3}$.

$$HH / 2\,CH = \sqrt{2} / \sqrt{3}$$
$$\rightarrow$$
$$HH = (\sqrt{2}/\sqrt{3})(2\,CH) = 178.6 \text{ pm}$$

(The sine of half the tetrahedral angle is equal to $\sqrt{2}/\sqrt{3}$.)

### A Check on the Self-Consistency
### of the Hydride-Ion Model of Methane

For simplicity, in the following calculation we place the protons of methane's C—H bonds at the centers of their spherical domains, as if the C—H bonds were undistorted hydride ions.

According to the Hellman-Feynman Theorem, that central location is not the best one for the protons. It doesn't correspond to an energy minimum for the model. Methane's protons are on the protonic side of pure hydride character, yet not greatly so. Methane is an exceedingly weak proton donor: much better than the hydride ions of sodium hydride, $Na^+H^-$, e.g., but much poorer than the O—H bonds of a water molecule, itself a weak proton donor.

The hydride-ion model of a C—H bond yields the following picture of a $CH_2$ group of methane.

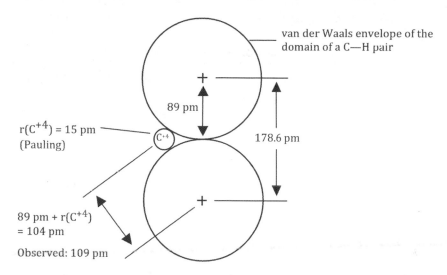

From the standpoint of the HH and CH distances in methane and Pauling's radius for the atomic core $C^{+4}$, the hydride-ion model of $CH_4$ is self-consistent to within about 5 percent.

The radius of the tetrahedral interstice formed by four domains of radius 89 pm is (by a famous radius-ratio rule*) 0.225 x 89 pm = 20 pm, in the same ballpark as, if somewhat larger than Pauling's radius for $C^{+4}$ of 15 pm. An atomic core of that size can support in its valence-shell without rattling four spheres with maximum radii of (15 pm)/0.225 = 67 pm, slightly larger than the 62 pm required to account for the 154 pm length of a carbon-carbon single bond (= 2x15 + 2x62). Shrinkage of the hydride-ion radius of 89 pm in the hydride-ion model of methane to smaller values, while leaving unchanged positions of the atomic nuclei, corresponds to adding protonic character to methane's C—H bonds.

* Reference to the relation of a tetrahedron to a cube yields (R = radius of C—H domain, r = radius of $C^{+4}$ core) –

$$2R/(R + r) = (\sqrt{2})/(\sqrt{3}/2) \rightarrow r/R = (\sqrt{3}/\sqrt{2}) - 1 = 0.225$$

### The Calculation

In calculating the energy of complete heterolytic dissociation of methane

$$CH_4 \longrightarrow C^{+4} + 4 H^-$$

based on the hydride model $C^{+4}(H^-)_4$ of five non-overlapping, spherically symmetrical charge distributions, one may represent the molecule's total charge distribution by five point charges.

### Point Charge Model of Methane

According to Coulomb's Law, two charges $Q_1$ and $Q_2$ at a separation r have a potential energy $V$ with respect to $V = 0$ at infinite separation of -

$$V = Q_1 Q_2/r$$

For charges of the same sign (which repell each other), V is positive (for r less than infinity). For unlike charges (which attract each other), V is negative. For the point charge model of methane (e = charge of an electron) -

$$
\begin{aligned}
V &= V(\text{core/-H}^- \text{ attraction}) + V(\text{H}^-\text{-H}^- \text{ repulsion}) \\
&= 4[(+4e)(-e)/109.4 \text{ pm}] + 6[(-e)(-e)/178.6 \text{ pm}] \\
&= e^2/\text{pm} (-16/109.4 + 6/178.6) \\
&= e^2/\text{pm} (-0.1463 + 0.0336) \\
&= e^2/\text{pm} (-0.1127) \\
&= -3743 \text{ kcal/mole*}
\end{aligned}
$$

*The calculated potential energy of $CH_4$, modeled as $C^{+4}(H^-)_4$, with respect to its five parts at infinite separation from each other.

The calculated increase in energy ($\Delta E$) on heterolytic dissociation of $CH_4$ to $C^{+4}$ and 4 $H^-$ at infinite separation from each other is +3743 kcal/mole.

$$CH_4 \longrightarrow C^{+4} + 4 \text{ H}^- \qquad \Delta E(\text{calculated}) = +3743 \text{ kcal/mole}$$

The electronic charge $e = 4.803 \times 10^{-10}$ esu and the standard conversion factors $(\text{esu})^2/\text{cm} = 1$ erg, $10^7$ erg = 1 Joule, and 4.184 J = 1 cal imply, jointly, with 1 mole = $6.023 \times 10^{23}$ entities, that $e^2/\text{pm}$ *per entity* = $3.321 \times 10^4$ kcal *per mole*.

### The Experimental Value

| Process | $\Delta E$/(kcal/mole) | Description |
|---|---|---|
| $CH_4(g) = C(gr) + 2 H_2(g)$ | +17.89 | Negative of energy of formation of methane from its elements in their standard states |
| $C(gr) = C(g)$ | +172 | Energy of sublimation of graphite |
| $C(g) = C^+(g)$ | +260 | Carbon's first energy of ionization |
| $C^+(g) = C^{+2}(g)$ | +562 | Carbon's second energy of ionization |
| $C^{+2}(g) = C^{+3}(g)$ | +1104 | Carbon's third energy of ionization |
| $C^{+3}(g) = C^{+4}(g)$ | +1487 | Carbon's fourth energy of ionization |
| $2 H_2(g) = 4 H(g)$ | +208 | Twice $H_2$'s bond dissociation energy |
| $4 H(g) + 4 e^- = 4 H^-(g)$ | -68.8 | Negative of four times H's electron affinity |
| $CH_4 = C^{+4} + 4 H^-$ | 3742 | |

CONCLUSION: *From a computational point of view, the localized electron-pair, ionic, hydride-ion/atomic-core model of methane appears to be a reasonable description of the molecule's charge cloud.*

The close agreement between the two numbers — 3743 calculated, 3742 observed — was unexpected. Hoped for, at best, at the outset, was an in-the-right-ballpark result. Prior to making the calculation, the author was prepared to rationalize a major discrepancy between $\Delta V$(calculated) and $\Delta E$(observed) in several ways.

For one thing, one might wonder: Should not the calculated change in the potential energy, V, be expected to be, by the Virial Theorem, twice the observed change in E? As noted at the outset, however, the $C^{+4}(H^-)_4$ model of $CH_4$ does not satisfy the Hellman-Feynman Theorem. Consequently, it does not satisfy the Virial Theorem. Therefore, it would probably be incorrect to set $\Delta E$(calculated) $\approx (1/2)\Delta V$(calculated).

Also, comparing the calculated $\Delta V$ to the observed $\Delta E$ would seem not to allow for a change (decrease) in electronic kinetic energy (T) on heterolytic dissociation of $CH_4$, particularly in the case of the electrons of the hydride ions, free of the powerful constrictive field of the $C^{+4}$ ion. A decrease on dissociation of T ($\Delta T < 0$) would tend to make the calculated $\Delta V$ greater than the observed $\Delta E$ (= $\Delta V + \Delta T$).

Also, one might question the physical reasonableness of the hydride ion model of methane on the grounds that, at first sight, it appears to place large formal charges on methane's hydrogen and carbon "atoms": –1 and +4, respectively. Actually, the notation "$H^-$" is merely a simplified way of speaking of the electron-domain model's charge distributions for C—H bonds that, for purposes of a calculation, may be taken to be point-charges. The domain that corresponds to an "$H^-$" (of a "C—H" bond) is, in the model, in the valence shell of *both* $C^{+4}$ and an $H^+$.

Favorable to a point-charge-model-calculation of methane's energy of dissociation to hydride ions and $C^{+4}$ is the calculation's allowance for existence of energetically important spherical — or nearly spherical — *cusps of electron density* about the hydrogen protons in the reactant and the products. A key assumption is: The *entire* charge distribution about a methane proton, due to the molecule's C—H shared-pair, is approximately spherically symmetrical.

One reason why the hydride-ion-model of methane works as well as it does in a calculation of $\Delta E$ of heterolytic dissociation based on point charges is that in both reactant and products the hydrogen protons are surrounded by (nearly) spherically-symmetric cusps of electron density, important for both E(reactant) and E(product), but, to a first approximation, unchanged on dissociation to hydride ions.

The Bottom Line: A point charge model of methane based on a valence sphere model of the molecule yields as one might hope a calculated energy of dissociation that seems to be in the right ball park.

# VSEPR Theory and CH$_4$: Planar or Tetrahedral?

*Is methane's shape governed by electron-electron repulsions, as implied by Valence Shell Electron Pair Repulsion Theory, or by electron-nucleus attractions?*

Consider potential energy terms for a simple model of methane: a point charge of +4, for C$^{+4}$, surrounded by four symmetrically protonated, uniformly charged, spherical electron-pair domains, net charges –1 (= -2 + 1), with diameters of unit length.

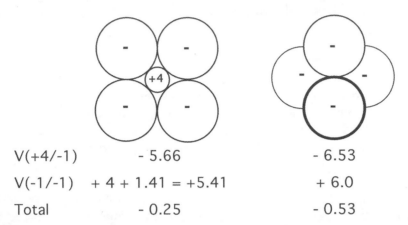

| | | |
|---|---|---|
| V(+4/-1) | - 5.66 | - 6.53 |
| V(-1/-1) | + 4 + 1.41 = +5.41 | + 6.0 |
| Total | - 0.25 | - 0.53 |

Protonated electron-pair/electron-pair repulsion is less for the square-planar arrangement (+5.41) than for the tetrahedral arrangement (+6.0), whereas core/electron-pair attraction is more negative for the tetrahedral arrangement (-6.53) than for the square-planar arrangement (-5.66). Overall, the tetrahedral arrangement is over twice as stable, with respect to the ions at infinite separation, as the square-planar arrangement, *owing to electron-nucleus attractions.*

*Valence-shell electron-pairs adopt locations that maximize nuclear/electron-pair attractions, not ones that minimize electron-pair/electron-pair repulsions.*

A more precise calculation would minimize total energies with respect to the radii of the electron-pair domains and with respect to locations of the protons within them. Since, however, the energy is a minimum for those resulting structures, passage from them to the structures pictured above is not expected to change *relative* values of the energy terms significantly. Nuclear-electron attraction, not electron-electron repulsion, is, in large part, responsible for molecular shapes. It may be time to retire VSEPR Theory, some investigators have suggested.

Were electron-electron repulsion truly the dominant reason for molecular shapes, molecules' parts would fly apart to infinite separations and hydrazine, H$_2$N—NH$_2$, with lone pairs on each nitrogen atom, would adopt in its configuration of least energy one in which its lone pairs are as far apart as possible, trans to each other, rather than, as observed, gauche. That configuration places the lone pairs trans to interior lobes of sigma antibonding NH orbitals, for energy-lowering electron-pair donor-acceptor interactions, driven by nuclear-electron attraction.

# Another Appraisal of VSEPR Theory

From the standpoint of VSEPR (Valence Shell Electron Pair Repulsion) Theory, why do two methylene molecules ($CH_2$) dimerize, to a single molecule (ethylene)? Why does bromine add to olefins? Fluorine to sulfur difluoride? And iodine to ammines, ethers, and ketones? Each instance of *association* creates an increase in Electron Pair Repulsion. From the standpoint of VSEPR Theory, *alone*, molecules should fly apart to electrons and atomic nuclei. By itself –

> VSEPR Theory is <u>not a **COMPREHENSIVE** theory</u> of molecular structure.

Something is missing. True, in the Points-on-a-Sphere Model of VSEPR Theory, the mutual repulsion of four point charges *on a sphere of a given size* is less for a tetrahedral arrangement of the charges than for a square-planar arrangement. Hence methane's shape? Begged is a BIG QUESTION:

> *Why are the points that represent electrons confined to a sphere — of fixed radius?*
>
> In the a more comprehensive Valence-Sphere Model of molecules (based on VSEPR Theory's missing feature), *variation with electron-domain arrangement* of the radius of the sphere on which the centroids of the electron domains' charge clouds reside accounts for methane's tetrahedral shape. The centers of four *close-packed,* hence *tetrahedrally,* arranged tangent spheres lie on a sphere of *smaller radius* than do the centers of four tangent spheres of the same size located at the corners of a square. A tetrahedral arrangement of electron-pair domains places electronic charge *closer* to an atomic nucleus than does a square planar arrangement of domains of the same size.

> *Missing in VSEPR Theory is explicit consideration of **nucleus-electron attraction**.*

Nucleus-electron attraction is the sole reason for formation of molecules from electrons and atomic nuclei. Other terms in a quantum mechanical molecular Hamiltonian — arising from electron-electron repulsion, nucleus-nucleus repulsion, and electron motion — are *positive*, with respect to dissociation of a molecule to nuclei and electrons at infinite separations. Only nuclear-electron attraction terms are negative and account for formation of molecules from nuclei and electrons.

$$E(\text{total}) = V_{ne} + V_{nn} + V_{ee} + T$$
$$-\quad\ +\quad\ +\quad\ +$$

Owing to joint operation of nuclear-electron attraction and an Exclusion Principle, chemistry has its *Octet Rule* and *"the tetrahedral atom",* for small atomic cores: $B^{+3}$, $C^{+4}$, $N^{+5}$, $O^{+6}$, $F^{+7}$, and $Ne^{+8}$. For cores of any size, chemistry has, in the words of professor Frank Rioux, a Valence Shell Electron-Pair/Nucleus-Attraction Theory of electronic structure.

Nucleus-electron attraction is the basis of Electron-Pair Donor-Acceptor Theory and the existence in chemistry of "electrophilic" and "nucleophilic" reagents. It supplies, also, an answer to another BIG QUESTION concerning VSEPR Theory, about which that Theory itself is silent.

*Why is VSEPR Theory expressed in terms of <u>electron pairs</u>?*

From the standpoint of an exclusive focus on *electron repulsion*, occurrence of spatially *paired* electrons is anomalous. Spatial *pairing* can't, in fact, occur in *odd-electron* molecules, such as NO and $NO_2$. And in Linnett's double-spin-set extension of Lewis's electron-pair interpretation of classical chemistry's bond diagrams, spin-sets are not spatially coincident in linear chemical structures, such as HCCH, HF, and OCO; and in molecules such as benzene that have two or more reasonable resonance structures. In non-linear, non-resonating structures, however, nucleus-electron attraction anchors each spin-set in (approximately) the same orientation and, thereby, forces formation of spin-and-spatially paired electrons.

Two Rules summarize the structural significance in chemistry of nuclear-electron attraction, and the Exclusion Principle.

### Pauling's First Rule of the Crystal Chemistry of Ionic Compounds

*A polyhedron of **anions** is formed about each **cation**.*

### The Sidgwick-Powell/Gillespie-Nyholm First Rule of the Molecular Chemistry of Covalent Compounds

*A polyhedron of **electron-pairs** is formed about each **atomic core**.*

VSEPR Theory *describes* (with its Points-on-a-Sphere Model) and *fine-tunes* (with its angularly large valence-shell lone pair domains) the results of the operation in chemistry of nuclear-electron attraction and an Exclusion Principle. As its name implies, Valence Shell Electron Pair Repulsion Theory is a theory of valence shell electron-pair repulsion. Period. It is not, also, except by implication, a theory of nucleus-electron attraction. It elevates one of the lesser terms in molecules' Hamiltonians to a structural principle of first rank, justified by use of an incomplete electrostatic, Points-on-a-Sphere model.

VSEPR Theory's popularity stems from its simplicity, owing to its limited scope. It yields right results without the need to understand the fundamental reasons for the results. It does not, of itself, promote understanding, in terms of nuclear-electron attraction, of existence of, e.g., $SF_6$ but not $OF_6$, planar $C_2H_4$ but nonplanar $Si_2H_4$, linear $C_2H_2$ but nonlinear $Si_2H_2$, the special stability of benzene and other conjugated aromatic systems, and an analogy between the electron-pair/atomic-core model of nonpolar compounds and the ionic model of highly polar compounds.

VESPR Theory's account of the structures of $NH_3$ and $PH_3$ is instructive. Both molecules have four valence shell electron pairs: three in heavy-atom/hydrogen bonds and one lone pair. Both molecules have HXH bond angles that are less than the tetrahedral angle, attributed in VESPR Theory to electron pair repulsion between a lone pair (lp) and bonding pairs (bp) being greater than electron-pair/electron-pair repulsion between bonding pairs and bonding pairs.

*VSEPR Theory's Fundamental Inequality Regarding Electron Pair Repulsions*

lp/bp > bp/bp

Since a phosphorus atom is larger than a nitrogen atom, one might suppose that lp/bp repulsion would be less in $PH_3$ than in $NH_3$, and that that might mean that the HPH angles of $PH_3$ are larger than the HNH angles of $NH_3$. In fact, the HPH angles, close to 90 degrees, are almost 20 degrees *smaller* than the HNH angles, which are only a few degrees less than the tetrahedral angle of 109.5 degrees.

The ammonia-phosphine comparison suggests that the physical origin of Valence Shell Electron Repulsion Theory's explanations of molecular geometry is not, as its name suggests, electron-pair/electron-pair *repulsion* — certainly present — but, rather, a larger *nucleus-electron attraction*, which leads to dispersal of lone pairs about surfaces of large atomic cores, such as $P^{+5}$ of $PH_3$.

The author is indebted to professor Frank Rioux for pointing out that methane's nonplanar tetrahedral geometry is paradoxical from the point of view of VSEPR Theory. Rioux supports that insight with calculations based on Kimball's Charge Cloud Model of Molecules. An excellent account of why he believes — with a number of other chemists — that it may be time to retire VSEPR Theory is available at www.users.csbsju.edu/~frioux/vsepr/NVSEPR.htm.

In their book *Discovering Chemistry with Natural Bond Orbitals* (Wiley-Interscience, 2012), Weinhold and Landis write that:

> "Despite its simple and intuitive character, Bent's rule is surprisingly successful in anticipating the subtle variations of s/p-character found in quantitative NBOs... The VSEPR model gives 'the right answer for the wrong reason' in selected main group examples (which are generally understood more satisfactorily in terms of Bent's rehybridization concepts). However, VSEPR-type concepts fail *spectacularly* for many transition metal species, whereas Bent's rehybridization rule, suitably generalized for s/d-type bonding, continues to account for molecular shape changes. . . [A beginning chemistry student who was indoctrinated with VSEPR-style rationalizations, but never introduced to Bent's rule, may therefore wish to consider a request for a tuition refund.]

> "For those who continue chemistry beyond freshman level, it is not surprising that VSEPR-type concepts play no significant role in more advanced quantum mechanical theories of organic and inorganic molecular structure. Judicious replacement of VSEPR concepts with equivalent Bent's rehybridization concepts (e.g., replacing "fat" by "more s-like" and "skinny" by "more p-like") would significantly improve the accuracy of current freshman-level pedagogy."

# Atomic Orbitals' Irrelevance for *Conceptual* Valence Bond Theory

*Sometimes it's useful to see how little theoretical machinery you need to obtain a given result.*

RICHARD FEYNMAN

Formation in MO Theory of molecular orbitals from linear combinations of atomic orbitals (LCAO), for reasons described below by C. A. Coulson, brings to mind the story of the mathematician who worked at home. Each afternoon he'd retreat to the kitchen to put on the stove a teakettle of water placed by his wife earlier on the sink's left drain, so that it would be hot when she returned from work. One afternoon he entered the kitchen and found the teakettle on the sink's *right* drain. A new problem! Back he went to his study. Then, inspired by a bright idea, he returned to the kitchen and moved the teakettle to the sink's *left* drain, muttering to himself: "I have hereby reduced the problem to one already solved."

Coulson describes in his book *Valence* the rationale behind the LCAO method in these words:

> "When [an] electron [of a diatomic molecule] is in the region of one of the nuclei the forces on it are those due chiefly to that nucleus and the other electrons near that nucleus. We may say that in the region of one nucleus A, the most significant parts of the system's Hamiltonian H are precisely those terms that would comprise the Hamiltonian of an electron in an isolated atom A. The other terms, associated with atom B, are not exactly zero, but they are small. Thus the wave equation near A resembles the wave equation of an isolated atom A. This means that in the neighborhood of one nucleus, e.g. A, the m.o. resembles an atomic orbital of A. Similarly in the neighborhood of the other nucleus B, the m.o. ensembles an atomic orbital of B. Since the complete m.o. has characteristics separately possessed by those two atomic orbitals, it is a natural step to describe it as a linear combination of those two atomic orbitals. That approximation is called the approximation of Linear Combinations of Atomic Orbitals, usually abbreviated to LCAO."

In the neighborhood of an atomic nucleus the LCAO approximation reduces the problem under consideration 'to one already solved'.

For calculations of molecular energies, good results near nuclei are important, as that's where the largest energy terms arise. For understanding intermolecular interactions and molecular shapes, however, *intimate details* of electron density distributions near nuclei are, for the most part, *irrelevant!* For most chemical purposes the most important parts of molecules' electron clouds are their *profiles*.

Recognition of the need in Conceptual Valence Theory for electron density profiles, to the exclusion of electron density magnitudes near nuclei, yields –

## A Major Simplification of Chemical Thought

*Not needed to understand **molecular structure and chemical reactivity** are atomic orbitals.*

Absence of atomic orbitals — and attendant absence of a need to address, in an account of molecular structure from first principles, solutions of Schrödinger's equation for the hydrogen atom — yields a student-friendly account of molecular structure and chemical reactivity.

# Chemically Modified "Atomic Obitals"

How do chemistry textbooks account for the fact that methane molecules are tetrahedral?

Before discovery of the electron?
*By recourse to chemical facts,*
*particularly the fact that dichloromethane has no isomers,*
*followed by an induction,*
*comprehensible to newcomers to chemical thought.*

After discovery of the electron?
*By recourse to "atomic orbitals".*
From where?
*Solution of Schrödinger's equation for the hydrogen atom.*
Goodbye comprehension!
*Hello faith-based chemistry courses!*

So why have modern chemistry textbooks forsaken the chemical explanation,
by way of chemical evidence and an induction,
for an atomic orbital explanation,
by way of formidable mathematics?

*In order to lend an air of deductive verisimilitude,* to paraphrase W. S. Gilbert, *to an otherwise perhaps bald and unconvincing induction.*

But atoms aren't molecules.
Their electron clouds often have angular momentum,
completely quenched in nonlinear molecules.
Orbitals from Schrödinger's equation for the hydrogen atom
are, for the most part, imaginary functions that don't account
for the directional character of chemical bonding.

*Choose their real and imaginary parts,*
*by taking linear combinations of those* Schrödinger *atomic orbitals.*
*Obtained from the nondirectional true "atomic orbitals"* $p_{+1}$ *and* $p_{-1}$
*are the chemically modified, more directional orbitals* $p_x$ *and* $p_y$,
*of the form* $xf(r)$ *and* $yf(r)$.

Those orbitals yield 90 degree bond angles, not the tetrahedral bond angles of methane.

*Take linear combinations of the* $p_x$, $p_y$, *and* $p_z$, *functions to form p-type orbitals that do point in the tetrahedral directions.*

Like all p orbitals, however, the hybrid p orbitals
  point in *two* directions.
    Jointly, four tetrahedrally-directed p orbitals
      point to the eight corners of a cube.

*Mix in s-character, for formation of one set of tetrahedrally directed, sp$^3$ orbitals. Q.E.D.*

Hold on. What was your motivation for mixing orbitals:
  unmodified true atomic orbitals of imaginary form
    to real forms that point at 90 degrees;
      to two sets of tetrahedrally directed p orbitals;
        to four sp$^3$ orbitals?

*A desire to account for the shape of CH$_4$.*

Not avoided, it seems, in your route to CH$_4$'s shape via Schrödinger's equation and chemically modified atomic orbitals is a need for inductions?

*One might say so.*

So why not cut to the chase at the outset, by way of the orbital-free, short, nonmathematical, chemical route to tetrahedral CH$_4$?

*Sometimes chemists like to leave the impression*
  *that their inductive science does not rest*
    *on a foundation of "murky chemical voodoo",*
      *but, rather, on physical inductions of broader scope. Also,*
        *sometimes it's useful to have mathematical descriptions*
          *of chemical bonds.*

In general chemistry?

*Perhaps not.*
  *Yet it's nice to know that they exist*
    *and may yield numerical values for molecular properties*
      *that rival or exceed in accuracy experimental data.*

The chemical and physical routes to molecular shapes are complementary?

*Indeed. The complementarity of classical conceptual valence bond theory*
  *and modern computational chemistry*
    *is one of the leading achievements of chemical thought,*
      *recently enhanced by wavefunction localization procedures,*
        *pioneered, e.g., by professor Weinhold and coworkers,*
          *for extracting from accurate molecular wavefunctions*
            *Lewis-type, exclusive orbital models of molecules.*

# Primary and Secondary Principles
## of
# Conceptual Valence Bond Theory

## Primary Principles

Close packing of electron domains (usually spherical) of *finite size* about sites of atomic cores

| EPCN* | POLYHEDRON |
|-------|------------|
| 3 | Triangle |
| 4 | Tetrahedron |
| 5 | Trigonal Bipyramid |
| 5 | Square Pyramid |
| 6 | Octahedron |
| 6 | Trigonal Prism |

$$\sum(n-1)B_n = \sum(EPCN)_i - V$$

$B_n$ = number of n-center bonds
$V$ = number of valence shell electron pairs

VSTR (Valence Stroke Termination Rule)**

\* EPCN: Electron Pair Coordination Numbers (of atomic cores)

\** VSTR: In valence stroke diagrams that exhibit no formal charges and in which lone pairs are represented by rabbit-ear valence strokes, the number of valence stroke terminations at the symbol of an element is equal to charge on the element's atomic cores.

## Secondary Principles

- Multicenter Bonding
- The Isoelectronic Principle
- Donor-Acceptor Interactions
- Different Structures for Different Spin Sets***
- Lone-Pair Dispersal about Large Atomic Cores
- Electron-Domain/Electron-Domain Steric Hindrance
- Electronegativities and Formal Charge Assignments
- Superposition of Alternative Structures (a.k.a. "Resonance")
- Core-Core Repulsion (with its explanation of the s-Character Rule)
- Occupancy by d- and f-Electrons of Nooks and Crannies in an Exclusive Orbital Model of an Electron Cloud

\*** Primary Principles are applied to each spin set separately if, for instance, they contain different numbers of electrons.

# $B_2H_6$, the Isoelectric Principle, and the Electronic Structure of Double Bonds

An important principle of Valence Bond Theory alluded to in the previous essay and used on the back cover in passage from potassium hydride to calcium metal is -

### The Proton/Electron-Pair Principle

*Protons of hydrogen atoms of stable species*
*are embedded in domains of electron pairs,*
*whose profiles are little changed by protonation.*

Valence sphere models of molecules of methane, ammonia, and water illustrate the Principle. From the fact that bond angles change by only a few degrees along the series, one infers that the molecules are "isoelectronic", in having essentially the same valence sphere models.

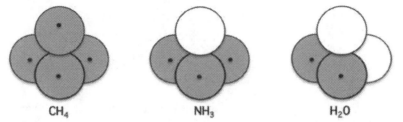

LEMMA 1: *Locations of protons indicate locations of domains of electron pairs.*

LEMMA 2: *Deprotonation of electron pairs does not change the overall articulation of electron clouds* (if anchored at at least three non-colinear sites).

The Lemmas and the Principle suggest an answer to the question:

*How should one picture the electronic structure of a double bond?*

As occupied σ and π orbitals? Or as occupied, equivalent, banana-shaped orbitals?

From a computational point of view, it does not matter, with an antisymmetric wavefunction, which set of orbitals are used in calculations: σ and π or σ+π and σ−π. Mathematically speaking they are equivalent to each other. From a conceptual point of view, however, with only one set of orbitals in mind, and not mindful of wavefunction antisymmetrization, one's choice, σ/π or σ+π/σ−π, may influence one's mental image of the electron density profile of a double bond, pictured below on the left for diborane.

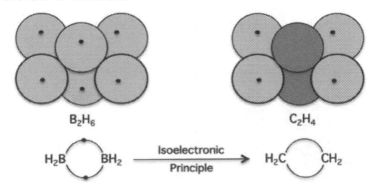

Except for locations of their protons, diborane and ethylene have the same valence sphere models. The molecules are, in a word, *isoelectronic*. Diborane's boron-boron bond is a protonated double CC bond. Ethylene's double bond is a depotonated double BHB bond.

# Four Routes to a Bent Bond Model of Double Bonds
### *Two Former and Two New Routes*

## 1. The Valence-Stroke/Hybrid-Orbital Route

Valence strokes represent hybrid atomic orbitals: $sp^3$, all around, for tetrahedral bond angles opposite a double bond; $sp^2$ (one third s-character) if that angle is $120°$, leaving for the double bond two $sp^5$ orbitals (one sixth s-character).

## 2. The Diborane/Isoelectronic-Principle Alchemical Route: $B_2H_6$ and $C_2H_4$

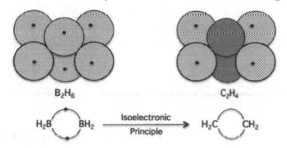

## 3. The Methylene Dimerization Chemical Route: $2 :CH_2 = C_2H_4$

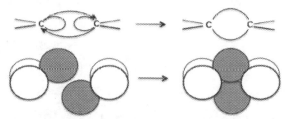

Shaded domains on the left represent singlet methylenes' lone pair domains. On the right they are domains of the double bond's equivalent orbitals. The mechanism is one of minimum motion of atomic cores and electron domains, not a head-to-head encounter, as suggested by the curly arrow representation.

## 4. The Methane/Atomic Carbon Chemical Route: $CH_4 + :C: = C_2H_4$

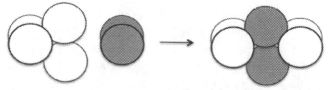

Shaded domains on the left represent a carbon atom's unshared valence shell electrons $s^2p^2$, formulated, equivalently, $(s+p)^2(s-p)^2$. White spheres represent protonated domains, two of which in $H_2CH_2$ are deprotonated by $:C:$, yielding for the latter carbon atom two C—H bonds and, for the initial methane moiety, two deprotonated pairs for the C=C double bond, shaded gray on the right.

All routes lead to the same equivalent orbital model of a double bond.

# Conceptual Valence Bond Theory and Fundamental Physical Forces

> You have no exact knowledge, Rutherford famously said (defining, in effect, "exact knowledge"), unless you can express it with numbers. Similarly, it's widely felt by physicists and chemists that you have no satisfactory *understanding* of chemical phenomena (defining, in effect, "understanding of chemical phenomena") unless you can express it in physical terms.

Before Thomson's invention of the electron and Rutherford's invention of the nuclear model of the atom, valence theory had no connections with physical thought. It was a purely phenomenological, chemical theory, encoding in the simplest manner possible (with valence strokes and symbols of the elements) chemical facts and inductions regarding molecular structure. From the point of view of physics — the science of *central* forces — chemistry's tetrahedrally directed affinities that, for multiple bonds' bent bonds, are not even directed toward each other!, seemed to be "murky chemical voodoo". G. N. Lewis's interpretation of bond diagrams in terms of electrons and atomic cores introduced the possibility of interpreting valence theory in terms of an Exclusion Principle for electrons and three fundamental physical forces.

| Physical Force | Leading Chemical Manifestation(s) |
|---|---|
| Nuclear-Electron Attraction | Formation of Molecules |
| | Doctrine of Coordination |
| | Nucleophilic and Electrophilic Sites |
| | Donor-Acceptor Interactions |
| Nuclear-Nuclear Repulsion | Small-Ring "Strain" |
| | s-Character Rule |
| Electron-Electron Repulsion | Spin-Set Anticoincidence |

The three forces create three potential energy terms (V), which, together with an electronic kinetic energy term (T), yield for a system's total energy (E) the expression -

$$E = V_{ne} + V_{nn} + V_{ee} + T$$

In stationary states:

- Total energy E of a system with respect to its parts at infinite separation satisfies a "Virial Theorem": $E = V/2 = -T$. Large negative V, and E, owing to close approach to each other of nuclei and electrons, moving rapidly, means a large positive kinetic energy T.

- According to a Hellman-Feynman Theorem, net forces experienced by a system's atomic nuclei owing to repulsion of other nuclei and to attraction of the system's electron cloud, treated as a classical charge distribution, vanish.

# Effects of Nuclear-Nuclear Repulsion on Bond Angles and Bond Lengths

Valence bond models of molecules whose heavy atoms satisfy the Octet Rule and have, accordingly, four electron pairs in their valence shells arranged tetrahedrally have hydrogen/heavy-atom/hydrogen bond angles equal to the tetrahedral angle, 109.5°. In ammonia, however, the HNH angle is a few degrees less than the tetrahedral value, whereas in methyl fluoride the HCH angle is a degree or so larger than the tetrahedral value; and in ethylene the HCH angles are some seven degrees larger than the tetrahedral angle. Discussed below are considerations suggested by valence sphere models of molecules relevant to explanations of departures of HXH angles from the tetrahedral angle.

**Anion Lattices as *Frames of Reference*.** Just as many oxides may be described as close-packed arrays of oxide anions with smaller cations occupying the lattices' tetrahedral and/or octahedral interstices, so, also, from the point of view of valence sphere models of molecules, many molecules may be viewed as fragments of close-packed arrays of "electride ions" (a.k.a. "electron pairs" or "electron domains") with smaller atomic cores occupying the lattices' tetrahedral and, in some cases of expanded octets, octahedral interstices. The electron clouds serve as *frames of reference* in locating molecules' atomic cores — in accordance with Density Functional Theory's Hohenberg-Kohn Theorem, according to which molecules' electron density distributions determine locations and charges of the molecules' atomic nuclei.

**The Hellman-Feynman Theorem.** For molecules in stationary states, the net electrostatic force exerted on an atomic nucleus by other nuclei and the molecule's electron cloud, viewed as a classical charge distribution, vanishes — as otherwise motion of the nucleus in the direction of a non-vanishing force would diminish the molecule's energy.

**Distortions Caused by Cation-Cation Repulsion.** According to Pauling (*Nature of the Chemical Bond*, 3rd ed., p561) "When coordinated polyhedra [of anions; or, here, electron pairs] about cations [or, here, atomic cores] with large charge share edges or faces with one another [in double or triple bonds, in the case of atomic cores and electron pairs], it is to be expected that the repulsion of the cations [or atomic cores] will lead to such a deformation of the polyhedra as to increase the cation-cation distance."

**The Isoelectronic Principle.** The profile and overall articulation of a molecule's electron cloud is little affected by addition of protons to lone pairs or removal of protons from protonated pairs.

Application of those considerations to ammonia is illustrated in Figure 1.

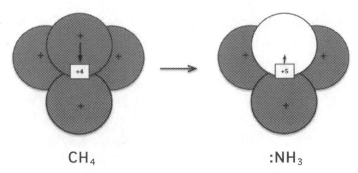

CH₄　　　　　　　　:NH₃

**Fig. 1.** Drawings of valence sphere models of $CH_4$ and $:NH_3$. The downward pointing arrow at the left indicates an alchemical transformation of a carbon core ($C^{+4}$) and a proton (+) into (at the right) a nitrogen core ($N^{+5}$), with, to judge by bond angles, the $N^{+5}$ core's subsequent slight relaxation upward.

The change from methane to ammonia has, to judge by bond lengths, little effect on the domains of ammonia's three nitrogen-hydrogen bonds, lengths 1.012 Å, compared to 1.094 Å in $CH_4$. The principal perturbation in passing from methane to ammonia occurs in the electron pair domain that changes from a protonated domain (in $CH_4$) to a lone pair (in $:NH_3$). Some but not all of the electronic charge equivalent to that of one electron follows the proton downward. (Ammonia's dipole moment is only 1.47 D.) Accordingly, attraction of the heavy atom core upward by the electronic charge of the uppermost domain increases in the cited alchemical transformation, but, as indicated by the short upward-pointing arrow on the right, absence of repulsion of the $N^{+5}$ core downward by a proton in the uppermost electron domain allows the $N^{+5}$ core to relax upward, thereby decreasing the HNH bond angles.

Changes pictured in Figure 1 are described by an s-Character Rule: Atoms tend to concentrate their s-character in orbitals directed toward substituents of low electronegativity, with a lone pair viewed as a substituent of zero electronegativity.

Application of the previously cited "considerations" to the case of bond angles opposite double bonds is pictured in Figure 2.

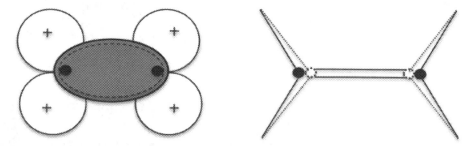

**Fig. 2. Left:** Electron domain model of $H_2C=CH_2$. Small black circles represent $C^{+4}$ cores. **Right:** Valence stick model of $H_2C=CH_2$. Dotted lines represent HCH angles of 109.5°. Corresponding solid lines represent the observed HCH bond angles.

Displacements caused by $C^{+4}/C^{+4}$ repulsion stretches domains of $C_2H_4$'s double bond, opens up the HCH angles, and shortens C—H bonds, from 1.094 Å in $CH_4$ to 1.085 Å in $C_2H_4$. In $C_2H_2$, continued $C^{+4}/C^{+4}$ displacements further shortens C—H bonds, to 1.059 Å. The decrease in CH bond length of 0.026 Å in going from $C_2H_4$ to $C_2H_2$ is greater than the decrease of 0.009 Å in going from $CH_4$ to $C_2H_4$ because in the former case $C^{+4}/C^{+4}$ repulsion thrusts the carbon cores *directly* into the domains of the C—H bonds.

# A Brief History of Localized Molecular Orbitals

*Sometimes a theory is most transparent in its simplest, least sophisticated forms.*

Chemistry's molecular orbitals were, in retrospect, first represented by the *one-dimensional valence strokes* of Alexander Crum Brown's bond diagrams, identified by Lewis as *electron pairs* of two-center bonds. That valence strokes truly represent, if highly schematically, *molecular* orbitals is, on reflection, apparent, inasmuch as, as mentioned previously, *divorced from molecules' bond diagrams, valence strokes are meaningless.* Valence strokes' chemical significance stems from their *collective particle behavior* in valence stroke diagrams, expressed mathematically, many years after Crum Brown, by Heisenberg with the expression $\Psi(1, 2, \ldots) = -\Psi(2, 1, \ldots)$.

Lewis' electron dots of his electron dot diagrams may be viewed as *zero-dimensional representations* of molecular orbitals.

Early mathematical descriptions of valence strokes included the *Heitler-London function* and overlaps of lobes of Pauling-Slater *hybrid atomic orbitals.* Possibilities of rescuing, so to speak, Lewis-type orbitals from a trash heap of concepts deemed by a newer Molecular Orbital Theory to be obsolete stem, from a physical point of view, from the *indistinguishability* of electrons and, as mentioned, above, the consequent *antisymmetric* character of electronic wavefunctions, which, accordingly, (i) *vanish* when two electrons of the same spin are at the same place at the same time, and which (ii) have the property of being expressible in terms of either localized or delocalized orbitals.

Localization procedures have included: Foster-Boys Localization, through minimization of orbitals' spatial extent; Edmiston-Ruedenberg Localization, through maximization of orbitals' self-energy; formation of Lennard-Jones' equivalent orbitals, from, e.g., linear combination of a double bond's sigma and pi orbitals; and Natural Bond Orbital Analyses of accurate antisymmetric wavefunctions by, e.g., Weinhold and coworkers.

Several routes lead to essentially the same Localized Molecular Orbitals.

The limiting instance of localized orbitals — short of Lewis's dots — are *exclusive orbitals*, induced from, e.g., as mentioned several times, *common sense impressions,* of matter's impenetrability, particularly the space-filling character of the electron clouds of helium's 2-electron atoms, dihydrogen's 2-electron molecules, lithium hydride's 2-electron ions, and elemental beryllium's 2-electron atomic cores and anionic "electride ions".

Called to mind is a Christmas toast at Cambridge's Cavendish laboratories in honor of its major-domo, J. J. Thomson, discoverer of a universal constituent of matter, with which he tried to explain all of chemistry. "Long live the electron!" went the toast. "May it never be of use to anyone!"

# Shapes of Exclusive Orbitals

*Try the simplest thing first. It might work.*
GENERAL PRINCIPLE OF INDUCTION

A sphere is an orbital's simplest shape. The simplest subset of Exclusive Orbital Models of Molecules is comprised, accordingly, of Valence *Sphere* Models. Spheres of different sizes fit the leading features of bond diagrams: small spheres for atomic cores (represented in bond diagrams by the symbols of the chemical elements) and larger spheres for the domains of valence shell electrons (represented in the diagrams by valence strokes: straight, for unstrained single bonds; curved for bonds of small-ring molecules, especially the two-member rings of multiple bonds; and rabbit-ear for the 1-member rings of lone pairs). Non-spherical shapes appear to be necessary to account, by induction, for, e.g., differences in lengths of single and double bonds (Figure 1) and the shapes of molecules that have unshared electrons in valence shells of large atomic cores (Figure 2).

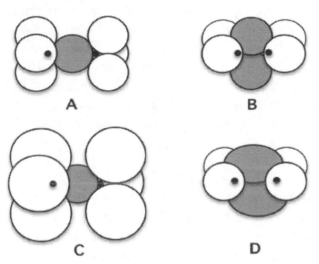

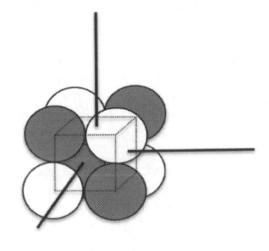

Fig. 1 (A,B,C,D). A & B: Equal-sphere-size models of ethane and ethylene. C: Large C—H model of ethane, to account for intra- and inter-molecular distances in crystalline ethane and (a side benefit) to account for the inertness of ethane's carbon-carbon bond. D: Stretched double bond domain model of ethylene, to account for its CC bond length compared to that of ethane.

Fig. 2. Anticoincident core model of phosphene, to account for its nearly 90° degree bond angles, compared to the nearly tetrahedral bond angles of ammonia. Its lone pair (not shown) is imagined to be delocalized in a non-spherical shape over the core's three hidden faces.

Packing of spherical exclusive domains about atomic cores leaves elecrophilic nooks and crannies, occupied in the d-block by electrons of semi-exclusive d-orbitals, in two sets, Figure 3.

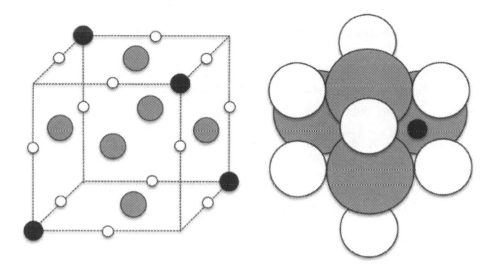

Fig. 3. Left: Small open circles represent relative locations in space, at edge-centers of a circumscribed cube, of centroids of charge of 12 semi-exclusive lobes of a set of three d-orbitals. Larger gray circles represent, similarly, 6 further space-filling, face-centered lobes of the remaining two d-orbitals. Black circles indicate the carbon cores of coordinated CO molecules of $Ni(CO)_4$, in which all 18 d-orbital lobes are occupied, by 4 pairs of electrons. Right: Exclusive domain model of the $d^{10}$ moeity of $Ni(CO)_4$. The indicated carbon core of a :CO: molecule (corresponding to the one at the front upper right at the left) donates a pair of electrons to one of the dimples, nooks, crannies, or pockets of the $d^{10}$ species and receives back from it into three dimples about the carbon end of a bent bond model of CO's triple bond electron density from the three adjacent d-orbital domains of three different d orbitals.

ADDED NOTE. The "exclusive orbitals" often referred to in this document are usually, also, and often referred to as such, "localized orbitals". Strictly speaking, they are *"semi-localized"* orbitals (perhaps particularly in the case of "d" and "f" electrons). Their finite sizes are of central importance in understanding stereochemistry and the saturation and directionality of primary and secondary chemical affinities, for picturing molecular electron density profiles, for modeling, approximately, electronic kinetic energies, and, thereby, for incorporating into Conceptual Valence Bond Theory the essence for chemistry of Schrödinger's wave equation. They are "delocalized Lewis dots" and, to a lesser degree, "delocalized valence strokes". They provide a modern, physical interpretation of chemistry's classical bond diagrams and, thereby, inject new life into classical structural theory.

# Exposure of Small Rings' Bent Bonds

The smaller a small ring, the more bent its bonds, the greater their exposure, and the greater their strength as nucleophilic electron-pair donors. The limiting case is a one-member ring: i.e., a lone-pair.

### Truncated Valence-Sphere Models of Small Rings' Bonds

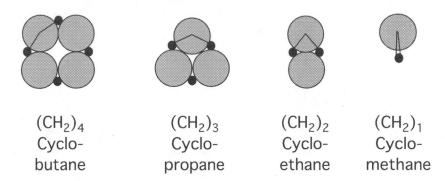

$(CH_2)_4$
Cyclo-
butane

$(CH_2)_3$
Cyclo-
propane

$(CH_2)_2$
Cyclo-
ethane

$(CH_2)_1$
Cyclo-
methane

**Gray Spheres:** domains of carbon-carbon bonds, except in the last instance. **Small Black Spheres:** $C^{+4}$ cores. **Bent Lines:** lines from pairs of bonded carbon cores to the centers of their carbon-carbon bonding domains. The highly bent "bond" of "cyclo-methane" is a lone pair.

Omitted for clarity are the two domains of the two C—H bonds of each $CH_2$ group. They are indicated below, one behind the other one in the case of "cyclo-ethane" (a.k.a ethylene). Indicated in the case of :$CH_2$ are the protons of its C—H bonds.

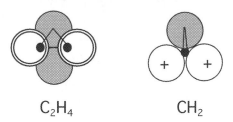

$C_2H_4$              $CH_2$

The exposed, unprotonated domains of the highly bent bonds of the smallest small rings, shown immediately above, are representations of their molecules' HOLMOs: Highest Occupied Localized Molecular Orbitals, a.k.a. the molecules' nucleophilic frontier orbitals, of lone pairs and the pairs of equivalent orbital representations of double bonds.

# A Teachable Topic

Simplicity of replacement of valence strokes by valence spheres renders Valence Sphere Theory highly teachable. Indicative of that remark was a comment by Professor Gabor Somorjai at a symposium at an ACS meeting in San Francisco in memory of Brian E. Bent, 1960 – 1996, professor of physical chemistry and surface science at Columbia University at the time of his sudden death. "Brian," said Gabor (he was Brian's research advisor at Berkeley), "had a wonderful feeling for how molecules behave." That's not surprising, thought his father. Brian had been introduced to valence sphere models of molecules at an early age.

After presents were opened, Christmas, 1967, Brian and his father retreated to their kitchen to assemble with rubber bands and bent brass paper fasteners strings of Styrofoam spheres, easily snapped together to form valence sphere models of molecules. With a card on how chemists count [1 (tetrahedral interstice) methane, 2 ethane, 3 propane, etc.], Brian named models made by his father. Then they switched roles: father naming, son constructing. After they'd run through the paraffins to hexane, they went on to the cyclic paraffins, beginning with cyclohexane (fun for showing the chair/boat interconversion). Down they went to smaller and smaller rings until, finally, they reached "cycloethane". What would Brian do for that?, wondered his father. No problem. Quickly he produced the valence sphere model of ethylene, one of his father's favorite models, for the ease with which it accounts for important properties of $C_2H_4$, including its chief nucleophilic and electrophilic sites and its HCH bond angles.

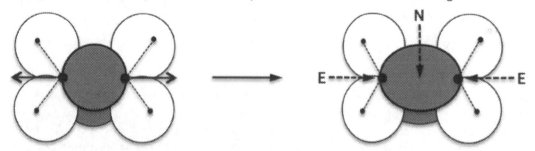

**Left**. Equal-sphere-size valence sphere model of ethylene, top view. White circles: domains of C—H bonds. Gray circles: domains of equivalent orbitals of C=C bond. Two black circles: Carbon $C^{+4}$ cores. Four smaller black circles: protons of CH bonds. Two outward-pointing arrows: directions of displacements of carbon cores from the centers of their tetrahedral interstices, owing to core-core repulsion. Dashed lines indicate tetrahedral HCH angles: 109.5°.

**Right**. Carbon cores' locations with respect to ethylene's electron cloud after outward displacements from the centers of their tetrahedral interstices, showing enlarged HCH angles, to 117.5°. **N**: nucleophilic site. **E**: Electrophilic site.

Conceptual Valence Bond Theory stands to the chemistry curriculum as the three R's stand to elementary education. They're included in curricula — or should be — for the same reasons. They're important. And they're teachable.

# A Pedagogical Hierarchy for Conceptual Valence Bond Theory

A pedagogically sound theory of valence should lend itself to progressively more advanced discussions at each stage of the curriculum, from high school through graduate school, wrote Professor William B. Jensen, noted chemical educator, historian of chemistry, and connoisseur of chemical thought, in a Foreword for a precursor to the present volume. A pedagogical hierarchy for Conceptual Valence Bond Theory might begin even earlier and unfold in the following fashion.

## Elementary School
- Free play with Styrofoam spheres connected to each other in strings of various lengths by rubber bands stretched through their diameters and held in place by paper fasteners.
- Construction of copies of models of molecules of paraffins and cyclic paraffins.
- Naming of constructed models, based on numbers of tetrahedral interstices.
- Construction of models of named hydrocarbons.

## Middle School
- Drawing of bond diagrams for molecules composed of the atoms C, H, and O, given chemical formulas and the conventions: 1 "valence stroke" from H, 2 from O, and 4 from C; and the rule: no dangling valence strokes.
- Creation of molecular formulas given bond diagrams (Step 4, p320).

## High School
- Evidence for nuclei, electrons, electron shells, lone pairs, the Octet Rule, the tetrahedral atom, and its use in construction of models of single, double, and triple bonds.
- Introduction of rabbit-ear valence strokes and the Valence Stroke Termination Rule.
- Construction of valence sphere models using a "Starter Kit" of spheres consisting of several single spheres and, preassembled, several digonal, trigonal, and tetrahedral sets.
- Creation of bond diagrams from valence sphere models of molecules (Step 5, p320).

## General Chemistry
- Isoelectronic species.
- Systematic discussion of evidence for localized molecular orbitals.
- Different Structures for Different Spin Sets and Bond Diagrams for NO and $O_2$.
- Derivation and uses of the Bond Number Equation.
- Formal charges, resonance, dispersed lone pairs about large atomic cores, and intermolecular donor-acceptor interactions.Creation of molecular formulas corresponding to valence sphere models.

## Organic Chemistry
- Valence sphere models of functional groups.
- Nucleophilic and Electrophilic sites.
- Intramolecular donor-acceptor interactions.
- Valence sphere models of curly arrow reaction mechanisms.

## Inorganic Chemistry.
- Expanded Octets.
- Multicenter Bonds.
- Additional applications of Conceptual Valence Bond Theory.

## Graduate School.
- Natural Bond Orbital analyses of accurate molecular wave functions.
- Development of software for creation directly from molecular formulas of Valence Sphere Models of approximate molecular electron density profiles (Step 3, p320).

# Conceptual Valence Bond Theory's Correspondence Principles
## *A Summary and Review*

Conceptual Valence Bond Theory developed from disparate points of view in the disciplines of general, organic, and inorganic chemistry, physical chemistry, and chemical physics. Each discipline contributed to the Theory distinctive concepts and models, rules and terminology yielding, on comparison, inter- and intra-disciplinary linkages in the form of analogies and correlations, connections and correspondence principles, cited below.

## Electron-Dot/Bond-Diagram Correspondence
Valence strokes correspond to electron pairs, atomic symbols to atomic cores, and additional valence shell electrons to lone pairs.

## Lone-Pair/Rabbit-Ear Convention
An unshared pair corresponds to two latent combining capacities, represented by a valence stroke whose ends terminate at the same atomic symbol.

## Lone-Pair/Bond-to-Hydrogen Structural Equivalence
Protonation and deprotonation of valence shell electron pair domains little affects overall molecular architecture.

## Valence-Stroke-Diagram/Valence-Sphere-Model Isomorphism
Valence-Sphere analogues of valence-stroke diagrams exist, so far as is known, for all molecules that have satisfactory valence-stroke diagrams.

## Nooks-and-Crannies/d-Electron Correspondence
Midpoints of the 12 edges and 6 faces of Lewis-Linnett cubes correspond to locations of d-orbitals' lobes. Reciprocally, d-orbital lobes define, collectively, locations of the 8 vertices of Lewis-Linnett cubes.

## Core-Charge/Absolute-Valence Convention
The two phrases designate the same concept.

## Valence-Stroke-Termination-Rule/Hohenberg-Kohn-Theorem
In bond diagrams numbers of valence stroke terminations at elements' symbols stand to charges of atomic cores as electron density distributions of molecular electron clouds stand to charges of the molecules' nuclei.

## Oracle/Editor Analogy
The equations $H\Psi = E\Psi$ and $\Psi(1, 2, \ldots) = -\Psi(2, 1, \ldots)$ stand to each other in Computational Valence Theory as the Bond Number Equation $\sum(n-1)B_n = \sum(EPCN)_i - V$ and Valence Sphere Models stand to each other in Conceptual Valence Theory. In each instance the former propose and the latter dispose.

## Ionic Model/Covalent Model Correspondence
All compounds may be viewed as ion compounds, formed by coordination of negative ions (anions or electron pairs) by positive ions (cations or atomic cores).

## Exclusive-Orbital/Wave-Function Correspondence
*Exclusive* Orbitals of *finite size* correspond in Computational Valence Theory to operation of, respectively, the equations $\Psi(1, 2, \ldots) = -\Psi(2, 1, \ldots)$ and $H\Psi = E\Psi$.

# Converging Lines of Evidence
## in support of
## *Exclusive Orbital Models of Molecules*
### A Recapitulation and Extension of Previous Remarks

Numerous lines of evidence suggest that to describe qualitatively molecular electron density *profiles* in order to understand conceptually the saturation and directional character of primary and secondary chemical affinities and, thereby, to understand molecular shapes, intra- and inter-molecular donor-acceptor interactions, and, accordingly, to understand curly-arrow reaction mechanisms, it is sufficient in a first approximation to picture electrons of molecules of compounds of elements of the *s*- and *p*-blocks of periodic tables as occupying, usually in spin-paired pairs, the exclusive, localized domains of valence sphere models of molecules (a.k.a. tangent sphere, charge cloud, and electron domain models) formed by replacement of valence strokes of classical bond diagrams by valence spheres. Supporting that conclusion are the two Master Equations of wave/particle mechanics: Schrödinger's equation $H\psi = E\psi$ and Heisenberg's equation $\psi(1, 2, \ldots) = -\psi(2, 1, \ldots) \rightarrow \psi(X, X, \ldots) = 0$. With Born's interpretation of the wave function $\psi$, the last equation states that two electrons of the same spin cannot be at the same place at the same time. Schrödinger's equation treats electrons as wavicles and suggests, with Heisenberg's equation, that two different electron-pair *domains* seldom occupy the same region of space. Cited below are "numerous lines of evidence" of disparate provenance that support the concept of exclusive molecular orbitals.

**Electron Pair Exclusion Principle. I.** On the assumption that most of the space occupied by condensed matter is occupied by its atoms' or molecules' electron clouds, one infers, from the space occupied by liquid helium, whose atoms contain one electron pair, and liquid hydrogen, whose molecules contain one electron pair, and crystalline lithium hydride, whose ions contain one electron pair, that, whereas two electrons can evidently occupy the same region of space at the same time, *two electron pairs cannot be in the same region of space at the same time.*

> The Electron Pair Exclusion Principle is a modern statement of Newton's explanation of matter's impenetrability in terms of "*hard* massy atoms". A physical model of such atoms assigns to electrons "a classically indescribable two-valuedness" (Pauli's words) called (today) "spin", and supposes that two electrons of the *same spin* cannot be at the same place at the same time nor even, owing to the continuity of probability densities, *in the same region of space* at the same time.

**Valence Stroke Exclusion Principle.** Valence strokes of satisfactory bond diagrams *never cross each other!* Never are they at the same place at the same time.

**Electron Pair Exclusion Principle. II.** According to G. N. Lewis, valence strokes represent *electron pairs*. Combined with the Valence Stroke Exclusion Principle, Lewis's induction implies that *for electron pairs two's a crowd.*

**Ionization Energies.** Energies required to remove an electron from (i) 1-electron hydrogen atoms, (ii) 2-electron helium atoms, and (iii) 3-electron lithium atoms are, respectively, 13.6, 24.6, and *merely 5.4 eV!* For electrons, *three's a crowd*.

**Localized Molecular Orbitals.** Because electronic antisymmetric wave functions may be expressed as determinants, unchanged (except for a proportionality constant) on replacement of their columns (or rows) by linear combinations of their columns (or rows) — because of that fact, electronic wave functions' orbitals may be expressed in different, mathematically, if not conceptually, equivalent ways.

A wave function composed, for instance, of the product A(1)B(2) of two orbitals A and B for two electrons "1" and "2" of the same spin, when rendered antisymmetric, by adding the term –A(2)B(1), may be written as a determinant, in several ways; e.g.,-

A(1)B(2) – A(2)B(1)  [= ‖ A   B ‖] = ‖ A+B   B ‖  = (-1/2)‖ A+B   A-B ‖

If A represents, e.g., a σ orbital of a double bond and B the bond's π orbital, then A+B and A-B represent two "equivalent orbitals": a somewhat localized upward curving "banana bond" and a similarly localized downward curving "banana bond".

One may for use, accordingly, delocalized canonical molecular orbitals for, say, computational purposes and mathematically equivalent localized molecular orbitals, for visualization and physical interpretation.

**Configurations of Maximum Probability.** Interpretation of a wave function consists in seeing by inspection of the forms of the wave function's orbitals the approximate locations of electrons that maximize the wave function's numerical value. Linnett and coworkers have called that configuration a molecule's *Configuration of Maximum Probability* (CMT). Its obvious physical significance explains why bond diagrams appear so widely in the chemical literature, as each valence stroke of a bond diagram represents schematically the domain of an exclusive spin orbital (or spatial pair of them), with location of an electron at each orbital's centroid representing the molecule's CMP. The same statement does not hold, however, for wave functions constructed from non-exclusive orbitals.

**Independent and Collective, Dependent Particle Models of Matter, and Bohr's Aufbau Process.** Broadly speaking, particulate models of matter are of two types: gaseous, independent-particle models and condensed state, collective-particle models. For particulate models of molecules there are, correspondingly, two theories: MO theory, which pictures electrons in a molecule as, before wave function antisymmetrization, independent, gas-like particles moving in an average field in delocalized orbitals that encompass entire molecules and are not altered as electrons are added in a Bohr aufbau process; and VB theory, which pictures electrons in molecules as occupying close confederations of localized orbitals whose configurations, owing to dependent particle behavior, change in an aufbau process.

On adding electrons to, for instance, $NO_2^+$, yielding $NO_2$ and subsequently $NO_2^-$, CMPs change, to judge by changes in the ONO bond angle: from 180° to 134° to 115°.

**Valence Theory and the Exclusion Principle.** Both MO and VB valence theory restrict occupancy of their orbitals to two electrons. In addition, at a computational level, both theories introduce, through use of antisymmetric wave functions, the restriction that two electrons of the same spin cannot be at the same place at the same time. An Exclusive Orbital Model of molecules adds to those restrictions the restriction that two *orbitals* occupied by electrons of parallel spin cannot occupy the same region of space.

**Charge Cloud Models.** Kimball and coworkers discovered that simple, Lewis-like "charge cloud" models of molecules yield ballpark-correct molecular energies.

Such energies emerge once one introduces into a calculation the charge of an electron, e, through calculation of coulombic potential energies, and Planck's constant, h, through use of de Broglie's relation, $\lambda = h/p$, in estimation of electrons' kinetic energies, where $\lambda$ is the diameter of an electron's domain.

**Natural Bond Orbitals.** Weinhold and coworkers have discovered that Natural Bond Orbital analyses of accurate molecular wave functions yield Lewis-like localized core, bonding, and lone pair orbitals.

**Oxide-Ion/Electride-Ion Structural Equivalence.** Just as hydride ions, $H^-$, are often structurally equivalent to fluoride ions, $F^-$, so, also, Exclusive Orbital Theory's postulated electride ions, $e_2^{-2}$, isoelectronic with $H^-$, are often structurally equivalent to oxide ions, $O^{-2}$, isoelectronic with $F^-$. Examples are the chloride-ion/perchlorate-ion series of ions, $[Cl(e_2^{-2})_{4-n}O_n]^-$, n = 0 – 4; the pair of molecules ethane, $H_3C—CH_3$, and dimethyl ether, $H_3COCH_3$; and crystals of calcium oxide, $Ca^{+2}O^{-2}$, and calcium electride, $Ca^{+2}(e_2^{-2})$, isoeletronic with potassium hydride, $K^+H^-$.

**Isoelectronic Molecules.** The similarity of bond angles in molecules of methane, ammonia, and water suggests that a bond to hydrogen, —H [an asymmetrically protonated electron pair (or polarized hydride ion, $H^-$)] is structurally equivalent, approximately, in its profile, to a lone pair.

**Transferability of Bond Properties.** Although the canonical molecular orbitals of, e.g., ethane and propane are significantly different from each other, C—H bond properties, such as length, strength, and vibrational frequency, are highly transferable, consistent with local orbital models of the molecules.

**Octet Rule.** From the standpoint of exclusive electron pair domains of approximately spherical shape, the first coordination polyhedron of such domains about an atomic core that shields the core from further coordination of electron domains is the tetrahedron, corresponding to the Octet Rule.

**Isomorphism of Valence Stroke Diagrams and Valence Sphere Models.** A one-to-one correspondence exists between valence stroke diagrams and valence sphere models. Every satisfactory diagram has a satisfactory model and conversely: if a satisfactory model can't be made, the corresponding molecule can't be synthesized.

**Stereochemistry of Primary Chemical Affinities.** Coordination by atomic cores of electron domains of *finite size* yields immediately chemical affinities' leading features: *saturation* and *directionality*.

**Stereochemistry of Secondary Chemical Affinities.** Exclusive orbital models of molecules with their nucleophilic "bumps" (of exposed electron domains of one-member rings of lone pairs and two-member rings of multiple bonds) and the models' electrophilic "pockets", "hollows", or "dimples" off faces of atomic cores' coordinated electron polyhedra account at a glance for the stereochemistry of inter- and intra-molecular electron pair donor-acceptor interactions and, accordingly, for curly arrow models of mechanisms of chemical reactions.

**Chemistry's *Lingua Franca*.** To understand what science is really about, said Einstein, pay attention to what scientists *do*, not to what they say they do. For many years MO theorists have urged chemists to use canonical molecular orbitals instead of classical bond diagrams. Yet a typical issue of *Chemical & Engineering News* (May 30, 2011) displays in nine articles and fifteen advertisements *205 bond diagrams* and not one canonical molecular orbital. For over a century bond diagrams have been chemistry's common language.

**Number of Trial Functions in MO Theory's Use of the Variation Theorem.** Computational Valence Theory's use of canonical molecular orbitals with the Variation Theorem is analogous, in some respects, to glassblowing's initial "get". Poor "gets" require huge corrective efforts. For obtaining good energy-estimates for some 99% of a system's energy, owing to good electron density estimates in the energetically important, but usually stereochemically unimportant, neighborhoods of atomic nuclei, beginning an application of the Variation Theorem with Canonical Molecular Orbitals formed from linear combinations modified [true] atomic orbitals, is currently the method of choice. From the point of view of Exclusive Orbital Models of molecular electron density *profiles*, however, mutually overlapping canonical MOs are exceedingly poor choices for chemical bonding regions. It's not surprising, accordingly, that highly accurate calculations require millions, even billions, of trial functions, to correct — it would seem — for initial poor "gets" regarding orbitals' character in bonding regions.

**Existence of a Deep-seated Consilience *Contingent on Use of Exclusive Semi-Localized Molecular Orbitals!*** Pauling's Rules for the structures of ionic compounds hold also, accordingly, for covalent compounds, if one changes the words "cations" and "anions" to the phrases "atomic cores" and "electron pairs", a.k.a. "electride ions". Created is a unified theory of the chemical bond in which all compounds — ionic, covalent, and metallic — are considered to be "ion compounds".

Existence of the extensive Consilience (pages 15-17) is absolutely contingent, to repeat, on use of exclusive, semi-localized molecular orbitals. No such simple correspondence between the concepts of structural inorganic and organic chemistry exists in MO theory. The Consilience is unique to Modern Conceptual Valence Bond Theory and its use of exclusive, semi-localized electron domains — a surprising result, in a way, in that MO theory has generally been considered to be a more comprehensive theory than Valence Bond theory. On the conceptual side, however, for ground states, VB theory, with, e.g., its "bonds", and its Consilience, has, it would seem, pride of place.

## Existence of *Many Disparate Lines of Evidence* for Exclusive Orbital Models of Molecules. But, to paraphrase Dalton, whether electrons occupy exclusive, semi-localized domains or not, this much is certain, granting that that be so, molecules would appear much as they do now.

SUMMARY. Exclusive Orbital Theory follows Heisenberg's recipe for successful revolutions (and not only in science!). *Change as little as possible.* Change "phlogiston lost" to "oxygen gained", "delocalized" to "localized", and "electron dots" and "valence strokes" to "electron domains".

From the point of view of Exclusive Orbital Theory, delocalized molecular orbitals are 20th century's phlogiston: a detour, for molecules' ground states, away from more realistic images of the collective particle behavior of close confederations of Fermions, described by the expression $\Psi(1, 2, \ldots) = -\Psi(2, 1, \ldots)$, the chief editor of chemial thought.

The Theory is crude — yet shrewd, *because crude!* It's the kind of theory that, like classical thermodynamics, achieves its usefulness *by what it leaves out:* inner details of electron density distributions, essential for accurate calculations of many molecular properties but not essential for a qualitative understanding of electron density profiles and, accordingly, for an understanding of molecular shapes, intermolecular interactions, and reaction mechanisms.

Conceptual Valence Bond Theory's traditional output — its bond diagrams — is the input to the Z-matrices of Computational Valence Theory, whose numerical output is Conceptual Valence Bond Theory's input for "creation of easy-to-use low end tools [such as valence stroke diagrams and valence sphere models] that allow scientists to rapidly generate [via] visualizations [exploratory] hypotheses"*.

* "Changing the Equation on Scientific Data Visualization," Peter Fox and James Hendler, *Science*, Vol. 331, 11 Feb. 2011, pp705-708.

CAVEAT. To repeat: A model of some thing, to be *useful*, must be *wrong,* in some respects, else it would be the thing itself, like a map the same size and shape of the terrain mapped. The trick in using *physical models* lies in focusing attention on their positive analogies and in ignoring their — <u>necessary</u> — negative analogies. The fleas (negative analogies) come with the dog (the positive analogies) — an example, suggests Professor Liebman, of "Hund's Rule".

# William Whewell on "The Fundamental Antithesis of Science"

William Whewell, born in Lancaster, England, 1794, studied at Trinity College in Cambridge where he later became a fellow and tutor; at 26 he was already a member of the Royal Society. His work in the realm of mechanics and dynamics was so important that it led to an appointment as professor of mineralogy at Cambridge in 1838. By 1841 he had become master of Trinity College; one year later he assumed the vice-chancellorship of Cambridge University. At the beginning of the thirties he began to study the history of the empirical sciences; the results of these investigations were published in his three-volume *History of the Inductive Sciences* in 1837. Three years later he published *Philosophy of the Inductive Sciences*.

JOSEPH KOCKELMANS, *Philosophy if Science: The Historical Background*

Faraday sought Whewell's advice on terminology with which to express results and inductions regarding his famous electro-chemical investigations. From their collaboration emerged three terms (in *italics*, shortly) central to discussion of Conceptual Valence Bond Theory's leading induction: namely, that all compounds are *ion*-compounds, in which the *cations* are atomic cores and the *anions* are electronically charged exclusive orbitals.

"[T]he whole of natural philosophy," wrote William Herschel (cited by Kockelmans), "consists entirely of a series of inductive generalizations [that, e.g., hydrogen, oxygen, and carbon have combining capacities of 1, 2, and 4], commencing with the most circumstantially stated particulars [that, e.g., the chemical formulas of water and "carbonic acid gas" are $H_2O$ and $CO_2$], and carried up to universal laws or axioms": that, e.g., in essentially all compounds of boron, carbon, nitrogen, oxygen and fluorine with sufficiently long life-times to be named and stored in bottles, the atoms of the cited elements have in their valence shells eight electrons in two spin-sets arranged tetrahedrally. That statement expresses the most general instance of the Isoelectronic Principle regarding electronic similarity in chemical difference.

Whewell offers for his "Fundamental Antithesis of Science," between sensations and ideas, things and thoughts, observation and reasoning, evidence and inductions, fact and theory, numerous aphorisms, including the following (sometimes slightly reworded for brevity).

- Conceptions by which Facts are bound together arise from exercises of the imagination.

- Fact-binding inductions' usefulness is demonstrated by their applications to other facts.

- Hypotheses [of which models are one class] may be useful, though involving much that is superfluous, and even erroneous.

- The Logic of Induction consists in stating Evidence and Inferences in such a manner, that the Evidence of the Inference is manifest; just as the Logic of

Deduction consists in stating the Premises and the Conclusion in such a manner that the argument for the Conclusion from the Premises is manifest.

- Although in Every Induction, a new conception is super-induced upon the Facts; yet once *effectually* done [emphasis added], the novelty of the conception is overlooked, and it is considered a fact. [Schrödinger's Equation, initially an induction, is, now, considered to be the "Oracle" of quantitative valence theory.]

- A true theory is a fact. A fact is a familiar theory.

- The distinction of Fact and Theory is only relative. Events and phenomena, considered as Particulars which may be colligated by Induction are Facts; considered as Generalities already obtained by colligation of other Facts, they are Theories.

In Whewell's terminology, the first part of this book concerns chiefly inductive ascents from particulars to generalities. The second part (that which follows) concerns chiefly deductive descents from generalities to particulars. Yet the distinction is only "relative". Any "ascent" may be made a "descent", and vice-versa, by changing an Induction to a Premise, or a Premise to an Induction.

Whewell raises an interesting point regarding his fundamental antithesis between fact and theory. We must ask, he says: *To whom is a fact a fact?* what habits of thought, what previous information, what ideas does it imply to conceive the fact as a fact?

- To astronomers the world is round. To flat-earthers it's flat.

- To biologists evolution is a fact. To a layperson it's a theory.

And, likewise, here? To whom is it useful to consider electrons in molecules to be localized? What habits of thought, what previous information, what ideas does it imply to conceive that induction to be (almost) a fact?

# Unsaturation and Hydrogenation

Molecules, in particular hydrocarbons, that have an excess connectivity owing to the presence of multiple bonds and/or rings are said to be "unsaturated". Addition of hydrogen reduces excess connectivity, EC, and unsaturation. For N Octet-Rule-obeying atoms sharing V pairs of electrons, in terms of the number of bonds B between octets

$$EC [= B - (N - 1) = (4N - V) - (N - 1)] = 3N - V + 1$$

Since each addition of a hydrogen molecule, H—H, increases the number of valence-shell electron-pairs, V, by 1 without changing the number of heavy atoms, N, it follows that $\Delta(EC) = -\Delta V$. A simple example is -

$$H_2C=CH_2 + H_2 = H_3C—CH_3.$$

Further hydrogenation reduces EC from 0 to –1. That is to say, it "cracks" ethane in the cited example into two molecules: $H_3C—CH_3 + H_2 = 2 CH_4$.

Atoms that have in their valence-shells lone-pairs (the smallest of small rings) *and* less than their maximum possible number of valence-shell electrons are sites of unsaturation, in the sense that two additional monovalent atoms can be bonded to them without "cracking". Usually the added atoms have relatively high affinities for electrons. The phosphorus atom of $:PCl_3$ is an instance of that kind of unsaturation.

$$:PCl_3 + Cl_2 = PCl_5$$

Reaction of methylene, $:CH_2$, with $H_2$ is a particularly simple instance of the saturation of unsaturation by way of hydrogenation.

*Valence-Sphere Representation of the Reaction*

$$:CH_2 + H_2 = CH_4$$

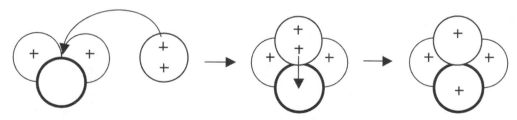

In the first step, $:CH_2$ acts as an electron-pair acceptor (a Lewis acid). $H_2$ (the doubly protonated electron-pair) acts as an electron-pair donor (a Lewis base). In the second step, the doubly-protonated electron-pair acts as a proton donor (a Brönsted acid) and the lone-pair acts as a proton acceptor (a Brönsted base). Replacement of $:CH_2$'s reaction partner H—H, above, by H—R, where R is an organic group, such as $CH_3$, yields the product $H_3C—R$ (rather than, as above, $H_3C—H$). The reaction is called, unrealistically, from a mechanistic point of view, an "insertion reaction", of $CH_2$ into the H—R bond, since the product may be written $H—CH_2—R$.

# Cyclopropane Formation from Ethylene and Methylene
## $(CH_2)_2 + CH_2 = (CH_2)_3$
### *A Localized Molecular Orbital Perspective*

Methylene, $CH_2$, is both a nucleophilic and an electrophilic reagent. It has both an exposed electron pair and an exposed atomic core.

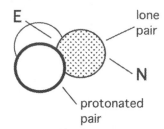

E: Site of exposed $C^{+4}$ core. Electrophilic site.
N: Site of exposed electron pair. Nucleophilic site.

Electron pairs of C—H bonds are exposed but are only weakly nucleophilic, owing to the presence within them of nucleus-repelling protons. Those protons, in turn, are only weakly electrophilic, because they are deeply embedded in the electron clouds of C—H bonds.

The arrangement of methylene's electrophilic and nucleophilic sites permits easy reaction of two $CH_2$ molecules with each other.

*Valence-Stroke Diagram and Valence-Sphere Model of $CH_2$'s Dimerization*

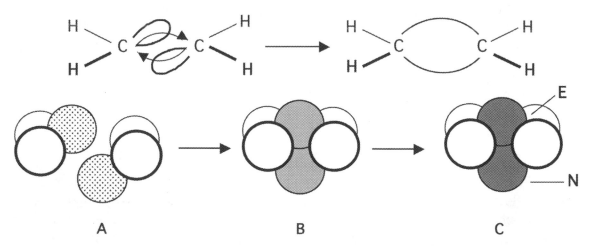

A B C

A: Nucleophilic lone pairs (the speckled domains) approach electrophilic sites. B: Lone pairs are not yet full-fledged bonding pairs if $C^{+4}$ cores have not yet moved from their initial trigonal interstices in A into the newly created tetrahedral interstices of B. C: With carbon cores in the tetrahedral interstices, the initial lone pairs of A have become bonding pairs of a double bond, shown in C in its "natural" twin (or equivalent) orbital representation.

Double bonds may be viewed as 2-membered rings, lone pairs as 1-membered rings. Exposure of ring-forming electron pairs increases with decreasing ring size: lone pairs are more nucleophilic than electron pairs of double bonds. Carbon $C^{+4}$ cores of double bonds, although surrounded by the electronic armor (toward nucleophilic reagents) of four electron pairs, are, nonetheless, somewhat attractive to nucleophiles, owing to relatively large, exposure-enhancing mutual repulsion of two $C^{+4}$ cores sufficiently close to each other to share the two electron pairs of double bonds.

Association of the powerful nucleophilic and electrophilic sites of $CH_2$ with, respectively, the weaker electrophilic and nucleophilic sites of $H_2C=CH_2$ yields cyclopropane.

*Valence-Stroke Diagram for the Reaction $H_2CCH_2 + CH_2 = (CH_2)_3$*

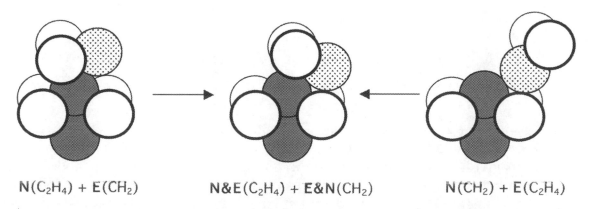

The valence-stroke diagram for formation of cyclopropane from methylene's "insertion", as it is called, into ethylene's double bond serves to book-keep rearrangements of electron domains, and suggests the manner in which reactant molecules may approach each other. Glossed over in the valence-stroke diagram are details regarding motions of atomic cores and spectator electron domains.

The reaction's first step is association of a nucleophilic site of one reagent with an electrophilic site of the other reagent (left and right figures below), followed (center) by a second N/E interaction.

$$N(C_2H_4) + E(CH_2) \qquad N\&E(C_2H_4) + E\&N(CH_2) \qquad N(CH_2) + E(C_2H_4)$$

On the left the top domain of the double bond is a 3-center CCC bond. Replacement of :$CH_2$ by isoelectronic $CH_3^+$ yields a model of the central 3-center AlCAl bonds of $Al_2(CH_3)_6$.

*Electron Domain and Atomic Core Rearrangements in Formation of Cyclopropane from Ethylene and Methylene*

White Spheres:        Domains of protonated C—H pairs, protons not shown.
Speckled Sphere:      Domain of methylene's lone pair.
Dark Grey Spheres:    Domains of electron pairs of carbon-carbon bonds.
Light Grey Spheres:   Domains of electron pairs of intermediate character, between that of a lone pair and a bonding pair.
Small Black Spheres:  Carbon $C^{+4}$ cores.

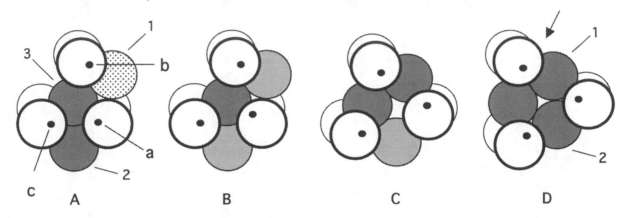

A: Initial molecular addition complex (previous figure). Domain 3 represents, as mentioned, a 3-center bond, two centers of which (the bottom two) are in a normal covalent bond relationship with the domain (electrostatic bond strengths equal to 1) and one of which (the upper one) is (with its $C^{+4}$ core shown still in its trigonal interstice of $CH_2$) in more of a dative bond relationship with it (electrostatic bond strength 0). The 3-center bond's valence-stroke representation appears in the following figure at the far right.

*Valence-Stroke Diagrams of Different Types of Electron Domains*

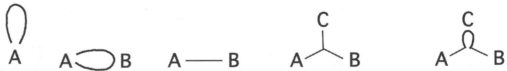

Lone Pair   Dative Bond   Covalent Bond   3-Center Bond   3c Dative/Covalent Bond

A to B: On the path to bringing electron domain 1 into the valence shell of atomic core **a** (at the initial expense of domain 2). Core **a** moves toward domain 1 and away from domain 2, as in a Walden inversion. It ends up in B surrounded by five electron pair domains in a trigonal bipyramidal arrangement. The two axial domains (light grey) are at a greater distance from it than the three equatorial domains (of a carbon-carbon bond and two C—H bonds). (Reversion of symmetrical B to A could yield ethylene and methylene with a $CH_2$ group interchange.) As the electrostatic interaction between core **a** and domain 1 increases and, simultaneously, that of core **a** and domain 2 decreases, that of domain 2 with core **c** increases and that of core **c** with domain 3 decreases as that of domain 3 and core **b** increases as core **b** moves from its initial trigonal interstice in methylene toward the tetrahedral interstice formed by methylene's three electron pairs and domain 3, all in the interests of maintaining energy-minimizing local electrical neutrality throughout the "insertion".

*Valence-Stroke/Curly-Arrow Representation of the Change A ⟶ B*

| In the change from A to B, domain 1, a lone pair domain in A, approaches in B the character of a domain of a dative bond. | 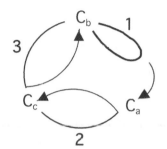 | Backside attack by domain 1 on $C_a$ induces some dative bond character in bond $C_aC_c$, rendering it somewhat polar, which induces similar character in bond $C_cC_b$. |
|---|---|---|

To repeat: As carbon atom $C_a$ becomes increasingly involved electrostatically with domain 1, it becomes less involved with domain 2, which, accordingly, becomes increasingly involved with atom $C_c$, which, in turn, becomes, therefore, less involved with domain 3, which, consequently, becomes more involved with atom $C_b$ as $C_b$ becomes less involved with domain 1 as domain 1 becomes more involved with atom $C_a$.

**B to C:** Several movements bring domains 1 and 2 (light grey in **B**, adjacent to each other in product **D**) closer together. Core **a** moves from its trigonal bipyramidal interstice in **B** to the nearby trigonal interstice formed by domain 1 and core **a**'s two C—H domains, as those C—H domains "slide" outward and upward on the "surface" of domain 1. Simultaneously domain 2 and the two domains of the C—H bonds of core **c** "slide" rightward, with their cores, on the "surface" of domain 3.

**C to D:** Continuation of cited domain slides and accompanying core movements yields product **D**: cyclopropane. Such is the choreography, or something similar to it, of methylene's "insertion into" double bonds, from the perspective of localized electron domain models of molecular structure.

Although domains of the C—C bonds of cyclopropane's 3-membered ring are less exposed in the ring's electron domain model than are those of models of the 2-membered rings of double bonds and the 1-membered rings of lone pairs, they are, nonetheless, somewhat nucleophilic toward electrophilic reagents such as $Ag^+$ whose $4d^{10}$ electrons can "back bond" to cyclopropane's external dimples. The arrow in Figure D indicates one such electrophilic site of $(CH_2)_3$.

# Planar Methane
## From the Point of View of Conceptual Valence Bond Theory

Flattening a valence sphere model of CH$_4$ yields, in the first instance, a structure that has, by the model's logic, a couple of bond lengths and bond angles, Figure 1.

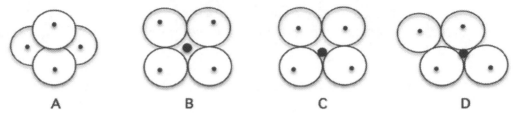

**Fig. 1.** Valence sphere models of tetrahedral (**A**) and planar (**B, C**, and **D**) methane. Large spheres represent domains of valence shell electron pairs of carbon-hydrogen bonds. Small black circles represent protons (of hydrogen atoms), larger black ones carbon atomic cores C$^{+4}$. **A:** The carbon core (not shown) is just about the right size (Pauling radius 15 pm) to occupy without rattling the tetrahedral interstice created by close packed domains of electron pairs of four CH bonds. **B:** A metastable structure. The carbon core is too small to occupy without rattling the interstice created by a square-planar arrangement of CH domains. **C:** A more stable arrangement than **B**. **D:** A still more stable arrangement.

Wasted in the structure represented by Figure 1**D** is occupancy of the low potential energy space for electrons about C$^{+4}$ above and below the plane of planar methane, remedied in Figure 2.

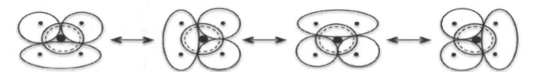

**Fig. 2.** Location of an *unshared electron pair* in an orbital centered above (solid circle) and, by resonance, below (dashed circle) the molecular plane. The remaining three pairs of valence shell electrons are located in two two-center CH bonds, and in a 3-centered HCH bond (the elliptical domain). Resonance renders the bonds equivalent to each other. In conventional orbital language the electrons may be described, approximately, as occupying in pairs a carbon 2p orbital, two carbon-sp$^2$/hydrogen-1s orbitals, and a 3-center carbon-sp$^2$/H-1s/H-1s orbital (or by some equivalent distribution of carbon's 2s character among its three bonding orbitals).

For the relation of the lone pair orbital to the bonding orbitals there are two possibilities, Fig 3.

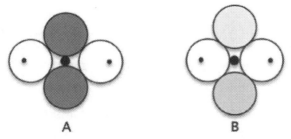

**Fig. 3.** Two conceivable arrangements for planar methane's lone pair domain (shaded) and its bonding domains. Transformation from arrangement **A** to arrangement **B** on ionization might account, schematically, for the extraordinarily low computed value for planar methane's ionization energy, reported to be about the same as the ionization energy of lithium!

# Additional Remarks Regarding Exotic Structures for Methane

**Liebman,** 5.10.12. The complementarity of which you speak [of computational MO Theory's *numbers* and conceptual VB Theory's *pictures*] is most fascinating . . . Did I mention to you the finding that pyramidal methane is calculated to be more stable than square planar methane?

**Bent.** 5.11.12. Of course! Of all people, your correspondent should have seen that result. By the *s*-Character Rule (a.k.a. "Bent's Rule") an atom tends to concentrate its *s*-character in orbitals directed toward substituents of low electronegativity. Lone pairs may be viewed as the limiting case: i.e., as bonds to substituents of zero electronegativity. They are *s*-seeking centers. Accordingly, the lone pair orbital of hypothetical planar methane will not, in principle, remain a pure p-orbital. It will capture a significant share of carbon's *s*-character, rendering the molecule non-planar, Figure 4.

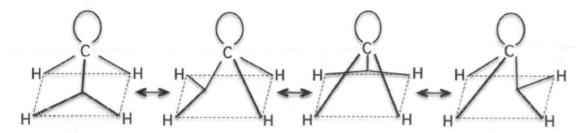

**Fig. 4.** Bond diagram for pyramidal methane, depicted as a resonant hybrid of structures that have two 2-center CH bonds and a 3-center HCH bond.

A single resonance structure of Figure 4 corresponds to the calculated transition state for the inversion of methane, formed by transfer of a proton from an electron pair domain of **Fig. 1A** (previous essay) to an adjacent domain, forming, thereby, simultaneously, a lone pair and a doubly protonated pair of a 3-center HCH bond, Figure 5: E --> F.

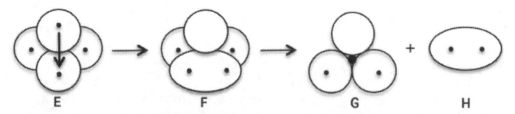

**Fig. 5.** Schematic depictions of distortions of $CH_4$. E: an incipient proton transfer in $CH_4$. F: A carbon core (not shown) with four electron pair domains in its valence shell: one not protonated (a lone pair), two singly protonated (more or less normal C—H bonds), and one doubly protonated (an HCH 3-center bond). G & H: Products of decomposition of F to methylene (G) and dihydrogen (H).

Calculated bond lengths reported for structure 5F are (in Å): CH of singly protonated domains 1.131; CH of the doubly protonated domain 1.316; and HH of the doubly protonated domain 0.847. The HH distance in dihydrogen is 0.742 Å.

# HCO

The HCO radical has an unusually short CO bond and an unusually long (and weak) CH bond. Both features may be understood in terms of Gauss-circuit mechanisms for homolytic loss of hydrogen atoms, starting with formaldehyde, $H_2CO$.

*Bond Diagrams for $H_2CO$, HCO, and CO*

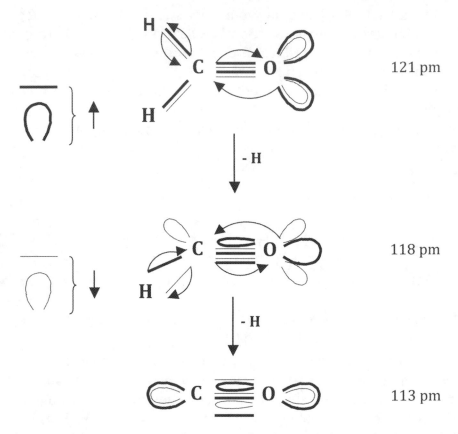

121 pm

118 pm

113 pm

Each valence-stroke represents one electron, each valence-stroke termination one-half an electron. In each diagram the number of valence-stroke terminations at "O" (which stands for $O^{+6}$) is 12, at "C" (which stands for $C^{+4}$) 8, and at "H" (which stands for $H^+$) 2, in accordance with Gauss's Law and the Principle of Local Electrical Neutrality.

Carbon-oxygen bond orders in $H_2CO$, HCO, and CO are, respectively, 2, 2 1/2, and 3. Bond lengths decrease in that order, with a marked shortening at CO, perhaps because it has 3x3 = 9 covalent/dative bond arrangements, whose superposition promotes electron-cloud-contracting electron correlation, whereas HCO has only 3 such resonant structures.

Two effects may contribute to HCO's long C—H bond (115 pm, compared, e.g., to 108 pm in $H_2C=CH_2$): predissociation (curly arrows, middle figure) and its splayed character, corresponding to the fact that HCO's 5-membered spin-set (middle figure) favors a linear HCO structure, whereas its 6-membered spin-set favors a bent structure. HCO's bond angle of 123° corresponds, suggests inspection of a valence-sphere model of CO, to the bond angle established by approach of a hydrogen atom to a CO molecule off a pocket or dimple of the triple bond.

# An Explanation for Formaldehyde's Low Bond Dissociation Energies

According to the *s*-Character Doctrine, bond strength increases with increasing *s*-character. C—H Bond Dissociation Energies of $CH_4$ and HCN are, respectively, 101 and 114 kcal/mole. Formaldehyde should have, accordingly, C—H BDEs in excess of 100 kcal/mole, for two reasons: its nominal hybridization at carbon is $sp^2$, compared to $sp^3$ for carbon of $CH_4$; and presence of the electronegative oxygen substituent should allow the carbon atom of $H_2CO$ to divert additional bond-strengthening *s*-character to its CH bonds. Nevertheless, *for formaldehyde BDE(H—CHO) is 78 kcal/mole and BDE(H—CO) is only 26 kcal/mole!* Conceptual Valence Bond Theory offers the following explanation for formaldehyde's low carbon-hydrogen bond dissociation energies.

**Legend.** Solid valence strokes represent electrons of alpha spin, dashed valence strokes electrons of (the opposite) beta spin.

**A & A':** Spin-set structures for formaldehyde: two (largely) coincident spin-sets.

**B & B':** Spin-set structures after loss of a proton with an alpha electron. Created in the first instance, prior to bond-dissociation energy-lowering electron reorganization, indicated (in part) by the two curly arrows, is an electrophilic vacancy in carbon's alpha spin set adjacent to the oxygen atom's nuclephilic unshared electrons, hence the indicated electrocyclic circuit and, consequently, as mentioned, a smaller than usual carbon-hydrogen bond dissociation energy.

**C & C':** Each spin-set is strained. The 5-membered spin-set (C) favors a linear HCO geometry, whereas the 6-membered spin-set (C') favors an HCO angle of approximately 120°. The weighted average — and predicted HCO bond angle — is $(5 \times 180° + 6 \times 120°)/11 = 147°$.

**D & D':** Spin-set structures after loss of the second proton, this time with a beta electron. Again a reorganization occurs (as in B) in the spin-set that loses an electron (the beta spin-set). It is accompanied by an additional reorganization in the alpha spin-set.

**E & E':** Two complete sets of spin-set quartets about each atomic core prior to a final BDE-lowering reorganization of the beta spin-set.

**F & F':** CO's bond is a triple bond, one-third dative bond character (yielding a nearly zero dipole moment). The bond's great strength, BDE(CO) = 257 kcal/mole, is borrowed, in part, so to speak, from the normal strength of two carbon-hydrogen bonds.

## Toward a Bond Diagram for C₂

The expression V(number of valence shell electron pairs) = 4(for the Octet Rule) x N(number of octets) – B(number of pairs in 2-center bonds counted twice in the product 4N), which implies that B = 4N – V, applied to $C_2$ yields the expression B = 4x2 – 4 = 4, a quadruple bond.

The quadruple bond structure is impossible, stereochemically, for a *tetrahedral model* of carbon atoms. And it is unlikely, on physical grounds, in that it leaves the back sides of the carbon cores electronically naked. A bond diagram that places a lone pair off each end of $C_2$ rectifies that deficiency and, moreover, lends itself to construction of a plausible valence sphere model.

The double bond model does not, however, satisfy the Octet Rule. The carbon cores' valence shells are incomplete. That deficiency can be rectified in one instance by "rolling up" a lone pair domain toward the adjacent carbon core, completing, thereby, that core's valence shell and becoming itself a bonding pair of a triple bond. Resonance renders the molecule's unshared electron density symmetrical.

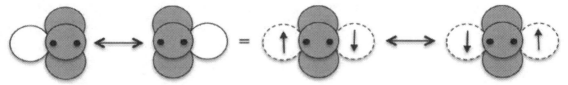

Unshared electron density is in anti-bonding regions, in the sense that as the internuclear distance decreases, for a fixed electron cloud, the energy of interaction between the atomic cores and unshared electron density becomes increasingly *positive*.

"There are many measures of bonding," writes Roald Hoffmann [1], "—distances, force constants, coupling constants, electron densities, difference densities, various magnetic and spectroscopic criteria. I prefer [as does the present author] to concentrate on the equilibrium bond length as the prime experimental criterion of bonding." $C_2$'s bond length, of 1.31 Å, is a shade less than ethylene's double bond length, 1.33 Å. The comparison suggests that the carbon-carbon bond of $C_2$ is chiefly a double bond with some triple bond character.

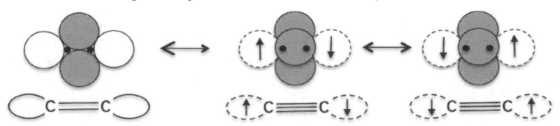

The carbon cores obey, to a small extent, the Octet Rule, in that, through a superposition of states, each core has in its valence shell, fractionally speaking, four electrons of each spin.

[1] In a manuscript about $C_2$ with Sason Shaik and Henry Rzepa titled "One Molecule, Two Atoms, and Three Views". The author is grateful to Professor Hoffmann for sharing with him the views of the manuscript's three authors. Their manuscript contains a bond diagram that is almost identical to the last two valence stroke diagrams above, on the right.

# C₃

From the standpoint of the conventional bond diagram for $C_3$,

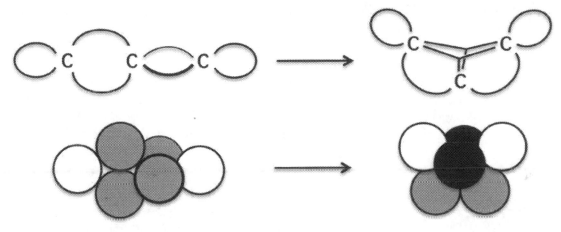

the molecule is a dicarbene, capable of dimerizing to linear $C_6$ and, thence, to linear $C_{3n}$. Alternatively, $C_3$ might complete the valence shells of its terminal carbon cores through formation of 3-center bonds.

In the valence stroke diagram at the left one may view the top component of the double bond on the left as attacking, in an electron pair donor-acceptor interaction, via molecular bending, in the plane of the paper, the vacant electron pair site of the carbon atom on the right. Formed is a 3-center bond. Similarly, in moving toward the valence stroke diagram on the right, the front component of the double bond on the right attacks the vacant site of the carbon atom on the left, via bending out of the plane of the paper. Formed is another 3-center bond.

In the valence sphere model on the left one may view the three domains on the left as rotating clockwise about an axis through its carbon core perpendicular to the plane of the page and simultaneously sliding rightward so as to place the upper domain of the double bond in the valence shell of the carbon core on the right, thereby becoming a 3-center bond, shown in black on the right for the molecule in a somewhat different orientation. Similar action at the other end of the molecule yields a second 3-center bond. The model's electron domains are not tangent to each other unless they are in the valence shell of the same atomic core. The structure contains a central carbon core bound to two flanking carbon cores by triple-bond-like arrangements. Each triple bond consists of one bent 2-center bond and two 3-center bonds. The model's six electron pair domains form jointly a bicapped tetrahedron. Correspondingly, for the equal-sphere-size-model the two triple bonds meet at an angle of 109° 28'. The 3-dimensional model is richer in its implications regarding details of the molecular rearrangement than is the corresponding 2-dimensional valence stroke diagram.

Favoring formation of the triple-bonded/coordinatively-saturated small ring structure over the coordinatively unsaturated linear structure is (as usual) a decrease in $V_{ne}$. Disfavoring (again, as usual) is an increase in $V_{nn}$ and $V_{ee}$, owing, in part, for $V_{ee}$, to an absence of spin-set anticoincidence for the cyclic structure. For the linear structure the $V_{ne}$ term favors a low vibrational bond bending frequency.

# Acetylenes

Acetylenes are the sweet spot for organic chemists — a class of compounds
energy rich yet kinetically persistent.                    ROALD HOFFMANN

Violent reaction of acetylene with oxygen in a eudiometer left observers marveling at their
dispersed equipment, reduced for the most part to a powder, and the fuel's thermodynamic
instability, despite its kinetic stability. The molecule's valence bond structure suggests two
reasons for that association, in terms of the influence that a triple bond has on the magnitudes
of two of the terms (in bold face below) in this expression for a molecule's energy:

$$E = V_{ne} + V_{nn} + V_{ee} + T$$

A triple bond's relatively short length creates thermodynamic instability through nuclear-nuclear
repulsion, as evidenced, e.g., by the molecule's relatively short carbon-hydrogen bonds. And the
bond's distinctive freedom for its spin-sets to become partially anticoincident in the triple bond
region creates kinetic stability, in a manner suggested by the following figures (reminiscent of
aromaticity owing to occurrence of Different Structures for Different Spin Sets).

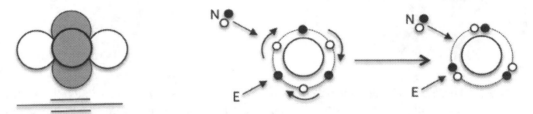

On the left are conventional valence sphere and valence stroke representations of acetylene's
electron cloud, shown in both instances with spatially coincident electron pairs.

In the middle is a view down acetylene's molecular axis, with the triple bond's three valence
spheres or strokes at the left replaced by six Lewis dots, black for those of one spin set and,
mutually anticoincident, owing to electron-electron repulsion between electrons of opposite
spin, white for electrons of the other spin set.

"N" and "E" represent nucleophilic and electrophilic reagents approaching acetylene in a manner
appropriate, in the case of "N", for the "black" spin set, and in the case of "E" for either spin
set. Access for the nucleophile's black spin set to an appropriate site in acetylene is blocked by
acetylene's white spin set. Attack on acetylene by an electrophile is compromised by absence of
localized electron pairs in the region of the triple bond.

On the right is a model after its partially anticoincident spin sets have rotated with respect to
each other about the molecular axis, with a destabilizing increase in potential energy, so as to
present reagent's "N" and "E" with suitable electrostatic sites.

It seems reasonable to suggest, therefore, that because of unusually high nuclear-nuclear
repulsion, owing to triple bonds' shortness, and because of unusually low electron-electron
repulsion between electrons of opposite spin, owing to triple bond's spin set anticoincidence,
"Acetylenes are," as Hoffmann says, "a class of compounds that are energy rich yet kinetically
persistent."

# Acetylene's First Excited State

The determination by Ingold and King (*Nature*, 1952, **169**, 1101) of -

### The Arrangement of Nuclei in Acetylene's First Excited State
(Distances in Å)

offers an opportunity to see if Conceptual Valence Bond Theory's diagrams and models designed to describe structures of molecules in their normal, ground states are useful, also, in rationalizing structures of excited states. Consider -

### *Acetylene's Frontier Orbitals*

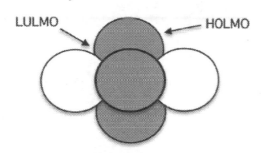

The molecule's HOLMOs (Highest Occupied Localized Molecular Orbitals) are the electron domains (shaded gray) of acetylene's carbon-carbon triple bond. The molecule's LULMOs (Lowest Unoccupied Localized Molecular Orbitals) are the pockets or dimples formed by two of the carbon-carbon domains and the white domain of a carbon-hydrogen bond.

Promotion of an electron from a HOLMO to a LULMO without nuclear rearrangement might be represented in the following fashion. (Solid and dashed valence strokes represent single electrons of opposite spin.)

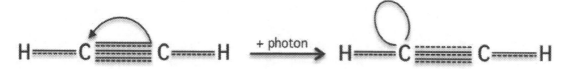

Resonance involving occupancy by the unshared electron of all equivalent LULMOs off both ends of the molecule yields doughnut-shaped rings of unshared electron density about the $C^{+4}$ cores. Energy-lowering movements of the cores toward that electron density localizes it, as conventional unshared electron density, represented by a rabbit-ear valence stroke. $V_{ne}$ (the potential energy of nuclear-electron attraction) becomes, thereby, more negative as T (electronic kinetic energy) becomes, owing to localization, more positive. If the $C^{+4}$ core on the left moves upward, then to minimize $V_{nn}$ (potential energy of nuclear-nuclear repulsion), the $C^{+4}$ core on the right moves downward. Produced is a trans-bent Structure, (A). Each rabbit ear represents one-half an electron.

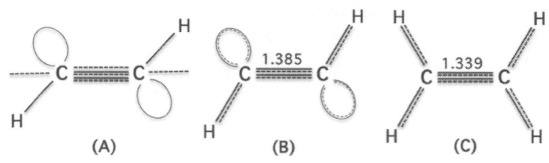

In Structure (A) the spin set represented by the dashed valence strokes favors, as shown, a linear arrangement of the atomic nuclei. Its potential-energy-lowering rearrangement yields Structure (B): a valence stroke representation of acetylene's first excited state. It's similar to the valence stroke diagram of the ground state of ethylene, Structure (C). The carbon-carbon internuclear distance is slightly longer in (B) than in (C) owing to the absence in (B) of carbon-core repelling protons in the unshared electrons' localized molecular orbitals. [Alternatively, one might say that by the s-Character Rule there is less bond-shortening s-character in the carbon-carbon orbitals in (B) than in (C).]

The structure of acetylene's excited state illustrates the statement that, owing to the delocalization of electron density in going to molecules' excited states from their ground states, an excited state structure is analogous to the structure that the ground state has on addition of an electron pair. Valence stroke diagram (B) is analogous to the valence stroke diagram for $C_2H_2^{-2}$. Below is a model of the addition of a protonated electron pair (a hydride ion) to acetylene, yielding a model of deprotonated ethylene.

*Valence Sphere Model of the Reaction*
*$C_2H_2 + H = C_2H_3^-$*

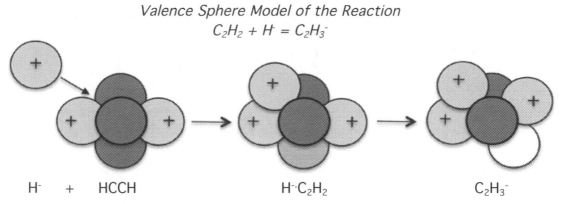

As the approaching hydride ion (upper left sphere) settles into one of acetylene's electrophilic pockets, or LULMOs (center figure), the adjacent carbon core moves up to meet it and its electrostatic hold on the domain of the carbon-carbon triple bond from which it departs (the bottommost domain) weakens. Counter clockwise rotation of that domain with the C—H domain on its right about the two dark gray domains of the original triple bond yields a model of $C_2H_3^-$.

# Structure of $C_2H_4^{+2}$

Discussions in the literature of the structure of the dication $C_2H_4^{+2}$ generally mention two isomers, planar and perpendicular, Figure 1.

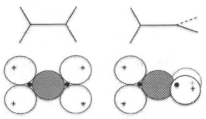

**Fig. 1.** Valence stroke and valence sphere models of the planar and perpendicular isomers of $C_2H_4^{+2}$. Valence strokes and large spheres represent valence shell electron pairs. Shaded domains represent carbon-carbon bonds. Other symbols represent atomic cores, of hydrogen and carbon atoms.

The consensus view considers the more stable isomer to be the non-planar one, owing to an agostic-type weak-donor/strong-acceptor interaction involving a C—H bond and an adjacent empty carbon 2p orbital. Not mentioned in the literature, to the author's knowledge, is the triple-bonded isomer formed by completion of two C—H/$C_{2p}$ interactions, Figure 2.

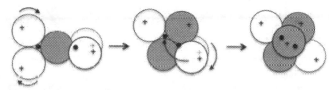

**Fig. 2.** Valence sphere models showing completion in two steps of two C—H/$C_{2p}$ donor-acceptor interactions in perpendicular $C_2H_4^{+2}$, yielding diprotonated acetylene, with two 3c/2e CHC bonds.

Another route to the triple bonded structure starts with di-protonated dinitrogen, $HNNH^{+2}$. Alchemical transfers of protons from its nitrogen nuclei to two of the domains of a bent bond model of nitrogen's triple bond yields, again, the triple bond model of $C_2H_4^{+2}$.

Yet another route to the triple-bonded isomer begins with a valence sphere model of ethylene. Removal of a hydride ion followed by a donor-acceptor interaction involving the vacated site and a C—H domain of the adjacent $CH_2$ group yields, on protonation of one of the domains of the original bent bond model of ethylene's double bond, the triple bond isomer.

Finally, the same Octet-Rule-satisfying structure is obtained on application of the Bond Number Equation $B_2 + 2B_3(= 0$ for a $C_2$ species$) = 4N – V$, where N = number of octets, V = number of valence shell electron pairs, and $B_n$ = number of n-center bonds irrespective of whether or not they are protonated. Accordingly, $B_1$(number of bonds to hydrogen, and/or lone pairs, if present) $= V – (B_2 + B_3)$ and $N_{CHC}$(number of protonated $B_2$ bonds) $= N_H$(number of hydrogen atoms) $– B_1$. For $C_2H_4^{+2}$, N = 2 and V = 5. Hence $B_2 = 3$, $B_1(=5-3) = 2$ and, consequently, $N_{CHC}(=4-2) = 2$. Those conclusions are summarized schematically in Figure 3.

**Fig. 3.** Valence stroke diagram for the Octet-Rule-satisfying double-protonated-triple-bond model of the five-electron-pair, electron deficient dication $C_2H_4^{+2}$, isoelectronic with diprotonated acetylene and dinitrogen. The two three-pronged valence strokes represent 3c/2e CHC bonds.

# The Cyclopropenyl Cation $C_3H_3^+$

The expression

$$B_2 + 2B_3 = 4N - V$$

where   $B_2$ = number of 2-center bonds between octets
$B_3$ = number of 3-center bonds between octets
$N$ = number of octets
$V$ = number of valence shell electron pairs,

yields for $C_3H_3^+$ ($N = 3$, $V = 7$) a relation

$$B_2 + 2B_3 = 5$$

that has, in terms of integers, two algebraic solutions:

$$B_2 = 5, B_3 = 0 \qquad B_3 = 1, B_2 = 2$$

Only the second solution corresponds to a reasonable valence stroke diagram, Figure 1.

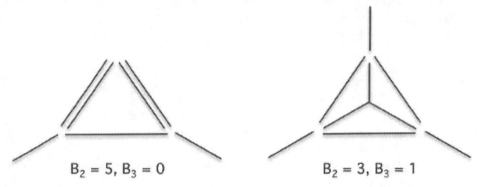

$B_2 = 5, B_3 = 0$ $\qquad\qquad$ $B_2 = 3, B_3 = 1$

**Fig. 1.** Octet-Rule satisfying bond diagrams for $C_3H_3^+$.

And for only the bond diagram on the right does a satifactory valence sphere model exist, Figure 2.

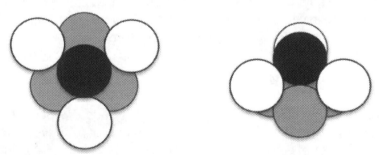

**Fig. 2.** Top view (at the left) and side view (at the right) of a valence equal-sphere-size model of $C_3H_3^+$: a tri-capped tetrahedron of seven valence shell electron pair domains. White spheres: C—H domains; gray spheres: C—C domains; black sphere: 3-center CCC domain.

The model, as it stands, corresponds to a nearly planar molecular structure. Inversion of the central tetrahedron yields a second electronic arrangement for essentially the same arrangement of atomic cores. The model may be viewed, accordingly, as either a model of one of two slightly nonplanar isomers of $C_3H_3^+$ or as one of two resonance structures of planar (and perhaps aromatic) $C_3H_3^+$.

# Electronic Structures of Cyclobutadiene Dianions of the Carbon Group

Size matters. Cation/anion coordination numbers of, for instance, the alkaline earth metal difluorides, $MF_2$, are 4/2, 6/3, and 8/4 for M = Be, Mg, and Ca, respectively. Similarly, structures of cyclo-$E_4R_4^{-2}$, R = $SiMe_3$ or $SiMe^tBu_2$, depend on whether E = C, Si, or Ge. For E = C, the $Me_3Si$-substituted $CBD^{-2}$ ring has a square planar delocalized aromatic structure (1), Figure 1.

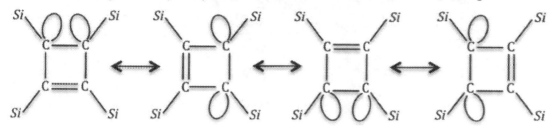

**Fig. 1.** Bond diagram for the square planar $SiMe_3$-substituted $CBD^{-2}$ structure. on the assumption that the carbon atoms obey the Octet Rule. $Si$ = $SiMe_3$. For the substituent "$Si$" = H, the number of valence shell electron pairs V = 11 = 4 (octets, N) x 4 (pairs/octet) – $B_2$ (number of pairs in 2-center bonds counted twice in the product 4N) $\rightarrow$ $B_2$ (= 4N – V) = 16 – 11 = 5 $\rightarrow$ Excess Connectivity EC [= $B_2$ – (N – 1)] = 5 – 3 = 2, such as a 4-membered ring and a double bond.

For E = Si and $Si$ = $SiMe^tbu_2$, the dianion is reported to have, again, a four-membered ring for which Lee et al. (1) assign the bond diagram pictured in Figure 2.

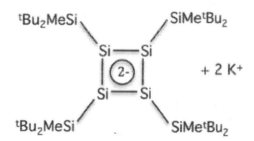

**Fig. 2.** Bond diagram assigned to the 4-membered ring of the $(^tBu_2Me)_4Si_4^{-2}$ dianion by Lee, et al. (1). The $Si_4$ ring has associated with it only 9 electron pairs, rather than 11 (legend, **Fig. 1**).

In the solid state the dianion is a folded four-membered ring, folding angle 34°, pictured by Lee et al. as in Figure 3.

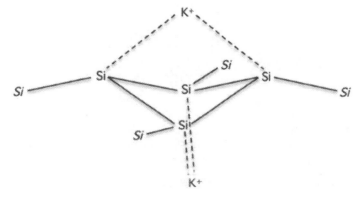

**Fig. 3.** Bond diagram assigned to the folded four-membered ring of the dianion $(^tBu_2Me)_4Si_4^{-2}$ by Lee et al. (1). Again, the ring has associated with it only 9 electron pairs.

Valence sphere models suggest explanations for the nonplanarity and "significantly pyramidalized" (1) endocyclic silicon atoms of $R_4Si_4^{-2}$, beginning with a model of Figure 2.

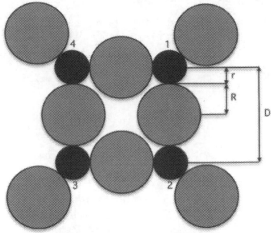

**Fig. 4.** Valence sphere model of the valence stroke diagram pictured in Figure 2. Black spheres represent $Si^{+4}$ cations (silicon's atomic cores), Pauling radius r = 0.41 Å (2). Gray spheres represent electron domains of silicon-silicon single bonds, radius R/Å = 0.60 + 0.4 r = 0.76 (3).

D(Si—Si bond length) = 2(r + R) = 2(0.41 + 0.76) = **2.34**. Observed (1): D = **2.30 – 2.36** Å.

Figure 4 shows schematically 8 of the 11 valence shell electron pairs associated with the 4 endocyclic silicon atoms. One seeks to place the remaining 3 valence shell electron pairs so as to complete the 4 silicon valence shells without increasing significantly, through multibond character (as in **Fig.** 1), the bond orders of the endocyclic silicon-silicon bonds. That goal can be achieved with the valence sphere model by rolling upward toward each other, in a manner of speaking, cores 1 and 3 and downward toward each other cores 2 and 4, and adding between them slightly stretched bond domains. Formed is a slightly folded 4-membered ring, Figure 5.

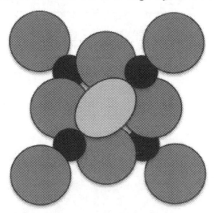

**Fig. 5.** Complete set of valence shell electron pair domains for the 4-membered ring of $R_4Si_4^{-2}$. The two elliptical, light gray, trans-annular domains at the center of the figure, with their major axes at right angles to each other, complete four octets in an approximately tetrahedral manner.

Figure 6 shows the corresponding valence stroke diagram.

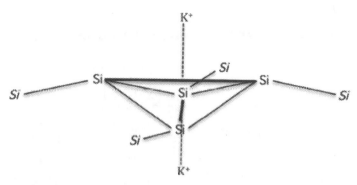

**Fig. 6.** Valence stroke diagram corresponding to the valence sphere model pictured in Figure 5. The two mutually perpendicular heavy valence strokes, between atomic cores 1 & 3 and 2 & 4 (**Fig. 4**), complete, with two pairs of THF molecules, the coordination shells of the potassium ions.

Figure 5 suggests for the electron density distribution of the dianion's 11th valence shell electron pair a delocalized streamer occupying those regions of space about the silicon cores not already assigned to more localized bonding pairs. In solution the behavior of $R_4Si_2Ge_2^{-2}$ suggests (1) that its negative charge is localized about the relatively large $Ge^{+4}$ cores, Figure 7.

**Fig. 7.** Valence stroke diagram (left) and valence sphere model (right) of the dianion $R_4Ge_2Si_2^{-2}$. The tendency of the germanium lone pairs (the white domains) to become "inert pairs" leads to the prediction that the bond angle Si(exo)GeSi(endo) is as small as permitted by the bulky R substituents.

In summary: An electronic model of the cyclobutadiene dianions of the carbon group that features largely localized, electron pair domains, together with, in two instances, delocalized orbitals, accounts for the dianions' leading geometrical features, including: different structures for carbon, silicon, and germanium species; normal silicon-silicon bond lengths; folded 4-membered rings with pyramidal ring atoms and ring angles slightly less than 90°; and reasonable electronic environments for potassium counter ions.

(1) Lee et al., *J. Am. Chem. Soc.*, 2004, 126, 4758-4759.
(2) Linus Pauling, *Nature of the Chemical Bond*, 3rd ed., 1960, Cornell University Press, Ithaca, NY, p514.
(3) Henry Bent, "Estimation of Internuclear Distances," *J. Chem. Ed.*, 1965, 42, 348-355.

# Interpretation of Bond Angles, Bond Lengths, and Energies of Rotamers of 1,3-Butadiene

Bond angles and bond lengths from "High Level ab Initio Energies and Structures for the Rotamers of 1-3-Butadiene" by David Feller and Norman C. Craig (*J. Phys. Chem. A* **2009**, *113*, 1601-1607) are reproduced in the following table.

| parameter | trans | 102°(TS) | 90° | gauche | cis(TS) |
|---|---|---|---|---|---|
| d(C1C2)/Å | 1.3389 | 1.3327 | 1.3329 | 1.3362 | 1.3371 |
| d(C2C3)/Å | 1.4549 | 1.4824 | 1.4818 | 1.4682 | 1.4696 |
| d(H1C1)/Å | 1.0825 | 1.0820 | 1.0819 | 1.0821 | 1.0819 |
| d(H2C1)/Å | 1.0799 | 1.0807 | 1.0808 | 1.0802 | 1.0799 |
| d(H3C2)/Å | 1.0848 | 1.0850 | 1.0852 | 1.0841 | 1.0833 |
| <(C1C2C3) | 123.5° | 123.8° | 123.8° | 124.4° | 126.3° |
| <(H1C1C2) | 120.8° | 121.3° | 121.2° | 121.3° | 122.1° |
| <(H2C1C2) | 121.5° | 121.1° | 120.2° | 121.1° | 120.8° |
| <(H3C2C1) | 119.8° | 117.0° | 119.3° | 116.6° | 118.2° |
| <(H1C1H2) | 117.7° | | | | 117.1° |
| <(H3C2C3) | 116.7° | | | | 115.5° |

Numbering of atoms is given in Figure 1.

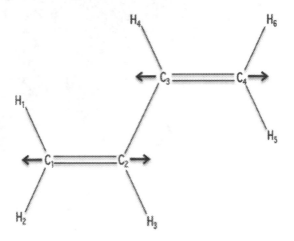

**Fig. 1.** Bond diagram for *s-trans* 1,3-Butadiene. Arrows show principal directions of atomic core displacements with respect to the molecule's electron cloud (treated as a rigid body), owing to $C^{+4}/C^{+4}$ repulsions across the molecule's double bonds.

This essay addresses the question: What interpretations does Conceptual Valence Bond Theory suggest for the calculated bond angles, bond lengths, and energies of the rotamers of 1,3-butadiene?

Lengths of the rotamers' C2C3 bonds, compared to that of ethane (1.534 Å), and magnitudes of the rotamers HCH angles, compared to the tetrahedral angle (109.5°), are evidence of core displacements (with respect to the molecule's electron cloud) indicated by the arrows in Figure 1. Listed below are additional suggestions regarding physical interpretations of the rotamers' structural features.

(1) **d(H1C1) > d(H2C1) for all rotamers.** The model of $C_1^{+4}/C_2^{+4}$ displacements owing to mutual $C_1^{+4}$-$C_2^{+4}$ repulsion implies, accordingly, that the left-pointing arrow on the extreme left points slightly downward, owing, it's suggested, to *mutual repulsion between cores $C_1^{+4}$ and $C_3^{+4}$.*

(2) **<(H1C1C2) < <(H2C1C2) for the *trans* rotamer,** in accordance with the displacement of C1 cited in (1).

(3) **<(H1C1C2) > <(H2C1C2)** for all rotamers other than the *trans* rotamer (2), especially for the *cis* rotamer, in accordance with displacements arising from steric repulsion between $H_1$ and $H_5$, Figure 2.

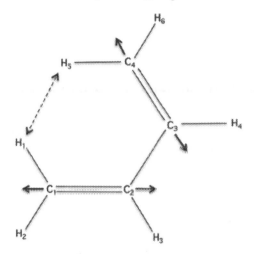

Fig. 2. Bond diagram for *cis* 1,3-Butadiene showing the relatively short distance between $H_1$ and $H_5$.

Rotations in concert counter clockwise of the H1C1 and H2C1 domains about C1, as indicated in Figure 3 below,

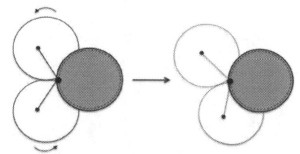

Fig.3. Rotation of the H1C1H2 group as a rigid body about C1 in the plane of the molecule.

(and likewise for the corresponding domains about C4, clockwise), without significant changes in bond lengths or the bond angle H1C1H2, increases the angle H1C1C2 and decreases the angle H2C1C2.

(4) In the *cis* isomer <(C1C2C3) is especially large and the <(H3C2C1) is the smallest angle involving hydrogen in all the rotamers, owing, in the present model (Fig. 2), to further relief of steric crowding between $H_1$ and $H_5$, in a manner described in the legend for Figure 2.

(5) The *trans* rotamer has the shortest C2C3 bond, owing, in the present model, to having the greatest number of maximum-strength banana-bond-donor/double-bond-acceptor ($\pi/\pi^*$) interactions across the C2C3 bond.

(6) The *gauche* rotamer has the second shortest C2C3 bond, for having across it the second most maximum-strength ($\pi/\pi^*$) donor-acceptor interactions.

(7) The *cis* rotamer has the third shortest C2C3 bond, for, although it has across it no maximum-strength ($\pi/\pi^*$) donor-acceptor interactions, it is the rotamer whose C2 and C3 vector displacements (Fig. 2) are oriented so as to produce the largest shortening of the C2C3 bond of any of the rotamers.

(8) d(C1C2) increases with an anticipated increase in participation in donor-acceptor interactions across the C2C3 bond, for four of the five cited rotamers.

*Order of Increase in Donor-Acceptor Interactions and d(C1C2)*
*in Rotamers of 1,3-Butadiene*

*90°/102°   <   gauche   <   trans*

(9) The *cis* rotamer is an exception to the trend cited in (8). Its C1C2 bond is longer than expected.

In the *trans* rotamer (Fig. 1), core-core repulsion between $C_2^{+4}$ and $C_4^{+4}$ acts to shorten the C1C2 bond. In the *cis* rotamer (Fig. 2), that repulsion has, however, little effect on the C1C2 bond length.

If energies of the rotamers follow in the negative direction degree of donor-acceptor interactions across bond C2C3, then the order of rotamer energies should be, as calculated, -

*trans   <   gauche   <   cis*

In summary: Expectations based on principles of Conceptual Valence Bond Theory yield inferences in qualitative agreement with high level ab initio energies and structures for rotamers of 1,3-butadiene.

**Acknowledgements.** The author is indebted to Professor Joel Liebman for confirming the author's hunch, based on examination of valence sphere models, that, contrary to conventional wisdom, 1,3-butadiene's *cis* rotamer may not represent a potential energy minimum; and to Professor Emeritus Norman C. Craig, of Oberlin College, for providing the author with reprints of his studies of butadiene's rotamers.

# trans, gauche, and cis Confomers of 1,3-Butadiene

If ever there's been a molecule that should showcase by its structure the virtues of the theory of π-electron delocalization it's been, arguably, 1,3-butadiene: $H_2C=CH-CH=CH_2$. Its central bond is unusually short for carbon-carbon single bonds (1.48 Å, compared to 1.53 Å for ethane). And presumed existence of *two planar confomers*, cis and trans, also has seemed for many years consistent with π-conjugation across the central CC bond. An alternative explanation exists for its length, however, as arising from a change in hybridization of the participating carbon atoms, from $sp^3$-$sp^3$ in ethane to $sp^2$-$sp^2$ in 1,3-butadiene. And, further, it now appears that *existence of a cis confomer for 1,3 butadiene is problematical!* — exactly as one might infer, however, from examination of its valence sphere models, Figure 1.

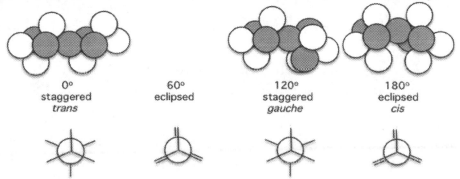

| 0° | 60° | 120° | 180° |
|---|---|---|---|
| staggered | eclipsed | staggered | eclipsed |
| *trans* | | *gauche* | *cis* |

Fig. 1. Valence sphere models of structures created by rotations about 1,3-butadiene's central carbon-carbon bond. Adjectives "staggered" and "eclipsed" refer to configurations of electron pair domains described in Figure 2.

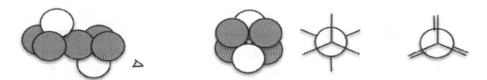

Fig. 2. **Left:** Ethane-like fragment of the valence sphere model of trans-1,3-butadiene. **Middle and Right:** Newman projection diagrams of a view along the fragment's carbon-carbon single bond of the domains at opposite ends of the bond, three at each end, in their staggered and (far right) eclipsed orientations.

Ethane has six pair/pocket, C—H/sigma-anti-bonding-orbital donor-acceptor interactions (thought to be responsible for its barrier to internal rotation). Butadiene, owing to the stereochemistry of its single and double bond domains, has, in the pockets or dimples at the interior ends of its double bonds, four significant acceptor sites for donor-acceptor interactions across its CC single bond. Inspection of the models reveals that in trans butadiene all four of those dimples are oriented so as to interact with the best donor sites: the electron pairs of the double bonds. Gauche butadiene has only two such interactions, cis butadiene none.

Construction of valence sphere models of trans and gauche 1,3-butadiene is relatively simple on a flat surface, in that, as for staggered ethane, the models consist of fragments of cubic close packed spheres. As oriented in Figure 1, numbers of spheres in horizontal layers for trans butadiene are 2 7 2, in an ABC arrangement, and for the gauche structure 1 6 4(fragmented as 1, 3). Both arrangements, tilted, yield close packed layers populated with 1 4 1 4 1 spheres. The ABC sequence 1 4 1 describes the valence sphere model of ethylene.

# Stereochemistry of Reduction of Butadiene with Sodium in Liquid Ammonia

Reduction of butadiene with sodium in liquid ammonia produces more *cis*- than *trans*-2-butene (although the *trans* isomer is said to be the more stable isomer, by about 2.9 kcal/mole).

No simple explanation for the 60/40 ratio exists, it's said, without reference to the molecular orbitals involved (1). Posed is a challenge for Conceptual Valence Bond Theory: Creation of a simple explanation for the reduction butadiene in terms of localized orbitals. [The explanation turns out to be very different than the one proposed in (1).]

The reactive system's most nucleophilic sites are sodium's solvated electrons — protonated slowly in liquid ammonia (in water rapidly) yielding dihydrogen molecules. The system's most electrophilic sites are modeled by the dimples off the ends of the double bonds of a valence sphere model of 1,3-butadiene, Figure 1.

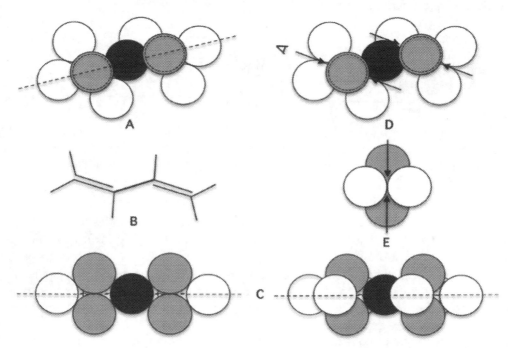

**Fig. 1. A** and **B.** Valence sphere model and valence stroke diagram of 1,3-butadiene. **C,** Right: The model in A rotated 90 degrees about the dashed axis. Left: The model at the right showing its "principal plane" of seven domains, before addition of four C—H domains, two in front of the "+" signs, two behind the (barely visible) "-" signs.

One sees in **A** and **C** that the 3 domains on the left of the domain of the C—C single bond (black) are, as in ethane, staggered with respect to the 3 domains on its right. In the less stable *cis* isomer those domains are in an eclipsed configuration. The model's eleven valence shell domains may be viewed as fragments of 3 cubic close-packed layers stacked in the *trans* isomer: A (2), B (7), C (2).

**D.** Arrows point to four of the model's eight dimples associated with its double bonds, in front of the plane of the page. Their nucleophilicity arises from exposure of their carbon cores owing to coulombic core-core repulsion of cores bonded to each other by relatively short, double bonds. (Relaxation of the cores outward shortens CH bonds and opens HCH angles, from 109.5° in $H_2CH_2$ to approximately 116° in $H_2CCH_2$.) Four similar nucleophilic sites lie behind the plane of the page.

**E.** One end of an end view of butadiene showing two of its eight nucleophilic sites.

Butadene's eight cited nucleophilic dimples correspond, in sets of four, to the lobes of molecular orbital theory's π antibonding orbitals of double bonds. Chemical reagents usually attack only one or two of a double bond's dimples, Figure 2. (In electronic transitions involving double bonds, all four lobes of their π antibonding orbitals are occupied.)

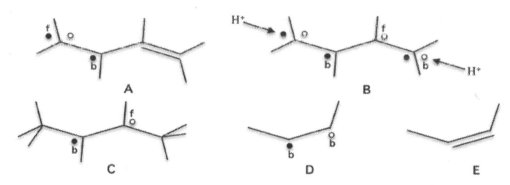

**Fig. 2. A.** $S_N2$-type attack by a solvated electron of positive spin (small *black* sphere) on the external, terminal dimple on the front side (f) of butadiene's double bond on the left. The "leaving group" is the electron of positive spin of the back domain (b) of the double bond on the left. Displacement from the double bond's back domain of positive spin density yields negative spin density (small *white* sphere) at the left end of the double bond on the left.

**B. A.** $S_N2$-type attack by a solvated electron of negative spin (small white sphere, extreme right) on the terminal dimple on the back side (b) of butadiene's double bond on the right. The "leaving group" in this instance is the electron of negative spin of the back domain (b) of the double bond on the right. Displacement from the double bond's front domain of negative spin density yields positive spin density (small black sphere) at the right end of the double bond on the right.

Of course, the second electron could attack butadiene from the same side as the first electron. But mutual coulombic repulsion favors attack at a second site as far as possible from the first site.

Also, solvated electrons could attack the double bonds at the sites of the bonds' interior dimples. Such attacks do not lead, however, to further reaction, namely, as depicted by the arrows, to proton transfers from ammonia molecules to the electron rich terminal sites of electronated butadiene, yielding carbon-hydrogen bonds and structure C.

In C the two spin-paired, spatially unpaired electrons from the two *trans* $S_N2$-type displacements by solvated electrons are *trans* to each other across butadiene's central carbon-carbon single bond. Rotation by 180 degrees about that bond yields structure D, prepared for formation of the central carbon-carbon double bond of 2-butene, preferentially in its *cis*-configuration, E.

Valence sphere models, such as those of Figure 1, partition the Euclidean space occupied by molecules into exclusive, localized, more or less space-filling domains. *They do not represent partitions into localized domains of the electrons themselves*, which, when represented by *antisymmetric* wave functions, occupy *simultaneously*, so to speak, all of a molecule's "occupied" domains. Charging the domains with charges equal to that of two spin-paired electrons yields approximate *electron density profiles* useful in understanding reaction mechanisms in terms of the concepts of classical valence bond theory, as illustrated here for the sodium reduction in liquid ammonia of 1,3-butadiene to, chiefly, *cis*-2-butene.

The term "cis-butadiene" is a stand-in, probably, for two *gauche*-conformers in which, as for the *trans*-conformer, the three domains on opposite sides of the CC single bond domain (one a domain of a C—H bond and two domains of an equivalent orbital model of a CC double bond) are *staggered* with respect to each other (as in ethane, owing, in both instances, to the cubic close packing character of their structures), rather than eclipsed, as in a *cis*-arrangement, which may not be an energy minimum.


(1) Ian Fleming, *Molecular Orbitals and Organic Reactions*, Wiley, London, 2010, pp x, 107.

# Oxirene

## (Oxacyclopropene)

### *An Explanation for Its Elusiveness*

Oxirene, **1**,

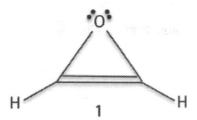

has not been isolated, emphasizes Errol Lewis in an interesting monograph (1), even though, to paraphrase slightly, "it looks at first glance like a normal molecule: no unusual stereochemical constraints are imposed, all atoms have their normal valence numbers, no octet limitations are transgressed, and the isoelectronic molecule cyclopropene exists." One possible explanation for **1**'s elusiveness, adds Lewis, is that "one electron pair on the oxygen is at least potentially able to enlist the assistance of the two π electrons of the double bond to confer antiaromaticity on the ring and thus to electronically destabilize it."

The term "antiaromaticity" names a phenomenon (illusiveness of a cyclic compound that has 4n π electrons) without, however, offering for that illusiveness — other than another name ("electronic destabilization") — any *physical* reason(s) for it, in terms of, e.g., the fundamental physical forces that appear in a molecule's Hamiltonian, namely: nuclear-electron attraction, nuclear-nuclear repulsion, and electron-electron repulsion. Nor does the term "antiaromaticity" offer any explanatory *chemical* reason(s) for the molecule's illusiveness, such as, e.g., an intramolecular donor-acceptor interaction that might lead to an isomerization of the strained structure to a more stable isomer of $C_2H_2O$, such as ketene, $H_2C=C=O$. That possibility has been considered in detail, *computationally*, by Lewis (1) and is examined, here, *conceptually*, to see what insights, if any, arise when one considers oxirene's elusiveness with the aid of a valence sphere model of the molecule's approximate electron density profile, Figure 1.

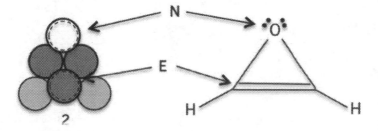

**Fig.** 1 Valence sphere model (left) and valence stroke diagram (right) of oxirene. N = nucleophilic site. E = electrophilic site. The two drawings are isomorphic. Oxirene's valence shell electron pairs are represented on the left by exclusive, spherical domains, on the right by non-crossing valence strokes (or pairs of dots).

Oxirene's most nucleophilic sites (its exposed oxygen lone pairs) lie near its most electrophilic sites (the four dimples in its electron cloud about the domains of its double bond; a.k.a. the lobes of its π* orbital). Because the nucleophilic lone pairs are in the valence shell of an atom of a conjugated ring, a cooperative electron, and atomic core, rearrangement is possible that, although it disrupts an octet (in forming a carbene) leaves formal charges unchanged, at zero, Figure 2.

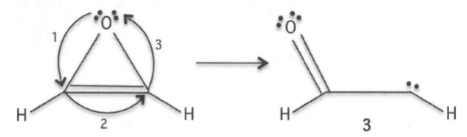

**Fig. 3** Curly-arrow/valence-stroke model of the molecular rearrangement of oxirene to a carbene.

An exclusive, localized orbital valence-*sphere* model of the electronic rearrangement pictured with valence strokes in Figure 3 suggests that the changes in affiliations of electrons and atomic cores, indicated incompletely in Figure 3 by the curly-arrows (1, 2, and 3), occur not sequentially (as Figure 3 might suggest) but, rather, more or less in concert, Figure 4.

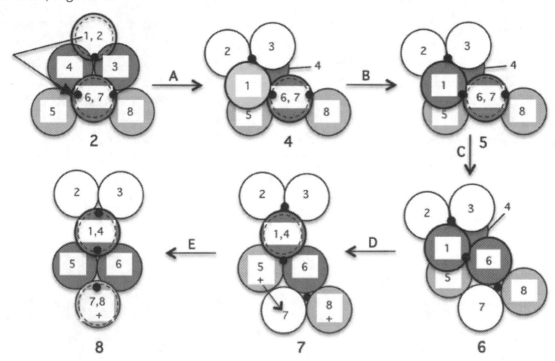

**Fig. 4.** Valence sphere model of a unimolecular rearrangement of oxirene (**2**) to ketene (**8**). White domains represent lone pairs; dark gray domains carbon-carbon or carbon oxygen bonds; light gray domains carbon-hydrogen bonds or, in the case of domain 1 of structure **4**, a donor-acceptor domain midway between the domain of lone pair and a bonding pair. Small black circles represent sites of the atomic cores: $C^{+4}$ and $O^{+6}$.

**Arrow A:** Attack of nucleophilic domain 1 on an electrophilic "dimple" in oxirene's electron density profile formed by domains 4, 5, and 6. Accompanying domain 1 are the oxygen core along with domain 2 and domain 3 (arrow 3 of **Fig.** 3). Formed by domain 1 with domains 4, 5, and 6 is a new, initially vacant tetrahedral interstice.

In rearrangement A the moiety $O^{+6}123$ moves as a unit counterclockwise on the surface of domain 4, thereby breaking the carbon-oxygen bond represented by domain 3, in order to maintain a quartet of electron pair domains about the electronegative core $O^{+6}$. Momentarily, oxygen has, consequently, a formal charge of -1. And the carbon atom of the broken carbon-oxygen bond has a formal charge of +1.

**Arrow B:** The $C^{+4}$ core on the left — the one attacked by domain 1 and its companions $O^{+6}23$ (arrow A) — moves through the trigonal interstice defined by domains 4, 5, and 6 into the newly created tetrahedral interstice defined by domains 1, 4, 5, and 6. Diminished is that carbon core's electrostatic hold on domain 7 (arrow 2 of **Fig.** 3).

**Arrow C:** Domain 7, in becoming a lone pair, moves — while remaining in the valence shell of the carbon core on the right — to a position in preparation for acceptance of a proton from protonated domain 4, forming, thereby, carbene **6**.

**Arrow D:** A proton transfer from domain 5 to domain 7 yields structure **7**. In passing from structure **6** to structure **7**, the model has been rotated slightly, about a vertical axis, counterclockwise.

**Arrow E:** Slight movement of the moiety $C^{+4}78$, as a unit, completes the carbene carbon atom's valence shell, yielding structure **8**, the valence sphere model of ketene.

The reaction schemes proposed for the elusiveness of oxirene, the reduction of butadiene, and formation of cyclopropane from methylene and ethylene share an important feature: absence along their reaction paths of major departures from tetrahedral quartets of electron spins about the sites of atomic cores.

From the point of view of the scheme pictured in Figure 4, Oxirene's elusiveness arises from a confluence of five factors:

o A nucleophilic site
o An electrophilic site
o Adjacency of the two sites
o A conjugated 3-membered ring
o A stable isomer

The cited features of classical conceptual valence bond theory raise a question: Is it necessary to invoke an alternative explanation, "antiaromaticity", for oxirene's elusiveness, with the implication that there exists in oxirene some mysterious "electronic destabilizing" physicochemical phenomenon, over and beyond the joint operation of the five cited factors?

(1) Errol G. Lewars, *Modeling Marvels: Computational Anticipation of Novel Molecules*, Springer, 2008. Highly recommended.

# Stability and Instability of OCCO and Related Species

## A Concordance between Computational Chemistry's Numerical Data and Conceptual Chemistry's Graphic Images Regarding Ethenedione

Ethenedione is a simple-looking molecule

$$O=C=C=O$$

There's no immediately obvious reasons why it does not exist, writes Lewars (1), and yet, he notes, it has defied decades of attempts to prepare it. Lewars reports the following data regarding ethenedione (1):

1. Theory predicts that ethenedione's ground state is a linear triplet.

2. $C_2O_2$'s ground state may easily "singletize" to a structure that on distortive motions away from linearity rapidly dissociates to 2 CO.

3. The ground state of isoelectronic OCCNH is calculated to be a singlet.

4. Both OCCNH and HNCCNH are predicted to be nonlinear.

5. Calculated barriers to decomposition of OCCNH to CO and HNC and HNCCNH to 2 HNC are, respectively, 14 and 81 kJ/mole, respectively.

6. The sulfur analogues OCCS and SCCS exist.

7. The oxime of ethenedione, OCCNOH, has been prepared by matrix isolation photolysis at 10 K.

Are those facts explicable, one may wonder, in terms of the qualitative concepts of Conceptual Valence Bond Theory?

For a molecule that contains 4 atoms that satisfy the Octet Rule and 10 valence shell electron pairs, the number of pairs shared by the octets is 4x4 (the number required for the octets without sharing) minus 10 (the number at hand), namely 6, sufficient for 3 double bonds.

However, owing to repulsions between electrons of opposite spin, $C_2O_2$'s 20 valence electrons, instead of being split 10 of one spin and 10 of the other spin, might be split in the ground state 9 of one spin and 11 of the opposite spin. With such a split it is still possible to have in the valence shell of each atomic core four tetrahedrally arranged electrons of a given spin, Figure 1.

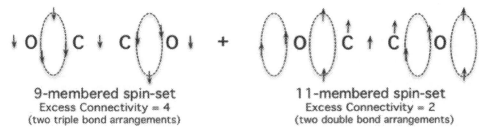

**9-membered spin-set**
Excess Connectivity = 4
(two triple bond arrangements)

**11-membered spin-set**
Excess Connectivity = 2
(two double bond arrangements)

**Fig. 1.** DSDSS (Different Structures for Different Spin-Sets) for triplet OCCO. To reduce formal charges for C and O of, respectively, -1/2 and +1/2, bonding electrons would be polarized slightly toward the oxygen cores.

The 9-membered spin-set favors a linear OCCO structure. The 11-membered spin-set favors an OCC angle of ca. 120°, unless the normally s-seeking unshared electrons are in pure *p*-orbitals, in which case chemical theory predicts for ground state triplet of OCCO a paramagnetic linear structure with an easy bending mode (Facts 1 and 2). For the record, the weighted average for the OCC angle for the 9-membered spin-set and a bent 11-membered spin set is predicted to be approximately $(9 \times 180° + 11 \times 120°)/20 = 147°$.

Isoelectronic OCCNH requires, *for a good bond to hydrogen*, a coincident electron pair: i.e., two 10-membered spin sets, Figure 2.

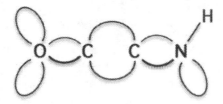

**Fig. 2.** A valence stroke diagram for OCCNH.

VB theory predicts that in its ground state OCCNH is a nonlinear singlet (Facts 3 and 4). One notes that at both ends of nonexistent OCCNH and OCCO their valence bond structures have exposed nucleophilic lone pairs adjacent to the four electrophilic dimples about the carbon-carbon double bond, perfectly located, jointly, for cooperative, dissociation-producing, intramolecular electrocyclic electron-pair donor acceptor interactions, Figure 3.

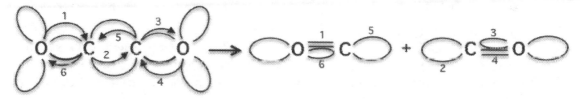

**Fig. 3.** Curly arrow representation of the dissociation OCCO = 2 CO. Valence strokes 3 and 6 in the products represent dative bonds.

> **Arrows 1 & 2.** An $S_N2$-type backside-type attack by of the electron density of an oxygen lone pair domain on the lower domain of the carbon-carbon double bond, the "leaving group": it changes from a bonding domain to a lone pair domain as the oxygen lone pair domain changes to a bonding domain as the carbon $C^{+4}$ core on the left migrates a short distance into the newly created tetrahedral interstice.

> **Arrows 2 & 3.** A second $S_N2$-type attack. The "leaving group" is one component of the carbon-oxygen double bond on the right, which becomes a component of carbon-oxygen partial dative bonding in a molecule of carbon monoxide.

> **Arrows 4 and 5.** A third $S_N2$-type attack, with the carbon $C^{+4}$ core on the right moving into a newly created tetrahedral interstice, thereby diminishing its electrostatic interaction with the electron density of the upper lobe of the carbon-carbon double bond.

> **Arrows 5 and 6.** This fourth $S_N2$-type attack completes the electrocyclic circuit.

In the product 2 CO as in the reactant OCCO formal charges are zero; i.e., numbers of valence stroke terminations at the symbols of the elements, C and O, are equal to, respectively, the charges on their atoms' cores, +4 and +6.

Replacing 1-dimensional valence strokes by 3-dimensional valence spheres yields approximate electron density profiles and a more intimate, specific, and realistic physical picture of a reaction mechanism, Figure 4.

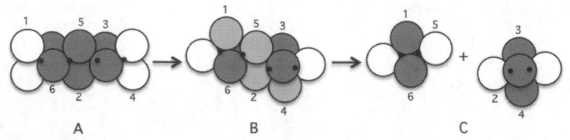

**Fig. 4.** Valence sphere models of the reactant, transition state, and product in the decomposition of ethenedione to carbon monoxide. Integers label regions of space, not individual electron pairs.

> **A.** VSM of OCCO. White spheres represent domains of oxygen atom lone pairs, dark gray spheres domains of the double bonds O=C=C=O. Small black spheres represent the atomic cores $C^{+4}$ and $O^{+6}$. Integers correspond to the numbered arrows of Figure 3.
>
> **A → B.** Formation of two intramolecular donor-acceptor interactions, by nucleophilic domains 1 and 4 (accompanied by adjacent lone pair domains) with adjacent electrophilic dimples opposite "leaving domains" 2 and 5. Carbon cores move outward and upward or downward through trigonal interstices toward newly created tetrahedral interstices.
>
> **B.** Transition state. Light gray domains represent lone pair domains on the way to becoming bonding domains (1 and 4) and bonding domains on the way to becoming lone pair domains (5 and 2) in the product C.

OCCNH and HNCCNH presumably decompose by mechanisms similar to that pictured for OCCO, with one difference. Instead of *lone pairs* that start off off-axis (in OCCO) and end up on-axis (in CO), the reactants start off with one or two off-axis *N—H substituents* that end up on-axis and require, one infers, activation-energy-contributing motion of one (in the case of OCCNH) or two (in the case of HNCCNH) protons (Fact 5).

Existence of OCCS and SCCS may reflect the activation-energy-raising reduction on dissociation of the number of *dispersed lone pairs about large $S^{+6}$ cores*, from two per $S^{+6}$ in OCCS and SCCS to one per $S^{+6}$ in CS (Fact 6).

Existence of OCCNOH (Fact 7) may reflect interference with the electrocyclic decomposition mechanism pictured in Figure 3 by the donor acceptor interaction pictured in Figure 5.

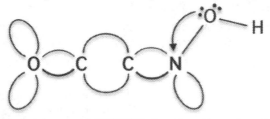

**Fig. 5.** Explanation for the existence of OCCNOH. Continuation of curly arrows with formation of an electrocyclic circuit yields instead of two fragments a single species with four dative bonds.

The present explanation for the nonexistence of ethenedione, owing to its ease of decomposition to carbon monoxide, assumes that CO is thermodynamically more stable than OCCO. Three physical effects contribute to CO's stability: (1) partial angular anticoincidence of its spin sets in the molecule's triple bond region; (2) partial longitudinal anticoincidence along the molecular axis owing to dative-bond/covalent-bond resonance; and (3) Coulombic repulsion of its atomic cores directly into the domains of its nucleophilic unshared electron pairs.

[1] Errol G. Lewars, *Modeling Marvels: Computational Anticipation of Novel Molecules*, Springer, 2008, Chapter 9.

# Unusual Acidity of Cyclopropene

## Valence-Sphere Model of Cyclo-$C_3H_4$

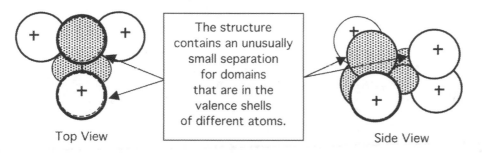

| Top View | The structure contains an unusually small separation for domains that are in the valence shells of different atoms. | Side View |

Stippled domains represent electron-pairs of carbon-carbon bonds.

Double-bond and protonated domains are larger than the two domains of the carbon-carbon single bonds.

Cyclo-$C_3H_4$ has an unusual feature, not apparent from its valence-stroke diagram. Domains of the $CH_2$ group's C—H bonds are unusually close to the domains of the electron-pairs of the carbon-carbon double bond. I.e., the proton of a C—H bond of the methylene carbon atom of a cyclopropene ring is unusually close to an *unprotonated* — hence highly nucleophilic — electron-pair in the valence-shell of another atom. The proton's removal is, consequently, unusually difficult. The cyclopropenyl anion formed by loss of the proton has only a fleeting existence.

The postulate that cyclopropenyl anion's instability arises from its being "antiaromatic", for having 4n, rather than 4n + 2, pi electrons, seems unnecessary.

# Cyclopentadienyl Anion and Cation

## Paradoxical Stabilities from the Standpoint of Number of Resonance Structures?

The cyclopentadienyl anion, $C_5H_5^-$, and cation, $C_5H_5^+$, are each represented in valence bond theory as superpositions of five equivalent, resonant-stabilizing structures, Figure 1.

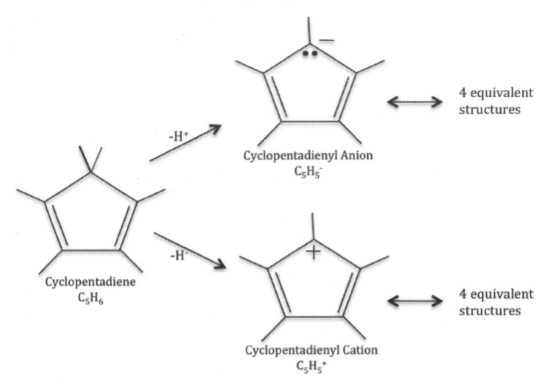

**Fig. 1.** Bond diagrams for cyclopentadiene and its ions formed by loss of a proton and a hydride ion. Resonance superposition of an ion's five equivalent bond diagrams distributes the ion's net charge equally over its five carbon sites.

And yet, although the anion is a well-recognized species, the cation, notes professor Joel Liebman, is highly reactive and difficult to prepare.

MO Theory's explanation for the contrasting character of cyclopentadiene's ions is based on the rule that species that have 4n+2 π-electrons (the case for the anion $C_5H_5^-$, n = 1, 4n+2 = 6) are stabilized, with aromatic character, whereas species (such as the cation, $C_5H_5^+$, which doesn't satisfy the 4n+2 rule) are "destabilized", being "antiaromatic". That explanation raises another question. How does valence bond theory account for the alleged "antiaromatic character"?

Valence bond theory accounts for aromatic character, as above for the cyclopentadienyl anion, by the fact that aromaticity always corresponds to occurrence, in valence bond theory, of *resonance* — and, accordingly, to whatever physical, energy-lowering effects one ascribes to that phenomenon. Absent, however, for valence bond theory, in the case of antiaromatic systems, is a corresponding physical basis for a corresponding energy-*elevating* effect.

The first step in addressing challenges to conceptual valence bond theory, to account for chemical phenomena, such as "antiaromaticity", is construction of a valence sphere model of the relevant species, Figure 2.

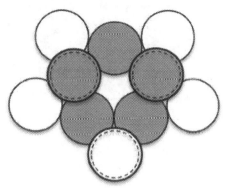

**Fig. 2.** Top view of a valence sphere model of cyclopentadiene. White spheres represent electron pair domains of carbon-hydrogen bonds, gray spheres domains of carbon-carbon bonds. Inner dashed circles represent domains directly beneath the corresponding upper domains. Each domain corresponds to a valence stroke in the molecule's corresponding bond diagram, oriented with its CH$_2$ group at the bottom and a carbon-carbon single bond at the top.

The second step is examination of the model for distinctive features, most notably steric effects, owing to the Exclusion Principle (as in the case of cyclobutadiene), and electron pair donor-acceptor interactions between nucleophilic sites (exposed electron pair domains) and electrophilic sites (exposed dimples in the model's electron density profile), Figure 3.

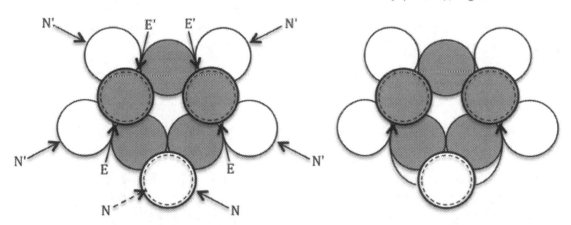

**Fig. 3. Left:** Cyclopentadiene's valence sphere model's electrophilic and nucleophilic sites, E and N. **Right:** Cyclopentadiene's principal, stereochemically allowed intramolecular donor-acceptor interactions, between its unprimed E and N sites. Dimples about double bonds are notably electrophilic, owing to outward displacements of the double-bonded atomic cores, owing to mutual core-core Coulombic repulsion.

Cyclopentadiene's donor-acceptor type interactions play prominent roles in the electronic structures of several species whose valence sphere models are isoelectronic with fragments of cyclopentadiene's valence sphere model, Figure 4.

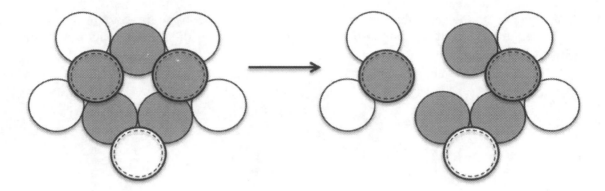

**Fig.** 4. Two fragments of cyclopentadiene's valence sphere model. The fragment on the far right becomes, with appropriate assignments for its electron pair domains and atomic cores, a valence sphere model of members of the propene/nitrosyl fluoride family of isoelectronic species.

The propene/FNO isoelectronic family includes formamide and formic acid, whose structures, together with those of other species that have lone pairs adjacent to double bonds, offer multiple geometrical evidence in their bond lengths and bond angles of tilts of the three domains at the lower left of the fragment on the right of Figure 4 about the domain of the single bond between heavy atoms, toward the adjacent electrophilic site (H. Bent, *Molecules and Chemical Bonds*, Trafford, 2012, pp255-258). The same interactions can occur in cyclopentadiene, if to a lesser degree, owing to the presence of a proton in the donor domain of a C—H bond.

Cyclopentadiene is distinctive in having a $CH_2$ group adjacent to *two* double bonds oriented in such a way, owing to the geometrical constraints of its five-membered ring, so as to favor donor-acceptor interactions between the weakly nucleophilic C—H domains of its $CH_2$ group and the adjacent electrophilic dimples of its two double bonds.

One is led, accordingly, and unexpectedly, to the thought that the difficulty in inducing cyclopentadiene to part with a hydride ion resides, not in an antiaromatic instability of the cyclopentadienyl cation, which is predicted to be aromatic, but, rather, in stability of the molecule itself, with respect to loss of a hydride ion from its $CH_2$ group.

Each instance of instability of a structure owing, according to MO theory, to a *common* cause, antiaromaticity, seems to arise, on the other hand, according to valence bond theory, from a *distinctive* cause: in, e.g., 4 π-electron systems, to a donor-acceptor interaction in the 5-membered ring of cyclopentadiene; to steric hindrance between domains of double bonds in the 4-membered ring of cyclobutadiene; and to an elevated transannular proton/carbon-carbon domain attraction in the 3-membered ring of cyclopropene.

In accounting for chemical phenomena with molecular orbital theory one relies on rules regarding orbitals, such as the 4n+2 rule. With valence bond theory one strives to account for chemical phenomena by relying on concepts related directly to fundamental physical principles (chiefly the Exclusion Principle, the Virial Theorem, Coulomb's Law, de Broglie's Relation, and energy minimization), augmented with structural principles related as closely and as simply as possible to empirical chemistry (such as the tetrahedral model for the valence shells of small atomic cores, dispersed lone pairs about large atomic cores, and minimum formal charges).

## Stabilities of Cyclopentadiene and Cycloheptatriene's Ions

Cyclopentadiene becomes aromatic on loss of a *proton* (yielding the stable anion $C_5H_5^-$), but not on loss of a hydride ion, although in simple resonance theory each ion has, as mentioned, the same number of leading resonance structures (5). In contrast, cycloheptatriene becomes aromatic on loss of a *hydride ion* (yielding the stable cation $C_7H_7^+$), but not on loss of a proton, although, again, each ion has the same number of leading resonance structures (7), Figure 1.

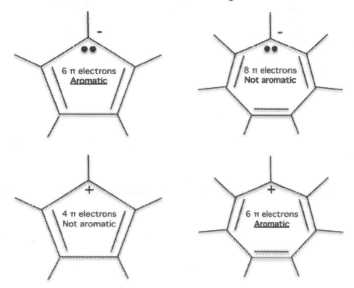

In MO Theory Huckel's Rule accounts for the results cited in the figure above. Cyclic conjugated planar species that have $(4n+2)$ π electrons (= 2, 6, 10, . . . ) are deemed to be stabilized, owing to "aromaticity", whereas similarly planar conjugated species that have $4n$ π electrons (= 4, 8, 12, . . . ) are deemed to be destabilized, owing to "antiaromaticity".

In Modern Conceptual Valence Bond Theory "aromaticity" corresponds, as mentioned, to enhanced stability owing to spatial anticoincidence between electrons of opposite spin, rendered possible by occupancy of different Kekule-like structures by a specie's different spin sets. To account for "antiaromaticity", however, one is forced, in Conceptual Valence Bond Theory, to seek some other explanatory molecular feature — such as, in the present instance, bond angles?

Angles of a regular planar pentagon are 108°, of a regular planar heptagon 128.6°. Angles of tetrahedrally-directed chemical affinities, such as at the pair of anionic sites above, are 109.5°, and of trigonally directed affinities, such as at the pair of cationic sites, 120°. The bond-angle character of anionic sites (109.5°) fits a pentagon's geometry (108°) much better than does the bond-angle geometry of a cationic site (120°), whereas the bond-angle character of cationic sites (120°) fits a heptagon's geometry (128.6°) better than does the bond-angle character of anionic sites (109.5°).

Stabilities of the ions of cyclopentadiene and cycloheptatriene are in harmony with their bond angles. The two compounds are, accordingly, candidates for a growing list of $4n$ π-electron systems that need not be considered to be "antiaromatic".

# Tricyclopentane
## *Extraordinarily Strained? Extraordinary Bonding?*

Removal of bicyclopentane's two bridgehead hydrogen atoms yields tricyclopentane, Figure 1.

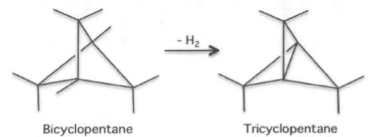

Bicyclopentane      Tricyclopentane

**Fig. 1.** Removal of an electron pair (as $H_2$) from $C_5H_8$, in the form of bicyclopentane, increases the species' excess connectivity, from two 4-membered rings to the three 3-membered rings of tricycopentane.

Tricyclopentane is considered to be super-strained, owing to its pair of inverted carbon atoms. In that regard the cyclopentanes' valence sphere models have an interesting feature, Figure 2.

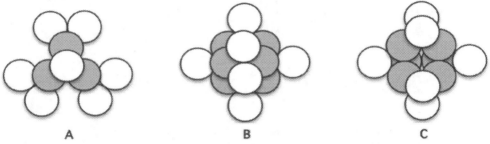

A            B            C

**Fig. 2.** Three views of an electron domain model of bicyclopentane. **A**: A view along the line of the two bridgehead C—H bonds. **B**: A view showing the trigonal prismatic arrantement of the domains of the molecule's six carbon-carbon bonds. The two bridgehead C—H domains (on the right and the left) cap the triangular faces of the C—C's trigonal prism. **C**: View **B** rotated 180 degrees about the bridgehead-bridgehead axis.

Inspection of a model constructed (as above) from domains of equal size reveals that the separation of the sites of the bridgehead carbon cores of tricyclopentane corresponds to the length of a normal carbon-carbon single bond, Figure 3.

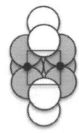

**Fig. 3.** Trigonal sites in the C—C trigonal prism, for the two bridgehead $C^{+4}$ cores (small black spheres) of tricycopentane. Their separation is equal to the diameter of the domain of a carbon-carbon single bond.

A normal C—C pair won't fit, however, into the available space between the two bridgehead cores. Part of its charge is evidently "squeezed out" to either side, as unshared charge; for the central bond's calculated bond order is said to be only 0.77. Its calculated bond length is reported to be 1.596 Å, compared to 1.516 Å for the ring CC bonds. That comparison suggests that the bridgehead carbon cores relax slightly outward with respect to their surrounding electron cloud.

# Bicyclic Pentalene

Many attempts to prepare bicyclic pentalene have failed because, it's said, the molecule is "antiaromatic", in having 4n π electrons, n = 2, Figure 1.

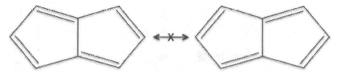

**Fig. 1.** Bond diagrams for Kekule-like structures for pentalene. Its t-butyl derivatives are said to exhibit bond alternation.

Pentalene tests –

## The Valence Sphere Theorem
*Satisfactory valence sphere models of molecules that do not exist do not exist.*

Inspection of a valence sphere model of pentalene suggests a *physical reason* — beyond the label "antiaromatic" — for its elusiveness, Figure 2.

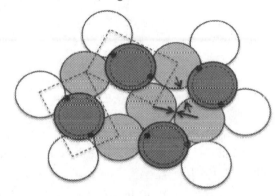

**Fig. 2.** Drawling of a top view of an equal-sphere-size version of a valence-sphere model of bicyclic pentalene. White circles represent domains of C—H bonds, light gray circles domains of C—C single bonds, and dark gray concentric circles dual domains of C=C double bonds. Small black circles represent domains of carbon $C^{+4}$ cores. Corners of the two dashed rectangles reside at the centers of the four electron pair domains about the two double bonds of the 5-member ring on the left. Arrows point to locations of regions in the model that are slightly or highly "unsatisfactory".

The unsatisfactory character of Figure 2 arises from excessive exclusion principle repulsions because the model fails to satisfy throughout -

## The Exclusive Orbital Condition
*Domains of satisfactory exclusive orbital models of molecules are not tangent to each other unless they reside in the valence shells of the same atomic cores.*

In Figure 2 the 5-member ring on the left is portrayed in its normal configuration, with the four domains about a double bond's pair of domains in their usual rectangular arrangement. However, rather than distributing the system's heightened strain — necessary for completion of the model —throughout the model, all of it has been assigned to the ring on the right, through unusual locations of the domains about that ring's double bonds. Presented for consideration is yet another 4n π-electron system whose instability can be attributed to something other than "antiaromaticity".

# Beware of Tidings of Delocalization

Aromatic systems are particularly stable, it's often said, owing to delocalization of their π-electrons. For with electron delocalization go increases in electrons' de Broglie wave lengths and, hence, by de Broglie's relation, $\lambda = h/p$, decreases of momentum, $p$, and, consequently, decreases of electronic kinetic energy, $T = p^2/2m$, and, therefore, decreases in total energy, $E$, provided potential energy, $V$, is constant, as for a particle in a potential energy "box" (below left), but not (below right) for a negatively charged electron moving in the field created by a positively charged atomic nucleus.

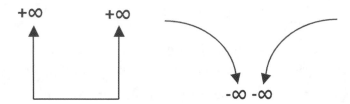

For potential energies, the difference in the two situations is the difference between plus and minus infinity. For total energies, it's the difference between $E (= T + V) = T$ (for $V$ = constant = 0) and, according to the Virial Theorem,

$$E (= T + V) = (1/2)V \quad \rightarrow \quad (1/2)V = -T \quad \rightarrow$$

$$\boxed{E = -T}$$

To minimize $E$ — negative with respect to a system's parts at infinite separation for stable systems governed by Coulomb's Law — minimize not $T$, by electron delocalization, but, rather, $V (= 2E = -2T)$, by maximizing $T (= -E)$.

Consider, e.g., an electron in a hydrogen atom. In going from a 1s orbital to a larger 2s orbital, $T$ decreases as $V$ and $E$ increase. $T$ is most positive and $E$ most negative for the smallest, *most localized orbital.*

In Modern Conceptual Valence Bond Theory an aromatic system such as benzene is considered to be unusually stable because its spin-sets in the carbon-carbon bonding regions are, to some degree, anticoincident (below left), rather than coincident (below right), as in hypothetical cyclohexatriene.

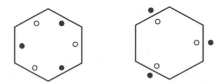

*Spatial anticoincidence allows nuclear-electron attraction to contract spin-sets' electron clouds, somewhat, without as great an increase in electron-electron repulsion as would otherwise occur between electrons of opposite spin.* And as $V$ becomes more negative, and, correspondingly, as $T$ becomes more positive, $E (= V/2 = -T)$ becomes more negative. *Benzene's unusual stability,* one is led to say, *arises not from unusual electron delocalization but, rather, in agreement with the Virial Theorem, from unusual electron <u>localization</u> about atomic nuclei.*

# Aromaticity's 4n+2 Rule

Passage from benzene — the prototypical aromatic system — to naphthalene involves, formally, addition of 4 carbon and 2 hydrogen atoms in the configuration of *cis*-1,3-butadiene.

Each new ring off an edge of a previous structure adds 2 double bonds, beginning with the original 3 of a Kekule structure. Thus the following table:

| Rings | Double Bonds | $\pi$ Electrons |
|-------|--------------|------------------|
| 1 | 3 | 6 |
| 2 | 5 | 10 |
| 3 | 7 | 14 |
| . | . | . |
| . | . | . |
| . | . | . |
| n | 2n+1 | 4n+2 |

Instead of beginning with a conjugated 6 member ring of 3 double bonds (benzene), one might begin with a 5-member ring with 2 double bonds and a $CH_2$ group (cyclopentadiene: $C_5H_6$) or with a 7-member ring with 3 double bonds and a $CH_2$ group (cycloheptatriene: $C_7H_8$), which, by loss of protons or hydride ions yield aromatic anions and cations, which, by addition of multiples of $C_4H_2$, yield, again, aromatic systems that satisfy the 4n + 2 rule.

Passage from $C_5H_6$ to $C_7H_8$ occurs on formal addition of $C_2H_2$ (acetylene, across a single bond). Removal of $C_2H_2$ from $C_5H_6$ yields $C_3H_4$, cyclopropene. Its loss of a hydride ion yields the stable cyclopropenyl cation, $C_3H_3^+$, a 4n + 2 system with n = 0, 2 $\pi$ electrons, and three resonance structures. The dication $C_4H_4^{+2}$ is also a $2\pi$ system, with four resonance structures. Both species may be formulated in terms of a single multicenter bond:

| | $4N - V$ | $= B_2 + 2B_3 + 3B_4$ | | | $V - (B_2 + B_3 + B_4)$ | $= B_1$ | | | |
|---|---|---|---|---|---|---|---|---|---|
| $C_3H_3^+$ | 12 | 7 | 3 | 1 | 0 | 7 | 3 | 1 | 0 | 3 |
| $C_4H_4^{+2}$ | 16 | 9 | 4 | 0 | 1 | 9 | 4 | 0 | 1 | 4 |

Black domains represent (left) a 3-center bond and (right) a 4-center bond. Gray domains represent 2-center carbon-carbon bonds. White domains represent bonds to hydrogen. The structures as they stand are nonplanar.

# An Interpretation of Naphthalene's Bond Lengths
## *The Role of Different Structures for Different Spin Sets*

Naphthalene introduces into valence bond theory a new feature: What should be the relative weights in a resonance hybrid of non-equivalent spin set structures? Whereas, e.g., benzene has two equivalent resonance structures, one for each spin set, given equal weights in a resonance hybrid model of benzene, naphthalene is represented in conventional valence bond theory by *three* spin-set arrangements, Figure 1.

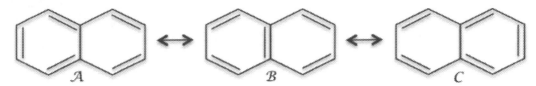

**Fig. 1.** Classical resonance structures for $C_{10}H_8$.

Figure 2 shows for the model of Figure 1 one set of bond orders, based on an assignment of equal weights for the three spin set arrangements $\mathcal{A}$, $\mathcal{B}$, and $\mathcal{C}$.

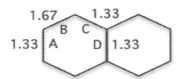

**Fig. 2.** Bond orders for naphthalene based on an order of 1 for a single bond, 2 for a double bond, and equal weighting of the three structures $\mathcal{A}$, $\mathcal{B}$, and $C$ of Figure 1.

Predicted is a pattern of bond lengths B < A = C = D. Observed bond lengths (based on studies prior to 2011) are shown in Figure 3.

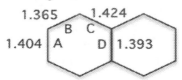

**Fig. 3.** Naphthalene's bond lengths, in Å, cited in the literature prior to 2011.

As expected from Figure 2, bond B is the shortest bond and the lengths of bonds A and D are about the same. Bond C, however seems too long, compared to bonds A and D. And compared to benzene (bond order 1.5, bond length 1.3969 Å), bonds A and D (with bond orders 1.33, Figure 2), seem too short.

To decrease bond C's bond order (to correspond to the bond's long length), one might increase the weight of structure $\mathcal{B}$ relative to the weights of structures $\mathcal{A}$ and $C$. That change destroys, however, the equality of the bond orders of bonds A and D. Using the three resonance structures of Figure 1, it is not possible, by changes in their relative weights in a superposition, to change the relative bond order of only one bond. Not considered to this point, however, is the possible role of spin set anticoincidence, Figure 4, not only for its explanation for the distinctive stabilities of aromatic molecules, but, also, for its role in determining the relative stabilities of a resonance hybrid's component spin set arrangements.

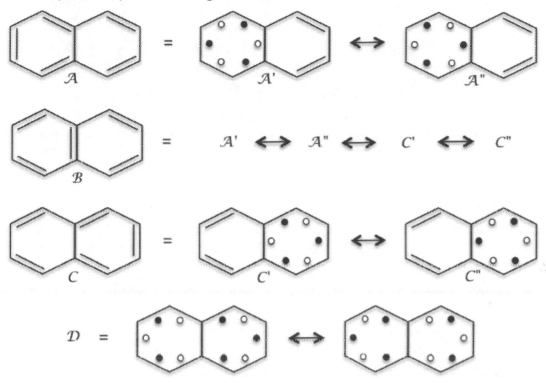

**Fig. 4.** Representation in conceptual valence bond theory of partially anticoincident spin set arrangements for naphthalene. Valence strokes represent two spin-paired electrons, small black circles electrons of one spin, small white circles electrons of the opposite spin. Introduction of the anticoincident representations of $A$, $B$, and $C$ (top three lines) does not alter the order of bond orders. The significant new feature of the figure resides in structure $D$ (bottom line). It provides a way of decreasing the bond order of bond D relative to the other bonds.

*Structure $D$ has no counterpart in conventional v.b. theory* (Figure 1). Yet it is the structure with the largest degree of anticoincidence and that, presumably, is, consequently, the structure with the least energy and, accordingly, the one that contributes most to a resonance hybrid representation of naphthalene, Figure 5.

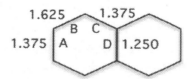

**Fig. 5.** Bond orders, for illustrative purposes, of the resonance hybrid $A + B + 2D$.

<u>Order of Bond Lengths</u>

Implied by $A + B + C$        B < A = C = D
Implied by $A + B + 2D$:     B < A = C < D
Observed Prior to 2011:       B < D ≈ A < C
Observed in 2011 (Fig. 6)   B < A ≈ C < D

139

In 2011 an ultrahigh resolution laser spectroscopy and *ab initio* calculation of the geometrical structure of naphthalene was reported [M. Baba, et al., *J. Chem. Phys.* **135**, 054305, (2011)], Figure 6.

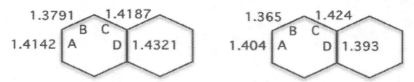

**Fig. 6.** Proposed geometrical structures of naphthalene. <u>Left:</u> Reported in 2011. <u>Right:</u> Reported prior to 2011. The largest change is in the length of Bond D, moved from being the second shortest bond (1.393 Å) to being the longest bond (1.4321 Å), a change of majpr significance for conceptual valence bond theory, in view of its earlier "failure" to account for naphthalene's reported bond lengths, prior to 2011.

Implications of the resonance hybrid  model $\mathcal{A} + \mathcal{B} + 2\mathcal{D}$ are in qualitative agreement with current experimental data:

- The predicted order of bond orders (Figure 5) is essentially the same as the observed order of bond lengths (Figure 6).
- Bond C, predicted to be the same length as bond A, is only 0.0045 Å (0.32 %) longer than bond A.
- Bond B (bond order 1.625, bond length 1.3791 Å) is shorter than benzene's carbon-carbon bond (bond order 1.5, bond length 1.3969 Å).
- Bond orders of bonds A, C, and D (1.250 – 1.375) are less than benzene's bond order (1.5) and, correspondingly, the bonds are longer than benzene's bond (1.1412 – 1.4321 Å compared to 1.3791 Å for benzene).

The results of this study lend credence to several ideas. Useful are:

- conceptual valence bond theory's classical bond diagrams
- the concept of resonance-superposition of classical bond diagrams
- fractional bond orders
- the idea that, unlike energy, bond lengths are bond-order-weighted *averages* of bond lengths of a resonance hybrid's contributing structures
- the concept of different structures for different spin sets
- the idea that different degrees of anticoincidence of a spin set's arrangements of spins correspond to different energies, energy decreasing with increasing anticoincidence
- the realization that classical valence bond theory, in limiting its bond diagrams to spatially coincident electron *pairs,* may overlook structurally significant spin set arrangements, as in the case, e.g., of naphthalene

Illustrated is the thesis, emphasized by Duhem, that a comparison of a theory with experimental data is, in principle, a test of the *entire* theory, not merely one aspect of it — albeit, in practice, one aspect of a theory may stand out as most in need of confirmation.

# Calculated Ring Currents for Cyclic Conjugated Hydrocarbons

Aromaticity is widely associated with the ability of a cyclic conjugated planar π system to support a ring current in the presence of a perpendicular external magnetic field (1). One might suppose, accordingly, that the magnitude of such a current would increase with increasing number of circulating electrons. Listed below are calculated magnetically induced ring currents, reported for eight hydrocarbons (1) that have, as listed, 0 to 18 conjugated π electrons.

Broadly speaking, calculated ring currents (the last figure in each instance, after multiplication by 100) are proportional to — in fact, nearly equal to — numbers of circulating π electrons if, for hydrocarbon **8**, allowance is made for the nonexistence of square planar cyclobutadiene.

That insight was a surprise: *Aromatic character suppressed by instability of a resonance hybrid.*

(1) P. W. Fowler and A. Sonici, Chemical Physics Letters, 383 (2004) 507-511.

# The Alkali Metals

A clue to the nature of the bonds in metallic sodium is provided by the existence in sodium vapor of sodium dimers: $Na_2$. A valence sphere model of the bond diagram Na—Na reveals its inadequacy.

The conventional covalent bond fails to locate electron density about major portions of the sodium cations. That issue is addressed by introduction of ionic character:

$$Na^+Na^- \longleftrightarrow Na^-Na^+$$

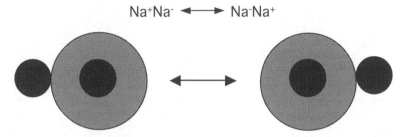

Superposition of the two structures yields an average electron density distribution about each $Na^+$ cation, radius 95 pm, equivalent to one electron, corresponding to a sodium atom. Overlap of the valence shells of two unaltered sodium atoms yields the following model of $Na_2(g)$, interatomic distance 309.7 pm. Resonance would make the net spin densities at the two atoms zero.

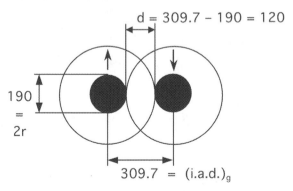

The structure of crystalline sodium is body centered cubic. Atomic spins at any instance might be pictured as arranged in the following manner.

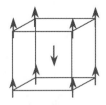

Below on the left is a view of the sodium atoms on one face of the unit cell and, at the right, along the unit cell's body diagonal, corresponding to weak bonding and, accordingly, to a low melting point.

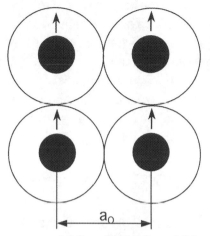
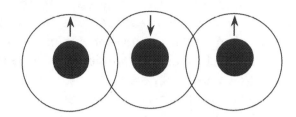

$$(i.a.d.)_g = 2r + d \rightarrow d = (i.a.d.)_g - 2r$$
$$a_0 = 2(r + d) = 2((i.a.d.)_g - r) \rightarrow$$
$$r = (i.a.d.)_g - a_0/2 \rightarrow$$
$$(i.a.d.)_g = r + a_0/2$$

$190 + 2 \times 120 = 430$ pm    Observed: 429 pm (20°C)

For lithium $(i.a.d.)_g = 267$ pm and $a_0 = 351$ pm $\rightarrow r(Li^+) = 91.5$ pm. Pauling's radius is 60 pm. Shannon and Prewitt's radius for the lithium ion for coordination number 6 is 90 pm.

Gas phase interatomic distances for $Rb_2$ and $Cs_2$ are not given by Herzberg in his volume on *Diatomic Molecules*. The elements' crystalline $a_0$ values are 560 and 604 pm, respectively. Pauling and S & P's ionic radii, listed below in that order (the latter for C.N. 6), yield the following predicted values for $(i.a.d.)_g$:

Rb: $r = 148, 166 \rightarrow (i.a.d.)_g = 428, 446$ pm

Cs: $r = 169, 181 \rightarrow (i.a.d.)_g = 471, 483$ pm

## Valence Sphere Models of Lithiated Boron Hydrides
## Isoelectronic with Ethane and Propane

Models live dangerously. They may be falsified. For, as remarked, to be useful, *a model must be wrong in some respects*, else it would be the thing itself, not a model. Associated with models' positive analogies are negative analogies — without which, of course, the positive analogies would not exist. The possibility always exists, therefore, that attempts to use models in situations that they were not explicitly designed to model may feature negative analogies that render the models in those situations useless. A possible case in point are valence sphere models of molecules and calculated structures of lithiated boron hydrides, reported by J. K. Olson and A. I. Boldyrev [Electronic Transmutation: Boron Acquiring an Extra Electron Becomes "Carbon", in press, *Chemical Physics Letters* (2011). The present author is indebted to professor Roald Hoffmann for calling this paper to his attention.]

Valence sphere models were designed initially to account for the structures of *covalent compounds* of *nonmetals* whose atomic cores are *small* (radii less than ≈ 20 pm) and whose electronegativities are relatively large (equal to or greater than ≈ 2.0). The models were not designed to account for structures that contain *ionic bonds* involving *metallic elements* whose atomic cores are relatively *large* (radii greater than ≈ 50 pm) and whose electronegativities are relatively small (less than ≈ 2.0). Locations in the molecules $Li_2B_2H_6$ and $Li_3B_3H_8$ of presumed cations $Li^+$ (radius 76 pm, electronegativity 1.0) with respect to presumed anions $B_2H_6^{-2}$ and $B_3H_8^{-2}$ (electronegativities of B and H equal to 2.0 and 2.2, respectively) provide, accordingly, rigorous tests of the usefulness of valence sphere models of molecules.

Since hydrogen is slightly more electronegative than boron, one expects the B—H domains of the two boron hydride anions, $B_2H_6^{-2}$ and $B_3H_8^{-2}$, isoelectronic with ethane and propane, respectively, to be nucleophilic with the counter ions $Li^+$ nestled in among the B—H domains, as pictured in Figure 1 for $Li_2B_2H_6$.

A                                        B

Fig. 1. Two valence sphere, large B—H models for $Li_2B_2H_6$. The energy of isomer **B**, Olson and Boldyrev calculate, is 15.0 kcal/mole greater than that of isomer **A**, owing, the models suggest, to the close approach of the $Li^+$ ion on the right (large black domain) to the $B^{+3}$ domain on the right (small black domain, almost hidden). (For $C_2H_6$, isoelectronic with $B_2H_6^{-2}$, C—H domains must be some 50% larger than C—C domains in order to fit inter-nuclear distances in the molecule and crystalline $C_2H_6$.)

The Li⁺ ions in the two models of Figure 1 are in contact with three B—H domains; i.e., the $B_2H_6^{-2}$ moiety is a tridentate ligand toward the Li⁺ cations. The larger ligand $B_3H_8^{-2}$ has, in addition to tridentate sites, a tetradentate site for Li⁺ — barely, without rattling, Figure 2.

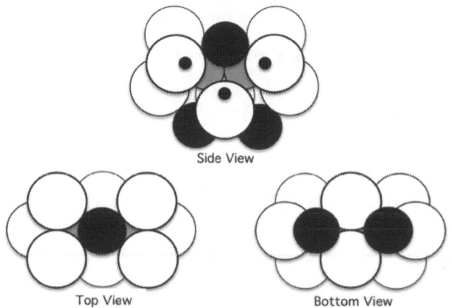

Side View

Top View          Bottom View

**Fig. 2.** Three views of a valence sphere model for $Li_3B_3H_8$. Gray domains are domains of BB 2-center bonds. Black domains, large and small, are domains of Li⁺ and B⁺³ ions, respectively. White domains are domains of BH bonds.

Each domain represents an electron pair, of increasing size with decreasing charge of its embedded atomic core or adjacent atomic cores, Figure 3.

B⁺³          B—B          Li⁺          H⁻

**Fig. 3.** From left to right: B⁺⁵-embedded pair; pair of a BB bond; Li⁺³-embedded pair; proton-embedded pair.

In summary: Valence sphere models model molecules' approximate electron density profiles, not their inner electron density contours. They depict molecular architecture (approximate bond angles and relative internuclear distances), the stereochemistry of intra- and intermolecular donor-acceptor interactions, and reaction mechanisms. Although they do not yield *numerical* values of molecular energies, they do yield most likely arrangements in space of, in the case of $Li_3B_3H_8$, domains of eight protonated electron pairs, three lithium ions, three boron cores, and two domains of 2-center BB bonds, in accordance with wave functions' exclusive orbital character — that two fermions of the same spin are seldom at the same place at the same time.

# Structures of the Carbenoids LiCH₂F

Quantum chemical calculations (MP4SDTQ/6-31G(d)//6-31G(d)+ZPE) on the simplest carbenoid, LiCH$_2$F (by Schleyer's group), have been reviewed in *Chemical Reviews* (Gernot Boche and John Lorenz, **201**, 101, 708). Relevant structures (bond lengths in pm) are shown in Figure 1.

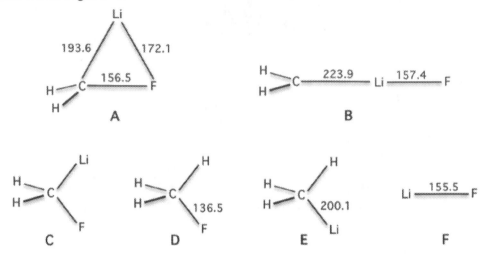

Fig. 1. Calculated structures for lithium methyl fluoride, LiCH$_2$F: **A** and **B**. (The other structures are for comparison.) The global minimum is **A**. It's HCF angle is 110.0°.

The most noteworthy features of structure **A** are said to be: "(i) the strikingly elongated C—F bond, from 136.5 pm in nonlithiated **D** to 156.5 pm (an increase of 20.0 pm, 14.7%)"; and "(ii) all four ligands lying in the same hemisphere".

The classical tetrahedral structure **C** does not correspond to a local minimum. How well, one might wonder, does *conceptual* valence bond theory account for the calculated structures?

LiCH$_2$F has two heavy-atom cores (C$^{+4}$ and F$^{+7}$) and seven pairs of valence shell electrons. In the absence of primary structure-determining qualities arising from the presence of Li$^+$ (treated below as an "add on"), one expects structure **A**'s qualitative valence shell electron density profile to be isoelectronic with $^-$CH$_2$F, Figure 2.

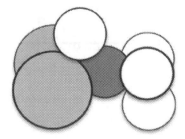

Fig. 2. Large C—H valence sphere model of the electron density profile of the valence shell electron pairs of $^-$CH$_2$F. White spheres: domains of lone pairs about the cores C$^{+4}$ and F$^{+7}$; dark gray domain: C—F bonding pair; light gray domains: C—H bonding pairs.

The best site for Li⁺ from the standpoint of lithium-ion/electron-domain attraction would seem to be for Li⁺ to be "tangent" to the carbon lone pair and to two of the fluorine lone pairs. That arrangement places Li⁺ close to, even in contact with, the C—F bonding pair, Figure 3.

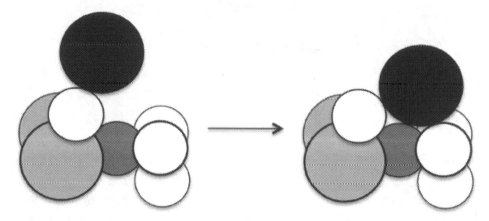

**Fig. 3.** Collapse of nonexistent structure **C** to structure **A**, placing thereby all ligands about $C^{+4}$ in the same hemisphere.

The order of interatomic distances in a model of structure **A** agrees with the calculated order:

$$C—F \ < \ Li—F \ < \ Li—C$$

Model **A**'s Li—C bond is bent, hence shorter in **A** than in **E**, Figure 4.

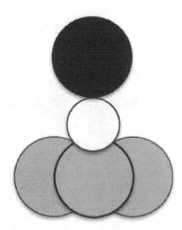

**Fig. 4.** Model of the linear C—Li bond of $CH_3Li$, longer than the bent C—Li bond of structure **A**.

The greater length of the C—F bond in **A** than in **D** ($H_3CF$) is attributed, here, to core-core repulsions between $C^{+4}$, $L^{i+}$, and $F^{+7}$. As Li⁺ approaches the anion $^-CH_2F$ in the manner indicated in Figure 3, it repels, somewhat, $C^{+4}$ and $F^{+7}$, outward.

Isomer **B**'s structure suggests the model in Figure 5.

**Fig. 5.** Valence Sphere Model of Structure **B**: a carbene (H$_2$C:)/lithium fluoride (Li$^+$F$^-$) complex. Light gray spheres: domains of C—H bonds; dark gray sphere: domain of C—Li bond; black sphere: Li$^+$ domain; white spheres: valence shell electron pair domains of F$^{+7}$.

Structure **B** raises the question: Why is its C—Li bond (223.9 pm) *longer* than the C—Li bond of CH$_3$Li (200.1 pm)?

In Figure 5, the model's lithium ion (black) is not coordinatively saturated, particularly on its carbon side. It might be expected, therefore, to steal electron density from neighboring C—H bonds. In structure B (Figure 1) lithium has only two donor C—H bonds from which to steal electron density. In the CH$_3$Li structure, however, it has three such bonds. One supposes — as usual — that an increase in electron density in a bonding region is accompanied by a decrease in bond length.

The lithiated species LiCH$_2$F, LiCH$_2$OH, and LiCH$_2$NH$_2$ all have as their most stable structures of type **A** (Figure 1). The explanation offered earlier for the increase in C—F distance in structure **A** over its value in CH$_3$F, by 17.7%, as arising from C$^{+4}$ - Li$^+$ - F$^{+7}$ repulsion, receives support from the fact that the corresponding bonds in LiCH$_2$OH and LiCH$_2$NH$_2$ are, indeed, longer than in CH$_3$OH and CH$_3$NH$_2$, but by only 11.5 and 7.8 percent, respectively. Cited below is additional support for an exclusive orbital model of approximate valence shell electron density profiles.

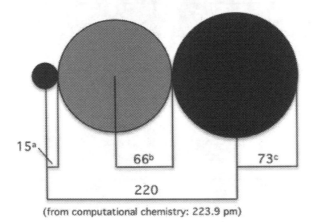

15[a]          66[b]          73[c]

220

(from computational chemistry: 223.9 pm)

**Fig. 6.** Estimate of the C—Li bond length in structure **B** of Figure 1.

a  Linus Pauling, "The Nature of the Chemical Bond," Cornell University Press, 3$^{rd}$ ed., 1960, p514.
b  H. A. Bent, "Estimation of Internuclear Distances," *J. Chem. Educ.*, **42**, 348-355, (1965):
   R(valence shell electron pair radius) = 60 pm + 0.4r(radius of atomic core)
c  Shannon and Prewitt, *Acta Crystallogr.* **B25**, (1969), 925-946.

## Relative Distances between a Regular Tetrahedron's Center, Corners, Edge-Centers, and Face-Centers

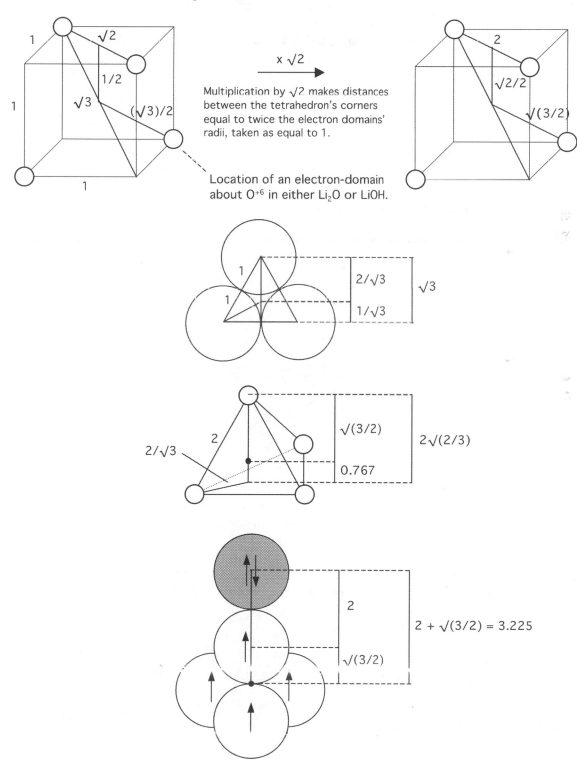

x √2

Multiplication by √2 makes distances between the tetrahedron's corners equal to twice the electron domains' radii, taken as equal to 1.

Location of an electron-domain about $O^{+6}$ in either $Li_2O$ or LiOH.

$2 + \sqrt{(3/2)} = 3.225$

# Calculated and Observed Lithium-Oxygen Distances in $Li_2O(s)$

Calculated and observed lithium-oxygen distances in body-centered $Li_2O(s)$ provide evidence of the transferability of valence sphere models' parameters and the supposition that the oxide ions' valence shell spin sets are angularly anticoincident.

Pauling's radius for $Li^+$ is 60 pm. The radius of an electron-pair in the valence shell of $O^{+6}$ (Pauling radius 9 pm) is about the same: 60 pm + 0.4 x 9 pm = 63.6 pm. Accordingly, to convert distances in valence sphere models for spheres of unit radius to interatomic distances in $Li_2O(s)$, multiply model distances by the approximate factor

$$(60 + 63.6)/2 \approx 62.$$

Interatomic distances for coordination of a cation, such as $Li^+$, that is about the same size as the electron domains of the coordinated anion, such as $O^{-2}$, are about the same whether the coordination is off an edge or a face of the anion's anticoincident spin-sets. Coordination off a corner yields, however, a significantly larger interatomic distance.

*Valence Sphere Model of an Anticoincident Oxide Ion and a Coordinated Lithium Ion in Body-Centered $Li_2O(s)$*

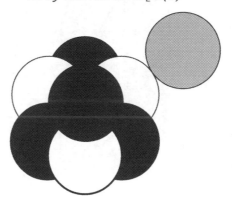

**Black:** Domains of electrons of one spin in the valence-shell of $O^{-2}$. **White:** Domains of electrons of the opposite spin. **Grey:** Domain of the two spatially coincident spin-paired electrons of $Li^+$.

In crystalline $Li_2O$, each oxide ion (shown above in a Lewis/Linnett configuration) is at the center of eight coordinated lithium ions at the corners of a surrounding cube.

Model i.a.d.: $2 + \sqrt{(3/2)} = 3.225$

Calc. i.a.d.: $3.225 \times 62$ pm = 200 pm

Observed i.a.d.: $200.0_1$ pm

An oxide ion's conventional radius of 140 pm (Pauling) corresponds to a model radius of 140 pm/62 pm = 2.258 $\approx$ (previous essay) $1 + \sqrt{(3/2)} = 2.225$.

# LiCO⁺ and COLi⁺

Li⁺ is a useful probe of the envelopes of molecules' electron clouds, since it has no valence-shell electrons of its own and, owing to the low electronegtivity of lithium, is unlikely to modify significantly envelopes of the electron clouds of molecules composed of atoms of elements more electronegative than lithium, such as the nonmetallic elements C, N, O, and F. Below are drawings of valence-sphere models of LiCO⁺ and COLi⁺.

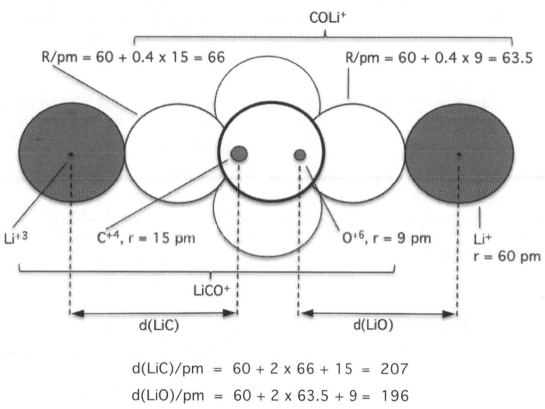

$$d(LiC)/pm = 60 + 2 \times 66 + 15 = 207$$

$$d(LiO)/pm = 60 + 2 \times 63.5 + 9 = 196$$

Corresponding calculated distances given by Weinhold and Landis (*Valency and Bonding*, p72) are 200 and 190 pm, difference 10 pm, compared to 11 pm above.

CO has a finite dipole moment. From the point of view of ion-dipole forces, only one of the species, LiCO⁺ and COLi⁺, should exhibit a potential energy minimum, yet both do.

*Chemical bonding is a highly localized phenomenon*. The most important electrostatic interactions in the present instances are attractive interactions between the Li⁺ ion and the CO molecule's *lone pairs*. Other electrostatic interactions — attractive and repulsive — drop off as the square of the distance.

Compared to the LiC and LiO distances depicted above, the figure's CO distance is significantly too small. C⁺⁴ - O⁺⁶ repulsion stretches along the molecular axis the triple bond's electron domains.

# Electron Domain Model of Dilithium Methane

_Breaking News_: $Li_2CH_2$ is a "square planar" molecule, thereby "BREAKING CARBON'S TETRAHEDRAL MOLD" (_C&EN_, Aug. 10, 2010, pp28-29). Actually, what's broken by "square planar" $Li_2CH_2$ (and not for the first time) is the thought that atomic positions always indicate positions of bonding electrons. ($H_2CO$, for instance, although "trigonal planar", does not, in valence bond theory, break carbon's "tetrahedral mold". Nor, e.g., does linear HCCH.

> _Nuclei's locations about an atomic core do not indicate directions of the core's chemical affinities unless all bonds to it are 2-center, single bonds not part of small rings._

_C&EN_'s error is an old error. In the pre-electronic era of valence bond theory, chemistry's tetrahedral carbon atom and its multiple bonds were paradoxical from the point of view of the central forces of physics. In the attraction for each other of two carbon atoms bonded by a multiple bond, _the atoms' tetrahedrally directed affinities do not point along the multiple bond's direction!_ Nor do they for the carbon-carbon bonds of cyclopropane. To bring chemical and physical theory into mutual agreement, it might be suggested, in retrospect, that in molecules positively charged atomic "cores" are surrounded by space-filling, approximately spherical negatively charged domains corresponding to the valence-stokes of bond diagrams. Produced for dilithium methane is the following figure.

_Valence-Stroke Diagram and Valence-Sphere Model for cis-$Li_2CH_2$_

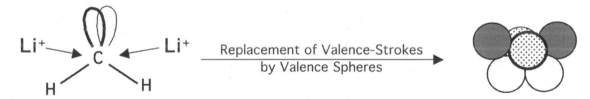

In the model at the right, the five atomic cores — 2 $Li^+$ and (not shown) $C^{+4}$ and 2 $H^+$ (of the C—H bonds) — lie in the plane of the page at the corners (for $Li^+$ and $H^+$) and the center (for $C^{+4}$) of a regular trapezoid. The carbon core is in its usual "mold", surrounded by four electron domains in a tetrahedral arrangement. The two $Li^+$ ions share a pair of domains, as in a double bond. Speckled domains represent 3-center LiCLi bonds. They are in the valence-shells of 3 atomic cores: $C^{+4}$ and 2 $Li^+$. White domains represent 3-center domains, also, being in the valence shells of $H^+$, $C^{+4}$, and $Li^+$. All domains are shown the same size. To fit inter- and intramolecular distances in crystalline paraffin's, one must suppose, however, that r(C—H pair) is some 50 percent larger than r(C—C pair), which is approximately equal to r($Li^+$).

> _Presence of multicenter bonds and a double-bond-like arrangement of domains means that locations of the atomic nuclei do not indicate, directly, the presence of a carbon core in its traditional "tetrahedral mode"_ (with respect to coordinated electron pair domains).

Bonding of $Li^+$ to $CH_2^{-2}$ is partially ionic, since reasonable electrostatic bond strengths for the large, lightly charged cores $Li^+$ relative to electrostatic bond strengths for the small, highly charged core $C^{+4}$ are small.

*Parameters for Assignment of Electrostatic Bond Strengths for*
*Dilithium Methane's 3-Center LiHC and LiCLi Bonds*

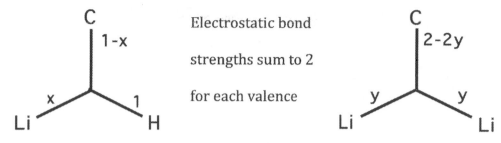

Electrostatic bond

strengths sum to 2

for each valence

Let L = formal charge (fc) of Li.
Then fc(C) = -2L if, as above, left, fc(H) is set equal to 0
since 2fc(Li) + 2fc(H) + fc(C) = 0
$$L = 1 - x - 2y \rightarrow y = (1 - x - L)/2$$
[For $C^{+4}$, -2L = 4 - 2(1-x) - 2(2-2y) yields the same expression for y.]
Because the electronegativity of H is greater than that of Li, one expects that
$$y > x \rightarrow x < (1 - L)/3$$
Also: $1-x > x \rightarrow x < 0.5$ and $2-2y > y \rightarrow y < 2/3$

Values of y for Different Choices for L and x

|  | A | B | C | D | E | F | G | H |
|---|---|---|---|---|---|---|---|---|
| fc(Li) = L | 0 | 0 | 0 | 0.2 | 0.4 | 0.6 | 0.8 | 1 |
| x | 0 | 0.1 | 0.2 | 0.1 | 0.1 | 0.1 | 0 | 0 |
| 1-x | 1 | 0.9 | 0.8 | 0.9 | 0.9 | 0.9 | 1 | 1 |
| y[=(1-x-L)/2] | 0.5 | 0.45 | 0.4 | 0.4 | 0.25 | 0.15 | 0.1 | 0 |
| 2-2y | 1 | 1.1 | 1.2 | 1.2 | 1.5 | 1.7 | 1.8 | 2 |
| fc(C) [= -2L] | 0 | 0 | 0 | -0.2 | -0.8 | -1.2 | -1.6 | -2 |

A, B, C: zero formal charges for Li. D - G: Increasing fc for Li. H: maximum fc for Li.

Because $Li_2CH_2$ has highly exposed nucleophilic sites (at C's lone pairs) and highly exposed electrophilic sites (at Li's cores), it easily dimerizes.

Planes of the two monomers are perpendicular to each other. $C^{+4}$ and $H^+$ cores are in conventional chemical environments: electron pair coordination numbers 4 and 1, respectively. Speckled electron pair domains represent 4-center LiLiLiC bonds.

$Li^+$ ions in the dimer have four electron pair domains in their valence shells, all in the same hemisphere. They are, therefore, still exposed, to a degree comparable to that of the double bond domains of ethylene.

# Localized Electron Domain Models of the Lithium Methyl Tetramer
## (LiMe)$_4$

Protons of the methide ion are somewhat hydridic. Consequently the ion's entire surface is nucleophilic — toward, e.g., a lithium ion.

*Possible Structures for the Ion-Pair (Li$^+$)(CH$_3^-$)*

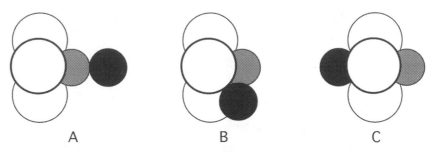

A           B           C

The ion-pair has exposed nucleophilic and electrophilic sites for all locations of the lithium ion. It forms a tetramer. In the tetramer the four lithium ions are arranged tetrahedrally, as are the four methide ions. Jointly the eight ions are arranged at the corners of a distorted cube.

*Two Tetrahedral Arrangements of Four Lithium Ions*
*and Four Electron-Pair Domains*

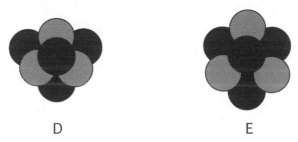

D                E

D: Close-packed tetrahedron of electron-pair domains (light grey) capped on its faces by lithium ions (black).

E: Electron-pair domains and lithium ions at alternate corners of a cube, viewed along a cube body diagonal

In structure D the electron-pair domains are in mutual contact, allowed if they are in the valence shell of the same atomic cores, here the lithium ions. One might wonder, however: Are the force fields of the four lithium ions (charges of +1, compared, e.g., to +4 for carbon cores) sufficiently intense to bring four electron-pair domains into close contact? Squeezing the lithium ions closer to each other, with expansion of the electron-pair domains' tetrahedral arrangement, yields structures such as E.

Capping corners of electron-pair tetrahedra of D and E with the three C—H domains of methide ions reveals a third defect in D: steric interference of the C—H domains with each other (indicated below by the arrows about structure F). The (grey) bonding domains in F and G represent 4-center LiLiLiC bonds.

*C—H Capped Structures D and E*

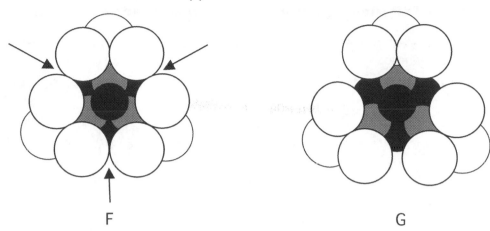

F                                       G

A structure between F and G, scaled, corresponds closely to observed internuclear distances: C—Li = 231 pm, Li—Li 268 pm.

The tetramer (LiMe)$_4$ has four somewhat exposed electrophilic lithium ions and four highly exposed somewhat nucleophilic hydride-ion-like domains of the methide ions. In crystalline lithium methyl an intermolecular association caps each lithium ion with the three C—H domains of a methide ion of an adjacent tetramer. Lithium ions acquire thereby octahedral arrangements of electron domains: three "lone pairs" of three methide ions and three C—H domains of one methide ion. All domains about Li$^+$ have large dative bond character with respect to Li$^+$; i.e., bonds to Li$^+$ are largely ionic, even for zero formal charges.

*Illustrative Electrostatic Bond Strengths for (LiMe)$_4$'s 3- and 4-Center Bonds*
*for Local Electrical Neutrality at Atomic Sites*

Li
|  0.1

0.9        1
C          H

In crystalline (LiMe)$_4$ there are three of these 3-center bonds in the valence shells of each C$^{+4}$ and Li$^+$ core.

Formal charges at lithium sites are
+1 – 3x0.1 3x(0.7/3) = 0.

Formal charges at carbon sites are:
+4 – 3x0.9 – 1.3 = 0.

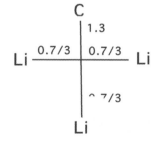

In (LiMe)$_4$ each C$^{+4}$ core has one and each Li$^+$ core has three of these 4-center bonds in its valence shell.

# The Alkali Halide Paradox
## Their Structures and Radius-Ratios

Forty percent of the alkali halides haven't the structures that they should have based on their cation-to-anion radius-ratios.

### Predicted Cation Coordination Numbers (CN) Based on Ions' Radius-Ratios

| $r^+/r$: | < 0.414 | 0.414 – 0.732 | > 0.732 |
|---|---|---|---|
| CN: | 4 | 6 | 8 |

### Cation and Anion Coordination Numbers of the Alkali Halides
#### Predicted/Actual

|   | Li | Na | K | Rb | Cs |
|---|---|---|---|---|---|
| F | 6/6 | 6/6 | 8/6 | 8/6 | 8/6 |
| Cl | 4/6 | 6/6 | 6/6 | 8/6 | 8/8 |
| Br | 4/6 | 6/6 | 6/6 | 8/6 | 8/8 |
| I | 4/6 | 6/6 | 6/6 | 6/6 | 8/8 |

Boxed are the 8 instances out of 20 that violate the radius-ratio rules. LiCl, LiBr, and LiI have larger coordination numbers than expected, KF, RbF, RbCl, RbBr, and CsF smaller coordination numbers than expected. *In each instance the NaCl (rocksalt) structure is unexpectedly stable.* One wonders: Might an explanation for the alkali halide paradox lie in departures in their crystals of their ions' most probable configurations (MPC) from perfect spherical symmetry?

The numbers 6 and 8 call to mind the cube, 6 faces, 8 corners, and the octahedron, 8 faces, 6 corners. (Each one is the other's dual.)

The cube's corners might correspond to the MPC of two anticoincident ion spin-sets.

The octahedron's corners might correspond to lobes of an ion's p-orbitals.

## A Donor-Acceptor Model of Cation-Anion Contacts in the NaCl Structure

### Black: spin up     White: spin down     Gray: Spin-paired

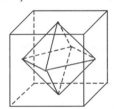

Cations, "core" charges +9 (except for Li), benefit more from angular anti-coincidence, through domain contraction, than do anions, "core" charges +7.

Region of conventional anion-anion overlap →

In the CsCl CN 8/8 structure anions would have the cubic anti-coincident structure donating electron density to faces of cationic octahedra.

Valence-shell $s^2$ pair.

Conventional anion envelope.

The p-orbital anion model makes anions smaller than ionic radii, in potential anion-anion overlap regions, hence the NaCl structure for, e.g., LiCl.

# Significance of Anomalous Crystal Structures of LiCl, LiBr, and LiI

Lithium halides have the sodium chloride, face-centered cubic structure. Each lithium ion is surrounded by six halide ions, although the Radius-Ratio Rules predict that, owing to the large sizes of $Cl^-$, $Br^-$, and $I^-$, compared to $Li^+$, lithium in LiCl, LiBr, and LiI should have coordination numbers less than six. Lithium ions are too small to occupy fully the interstices formed by close-packed $Cl^-$, $Br^-$, and $I^-$ ions. Radii of those interstices are given in the following table, column (5). Distances are in pm. Ionic radii are from Pauling, *Nature of the Chemical Bond:* $r(Li^+)$ = 60 pm.)

| (1) | (2) | (3) | (4) | (5) | (6) | (7) |
|-----|-----|-----|-----|-----|-----|-----|
| LiX | $r(X^-)$ | $2r(X^-)$ | $d(X^-...X^-)$ | $(0.414)r(X^-)$ | $d(M—X)$ | $d(M—X) - r(X^-)$ |
| LiF | 136 | 272 | 284 | 56 | 201 | 65 |
| LiCl | 181 | 362 | 362 | 75 | 256 | 75 |
| LiBr | 195 | 390 | 388 | 81 | 275 | 80 |
| LiI | 216 | 432 | 424 | 89 | 300 | 84 |

Comparing columns (3) and (4), one sees that the halide ions are close-packed in LiCl, but seemingly overlap, slightly, in LiBr; and still more so in LiI.

Column (7) gives *the apparent sizes of the species at the lithium sites.* The smaller the halogen's electronegativity, the larger the lithium species appears to be. That fact suggests *leakage of charge from the halogen ions to the lithium ions,* in an amount LiI > LiBr > LiCl > LiF. The lithium halides in that charge-leakage model might be represented as resonance hybrids of an ionic structure and a structure composed of atoms.

$$Li^+X^- \longleftrightarrow LiX$$

The atomic-like "Li" may be pictured as a lithium core, $Li^+$, surrounded by a cored spherical domain occupied by a fraction of the charge of an electron-pair.

Owing to the Exclusion Principle, electron clouds of halide species do not penetrate the augmented lithium ions' electron clouds. Produced, accordingly, are metal-halogen distances greater than the sums of ionic radii.

The corresponding halogen species, "X", being somewhat atomic-like, are postulated able to overlap each other, slightly, presumably the more so the larger the charge leakage from halogen ions to lithium ions. Since that leakage has been deemed to be greatest for LiI, column (7) [= (6) – (2)], the difference, column (3) – column (4), is, accordingly, the greatest for lithium iodide. The charge-leakage model seems to be self-consistent.

Charge-leakage should occur for all cations surrounded by electron-donors. The greater the donors' donating tendencies and the greater their number, the greater will be, presumably, a given cation's apparent size. For a given donor, in other word, *a cation's (apparent) radius should increase with increasing coordination number.* There appear to be no exceptions to that rule. Also, for given donors, the smaller a spherical cation is and the larger its charge, the greater should be radius-enlarging charge-leakage. That, also, seems to be the case, broadly speaking, for the cations of Groups I(s) and II(s).

# Remarks Regarding the "Charge-Leakage" Model of Lithium Halides

The resonance hybrid, charge-leakage model of LiBr and LiI is illustrated schematically below (X = Br or I, the black circle = $Li^+$, the large circle = $X^-$).

$$Li^+X^- \longleftrightarrow LiX$$

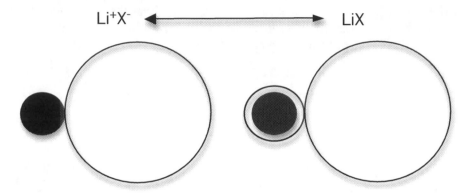

It is not an example of ionic-covalent resonance, for the covalent component of ionic-covalent resonance is represented schematically as follows:

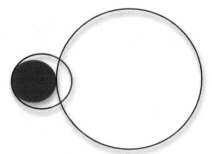

Charge-leakage from anion to cation yielding covalency wouldn't make the cation-anion distance longer. It would, if anything, shorten it.

The charge-leakage illustrated schematically immediately above does occur, however, in gaseous fluorides (Weinhold and Landis, *Valency and Bonding*, p49). But insofar as that covalency involves spin-paired electron density, it is impossible, owing to the Exclusion Principle, in the solid state, with multiple electron-pair donor ligands about cations.

The postulated charge-leakage in crystalline LiBr and LiX is analogous to the "inert pair" phenomenon of inorganic chemistry. In both instances a cation's formal charge decreases, its size increases, and bond lengths increase.

$Li^+X^-$/LiX resonance may be viewed as increasing bond lengths, and, accordingly, as increasing the ease of atomization, by way of pre-dissociation of an ionic compound to neutral atoms.

# Dimerization of (Hypothetical) Be$_2$

Beryllium atoms do not dimerize.

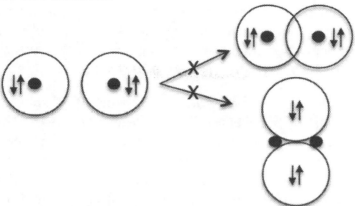

The upper structure on the right is forbidden by the Exclusion Principle. The lower structure (corresponding to a double bond: Be=Be) is unlikely, owing to its poor use of the low potential energy space for electrons about the backsides of the Be$^{+2}$ cores and to the high exposure of the electron pair domains, compared, in both instances, to the situation on the left for two s$^2$ beryllium atoms. To put it another way: the lower structure on the right has two powerful electrophilic sites and two powerful nucleophilic sites stereochemically poised to form by way of four electron pair donor-acceptor interactions four 3-center bonds of a tetramer, said by professor Joel Liebman (private communication) to be the first bound beryllium oligomer.

### Two Views of a Valence Sphere Model of Be$_4$

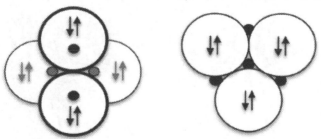

A beryllium core is surrounded in the model by the electron density of electron pairs in three of the four tetrahedral directions from the core. Addition to Be$_4$ of four molecules of dihydrogen,

one molecule of H$_2$ going to each exposed face of the model, yields, on alchemical transfer of a proton into each Be$^{+2}$ core, a valence sphere model of B$_4$H$_4$, isoelectronic with Be$_4\cdot$4H$_2$.

# Valence Sphere Model of $Be_4B_4H_8$

Useful theories account for known facts and predict new ones. One way to construct reasonable-looking valence sphere models that might correspond to unknown yet plausible molecular species begins with construction with spheres of deltahedra and concludes with capping their triangular faces. Inner spheres correspond to multicenter bonds, outer spheres to bonds to hydrogen; or to lone pairs.

The simplest example is a tetracapped tetrahedron of 8 spheres (16 valence shell electrons). It's a model of tetrahedral $C_4$ and isoelectronic $B_4H_4$. The next deltahedra, a trigonal bipyramid, hexacapped, is not a "reasonable-looking" model, inasmuch as its face-capping domains are too close to each other. An octacapped octahedron, however, is, "on the face of it", reasonable-looking. Its $6 + 8 = 14$ electron pairs (28 valence shell electrons) correspond, if all caps are bonds to hydrogen, to $28 - 8 = 20$ electrons per 8 heavy atoms or, on the average, to 2 1/2 valence shell electrons per heavy atom: say 4 Be atoms and 4 B atoms (arranged, for maximum symmetry, as two interpenetrating tetrahedra). For Octet-Rule-satisfying structures, heavy-atom/heavy-atom bonds are calculated to be 4-center bonds.

$$B_2 + 2 B_3 + 3 B_4 = 4N - V = 4 \times 8 - 14 = 18 \qquad B_1 = V - (B_2 + B_3 + B_4)$$
$$\phantom{B_2 + 2 B_3 + 3 B_4 = }0 \quad\; 0 \quad\; 6 \qquad\qquad\qquad\qquad\quad 8$$

Other B-values yield $(B_2 + B_3 + B_4) > 6$ and, consequently, $B_1 < 8$.

### *Two Views of an Equal-Sphere-Size Model of $Be_4B_4H_8$*

Face View

Corner View

From the corner view of the model of the octacapped octahedron one sees that it may be described as four close packed layers of spheres that consist, in planes parallel to the page, of 1, 6, 6, and 1 sphere(s), respectively, in a face-centered cubic ABCA stacking arrangement. The structure is expected to correspond to a local potential energy minimum in the configuration space of 4 beryllium atoms, 4 boron atoms, and 8 hydrogen atoms.

# Bond Diagrams for HBCBH

*A Bond Diagram That Satisfies the Valence Stroke Termination Rule
(No Formal Charges)
But Not the Octet Rule for the Boron Atoms*

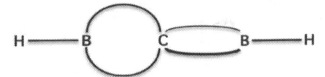

*Incipient Donor-Acceptor Interactions*

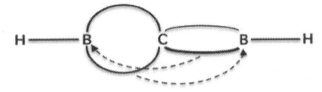

*Weak Donor-Acceptor Interactions*

For local electrical neutrality (zero formal charges) electrostatic bond strengths, indicated in four instances as 0.1 and 0.9, are 1.0 in the other instances.

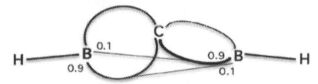

*Stronger Donor-Acceptor Interactions:
Formation of Two 3-Center BCB Bonds*

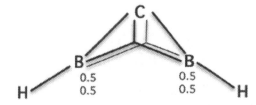

A donor-acceptor interaction in which the donor is an electron-pair of a 2-center bond becomes in the limiting case of increasing strength a 3-center bond.

Valence sphere models can be made for all of the valencer stroke diagrams pictured above, but not for all numerical solutions of HBCBH's Bond Number Equations.

## Solutions for Bond Number Equations for HBCBH

$$\sum(EPCN)_i - V = B_2 + 2B_3 \qquad\qquad B_1 = 6 - (B_2 + B_3)$$

*Bond Numbers for a Quartet of Pairs for C and Two Sextets for the B's*

$$\sum(EPCN)_i = 4 + 3 + 3 = 10$$

| $\sum(EPCN)_i - V$ | $B_2$ | $B_3$ | $B_1$ | |
|---|---|---|---|---|
| 4 | 4 | 0 | 2 | (1) |
| 4 | 2 | 1 | 3 | (2) |
| 4 | 0 | 2 | 4 | (3) |

*Bond Numbers for Three Quartets*

$$\sum(EPCN)_i = 3 \times 4 = 12$$

| | | | | |
|---|---|---|---|---|
| 6 | 6 | 0 | 0 | (4) |
| 6 | 4 | 1 | 1 | (5) |
| 6 | 2 | 2 | 2 | (6) |
| 6 | 0 | 3 | 3 | (7) |

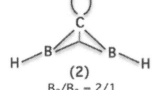

**(1)**
$B_2/B_3 = 4/0$

Excess Connectivity = $B_2 - 2 = 2$ = two double bonds or a double bond and a 3-member ring.

All four non-octet structures (1), (1'), (2), and (3), have valence sphere models. Electron clouds of (1') and (3) are isoelectronic with that of ethylene. Atomic cores are especially close to each other (2) and (3).

**(1')**
$B_2/B_3 = 4/0$

**(2)**
$B_2/B_3 = 2/1$

Light valence strokes in (2) and (3) repesent dative bonding, for zero formal charges.

**(3)**
$B_2/B_3 = 0/2$

**(4)**
$B_2/B_3 = 6/0$

**(5)**
$B_2/B_3 = 4/1$

**(6)**
$B_2/B_3 = 2/2$

In figures (4) and (5) the symbols "H" represent protonated C—B bonds; i.e., 3-center CHB bonds, counted as $B_2$-type bonds (i.e., as bonds between two heavy — nonhydrogen — atoms). For local electrical neutrality those bonds are dative bonds at their boron ends.

Of the Octet-Rule-satisfying structures (4), (5), and (6), only structure (6) has a satisfactory valence sphere model: a bicapped tetrahedron (isoelectronic with the model suggested for $C_3$), bond angle BCB = 109.5°; calculated by Weinhold: 104.2° (private communication).

# Multicenter Bonding in the Boron Hydrides

Consider a molecule that contains –

$V$ valence-shell electron pairs (= number of valence strokes in its bond diagram)
$N$ octet-rule-satisfying "heavy atoms": B, C, N, O, and/or F (= number of octets)
$B_1$ lone pairs and protonated lone pairs (= bonds to hydrogen)
$B_2$ 2-center bonds between octets, and protonated 2-center bonds
$B_3$ 3-center bonds between octets, and protonated 3-center bonds
$B_4$ 4-center bonds between octets, and protonated 4-center bonds

The total number of valence shell electron pairs, $V$, is given by the expressions

$$V = B_1 + B_2 + B_3 + B_4$$
$$= 4N - B_2 - 2B_3 - 3B_4$$

$4N$ is the sum of the number of electron pairs reported by $N_{octets}$ with, however, each pair in an n-center bond or protonated n-center bond reported n times instead of once, as for lone pairs and protonated lone pairs. Rearrangement yields

$$B_2 + 2B_3 + 3B_4 = 4N - V$$
$$B_1 + 2B_2 + 3B_3 + 4B_4 = 4N$$

For $B_3 = B_4 = 0$, the first relation reduces to $B_2 = 4N - V$.

Bonding in the boron hydrides is often specified by *styx* numbers.

$s$ = no. BHB bonds    $t$ = no. BBB bonds    $y$ = no. BB bonds    $x$ = no. BH$_2$ groups
$t = B_3$    $s+y = B_2$    $N_H$(no. H atoms)$-s = B_1$    $s+2x = N_H - N_{BH}$(no. H atoms in BH bonds)

Tabulated below are $B_n$-values and some corresponding *styx*-values for three boron hydrides.

| | N/V | 4N – V | = B$_2$ + 2B$_3$ | | = s | + y | + 2t | |
|---|---|---|---|---|---|---|---|---|
| B$_4$H$_{10}$ | 4/11 | 5 | 5 | 2x0 | 4 | 1 | 2x0 | = 5 |
| B$_5$H$_9$ | 5/12 | 8 | 6 | 2x1 | 4 | 2 | 2x1 | = 8 |
| B$_5$H$_{11}$ | 5/13 | 7 | 3 | 2x2 | 3 | 0 | 2x2 | = 7 |

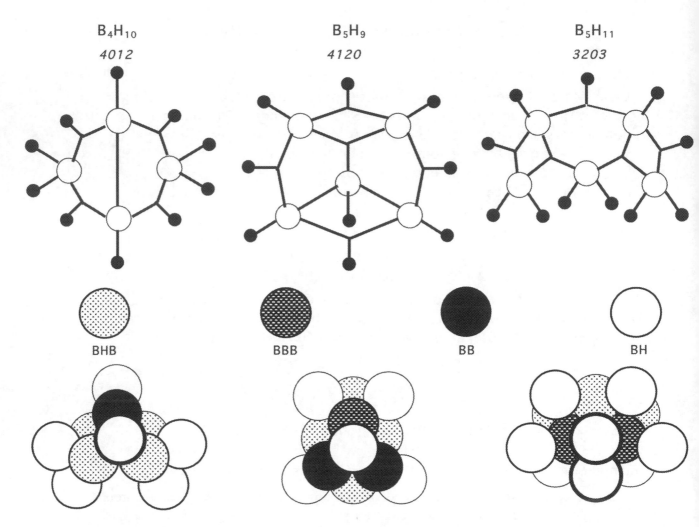

$B_4H_{10}$
*4012*

$B_5H_9$
*4120*

$B_5H_{11}$
*3203*

BHB    BBB    BB    BH

In the valence stroke diagrams (top row) large white circles represent boron atoms, smaller black circles hydrogen atoms. In the valence sphere models (bottom row) there are for $B_4H_{10}$ four tetrahedral interstices formed by the large domains and for $B_5H_9$ and $B_5H_{11}$ five tetrahedral interstices, occupied in each instance by boron $B^{+3}$ cores (not shown). Large white and lightly speckled domains are protonated. Only if they reside in the valence shell of the same atomic core are electron pair domains in contact with each other.

Occurrence of multicenter bonds is consistent with the view that compounds are ion compounds. Like conventional ions, anionic electron pairs may have more than the two coordinated cationic atomic cores of conventional 2-center bonds.

Valence strokes must be modified in going from 2- to 3-center bonds, and are seldom used for bonding of higher degrees of "centeredness". Valence spheres, however, handle bonding of any degrees of "centeredness".

# Bond Diagram for the Borane Carbonyl
## $B_2(CO)_2$

Every newly recognized molecule composed of the *p*-block's nonmetallic elements is a challenge for classical valence theory. Does the molecule have a conventional valence stroke diagram? One way to identify such diagrams for instances in which the molecule's elements, such as B, C, and O, are from the *p*-block's first row and, consequently, usually satisfy the Octet Rule, is to reduce the exercise to finding a bond diagram (or diagrams) for the corresponding isoelectronic hydrocarbon(s).

$B_2(CO)_2$, with 13 valence shell electron pairs, is, nominally, isoelectronic with $C_6H_2$. The only Octet-Rule-satisfying hydrocarbons that have only 2 hydrogen atoms are the acetylenes, $(C_2)_nH_2$. For n = 3, the bond diagram is -

$$H\!\!-\!\!\!-\!\!\!-\!\!C\equiv C\!\!-\!\!\!-\!\!\!-\!\!C\equiv C\!\!-\!\!\!-\!\!\!-\!\!C\equiv C\!\!-\!\!\!-\!\!\!-\!\!H$$

$C_6H_2$ has an excess connectivity, EC, of 6, in agreement with the usual calculation for a molecule that has 6 octets and 13 valence shell electron pairs:

$$EC = (4 \times 6 - 13) - (6 - 1) = 6$$

One step in passing alchemically from $C_6H_2$ to $B_2(CO)_2$ is transformation of the terminal C—H groups to terminal nitrogen atoms.

$$N\equiv C\!\!-\!\!\!-\!\!\!-\!\!C\equiv C\!\!-\!\!\!-\!\!\!-\!\!C\equiv N$$

Such species, $NC(C_2)_nCN$, have been observed in interstellar space.

Next, transform the terminal CN groups to isoelectronic BO entities, with, simultandously, transformation of a bonding pair into a dative bond (as the "lines of force" represented by the N—C valence strokes following the alchemically migrating protons into their new nuclear sites).

$$O\equiv B\!\!-\!\!\!-\!\!\!-\!\!C\equiv C\!\!-\!\!\!-\!\!\!-\!\!B\equiv O$$

Finally, transform in a similar manner the BC and CB entities into CB and BC entities, and dative bonds.

$$O\equiv C\!\!-\!\!B\equiv B\!\!-\!\!C\equiv O$$

"Combined matrix isolation infrared spectroscopy and quantum chemical computations [have] established $[B_2(CO)_2]$ to have a linear singlet ground state with some boron-boron triple bond character" (1).

Satisfied at each step of the alchemical transformation of linear $C_6H_2$ into linear $B_2(CO)_2$ is the Valence Stroke Termination Rule: that for bond diagrams of no formal charges in which "rabbit-ear" valence strokes represent lone pairs and dative bonds, *the number valence stroke terminations at the symbol of an atomic core is equal to that core's charge.*

(1)   Zhou, M; Tsumori, N.; Li, Z.; Fan, K.; Andrews, L.; Xu, Q. *J. Am. Chem. Soc.* 2002, *124*, 12936.

# Borazine

Ring bonds of borazine, $(BH)_3(NH)_3$, like those of isoelectronic benzene, are all the same length, yet, unlike benzene, the molecule itself is not significantly aromatic, Figure 1.

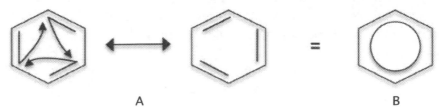

A                                                                 B

**Fig. 1. A:** Classical curly-arrow representation of the prototypical aromatic system. The three curly arrows function as a *unit* on covalent bonds. **B:** A shorthand representation of "aromaticity".

Use of scheme A for $(BH)_3(NH_3)$ yields the first column of Figure 2.

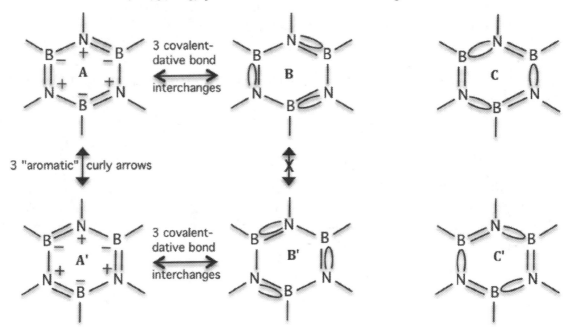

**Fig. 2.** Valence stroke diagrams for borazine. Local electrical neutrality is incomplete for structures A and A', as indicated by their formal charges (+ and -). Structures C and C' are presumably less stable than structures B and B', owing to "resonance" of the type –

for B and B' but not for C and C'.

Not possible for structure B and B', however, is simple, 3-curly-arrow resonance of the type depicted for aromaticity in Figure 1A. The route to B' from B is via the high-energy structures A and A': B → A → A' → B'. Inappropriate for borazine, accordingly, is the aromatic sextet notation of Figure 1B.

# Local Orbital Models of the Δ-hedral *Closo*-Boranes $B_nH_n^{-2}$
## (n = 6-12)

The boron atoms of the *closo*-boranes $B_nH_n^{-2}$ are arranged at the vertices of polyhedra that have exclusively *triangular faces* (hence their name: "delta-hedra"), suggestive of the occurrence of localized 3-center BBB bonds.

**Δ-hedra.** For *n* = 6 and 12, the nuclei of the boron atoms occupy the vertices of an octahedron and an icosahedron with, respectively, 8 and 20 triangular faces.

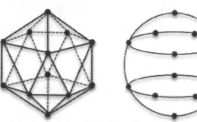

$B_6H_6^{-2}$                                $B_{12}H_{12}^{-2}$

A Bicapped Square              A Bicapped Pentagonal Antiprism

Each boron atom contributes one electron to an outward-pointing boron-hydrogen bond and, consequently, two electrons, or one electron pair, to the boron framework.

Since each triangular face has 3 edges and each edge is shared by two faces, the total number of edges, E, of a Δ-hedra of F faces is 3F/2. By Euler's Theorem, E = F + C(number of corners or vertices, *n*) – 2. Consequently F = 2*n* – 4. For *n* > 4, F > n.

| *n*: | 4 | 5 | 6 | 7 | 8 | 9 | 10 | 11 | 12 |
|------|---|---|---|---|---|---|----|----|----|
| F:   | 4 | 6 | 8 | 10 | 12 | 14 | 16 | 18 | 20 |

*The closo-boranes have more locations for 2e/3c BBB bonds than they have framework electron pairs.* Equal occupancy of all F framework 3-center bonding sites by *n* localized electron pairs of $B_nH_n^{-2}$ can occur by way of *resonance* among various valence bond structures in which each framework bonding site corresponds to the fraction *n*/F of an electron pair: 6/8 for $B_6H_6^{-2}$, 12/20 for $B_{12}H_{12}^{-2}$.

**Implications of the Octet Rule.** The Octet-Rule expressions

$$B_2 + 2B_3 = 4N - V \quad \text{and} \quad B_H = V - (B_2 + B_3)$$

where:    $B_{2 \text{ or } 3}$ = number of 2- or 3-center bonds
$B_H$ = number of B—H bonds = *n*
N = number of octets = number of boron atoms = *n*
V = number of valence shell electron pairs = 2*n* for $B_nH_n$
= 2*n* +1 for $B_nH_n^{-2}$

yield these results:

|          | $B_2$ | $B_3$ |
|----------|-------|-------|
| $B_nH_n$ | 0 | *n* |
| $B_nH_n^{-2}$ | 3 | *n* - 2 |

**2-Electron/*n*-Center Models.** The closed cage *closo*-boranes $B_nH_n^{-2}$ have the distinctive property that the main lobes of their B—H antibonding orbitals, off the least electronegative, boron ends of their B—H bonds, point exactly (for $n = 6$, 7, and 12) or, in some instances, approximately (for $n = 8 - 11$) toward their polyhedra's centers.

> Alternatively, conceptual molecular orbital theory describes those interior lobes as inward-pointing s-$p_z$ hybrids (companions to outward-pointing s+$p_z$ hybrids of B—H bonds) and forms from their sums low-lying 2-electron/*n*-center molecular orbitals, $a_{1g}$.

Location of an electron pair within a $B_nH_n^{-2}$'s polyhedron that contains $n$ 3-center bonds yields an alternative to the $B_2/B_3 = 3/(n-2)$ arrangements of framework electron pairs, namely $B_2/B_3 = 0/n,1$ (for the central electron pair in its *n*-center orbital).

**Hybrids of Hybrids.** The two types of arrangements of *closo*-boranes' framework electron pairs, $B_2/B_3 = 3/n-2$ and $B_2/B_3 = 0/n,1$ are each resonance hybrids. The species themselves are, accordingly, resonance hybrids of resonance hybrids.

*Resonance Hybrid Model of $B_nH_n^{-2}$*

$3/n\text{-}2 \longleftrightarrow 0/n,1$

**$B_6H_6^{-2}$.** Pictured below are valence stroke diagrams and a valence sphere model of a resonance hybrid of $B_6H_6^{-2}$.

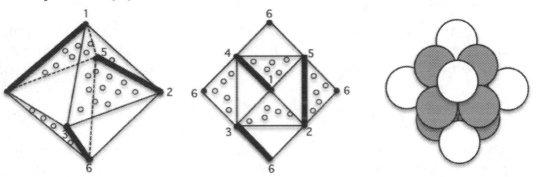

Left: Perspective view of one arrangement of bonds for an Octet-Rule-satisfying $B_2/B_3 = 3/n\text{-}2(=4)$ structure of $B_6H_6^{-2}$. Middle: Exploded view of the octahedron to its left. Right: Electron domain model of the ion's 0/*n* structure. White domains represent B—H bonds, gray domains eight possible sites of 3-center BBB bonds, occupied by the ion's six framework electron pairs through resonance. Each gray domain represents, accordingly, 6/8ths = 0.75 of an electron pair.

One sees at the right that an octahedron and a cube are each others' duals. The octahedron's faces (occupied by the gray spheres) correspond to the cube's corners. The cube's faces (occupied by the white spheres) correspond to the octahedron's corners.

**$B_nH_n$?** The resonance hybrid model of the closo-boranes $B_nH_n^{-2}$ offers an explanation for why the corresponding hydrides $B_nH_n$ do not exist. Protonation of BB and/or BBB bonds of $B_nH_n^{-2}$ would lock the species' boron framework into a single electron pair arrangement, thereby causing it to lose its resonance energy stabilization.

**CaB$_6$.** In crystaline CaB$_6$, 2-center BB bonds (the black domains in the two figures below) replace the 2-center BH bonds of B$_6$H$_6^{-2}$.

 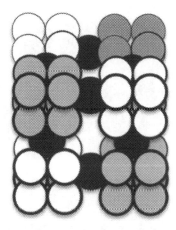

Two views of a valence sphere representation of a unit cell of CaB$_6$. Left: view off a corner. Right: view off an edge and a face. Black spheres: 2-center BB bonds (corresponding to the B—H bonds of B$_6$H$_6^{-2}$). Other spheres: domains of 3-center BBB bonds (as in B$_6$H$_6^{-2}$), white or gray, to indicate alternate B$_6$ octahdra. Each white or gray sphere represents, by way of resonance, 6/8ths of an electron pair. Within each B$_6$ octahedron is an electron pair domain of a 6-center BBBBBB bond (not shown), in the B$_2$/B$_3$ = 0/$n$ (= 6),1 arrangement of electron domains of the boron octahedral resonance hybrids. CaB$_6$'s calcium ion Ca$^{+2}$ (also not shown) resides within the large central cavity in contact with eight domains of eight B$_6$ polyhedra.

In the formulation above, CaB$_6$ has several kinds of bonds:

- 2e/2c covalent BB bonds between B$_6$ polyhedra

- 2e/2c covalent BB bonds of 3/4 resonance hybrids

- 2e/3c covalent BBB bonds of 3/4 resonance hybrids

- 2e/3c covalent BBB bonds of 0/6 resonance hybrids

- ionic bonding between Ca$^{+2}$ and eight domains of eight surrounding B$_6$ polyhedra

Boron atoms in the ionic formulation Ca$^{+2}$B$_6^{-2}$ have formal charges of -1/3; or, again, on adding up contributions from their atomic cores (+3) and contributions from four (2 x 6/8)e/3c bonds, one 2e/6c bond, and one 2e/2c bond, formal charges of -

$$+3 - [\{(2 \times 6/8) \times 1/3 \times 4\} + 2 \times 1/6 + 1] = -1/3$$

**$B_7H_7^{-2}$.** Pentagonal bipyramidal $B_7H_7^{-2}$ has two sets of BH groups: five equatorial and two polar (of which only one is shown in the valence sphere model pictured below).

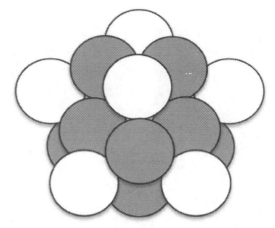

Electron domain model of $B_7H_7^{-2}$'s $0/n,1$ structure. White domains represent B—H bonds, gray domains ten possible sites of 3-center BBB bonds, occupied by the ion's seven framework electron pairs through resonance. Each gray domain represents, accordingly, 7/10ths = 0.70 of an electron pair.

One sees that a pentagonal bipyramid and a pentagonal prism are each others' duals. Each one has 15 edges (= 7 + 10 - 2).

In the figure above the number of electron pair domains in the valence shells of the boron cores (not shown) is five for the equatorial cores and six for the polar cores. In accordance with the Octet Rule, however, only four domains are occupied at any instant. Resonance among such structures yields occupancy of all five or six domains.

Taking, at the outset, formal charges of the hydrogen atoms to be zero, and assuming that all of the boron framework domains are equally occupied, one calculates for the boron atoms the following formal charges:

Equatorial: $+3 - [(2 \times 7/10 \times 4 \times 1/3) + 1 + 2/7] = -0.154$

Polar: $\quad +3 - [(2 \times 7/10 \times 5 \times 1/3) + 1 + 2/7] = -0.620$

As a check: $5(-0.154) + 2(-0.620) = -2.0$

A majority of the cited formal charges should probably be assigned to the hydrogen atoms, usually considered to be slightly more electronegative than boron atoms. One anticipates, accordingly, that the polar hydrogen atoms are more hydridic than the equatorial hydrogen atoms.

Although in the presence of water the *closo*-boranes are thermodynamically unstable with respect to formation of hydrogen and boric acid, via protonation of hydridic B—H bonds and backside attack on B—H bonds by water molecules' nucleophilic lone pairs, the *closo*-boranes are extremely stable toward nucleophiles, owing to the hydridic character of their B—H bonds and to the inaccessibility of the B—H bonds' backsides.

$B_{12}H_{12}^{-2}$. A local orbital model of the highest *closo*-borane has many resonance structures, for both its 0/12,1 structure type and its 3/10 structure type, one of which is pictured below.

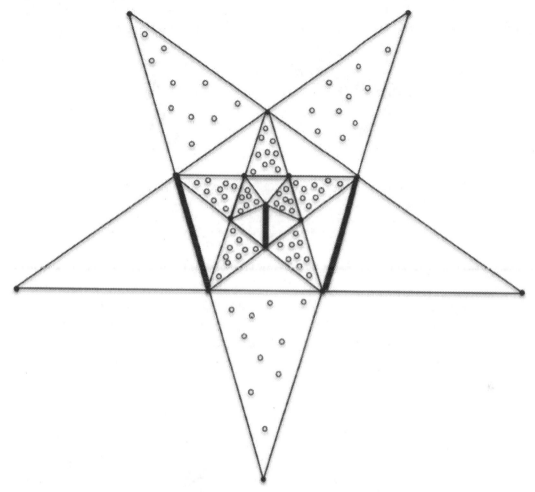

An exploded top view of an icosahedron: 12 vertices, 20 faces. It may be viewed as a pentagonal antiprism of ten vertices (those of the inner and outer pentagons) whose two pentagonal faces are capped (by the innermost vertex and the "exploded one, repeated five times (at the outer vertices of the large star). Thick lines represent a 3/n-2 structure's three 2-center bonds, filled faces its ten 3-center bonds. Shown associated with each vertex are three electron pairs: either a 2-center bond and two 3-center bonds or three 3-center bonds. Completing each $B^{+3}$ octet is a B—H pair (not shown). Formal charges are, at any instant, -1/3 for the six atoms involved in single bonds, 0 for the other six atoms.

Weinhold and Landis report (*Valency and Bonding*, Oxford, 2005, pp340-341) that "by any criterion of delocalization density or number of contributing resonance structures, $B_{12}H_{12}^{-2}$ exhibits a more impressive degree of electronic delocalization than benzene and other 'aromatic' prototypes of organic chemistry."

**Δ-hedral Bipyramids and Their Dual Prisms.** For $n = 6$ and 7, the boron cores of the *closo*-boranes $B_nH_n^{-2}$ are located at the vertices of square and pentagonal Δ-hedral bipyramids, respectively, with their 3-center bonding sites located at the vertices of the bipyramids' dual square and pentagonal prisms. The simplest instance of such structures is the case $n = 5$: a trigonal bipyramid and its dual the trigonal prism.

Two Views of the Trigonal-Bipyramid/Trigonal-Prism Duals. The bipyramid's vertices (white spheres) lie off the the faces of the prism (gray spheres), and vice-versa. The figures contain 11 spheres, the number of valence shell electron pairs of $B_5H_5^{-2}$.

$B_5H_5^{-2}$? Pictured immediately above is an electron domain model of hypothetical $B_5H_5^{-2}$. It is not, however, a satisfactory structure, for all six of its framework bonding domains are fully occupied by electron pairs: five from the boron atoms, plus an additional pair for the ion's net charge of -2, since there is not sufficient room for an electron pair in an interior 5-center BBBBB bond. Placed about the equatorial boron cores are, accordingly, five electron pairs. The Octet Rule is not satisfied for three of the ion's five boron atoms.

$B_4H_4^{-2}$? The tetrahedron is Nature's simplest Δ-hedron. It's its own dual: $F = C = 4$.

Two views of a tetracapped tetrahedron. An electron domain model of hypothetical $B_4H_4$.

A tetracapped tetrahedron has 8 electron pair domains. $B_4H_4^{-2}$ has, however, 9 valence shell electron pairs: 4 for four B—H bonds leaving $9 - 4 = 5$ for the boron framework. The number of framework electron pairs is *greater* than the number of 3-center sites. Where, then, might the 9th pair go? A $B_2/B_3 = 0/4,1$ arrangement is impossible, since the central tetrahedral cavity is too small for the domain of a 4-center BBBB bond. And a $B_2/B_3 = 3/n\text{-}2\text{=}2$ arrangement based on a tetrahedral arrangement of framework bonds is likewise impossible, as the following figure shows.

172

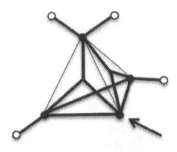

An Octet-Rule-satisfying valence stroke diagram for hypothetical $B_4H_4^{-2}$. The bond diagram has the required 9 valence strokes (3 for 2-center BB bonds, 2 for 3-center BBB bonds, and 4 for B—H bonds). As required by the Octet Rule, it has 4 valence stroke terminations at the site of each $B^{+3}$ core. The arrow points, however, to a non-tetrahedral arrangement of electron pair domains about the site of the $B^{+3}$ core at the lower right.

Construction of a satisfactory valence sphere model of $B_4H_4^{-2}$ *based solely on 2- and 3-center bonds* appears to be impossible. However, the usual Octet-Rule relations

$$B_2 + 2\,B_3 + 3\,B_4 = 4N - V = 4\text{x}4 - 9 = 7 \quad \text{and} \quad B_H = V - (B_2 + B_3 + B_4)$$

with $B_4 = 1$, $B_2 = 4$, $B_3 = 0$, and, consequently, $B_H = 4$ yield the following non-*closo* bond diagram and molecular model for $B_4H_4^{-2}$.

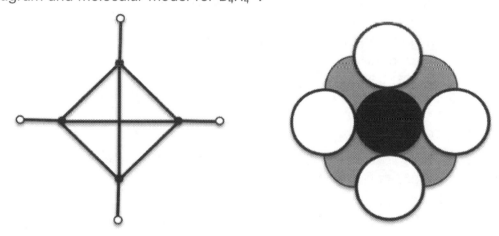

Left: 9-stroke valence stroke diagram for $B_4H_4^{-2}$ featuring 4 2-center BB bonds and 1 central 4-center BBBB bond. Boron formal charges are $+3 - (3 \times 1 + 2 \times 1/4) = -1/2$. Right: Top view of a 9-sphere tetracapped square pyramid electron domain model for $B_4H_4^{-2}$. Gray: domains of 2-center BB bonds. Black: domain of the central 4-center BBBB bond. White: domains of 2-center BH bonds. Boron $B^{+3}$ cores are in a square planar arrangement. Hydrogen $H^+$ cores lie in a second, larger square planar arrangement slightly above the plane of the boron cores. Removal of the three northeast domains (two white, one gray) leaves six electron pair domains arranged as in the electron domain model of ethylene.

The hypothetical $B_4H_4^{-2}$ molecule has a reasonable valence sphere model that is expected to correspond to a potential energy minimum in the configuration space of four boron atoms, 4 hydrogen atoms, and two additional electrons.

**B$_4$H$_4$ and B$_4$Cl$_4$.** B$_4$H$_4$, like B$_4$H$_4^{-2}$, has what appears to be, at first sight, a reasonable electron domain model, but not (yet) a reported existence. Its chloro-derivative, B$_4$Cl$_4$, does, however, exist. A valence sphere model for it suggests a reason why its existence is more likely than the existence of B$_4$H$_4$.

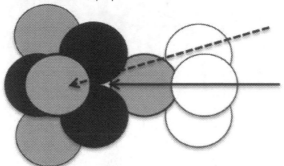

VSM for B$_4$Cl$_4$. Black: electron pair domain of a 3-center BBB bond. Gray: domain of a 2-center B—Cl bond. White: domain of a chlorine lone pair. Shown are the lone pairs for only one of the four chlorine atoms.

In B$_4$Cl$_4$, with its four mutually tangent 3-center bonds, locations of chlorine atoms' nucleophilic lone pairs with respect to electrophilic sites is unique. B$_4$Cl$_4$'s geometry places near the usual internal pocket across a single bond (indicated by the solid arrow above) a second electrophilic pocket (indicated by the dashed arrow). *B$_4$Cl$_4$ has twelve energy-lowering donor-acceptor pair-pocket interactions absent in B$_4$H$_4$.* Stability of BF$_3$ (owing to multiple-bond character of its BF bonds) works against existence of B$_4$F$_4$.

**Summary.** The previous discussion brings forward –

- Valence bond diagrams and valence sphere models for the *closo*-boranes, B$_n$H$_n^{-2}$, $n = 6 - 12$, based on resonance among B$_2$/B$_3$ = 0/$n$,1 and 3/$n$-2 structures.

- A mathematical proof, based on the Octet Rule and geometrical properties of delta-hedra, for why for one set of resonance structures B$_2$ = 3 and B$_3$ = $n - 2$.

- Reasons for the non-existence of:

  - B$_n$H$_n^{-2}$ closo-boranes for n = 4 and 5.

  - The protonated species B$_n$H$_n$, $n = 6 - 12$.

- Reasons for the existence of:

  - Non-*closo* B$_4$H$_4^{-2}$, with no 3-center bonds and one 4-center BBBB bond.

  - B$_4$Cl$_4$, in the absence of the existence of B$_4$H$_4$.

Those results are significant for Valence Bond Theory, in that the electronic structures of the *closo*-boranes usually have been considered to be the exclusive province of Molecular Orbital Theory.

# Why Does $B_4Cl_4$ Exist but Not $B_4H_4$?

The only Octet-Rule-satisfying valence stroke diagram for $B_4H_4$ that corresponds to a satisfactory valence sphere model is the structure $B_2B_3B_4$; $B_1$,BHB = 040; 4,0, Figure 1.

**Fig. 1.** Valence sphere model for $B_4H_4$'s structure 040; 4,0. White domains represent 2-center B—H bonds, gray domains 3-center BBB bonds. All four tetrahedral interstices are occupied, by $B^{+3}$ cores (not shown); and each of the four white domains (of which three are shown) contains a proton (also not shown).

There is, as mentioned, a leading problem for Figure 1. *The corresponding molecule does not exist* —although, to repeat, its chloro-derivative does, Figure 2.

**Fig. 2.** Equal-sphere-size model of $B_4Cl_4$. Dark gray spheres represent 3-center BBB domains, light gray B—Cl domains, white Cl lone pairs. Boron $B^{+3}$ and chlorine $Cl^{+7}$ atomic cores (not shown) reside in the eight tetrahedral interstices (of which locations for six are shown).

The Valence Sphere Models of Figures 1 and 2 suggest yet another reason for the existence of $B_4Cl_4$ and the nonexistence of $B_4H_4$.

**Special Features of $B_4X_4$ Structures.** The boron skeletons of valence sphere models of $B_4H_4$ and $B_4Cl_4$ are unusual. Mutual adjacency of the mutually repelling $B^{+3}$ cores calls to mind a valence sphere model of a *triple bond*. From the point of view of core-core repulsions, the $B_4$ tetrahedra of equal-sphere-size models of $B_4H_4$ and $B_4Cl_4$ are *highly strained* — six times (once for each edge of the inner tetrahedron of 3-center domains). The boron cores are, in fact, some 16 percent closer to each other than they would be if they were sharing faces of triple bonds of equal-sphere-size models. Their arrangement greatly exaggerates the unrealistic bond shortenings that occur — when all domains are the same size — in going from single bonds to triple bonds, Figure 3.

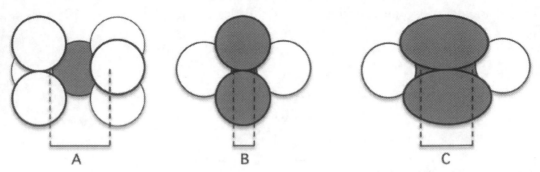

**Fig. 3.** Changes in models' bond lengths on passing from single to triple bonds. **A** and **B**: equal-sphere-size models. **C**: stretched triple bond domains, owing to core-core repulsion.

With a cue from Figure 3C, Figure 4 below may be more realistic than Figure 2, if still a highly schematic model of $B_4Cl_4$.

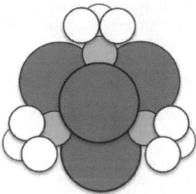

**Fig. 4.** Valence Sphere Model of $B_4Cl_4$. Large spheres: stretched domains of BBB 3-center bonds. Smaller gray spheres: domains of B—Cl bonds. White spheres: domains of Cl lone pairs.

Figure 4 suggests why $B_4Cl_4$ exists and $B_4H_4$ does not. Chlorine can expand its octet (in a physical sense), thereby stabilizing, by electron pair donor-acceptor interactions, $B_4Cl_4$'s stretched 3-center BBB domains.

In summary, $B_4Cl_4$ exists but not $B_4H_4$ for perhaps these reasons:

- Destabilizing, core-core repulsions, owing to unusual, triple-bond-like orientations of $B^{+3}$ cores, present in both compounds, but not compensated for in $B_4H_4$ as they may be (see following remarks) in $B_4Cl_4$.
- Lone-pair/antibonding energy-lowering interactions in $B_4Cl_4$ but not in $B_4H_4$.
- BBB/vacant-Cl-d-orbital energy-lowering interactions in $B_4Cl_4$ but not in $B_4H_4$.

This essay brings forward the idea that synergistic electron pair interactions, forward from boron BBB bonds to Cl 3d space and backward from Cl lone pairs to boron antibonding orbitals, stabilize $B_4Cl_4$.

# Bis(triphenylphosphoranylidene)methane
## Bent $Ph_3P=C=PPh_3$

"The curious yellow compound $Ph_3=C=Ph_3$ should be noted: unlike allene, $H_2C=C=CH_2$, which has a linear [geometry about the] central carbon atom, the molecules are bent and the structure is unique in having 2 crystallographically independent molecules in the unit cell which have substantially different bond angles, 130.1° and 143.8°. The short P=C distances (163 pm compared with 183.5 pm for P—C(Ph)) suggest double bonding, but the nonlinear P=C=P unit and especially the two values of the bond angle, are hard to rationalize."

Greenwood and Earnshaw, *Chemistry of the Elements*, 1984, p636.

Added Note: The difference (183.5 – 163) pm = 20.5 pm is almost exactly the difference between CC single and double bonds: (154 – 134) pm = 20 pm.

The title molecule may be thought of as composed of 2 $Ph_3P$: molecules and a carbon atom.

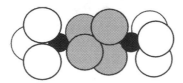

The chief difference between the molecule's valence-sphere model in the neighborhood of its central carbon core and that of allene lies in the *large size of $P^{+5}$* (Pauling radius 34 pm), over half the size of the domain of a valence sphere model's carbon-carbon single bond (66 pm)! *A linear molecule at carbon uses inefficiently the low potential energy space for electrons about $P^{+5}$.*

Shown are two $P^{+5}$ cores (black) coordinated off opposite edges of a polyhedron of four electron-pair domains (gray) about $C^{+4}$ (not shown) of the central carbon atom. Domains of P—C(Ph) bonds (white) are crowded together to exhibit the total amount of nominally "empty space" about a $P^{+5}$ core when it coordinates 5 electron-pair domains all of which are shared with $C^{+4}$ cores (two with the central carbon atom and three with the three carbon cores of the three single (white) P—C bonds).

The $P^{+5}$ cores become coordinatively saturated, in the model, if they are located off the faces, rather than the edges, of the tetrahedron of electron-pairs about the central $C^{+4}$ core.

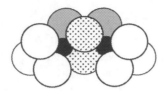

Shown is a valence sphere model with six electron-pair domains in the valence-shell of each $P^{+5}$ core. Speckled domains represent 3-center PCP bonds, gray domains bent PC bonds, white domains straight P—C(Ph) bonds. The model, as it stands, yields a PCP bond angle of $109.5^{\circ}$. Severe steric crowding of ortho C—H domains of the phenyl groups bonded to the $P^{+5}$ cores by the two bottom domains would open up the PCP angle, toward $130^{\circ}$.

A hybrid model with one $P^{+5}$ core coordinated off a face of $C^{+4}$'s tetrahedron (second figure above) and one off an opposite edge (first figure), plus its mirror image, to make, by resonance, both PC bonds equivalent to each other, yields a PCP bond angle of $144.7^{\circ}$, compared to an observed angle of $143.8^{\circ}$.

From the point of view of valence sphere models of molecules, the structure of the title compound illustrates an important point. Size matters! — not in drawing valence stroke diagrams of molecules, or in constructing valence stick models of them, but very much so in constructing space-filling valence sphere models of molecules.

Cations of different sizes, together with anions of different sizes, have long been used, of course, to rationalize structures and internuclear distances of ionic compounds. Yet even after G. N. Lewis introduced, nearly a century ago, his electron-pair/atomic-core interpretation of organic chemists' valence stroke diagrams, chemists generally have not viewed covalent compounds as "ion compounds", although once that is done, analogies between the principles of organic and inorganic structural chemistry spring to view immediately.

The chief impediment to development of a treatment of the electronic structures of organic and inorganic compounds in which all compounds are viewed as "coordination compounds", of anions by cations (usually large atomic cores) and electride ions by atomic cores (usually small cations) seems to have been the belief that "covalent bonding", in being "directional", is different than "ionic bonding", widely deemed to be "nondirectional".

Sometimes models influence thought more than we may realize. Skinny, one-dimensional valence sticks of a valence-stick model of methane indicate distant-independent relationships among four valence sticks with their specified angular dispositions, whereas corresponding space-filling, three-dimensional valence spheres of a valence-sphere model of methane specify less obviously a distance-independent angular relationship among the four valence spheres with respect to each other. It's the difference between pointing with a stick and pointing with a sphere, whose diameter from where the sphere touches the pointer corresponds to the stick. Four close-packed spheres' diameters that point toward the spheres' interstice correspond to the four tetrahedral directions of "covalent" bonding.

# Bond Angles and Bond Lengths in NH$_n$ Species, n = 1, 2, and 3

From the point of view of Conceptual Valence Bond Theory, NH$_2$'s bond angle of 103.3° is, at first sight, puzzling. Its 4 valence shell electrons of one spin favor an angle of approximately 109.5°. Its 3 electrons of the other spin favor an angle of approximately 120°. The weighted average is 114°.

$$(4 \times 109.5° + 3 \times 120°)/7 = 114°$$

Allowing for the s-character-preempting character of unshared electrons and reducing, accordingly, the models' bond angles from, say, 109.5° to 107° and from 120° to 116° only reduces the calculated 114° HNH bond angle of the superposition to 110.9°. Some other effect, it seems, is operative. With Conceptual Valence Bond Theory's "Secondary Principles" in mind, examination of the valence stroke diagram for the superposition model suggests what that effect might be.

*Electron-electron repulsion between unshared electrons of opposite spin is minimized by assigning all of nitrogen's s-character of its 4-membered spin set to its unshared electrons, in sp (rather than sp$^3$) orbitals.* That assignment places the spin-set's bonding electrons in pure p orbitals. The calculated HNH bond angle is now 102.9°.

$$(4 \times 90° + 3 \times 120°)/7 = 102.9°$$

(Observed: 103.3°)

In the present model of NH$_2$'s bent ground state, the average s-character of the nitrogen hybrid orbital of an N—H bond is nominally (0% + 33%)/2 = 16.5%. Its length is 102.4 pm. The corresponding values for NH$_3$ are 24.5% and 101.4 pm. An increase of ≈ 8% in s-character appears to correspond in the nitrogen-hydrogen system to a bond length decrease of ≈1.0 pm.

NH$_2$ has a linear excited state, d(N—H) = 98 pm. That decrease in bond length from NH$_3$ of (101.4 – 98) pm ≈ 3 pm corresponds, by the calculation of the previous paragraph, to a increase in s-character of ≈ 8%/pm x 3 pm ≈ 24%, corresponding to a nitrogen hybrid orbital whose s-character is ≈ 24.5% + 24% ≈ 48.$_5$% ≈ 50%. The molecule's two shared pairs are, as expected, from the molecule's geometry, in essentially sp orbitals with the molecule's three unshared electrons in, accordingly, essentially pure p orbitals.

NH's bond length of 103.8 pm, compared with that of ammonia, 101.4 pm, implies, by the same proportionality, that the percent s-character in the nitrogen hybrid orbital of NH's bond is ≈ 24.5% – 8%/pm x (103.8 – 101.4) pm ≈ 5.2%, for 2 bonding electrons competing for s-character against 4 unshared electrons, compared to the case for NH$_2$ of 16.5% for 4 bonding electrons competing against only 3 unshared electrons, where, accordingly, 5.2% x 4/2 x 4/3 = 14% ≈ 16.5%. Cited below are -

### Bond Angles, Lengths, and Approximate s-Character for NH$_n$ Species

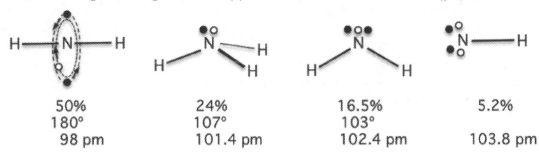

| 50% | 24% | 16.5% | 5.2% |
|-----|-----|-------|------|
| 180° | 107° | 103° | |
| 98 pm | 101.4 pm | 102.4 pm | 103.8 pm |

As expected, as nitrogen-orbital s-character decreases, bond angle decreases and bond length increases, by about 1 pm per 8% change in s-character.

$$\Delta(\% \text{ s-character})/\Delta(\text{bond length})$$

(50–24)/(101.4–98) = 7.6    (24–16.5)/102.4–101.4) = 7.5    (16.5–5.2)/(103.8–102.4) = 8.1

The Newtonian "Synthesis" of this essay consists, in summary, of -
- A splayed-bond/maximally-anticoincident-unshared-electrons model of NH$_2$'s ground state.
- A model of NH$_2$'s linear excited state.
- A hybrid orbital model of bond angles and bond lengths of NH$_n$ species.

# Ammonium Ion's Unusual Bond Lengths

Bent's Rule predicts that protonation of ammonia's lone pair should lead to a redistribution of atomic s-character, from nitrogen's lone pair orbital to its orbitals of its bonds to hydrogen, with, consequently, bond-shortening for those bonds of increased s-character. In fact, however, *on lone-pair protonation, ammonia's NH bonds become longer, not shorter, changing in length from 101.24 pm to 103.2 pm.*

Consideration of nuclear-nuclear repulsions yields the same contradiction. Introduction of a proton into ammonia's lone pair increases the Coulombic force acting on the nitrogen atomic core $N^{+5}$ directed directly away from the added proton. Relaxation of the $N^{+5}$ core toward, simultaneously, the other three protons opens up HNH angles, from 107° to the tetrahedral angle of 109.5°, as observed, but, as is not observed, shortens the original NH bonds. Thus the paradox: bond lengthening rather than an expected bond shortening. Conventional bond diagrams for $NH_3$ and $NH_4^+$ suggest a reason for that behavior.

A +1 formal charge on the electronegative nitrogen atom bonded to less electronegative hydrogen atoms is unrealistic. The ion's positive formal charge, suggest bond lengths, is shared largely by the hydrogen atoms, through dative bonding.

Formal charges on the partially dative-bonded hydrogen atoms are +1/4, for dative bond character of 1/4. In the dication of hydrazine, $H_2N—NH_2^{+2}$, corresponding hydrogen formal charges and dative bond character are +1/2; and bond length is 1.06 pm. Bond lengthening owing to dative bonding appears to be approximately proportional to fractional increases in dative bond character: i.e., a 2 pm increase in bond length for an initial increase of 1/4 in dative bond character; and $\approx$ 2.8 pm bond-length increase for a further increase of 1/4 in dative bond character.

Bond lengths for the corresponding nitrogen-fluorine species, for which dative bonding is not expected,

obey Bent's Rule.

# Bond Diagrams for Nitric Oxide

Figure 1 shows a commonly seen bond diagram for nitric oxide.

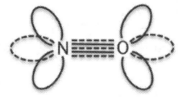

**Fig. 1.** Conventional bond diagram for nitric oxide.

Formal charges for the N and O atoms are zero, in accordance with the molecule's small dipole moment, 0.153 D. The diagram is, however, unsatisfactory in three respects. (1) The molecule's bond length lies between that of a double and a triple nitrogen-oxygen bond.

|              | HNO     | NO        | NO$^+$  |
|--------------|---------|-----------|---------|
|              | 1.212 Å | 1.150 Å   | 1.062 Å |
| Bond Order:  | 2.0     | ($\approx$ 2.5?) | 3.0     |

(2) All of the molecule's net spin density does not reside on the nitrogen atom. And (3) the nitrogen N$^{+5}$ core is, with respect to one spin-set, *coordinatively unsaturated, yet adjacent to unshared electrons!*, Figure 2 below, first figure.

**Fig. 2. Left:** Usual Lewis electron dot diagrams for NO. The small curly arrow indicates a donor-acceptor interaction that completes the nitrogen atom's valence shell with respect to the black spin-set. **Center:** Each atomic core (indicated by the symbols "N" and "O", meaning N$^{+5}$ and O$^{+6}$) has in its valence shell four electrons of each spin; i.e., the Quartet Rule for electron pairs has been applied twice, once for each spin-set. **Right:** Schematic representation of the two spin-sets' stereochemistry: a triple-bond-like arrangement for the 5-member black spin set [number of electrons, V = 5, hence, number of electrons in the bonding region, B (= 4N – V) = 4x2 – 5 = 3); and a double-bond-like arrangement for the 6-member spin-set (B = 4x2 – 6 = 2).

Passage from the Lewis-like diagram of *zero-dimensional* dots of Figure 2 to a diagram of *one-dimensional* valence-strokes yields the bond diagram of Figure 3.

**Fig. 3.** Double-Quartet bond diagram for NO. Each valence stroke represents *one* valence shell electron. The number of valence-stroke terminations at the symbols "N" and "O", divided by 2, is 5 1/2, corresponding to unrealistic formal charges, for "N" and "O", of, respectively, -1/2 and +1/2. Those formal charges may be improved by indicating, diagrammatically, in one of two ways, that the five bonding electrons are polarized, somewhat, toward "O", Figure 4.

Etc.

**Fig. 4.** Valence stroke diagrams for polar covalent and partially dative bonding models of NO.

# Molecular Modeling of the Gas Phase Hydration of NO⁺ with Formation of HONO and H₃O⁺

A recent experimental and theoretical study on "How the Shape of an H-Bonded Network Controls Proton-Coupled Water Activation in HONO Formation" in the gas phase (*Science*, 15 Jan. 2010, VOL. 327, 308-312), reports detailed information regarding the reaction

$$NO^+ + 4\,H_2O = HONO + H_3O^+ \cdot 2H_2O$$

Presented is an opportunity to test the usefulness of valence-sphere models of molecules. Do their bumps-and-hollows' representation of species' frontier orbitals provide reasonable rationalizations of the reported information? The following discussion assumes no prior familiarity with valence sphere models of molecules.

The system's leading nucleophilic sites are the water molecules' lone pairs. Candidates for being considered electrophilic sites are the hydrogen-bonding sites off water molecules' O—H bonds and the pockets, hollows, or dimples associated with the nitrogen-oxygen triple bond of NO⁺ at its terminal atom that carries most of the species' positive charge.

*Valence-Stroke Diagram and Valence-Sphere Model of NO⁺*

**Left:** The N/O bond depicted as a triple bond with one-third dative bond character, which places the ion's positive charge on the N atom. **Right:** Gray circles represent the triple bond's electron-pair domains. N's lone-pair domain is slightly filled, for ease of identification in the following figures.

*Valence-Sphere Model of a Water Molecule*

White circles: lone-pair domains. Gray circles: domains of O—H bonding pairs. "+": proton of an H atom of an O—H bond.

## Interactions of the NO⁺/H₂O System's Frontier Orbitals

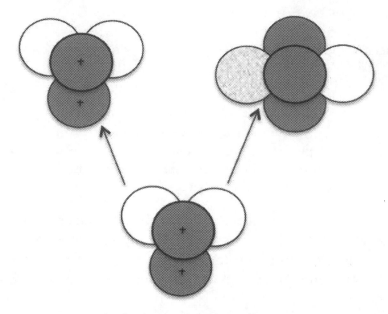

**Left Arrow:** Formation of a hydrogen bond. **Right Arrow:** Formation of a "pair-pocket" bond. The system's HOLMOs (Highest Occupied Localized Molecular Orbitals) are the water molecules' lone-pairs. Its LULMOs (Lowest Unoccupied Localized Molecular Orbitals) are the pockets formed by N's lone-pair and two domains of the NO⁺ triple bond.

## Two Views of the Valence-Sphere Model of the Monohydrate NO⁺·H₂O

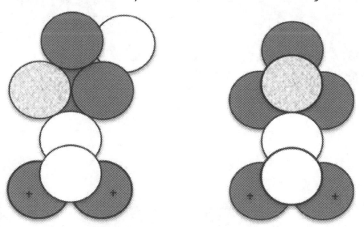

The NO⁺ ion on the right is viewed along its N—O axis. The water molecule is in an eclipsed configuration with respect to the three domains of the NO⁺ pocket. On the left it is in a staggered configuration. Presumably there's nearly free rotation about the donor-acceptor bond.

*Valence-Sphere Models of Two Isomers of the Dihydrate of NO⁺*

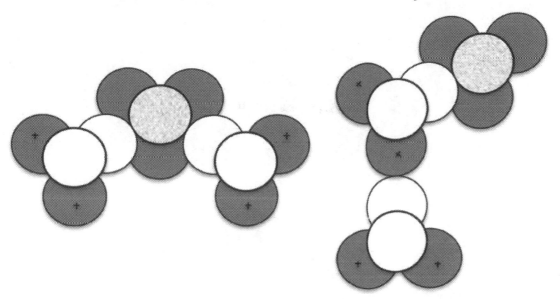

The reported structure of $NO^+ \cdot 2H_2O$, on the left, implies that the nitrosonium-ion/water-molecule pair-pocket bond is stronger than a hydrogen-bond between two water molecules. A third water molecule coordinated as on the left yields one of three reported isomeric structures for the trihydrate of $NO^+$.

*Valence-Sphere Model of NO⁺ Coordinating Three Water Molecules*

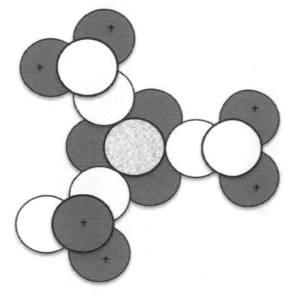

The other two isomers of $NO^+ \cdot 3H_2O$ contain hydrogen bonds and have consequently lower coordination numbers for $NO^+$: namely (see below), 2 and 1.

The three isomers are named, according to their nitrogen-atom coordination numbers, N3 (above), N2 (immediately below), and N1.

*Valence-Sphere Model of the N2 Isomer of the Trihydrate of NO⁺*

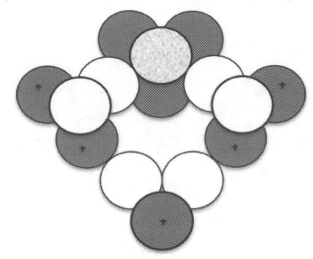

In this cyclic N2 isomer a three-molecule hydrogen-bonded "water wire" acts as a chelating agent toward NO⁺. The isomer contains four donor-acceptor interactions.

*Valence-Sphere Model of the N1 Isomer of the Trihydrate of NO⁺*

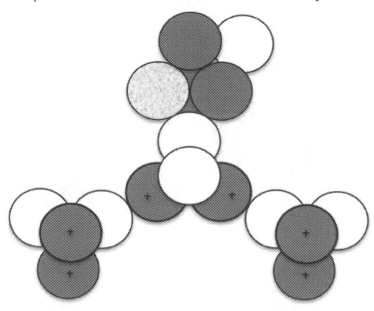

In this (inverted) Y-shaped N1 isomer of the trihydrate of NO⁺, the "water wire" is monodentate toward NO⁺. Like N3, this N1 isomer contains three intramolecular donor-acceptor interactions.

Cyclic N2 with four donor-acceptor interactions is calculated to have the lowest energy of the three isomers, by approximately 1.7 kcal/mole over the highest energy isomer, N1.

*Donor-Acceptor Interactions and Relative Energies of Isomers of NO⁺·3H₂O*

| Isomer Name | Relative E (1 lowest) | DA Interactions (Total Number) | Type of DA Interactions O···N | OH···O |
|---|---|---|---|---|
| N2 (cyclic) | 1 | 4 | 2 | 2 |
| N3 | 2 | 3 | 3 | 0 |
| N1 (Y-shaped) | 3 | 3 | 1 | 2 |

The two types of DA interactions are evidently of comparable strength. For if intermolecular interaction O···N were significantly stronger than OH···O, isomer N3 would have the least energy. And if the reverse were true, isomer N1 would lie lower in energy than N3. That N3 lies lower in energy than N1 implies that the O···N interaction is stronger than the OH···O interaction, as inferred near the outset from the structure of the dihydrate of NO⁺ (which has two N···O interactions, rather than one N···O interaction and one OH···O interaction).

Observed NO vibrational frequencies and calculated NO distances suggest that the isomer N1 is similar in structure to the immediate precursor of HONO and hydrated $H_3O^+$.

*Observed NO Frequencies and Calculated NO Distances for Isomers of NO⁺·3H₂O*

| Species | NO Frequency | r(NO) | r(ON···O) |
|---|---|---|---|
| NO⁺ | 2344 | 1.0619 | |
| N3 | 2312 | 1.075 | 2.421 |
| N2 | 2264 | 1.078 | 2.334 |
| N1 | 2055 | 1.093 | 1.987 |
| NO | 1876 | 1.150 | |
| HONO | | 1.173 | 1.441 |

In passing from NO⁺ (bond order 3) through its hydrates to HONO (terminal NO bond order 2, compared to 2.5 for NO), the NO frequency decreases; the NO bond length increases, from that of a nitrogen-oxygen triple bond, 1.062 Å, to that of a nitrogen-oxygen double bond in HONO, 1.173 Å; and the length of the initial nitrogen-oxygen donor-acceptor interaction, 2.421 Å, decreases to that of a nitrogen-oxygen single bond in HONO, 1.44 Å.

Completion of addition of water to NO⁺ with production of HONO requires, as indicated below, loss by one of the water molecules of a proton to another water molecule, yielding $H_3O^+$, stabilized if it is hydrogen-bonded to additional water molecules, over whose protons the species' positive charge can be delocalized.

## Schematic Valence-Stroke Diagram of a Mechanism for the Reaction

$$NO^+ + 4\,H_2O = HONO + H_3O^+ \cdot 2H_2O$$

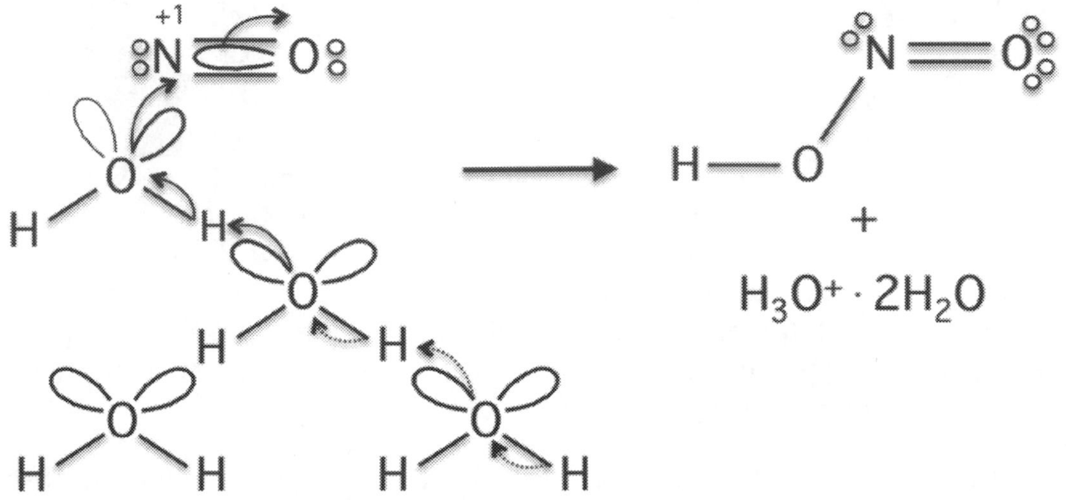

Curly arrows indicate migration of negative charge upward concomitant, accordingly, with migration downward of the positive charge on $NO^+$ to the underlying water molecules. Formed on transfer of the attacked proton (of the water molecule added to $NO^+$) to the adjacent hydrogen-bonded water molecule is a dihydrate of $H_3O^+$.

$H_3O^+ \cdot 2H_2O$ is the "water wire" of isomer N1, protonated. Dotted curly arrows, above, indicate the manner in which its positive charge is spread out over all seven of its hydrogen atoms through an "inductive effect" produced by superposition of resonance structures that involve dative bonds between hydrogen and oxygen.

Owing to hydrogen-bonding, the 3-molecule "water wire" is a better proton acceptor, particularly by its middle molecule, than is a single water molecule.

The following figure is another view of the reaction mechanism. The figure is isomorphic with the valence-stroke diagram. Each valence-stroke, straight or rabbit-ear, has been replaced, along with the lone-pairs shown as pairs of dots, by a valence-sphere. Not shown, as usual, are the relatively small heavy-atom cores, $N^{+5}$ and $O^{+6}$, which reside in the model's tetrahedral interstices. Electron-pair domains, represented by circles, do not touch each other unless they are part of the valence-shell of the same atomic core.

*Valence-Sphere Model of the Valence-Stroke Diagram*
*of a Mechanism for the Reaction*

$$NO^+ + 4\,H_2O = HONO + H_3O^+ \cdot 2H_2O$$

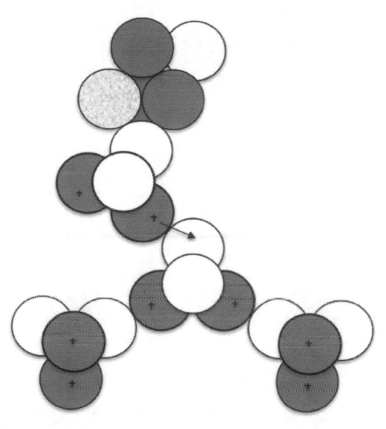

The five spheres at the top represent the NO⁺ ion. The three tetrahedrons at the bottom represent the "water wire" of isomer N1. Bridging those two moieties is a fourth water molecule.

The arrow indicates "the intracluster proton transfer at the heart of this process" — by which the nitrosonium ion and water yield nitrous acid and a hydrated proton.

The authors ask: What is the most likely path for formation of the tetrahydrate pictured above:

- Addition of a water molecule to isomer N1 by an insertion reaction?
- Addition of a 3-membered "water wire" to the monohydrate?
- Something else?

The classic answer from chemical kinetics is: Determine experimentally the dependence of rates of formation and disappearance of various species on concentrations of NO⁺ and H₂O. To determine energies of activation, repeat the rate measurements at different temperatures.

Pictured below are drawings of -

*Valence-Sphere Models of the Products of the $NO^+$/$H_2O$ Reaction*

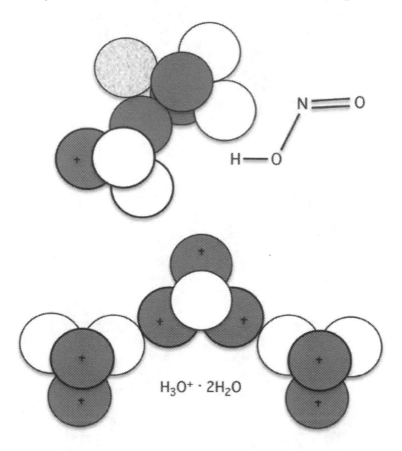

Concomitant with the proton migration pictured in the previous figure is migration — with respect to the "electride ion lattice", used as a frame of reference (analogous to the close-packed anion lattices of inorganic crystal chemistry) — of the $N^{+5}$ core of $NO^+$ through the trigonal interstice formed by its lone pair and two domains of the triple bond into the new tetrahedral interstice formed by those domains and the electron-pair donated by the added water molecule in its donor-acceptor interaction with $NO^+$.

The reaction may be described as water-catalyzed back-side attack on an electron-pair of $NO^+$'s triple bond. That attacked pair, "the leaving group", enhanced in that role in having partial dative bond character, becomes a lone-pair on the terminal oxygen atom of HO—N=O.

*Paths from $NO^+$ ("N") and $H_2O$ ("W") to HONO and $H_7O_3^+$*

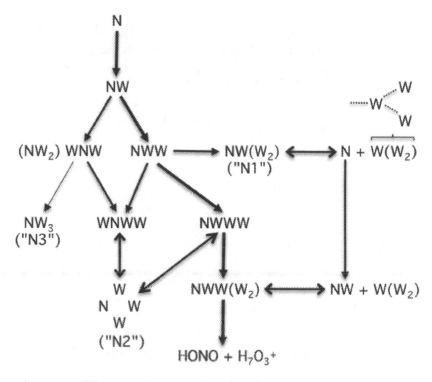

Each arrow indicates addition of one molecule of water (W).

The two-headed arrows indicate equilibria with respect to the making or breaking of a single donor-acceptor interaction.

The route at the right — dissociation of "N1" followed by addition of a water molecule to "N" followed by association of NW with the "water wire" $W(W_2)$ through its central water molecule is a mechanism for the "insertion" of a water molecule into "N1".

Heaviest arrows indicate what may be the most probable route from N + 4W to HONO + $H_7O_3^+$.

*Anomalous NO Stretching Frequencies in the Simple Hydrates of $NO^+$*

NO stretching frequencies of $NO^+ \cdot nH_2O$, n = 0, 1, 2, and 3 (as $NW_3$, isomer "N3") are, respectively, 2344, 2294, 2306, and 2312 cm$^{-1}$. The last two frequencies seem, at first glance, to be abnormally high compared to the second one. Hydration of $NO^+$ at its oxygen end owing to oxygen's slight positive charge would increase the contribution to the ion's superposition of states of the structure on the right below, in which the triple bond has no dative bond character.

# Nitrogen Dioxide
## $NO_2$

Nitrogen dioxide's structure is usually considered unusual. Although its bond length, 119.7 pm, lies almost exactly between the bond lengths of $NO_2^-$, 123.6 pm, and $NO_2^+$, 115 pm [(115 + 123.6)/2 = 119.3), its bond angle lies outside the normal ranges of bond angles.

*Ranges of Normal Bond Angles*

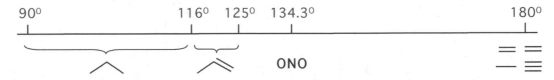

Among bent bonds ONO's bond angle is one of the largest.

$NO_2$ has 17 valence-shell electrons, split 8 of one spin, 9 of the other spin.

The 9-member spin-set has, for a quartet of spins about each atomic core, 3 electrons in bonding regions (the same number as the number of bonding electron-pairs in 9-electron-pair, 3-heavy-atom propylene).

$$B_2 (= 4N - V) = 4 \times 3 - 9 = 3$$

Favored is a single-bond/double-bond bond angle in the range $116^0 - 125^0$.

$NO_2$'s 8-member spin-set has 4 electrons in bonding regions (the same number as the number of bonding electron-pairs in 8-electron-pair, 3-heavy-atom allene and carbon dioxide). It favors a double-bond/double-bond bond angle of $180^0$.

Total bond order is $(1/2)(3 + 4)/2 = 1.75$, in agreement with the bond order inferred from bond lengths: namely the average of 1.5 (of $NO_2^-$) and 2 (of $NO_2^+$). The weighted average of the natural bond angles of the two spin sets is $(8 \times 180^0 + 9 \times 115.5^0$ (of $NO_2^-$)/17 = 145.8O.

ONO's observed bond angle of $134.3^0$ is closer to that of bent ONO$^-$ than to that of linear ONO$^+$ because, presumably, it's easier to bend linear configurations than the corresponding bent configurations, for the following reason.

$NO_2$'s $134^0$ bond angle is not optimal for either its 8- or its 9-member spin set. Both spin sets of $NO_2$ are strained. But the strain energy for the 9-member spin set on its departure from its optimal, bent geometry rises faster than the strain energy of the 8-member spin on its departure from its optimal, linear geometry, and not only because the 9-member spin set has the greater number of electrons, taken into account in calculation of the weighted average angle of 145.8°, but also because of increasing importance of an energy-lowering, donor-acceptor interaction for the 8-member spin set as it departs from its optimal linear geometry.

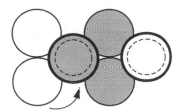

Shown is a valence sphere model of the optimal geometry of $NO_2$'s 8-member spin set. The curly arrow indicates a "pair-pocket", donor-acceptor interaction that helps to account for the fact that ONO's bond angle of 134.3° lies further from the optimal angle of 180° for the 8-member spin-set than from the optimal angle for the 9-member spin set, even after allowing for numbers of electrons in each spin set — which, alone, lead one to expect a bond angle of 145.8°. The observed angle, it's suggested, stems from occurrence of an energy-lowering, intramolecular, donor-acceptor interaction, indicated by the arrow.

The 9-member spin set, also, has intramolecular donor-acceptor interactions between terminal unshared electrons and the internal dimples about the domains of its double bonds. As in the case of the 8-member spin set, those energy-lowering interactions increase as the structure departs from its optimum geometry (toward linearity). They are less significant, however, than in the case of 8-member spin set, owing to their action over greater distances.

Below are remarks regarding nitrogen dioxide by the father of the theory of different structures for different spin sets, particularly in odd-electron molecules.

"It is interesting that this bond angle of 134° for $NO_2$ is much larger than is usually found for 'bent' molecules, involving atoms of elements of the First Short Period (e.g. $O_3$) and hydrogen (e.g. $H_2O$). Consequently there is some significance in the fact that the [double spin set] structure would lead to the expectation that the angle would be abnormally large; though not 180°." J. W. Linnett, *The Electronic Structure of Molecules: A New Approach*, Wiley, 1964, page 72.

# Structure and Reactivity of Nitrous Oxide

Nitrous oxide's atoms in compounds generally satisfy the Octet Rule. Two Octet-Rule-satisfying structures exist for linear NNO: one with a triple NN bond and a single NO bond (Structure A below) and one with two double bonds (Structure B).

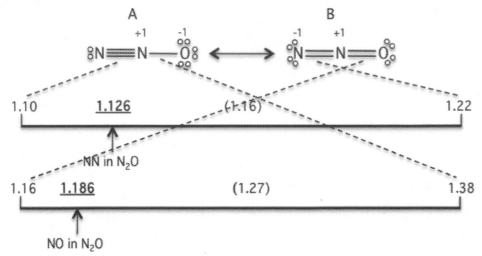

Both structures, drawn without dative bonds, have formal charges, best in A. Since NNO has essentially no dipole moment, its bond diagram is usually pictured, as shown above, as a resonance hybrid that's 50% A in character and 50% B. However, NNO's bond lengths (underlined above) do not lie midway (at 1.16 and 1.27) between the lengths (shown at the ends of the dashed lines) expected for Structures A and B. A 75/25 blend fits the NN length but not the NO length, unless its "expected value" of ca. 1.38 is reduced to 1.19. An argument for that reduction is pictured below.

$N^{+5}/N^{+5}$ repulsion thrusts dinitrogen's cores into its lone pairs (white domains). Addition of an oxygen atom then yields a short NO single bond.

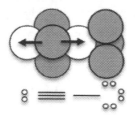

Evidence of such core/core repulsion includes: NN's low bascicity; HCCH's acidity and relatively short CH bond; and in diverse situations the s-character rule.

A reduction in NO single bond length of 1.38 - 1.19 = 0.19 Å may be reasonable. Consider the case of ethylene.

$C^{+4}/C^{+4}$ repulson thrusts ethylene's carbon cores along the bisectors of its HCH bond angles, opening up those angles.

An outward displacement of 0.076 Å increases an HCH angle from 109.5° to the observed angle of 116°.

For ethylene the outward thrust is proportional to $4 \times 4/(1.34)^2 = 8.88$ for an assumed displacement of 0.076. Their ratio is 8.8/0.076 = 120. The corresponding numbers for dinitrogen are $5 \times 5/(1.10)^2 = 20.7$, 0.19, and 109. The modest agreement between 109 and 120 is modest support for the physical picture of core displacements within electron clouds owing to core-core Coulombic repulsions, particularly between the two cores of a triple bond, as in dinitrogen, structure A, hydrogen cyanide, and acetylene.

Accounting for a zero dipole moment with a 75/25 blend of structures A and B requires introduction of a dative bond into each structure so as to reduce formal charges to zero.

*Final Valence Stroke Diagram for Nitrous Oxide*

The molecule's nonpolar character accounts for its solubility in vegetable fats and use as an "aerating" agent in whipped cream.

Presence of the NO dative single bond in dominant Structure A' is consistent with the ability of nitrous oxide to support combustion of easily flammable materials, although its mode of thermal decomposition, directly to dinitrogen and atomic oxygen, NNO --> NN + O, has a relatively high activation energy, owing, it's supposed, to the contribution to the molecule's ground state of Structure B', in which the NO bond is a double bond.

A curly arrow circuit transforms one structure into the other one.

One of nitrous oxides' most remarkable reactions, say Greenwood and Earnshaw in their textbook *Chemistry of the Elements*, is with molten alkali metal amides, forming azides. Reaction mechanisms of organic chemistry suggest that NNO's most likely resonance form at the reaction's outset is Structure B'. The dashed arrow below indicates one of its Lowest Unoccupied Localized Molecular Orbitals. The reaction's first step (below) is isoelectronic with the reaction of carbon dioxide with water, yielding carbonic acid: OCO + HOH = $(HO)_2CO$.

Subsequent backside attack on the NO bond by a lone pair on the amide's nitrogen atom, followed by a proton transfer (as in the first step above), yields a molecule of water and the azide ion, NNN⁻, isoelectronic with Structure B'.

# Explanations of Selected Properties of $N_2F_2$

## Observed Properties

P1  $N_2F_2$ is formed on heating fluorine azide:

$$2 N_3F = 2 N_2 + N_2F_2$$

P2  Like $N_2H_2$, $N_2F_2$ has *cis* and *trans* forms.

P3  Unlike $N_2H_2$, the *cis* form is favored.

P4  NN distances are: *cis* 1.209 Å, *trans* 1.224 Å.

P5  FN distances are: *cis* 1.409 Å, *trans* 1.398 Å.

P6  FNN angles are: *cis* 114°, *trans* 106°.

P7  The *cis* isomer, although more stable than the *trans* isomer, is more reactive. Unlike the *trans* isomer, the *cis* isomer –
  A  Slowly etches glass
  B  Reacts with $AsF_5$, yielding the salt $N_2F^+AsF_6^-$

P8  The $N_2F^+$ ion –
  A  Is linear
  B  Has an NN distance of 109.9 Å
  C  Has an NF distance of 1.217 Å

P9  The partially chlorinated derivative FNNCl is highly explosive.

## Qualitative Explanations

P1  For structures whose atoms (such as N and F of the first row of the *p*-block) satisfy the Octet Rule, V(number of valence shell electron *pairs*) equals 4 times N(number of octets) minus B(number pairs shared by octets in 2-center bonds and, accordingly, counted twice in the product 4N) → B = 4N – V.

For $N_3F$, N = 4 and V = 11 → B = 5 → Excess Connectivity [= B – (N – 1)] = 2 → a structure with (i) a double bond and a 3-membered ring, (ii) two double bonds, or (iii) a triple bond, Figure 1.

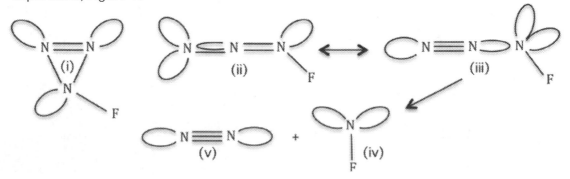

Fig. 1. Valence stroke diagrams for $N_3F$ that satisfy the Octet-Rule and the Valence-Stroke-Termination-Rule. Structures (ii) and (iii) are resonance hybrids. Rabbit-ear valence strokes in bonding regions represent dative bonds. Structure (iii) suggests, accordingly, that latent in $N_3F$ is the ability to dissociate on heating (long arrow) to NF (iv) and dinitrogen (v). Dative bonds are used in (ii) and (iii) to yield formal charges of zero. Isomer (i) is less stable than the resonance hybrid (ii)/(iii) owing chiefly, presumably, to a relatively large core-core repulsion term, and absence of resonance.

Formation of FNNF from NNNF occurs in two steps: formation of NN and NF (Figure 1), followed by dimerization of NF to FNNF, Figure 2.

**Fig. 2.** Highly schematic "curly arrow" representation of an electrocyclic mechanism for dimerization of NF to *cis* FN=NF. For formation of *trans* FN=NF, invert one of the monomers.

Replacement of valence strokes in Figure 2 by valence spheres yields a more realistic representation of NF dimerization. The monomers do not react side-by-side (Figure 2) nor head-to-head (FN + NF) but, rather, face-to-face, Figure 3.

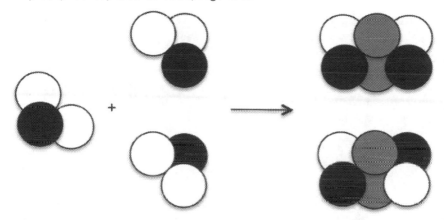

**Fig. 3.** Valence sphere models of dimerization of NF to *cis* FN=NF (top line) and, on rotation of the second NF monomer 180°, to *trans* FN=NF (bottom line). White spheres represent domains of lone pairs in the valence shell of $N^{+5}$ cores. Not shown are atomic cores and lone pair domains about $F^{+7}$ cores. Black spheres represent domains of N—F single bonds, gray spheres domains of FN=NF double bonds. On dimerization a lone pair of each monomer becomes a bonding pair of a double bond. Each NF monomer acts simultaneously, in the relative orientation shown above and below (confirmed by theoretical calculations), as an electron pair donor (origin of the short diagonal arrow at the far left below) and as an electron pair acceptor (terminus of the other short arrow).

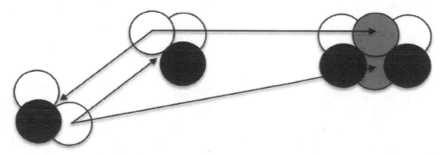

Owing to relatively large electrostatic repulsions between $N^{+5}$ cores and adjacent $F^{+7}$ cores, additional electron donor-acceptor interactions are expected to occur in *cis* FN=NF, Figure 4.

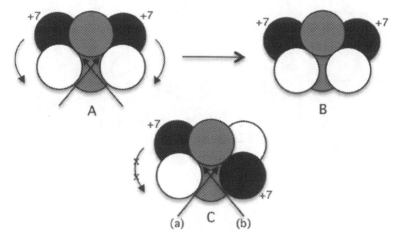

**Fig. 4.** Intramolecular electron pair donor-acceptor interactions in *cis* and *trans* FN=NF.

    **A** *cis* FN=NF. Straight arrows point to electrophilic sites, described in orbital language as nitrogens' domains of nitrogen-fluorine sigma antibonding orbitals. Curved arrows indicate, in each instance, the direction of rotation (about vertical axes), as a unit, of a nitrogen lone pair (white domains), a nitrogen-fluorine bonding pair (black domains), together with a $N^{+5}$ core, in a manner that brings the nucleophilic nitrogen lone pairs closer to the cited electrophilic sites, whose electron-density acceptor strengths are enhanced by electrostatic repulsions by the $F^{+7}$ cores of the $N^{+5}$ cores, toward the electrophilic dimples off the nitrogen ends of the NF bonds.

    **B** Configuration of *cis* $N_2F_2$'s electron pair domains (excluding, as before, fluorines' lone pair domains), after occurrence of the donor-acceptor interactions cited in **A**.

    **C** *Trans* FN=NF. Straight arrow (b) points to a previously cited electrophilic site: a dimple in the molecule's electron density profile opposite a bond to a highly electronegative substituent. In the molecule's *trans* isomer it's most electrophilic sites and its most nucleophilic sites are, for the exhibited stereochemical reasons, unable to interact with each other. Straight arrow (a) points to a dimple in the molecule's electron cloud that is stereochemically accessible for a donor-acceptor interaction, but that, being opposite a lone pair, is an electrostatically weak electrophilic site.

Valence stroke diagrams, which show atomic cores' locations explicitly (In that regard the diagrams and the corresponding valence sphere models are complementary representations of molecules), highlight the geometrical implications of the previously cited donor-acceptor interactions, Figure 5.

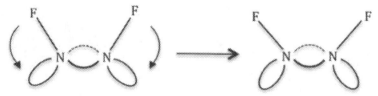

**Fig. 5.** A valence stroke diagram for cis FN=NF, showing that for N(lone pair)/σ*(N—F) interactions to occur, the lone pairs must be trans to the N—F bonds.

P2    For $N_2F_2$, the number of octets, N, is 4, the number of valence shell electron pairs, V, is 12, and thus the number of pairs shared in 2-center bonds, B (= 4N – V) is 4 and, consequently, the excess connectivity [= B – (N – 1)] is 1. Of the possible 2-, 3-, and 4-membered rings, only a structure with a 2-membered ring, Figure 5, satisfies for $N_2F_2$ the valence stroke termination rule: that for zero formal charges the number of valence stroke terminations at the symbol for an element is equal to the charge on the element's atomic cores, Figure 6,

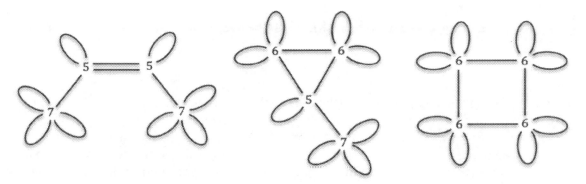

**Fig. 6.** Octet-rule-satisfying valence stroke diagrams for molecules that contain no hydrogen atoms and for which N (number of octets) is 4 and V (number of valence shell electron pairs) is 12. Shown are atomic core charges for zero formal charges. The first structure, with the double bond, and, therefore, the possibility of *cis* and *trans* isomers, is the only satisfactory structure for $N_2F_2$ with its core charges of +5, +5, +7, and +7.

The donor-acceptor interaction in *cis* FN=NF pictured in Figure 4B accounts for facts **P3-P9** in the following fashion. It -

- o lowers the energy of *cis* FN=NF relative to the energy of *trans* FN=FN, in which the donor-acceptor interaction is essentially absent (Figure 4C), but does not lower significantly the energy of *cis* HN=NH relative to *trans* HN=HN, since the N(lone pair)/antibonding orbital interaction is weak in both isomers of HN–NH because repulsion of $N^{+5}$ cores of the electrophilic sites by the $H^+$ cores of HN=NH is less than the repulsion of $N^{+5}$ cores by the $F^{+7}$ cores of FN=NF.

- o shortens, in *cis* FH=NF, the NN distance; increases the FN distances, as the $N^{+5}$ cores move away from the $F^{+7}$ cores toward the approaching lone pairs (in an incipient $S_N2$ reaction); and increases FNN angles. Also, the cited donor-acceptor interaction -

- o leads to dissociation of FN=NF to $F^-$ and $FN_2^+$ (isoelectronic with OCO and NNO), which yield, by $S_N2$ attack of $F^-$ on the F—N bond of $FN_2^+$, dinitrogen and glass-attacking difluorine, along with, in the presence of $AsF_5$, the salt $(FN_2^+)(AsF_6)^-$.

$$F \longrightarrow \overset{+}{N} === N \bigcirc + F^- \longrightarrow F_2 + N_2$$

$$\downarrow AsF_5$$

$$(FN_2^+)(AsF_6)^-$$

The first step above is especially facile in the explosive decomposition of FNNCl, in which the leaving group (at the left above) is $Cl^-$ (instead of $F^-$). In $FN_2^+$ the NN bond is as short as a normal triple NN bond and the FN bond is nearly as short as a double bond, analogous to the situation in isoelectronic $ON_2$. $S_N2$ attack of $F^-$ on the F—N bond of $FN_2^+$ yields difluorine and dinitrogen.

# Valence Stroke Diagrams for H₂O⁺

"Reorganization! That's what I say."
HUMPTY DUMPTY paraphrased

MO theorists have criticized BO Theory (Bond Orbital Theory) for its use of localized orbitals, its inability to account for $O_2$'s paramagnetism, and its alleged inability to account for $H_2O$'s photoelectron spectrum. Recognition of the mathematical equivalence in determinantal wave functions of delocalized MOs and (linearly related) localized BOs addresses, in large part, the first criticism. Linnett's Double Spin-Set Theory responds to the second criticism. A response to the third criticism resides in recognition that, from the point of view of Conceptual Valence Bond Theory, owing to *close-packing* of electron domains about atomic cores, removal of an electron, and its domain, from a set of molecular domains for electrons of a given spin may lead to a significant *reorganization* of the spin set's remaining domains. An example is the sequence of structures $NO_2^-$, $NO_2$, and $NO_2^+$. On passage from the anion to the cation, the ONO bond angle increases from 116° through 134° to 180°.

Consider removal of an electron from a water molecule's HOLMO ("Highest"— i.e., most nucleophilic — Occupied Localized Molecular Orbital), for the case of a *frozen electron cloud*, before it has had time to relax to a stationary state. (In the following valence stroke diagrams, solid valence strokes represent electrons of one spin, dashed valence strokes electrons of the opposite spin.)

The 3-membered spin set about $O^{+6}$ can relax from its frozen configuration, from ionization of a lone pair (lp), in two ways: through resonance, yielding a tetrahedral configuration, te-cf; and through rearrangement to a trigonal configuration, tr-cf. ["cf(lp)" below means "from a configuration derived from a lone pair".]

The trigonal configuration of the 3-membered spin set, formed in ionization of an unshared electron from $H_2O$, places the centroids of the spin set's electron domains closer to the oxygen $O^{+6}$ core than does the tetrahedral configuration. Accordingly, it is expected to be the structure of $H_2O^+$'s ground state, once one has moved the formal charge of +1 on oxygen to the more electropositive hydrogen atoms, through formation of bonds that have partial dative bond character.

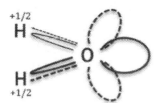

The number of (half) valence stroke terminations at "O" is 12. Division by 2 yields 6, the correct number of terminations of full valence strokes for zero formal charge at the site of $O^{+6}$. The HOH bond angle is expected to be larger than for water: perhaps about $[3\times116 + 4\times104)]/7 = 109$ degrees.

Conceptual Valence Bond Theory yields in an analogous manner for ionization from $H_2O$ of a bonding electron (bp) the following valence stroke diagrams.

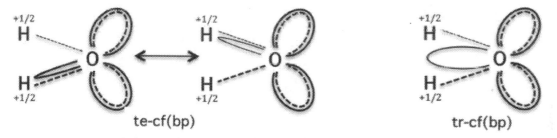

te-cf(bp)          tr-cf(bp)

Both HOH bond angles are expected to smaller than that of water.

Ionization of an electron from a bonding pair (bp) is presumably more difficult than ionization of an electron from a nonbonding lone pair (lp), particularly in the case of the trigonal configuration, tr-cf(bp), which has only two electrons in conventional bonding regions. One is led to expect ionization energies, therefore, in the order:

$$\text{tr-cf(lp)} < \text{te-cf(lp)} \ll \text{te-cf(bp)} \lll\!\!< \text{tr-cf(bp)}$$

### Observed IEs of $H_2O$
(in eV)

12.6  13.8    17.2                          33.2

A description in terms of atomic orbitals yields similar conclusions. For simplicity, take oxygen's contributions to the bonding orbitals to be pure p orbitals: $2p_x$ and $2p_y$. MO Theory's orbitals for the lone pairs are, correspondingly, oxygen's 2s and $2p_z$ orbitals, yielding, directly, two ionization energies, with ionization of an s electron more difficult than ionization of a p-electron. VB Theory's lone pair orbitals are sp hybrids: $2s + 2p_z$ and $2s - 2p_z$. Ionization followed by resonance corresponds to taking the sum or the difference of those two hybrids. Their sum yields the 2s orbital, corresponding to ionization of a $2p_z$ electron. Their difference yields the $2p_z$ orbital, corresponding to ionization of a 2s electron.

# Structures of FOF, HOF, and HOH

HOF has the smallest bond angle recorded for 2-coordinate oxygen in an open chain and its hydrogen-oxygen bond is slightly longer than the H—O bonds of HOH, contrary to the s-character rule. In agreement with the s-character rule, $OF_2$'s F—O—F bond angle is slightly smaller than the H—O—H bond angle of HOH and its O—F bonds are shorter than the O—F bond of HOF.

140.5 pm    F / O )103°    \ F

144.2 pm    F / O ) 97°    96.4 pm \ H

H / O ) 104.5°    95.7 pm \ H

Those bond length and bond angle differences and departures of bond angles from the ideal tetrahedral angle of 109.5° are in the direction expected from displacements of cores from the centers of their tetrahedral interstices owing to –

1. Core-core repulsion, particularly between small cores of large charge, such as $F^{+7}$ and $O^{+6}$.

2. Core-electron attraction, in the form of "pair-pocket" interactions across single bonds between lone pairs and interior pockets off the backsides of vicinal trans bonds.

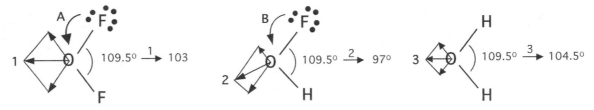

Forces 1, 2, and 3, arising from core-core repulsions, tend to diminish bond angles and increase bond lengths, in the order 1 ≈ 2 > 3. Interactions A and B ("tilts" at F) tend to (1) decrease the lengths of bonds to the donor atoms; (2) increase to a lesser extent the lengths of vicinal trans bonds, as $O^{+6}$ moves slightly in the direction of the approaching lone pairs, making, therefore, O—H in HOF longer than O—H in HOH; and (3) increase bond angles, in the order A >> B (in part because $F^-$ is a better leaving group than $H^-$), making, therefore, the angle F—O—F in FOF greater than the angle H—O—F in HOF.

Depicted below is a valence-sphere model of FOF before and after fine-tuning to allow for expected effects of core-core repulsions and core/trans-vicinal-electron-pair attractions.

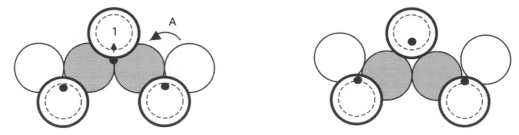

To account for the observed F—O—F bond angle in FOF, one supposes that the angle-closing effect of force 1 is greater than the angle-opening effect of interaction A.

# Electronic Structures and Molecular Geometries of $O_2$, $O_2^-$, and $O_3^-$

Oxygen posed a problem for classical valence bond theory in several respects, including the paramagnetism of $O_2$, the absence of cyclo-$O_4$ with OO bonds of normal strength, and the absence of the ions $O_4^{-2}$ and $O_5^{-2}$ valent isoelectronic with $SO_3^{-2}$ and $SO_4^{-2}$. MO theory and Hund's rule accounted for triplet $O_2$. Later Linnett, addressing the same issue, hybridized Hund's Rule, so to speak, yielding "double quartets" of electron spins, sometimes in partially anticoincident energy-lowering arrangements about cores of atoms that satisfy the Octet Rule, Figure 1.

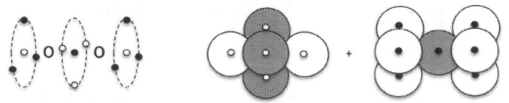

**Fig. 1.** Electron dot diagram (left) and drawing of a valence sphere model (right) of a molecule of triplet $O_2$ whose valence shell electrons are split 5 of one spin (small white circles on the left, arranged as for a triple bond) and 7 of the other spin (small black circles on the left, arranged as for a single bond). Large white circles on the right represent domains of the 6 unshared electrons of the 7-membered spin set and the 2 unshared electrons of the 5-membered spin set. Large gray circles represent domains of the 4 bonding electrons. Each spin-set has a quartet of tetrahedrally arranged spins about each atomic core (not shown).

Linnett's model of triplet $O_2$ explains why it does not dimerize to a 4 membered ring of four single bonds, isoelectronic with cyclobutane, for dimerization would decrease anticoincidence (as in the case of normal homolytic bond formation) without, however, increasing the number of bonding electrons. Linnett's model also accounts for structures of the two oxygen-rich species $O_2\text{-}M^+O_2^-$ and $O_2\text{-}M^+O_3^-$ produced unexpectedly in attempts to create charge-stabilized $O_4^{-2}$ and $O_5^{-2}$ as $MO_4^-$ and $MO_5^-$ (M an alkali metal) by laser vaporization of $M_2CO_3$ with helium carrier gas seeded with oxygen (1). Bond diagrams for the odd-electron species $O_2^-$ and $O_3^-$ may be created by applying, after Linnett, a Quartet Rule to each species' spin sets separately [V(number of valence shell electrons of a given spin) = 4N(number of quartets of the specified type) – B(number of spins of that type shared by quartets) → B = 4N – V]; or by adding an electron to $O_2$ and $O_3$ in the style of physical organic chemistry, Figure 2.

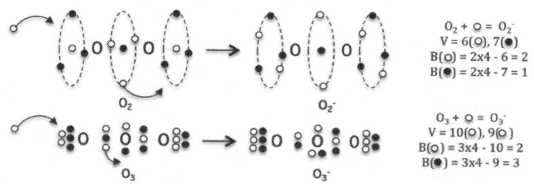

$$O_2 + O = O_2^-$$
$$V = 6(O), 7(\bullet)$$
$$B(O) = 2\times4 - 6 = 2$$
$$B(\bullet) = 2\times4 - 7 = 1$$

$$O_3 + O = O_3^-$$
$$V = 10(O), 9(O)$$
$$B(O) = 3\times4 - 10 = 2$$
$$B(\bullet) = 3\times4 - 9 = 3$$

**Fig. 2. Top Row.** Double quartet structures for $O_2$ (left) and $O_2^-$ (right). **Second Row.** Double quartet structures for $O_3$ (left) and $O_3^-$ (right). Number of electrons per bond are: $O_2$ 4, $O_2^-$ 3; $O_3$ 3, and $O_3^-$ 5 per two bonds = 2.5 per bond. Corresponding bond orders are 2, 1.5, 1.5, 1.25. Ozone (b.o. 1.5) is usually shown as a hybrid involving single-bond/double-bond resonance. Formal charges for $O_2$'s atoms are -1/2, +1, -1/2, for $O_3$'s atoms -3/4, +1/2, -3/4.

Below are bond orders and bond lengths (in Å) for the four oxygen-containing species of Figure 2 and for HOOH (by calculation for $O_2^-$ and $O_3^-$)(1).

| $O_2$ | $O_3$ | $O_2^-$ | $O_3^-$ | HO—OH |
|-------|-------|---------|---------|-------|
| 2 | 1.5 | 1.5 | 1.25 | 1 |
| 1.207 | 1.278 | (1.34) | (1.35) | 1.48 |

Bond length for –
 (1)  $O_2^-$ seems about right compared to those for $O_2$ and HOOH.
 (2)  $O_3$ seems short compared to that for $O_2^-$ and those for $O_2$ and HOOH.
 (3)  $O_3^-$ seems short compared to that for $O_2^-$.
 (4)  HOOH seems long compared to those for $O_2$ and $O_3$ and for $O_3^-$.

Those facts can be accounted for as follows:

 (1)  $O_2^-$'s bond order and bond length lie midway between those of $O_2$ and HOOH.

 (2)  Formal charges for $O_3$'s atoms in the usual bond diagram for $O_3$ are -1/2 for its terminal atoms and +1 for its apex atom. One expects for the molecule, therefore, a high degree of bond-shortening owing terminal-unshared-electron/$\sigma^*_{OO}$ donor-acceptor interactions.

 (3)  The same bond-shortening interaction that occurs in (2) for $O_3$ occurs also, here, for $O_3^-$.

 (4)  Onset of anticoincidence in HOOH on dissociation creates a degree of pre-dissociation in HOOH with a lengthened (and weakened) OO bond.

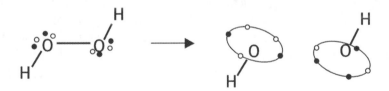

In $O_3^-$ (**Fig. 2**, lower right) the 9-membered spin set favors the geometry of ozone, OOO bond angle 116.8°, whereas the 10-membered spin set with two unshared domains on the central atom favors the geometry of dimethyl ether, COC bond angle 111.5°. The weighted average of the two angles is 114 degrees. Reported for the OOO bond angle of $O_3^-$ of $LiO_5^-$, $NaO_5^-$, and $KO_5^-$, are angles of, respectively, by calculation, 112.2°, 113.8°, and 114.6° (1). Presumably the last angle corresponds most closely to that of a hypothetical free $O_3^-$, in the absence of a bond angle-constricting cation, Figure 3.

**Fig. 3.** Geometrical structures of $MO_4^- = O_2^-M^+O_2^-$ (M = Li, Na, and K) and $MO_5^- = O_2^-M^+O_5^-$.

Dimensions of $O_2^-M^+O_2^-$ for M = Li, Na, and K are cited in Table 1.

Table 1. O—M—O Bond Angle and M—O Bond Length in $O_2^-M^+O_2^-$ (1)

| M | R(M⁺) | | <(O—M—O) | (M—O)/Å | |
|---|---|---|---|---|---|
| Li | 0.60 | | 41.5° | 1.899 | |
| | | 0.35 | | | 0.364 |
| Na | 0.95 | | 34.7° | 2.263 | |
| | | 0.38 | | | 0.331 |
| K | 1.33 | | 30.0° | 2.594 | |

M—O bond lengths of $O_2^-$ of $O_2^-M^+O_2^-$ tracks closely the radius of the ion M⁺. Given r(M⁺), the bond length O—O, and the overall geometrical structure of $O_2^-M^+O_2^-$, as pictured in Figure 3, one might estimate the bond angle O—M—O from a valence sphere model of the M⁺/$O_2^-$ interaction along an expression for the radius of electron domains in the valence shell of $O^{+6}$ cores, Figure 4.

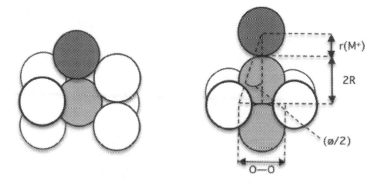

**Fig. 4. Left:** An alkali metal cation (dark gray sphere) in contact with a valence sphere model of the 7-membered spin set of $O_2^-$. **Right:** The same cation in contact with a model of $O_2^-$'s 6-membered spin set. Light gray circles signify domains in bonding regions. Domains' radii R are given by the expression $R/Å = 0.60 + 0.4r(O^{+6}) = 0.63$. If the minimum distance of approach of M⁺ to $O_2^-$ is determined as pictured on the right in **Fig. 4**, $\tan(ø/2) = [r(M^+) + 2R]/[(O—O)/2]$. For M = Li, r = 0.60 Å (according to Pauling) → $ø[= <(O—M—O)] = 39.8°$. The calculated value reported in reference (1) is 41.5°.

Conclusions: Modern Conceptual Valence Bond Theory appears capable of accounting for the leading features of the structures of $O_2^-$ and $O_3^-$. Use of the lithium ion, e.g., as a probe of the ions' electron density profiles in directions perpendicular to the axis of a double bond at its mid-point in a plane perpendicular to the molecular plane yields, for the length of a bond with double bond character, a picture of stretched double bond domains, Figure 5.

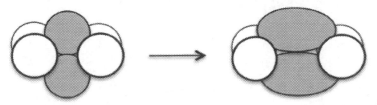

**Fig. 5. Left:** Equal-sphere-size valence sphere model of a double bond. **Right:** The previous model modified to fit a structure calculated for $O_2^-$.

(1) Hau-Jin Zha et al. "In Search of Covalently Bound Tetra- and Penta-Oxygen Species, JACS, 2002, 124, 6742-6750

## Geometrical Structure and Valence Stroke Diagrams for $O_4^-$

Agreement between B3LP/6-311+G* calculations and infrared spectra for $O_4^-$ in argon matrices has led to the suggestion that the anion $O_4^-$ has a rectangular structure with two short O—O distances (1.267 Å) and two long O—O distances (2.073 Å). Conceptual Valence Bond Theory accounts for those conclusions in the following manner.

$O_4^-$ has 25 valence shell electrons: 12 of one spin (+), 13 of the opposite spin (-). If each spin set places four spins about each $O^{+6}$ core, the number of shared spins in 2-center bonds for each spin set, B(+) and B(-), and corresponding Excess Connectivities, C(+) and C(-), are given by the expressions:

$$12 = 4 \times 4 - B(+), \quad 13 = 4 \times 4 - B(-) \;\rightarrow\; B(+) = 4, \; B(-) = 3 \;\rightarrow\; C(+) = 1, C(-) = 0$$

In the corresponding valence stroke diagrams each valence stroke represents one electron.

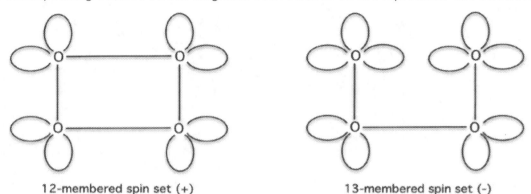

| 12-membered spin set (+) | 13-membered spin set (-) |

The 13-membered spin is a resonance hybrid of two structures.

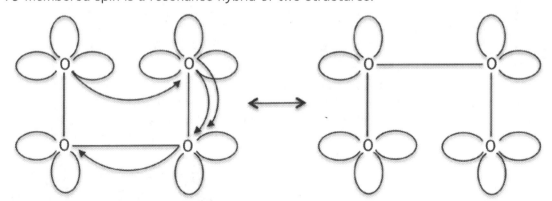

Bond orders are: for the long bond (LB) 1/2 + 1/2(1/2) = 3/4, for the short bond (SB) 1.0. Corresponding bond lengths seem unusually long and unusually short.

*OO Bond Lengths (pm) and Formal Bond Orders*

| O=O | $O_4^-$ SB | HO—OH | $O_4^-$ LB |
|-----|-----------|-------|-----------|
| 121 | 127 | 148 | 207 |
| (2) | (1) | (1) | (3/4) |

The bond length comparisons support the supposition that, owing especially to formal charges of -1/2 on the oxygen atoms, significant n/σ* donor/acceptor interactions occur in $O_4^-$ across its short bonds, which tend to shorten the short bonds and lengthen the long bonds.

# Exclusive Orbital Models for the Dianion $Al_4^{-2}$

What happens if an attempt is made to apply Modern Conceptual Valence Bond Theory, developed to account for structures of small-core, covalent molecules, such as those encountered in organic chemistry, to a large-core, inorganic species, such as the metallic dianion $Al_4^{-2}$, discussed at length by Boldyrev and Wang (1)? The analysis begins (as usual) with the Bond Number Equations -

$$\sum (n-1)B_n = \sum (EPCN)_i - V \tag{1}$$

$$B_1 = V - \sum B_n \ (n > 1) \tag{2}$$

where:   $B_n$ = number of n-center electron-pair bonds
   $B_1$ = number of lone pairs
   $(EPCN)_i$ = Electron Pair Coordination Number of Atomic Core i
   $V$ = number of valence shell electron pairs

Equations (1) and (2) play the role in Conceptual Valence Bond Theory that Schrödinger's equation plays in Computational Valence Theories.

For $Al_4^{-2}$ the maximum value of n is 4. $V = 7$. And if each atom satisfies the Octet Rule, $(EPCN)_i = 4$. Thus, equations (1) and (2) become [together with algebraically possible $B_n$-values (beginning, in thought, with values for $B_4$)] —

| $B_2$ | $2B_3$ | $3B_4$ | $= 4 \times 4 - 7 = 9$ | $B_1 = 7 - \sum B_n$ |
|---|---|---|---|---|
| 0 | 0 | 3 | | 4 |
| 1 | 1 | 2 | | 3 |
| 3 | 0 | 2 | | 2 |
| 0 | 3 | 1 | | 3 |
| 2 | 2 | 1 | | 2 |
| 6 | 0 | 1 | | 0 |
| 1 | 4 | 0 | | 2 |
| 3 | 3 | 0 | | 1 |
| 5 | 2 | 0 | | 0 |

The only set of $B_n$-values for which a satisfactory valence sphere model exists is the $B_1B_2B_3B_4 = 0601$ set, Figure 1.

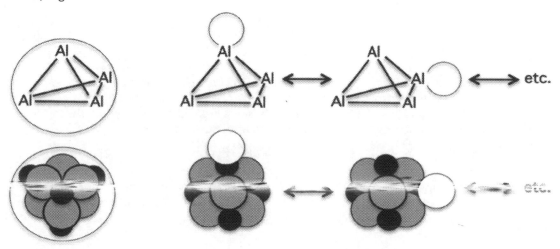

**Fig. 1. TOP ROW.** Valence stroke diagram of the 0601 structure for an Octet-Rule-satisfying $Al_4^{-2}$ species. **Left:** The circular valence stroke represents, schematically, a 4-center orbital that embraces the entire ion. **Right:** An alternative representation of the 4-center orbital, via resonance.

**BOTTOM ROW.** Valence sphere model of the 0601 structure for $Al_4^{-2}$. Black spheres represent domains of $Al^{+3}$ cations. Gray spheres represent domains of 2-center electron-pair Al—Al bonds. And white spheres represent domains that, by resonance, represent the ion's 4-center orbital. The six Al—Al domains are arranged octahedrally, with four of the octahedron's eight triangular faces capped by $Al^{+3}$ ions.

Figure 1 illustrates —

*Three Strategies Electron Deficient Species Use to Fill Their Valence Shells*

Use of —

- Multicenter electron domains
- Multi-sited electron domains, a.k.a. "bond/no-bond resonance"
- Dispersal of lone pair domains about large atomic cores

Although structure 0601 may represent a potential energy minimum on the ion's potential energy surface, it probably does not represent the ion's global minimum, owing to the small accumulation of electron density about the outward-facing portions of its aluminum ions, rectified by placing an electron pair in each aluminum ions' valence shell, leaving $7 - 4 = 3$ electron pairs for formation of aluminum framework bonds, Figure 2.

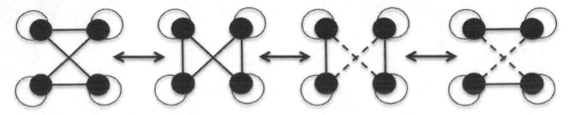

**Fig. 2.** A valence stroke diagram for $Al_4^{-2}$ with lone pairs (white domains) in the valence shells of each $Al^{+3}$ atomic core (black domains). The 4-center orbital (X) resides, by "resonance", above (solid lines) and below (dashed lines) the plane of the ion, in a π-type orbital, Figure 3.

**Fig. 3.** Schematic representation of the local electronic environment of an aluminum ion, $Al^{+3}$ (the black circle), in the valence stroke diagram of Figure 2. The ion's Electron Domain Coordination Number is, in effect, 5. (Valence *sphere* models, it's seen, from the nonspherical shapes of the lone pair domain and the 4-center domain, are a subset of exclusive orbital models.)

Each valence "stroke" (linear or "X-shaped") in Figure 2 corresponds to an electron domain, which, in the case of resonance, is not fully occupied. In effect, the number of domains corresponding to the bond diagram pictured in Figure 2 is increased from the 7 of Figure 1 to 10. Correspondingly, the Electron Domain Coordination Numbers of the $Al^{+3}$ ions increases from 4 of Figure 1 to 5 of Figure 3. Accordingly, the Bond Number Equation becomes -

$$B_2 + 2B_3 + 3B_4 = 4 \times 5 - 10 = 10 \qquad B_1 = 10 - \sum B_n \qquad (3)$$
$$\quad 4 \quad\;\; 0 \quad\;\; 2 \qquad\qquad\qquad\qquad\qquad\quad 4$$

Integers beneath equation (3) correspond to numbers of valence strokes in Figure 2.

Figure 4 (below) gives an estimate of the lengths of the aluminum-aluminum bonds in the $B_1B_2B_3B_4 = 4402$ isomer of $Al_4^{-2}$ pictured in Figure 2

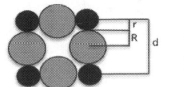

r = 0.50 Å (Pauling, "Nature of the Chemical Bond," p514)
R = 0.60 Å + 0.4(r) = 0.80 Å [Bent, *JCE*, 42, 348 (1965)]

d = 2(r + R) = 2.60 Å
d[B3LYP/6-311+G (1)]: 2.592 Å

**Fig. 4.** Valence sphere model of $Al_4^{-2}$'s 4402 isomer (Figure 2) sans domains of its lone pairs and 4-center domains.

Bond orders of the aluminum-aluminum bonds of the 4402 isomer of $Al_4^{-2}$ pictured in Figure 4 are 1/2 (for 2 electron pairs in 4 domains of the ion's σ bonds) + 1/2 (for single electron pairs in 2 domains of the ion's π bond), yielding a net bond order of 1, corresponding to a single Al—Al bond with an estimated length, based on an empirical "R-equation", of 2.60 Å (Figure 4), compared to a quantum-chemical calculated value of 2.592 Å (1).

In summary: $Al_4^{-2}$'s 4402 isomer utilizes all three of the cited strategies for completing the valence shells of its $Al^{+3}$ cores. It has: a multicenter bond; dispersed lone pairs about its four $Al^{+3}$ cores; and resonance, in both its σ and π framework bonds, giving rise to two types of aromatic character, with calculated ring currents reported (1) to be larger for its four σ electrons than for its two π electrons.

One remaining feature of the dianion's geometrical structure remains to be accounted for: its square-planar structure. Boldyrev and Wang write (emphasis added): —

> *The perfect square structure of the $Al_4^{-2}$ global minimum is unexpected*, because all alternative structures present better charge separation, expected to be important in determining the relative stability of the doubly charged anion. . . The question now is why the planar structure is so stable compared with the alternative structures. *There must be some unique features of chemical bonding in $Al_4^{-2}$ that give rise to the stability of the favored square-planar structure* (1).

The "unique features" stem, it's suggested, from Pauli repulsions among electrons of parallel spin in the aluminum ions' L shells, which forces the electrons of each spin-set into tetrahedral arrangements, combined with Coulombic repulsions between core electrons of opposite spin, which renders the two spin-sets as anticoincident as possible, Figure 5.

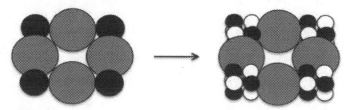

**Fig. 5.** Figure 4 in more detail, viewed part way between a top view, as in Figure 4, and a view off one edge. **Left:** $Al_4^{-2}$'s σ-bonding framework with, as before, spherical $Al^{+3}$ ions. **Right:** The same framework with partially anticoincident L-shell spin-sets nestled as close as possible to the bonding electron domains and showing why, accordingly — owing anticoincidence and atomic-core/electron attraction — the dianion favors a square planar structure with 90° AlAlAl angles.

# Calculated Structure of the Chain-like Dianion Si(C₄)₂⁻²

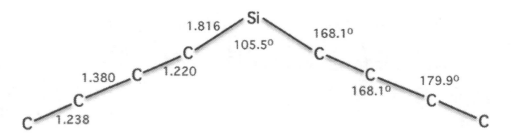

Lengths of the four short CC bonds, 1.238 and 1.220 Å, are close to the length of the CC triple bond of acetylene, 1.21 Å. The length 1.380 Å is almost exactly the length expected for a standard carbon-carbon single bond (1.54 Å) foreshortened 0.04 Å for each degree of bond order of flanking multiple bonds (for an estimated length of 1.54 – 4x0.04) Å = 1.38 Å). And 1.816 Å is approximately the length expected for a carbon-silicon single bond:

$$d(C—Si) = 2R(C—Si) + r(C^{+4}) + r(Si^{+4}) = 2[0.6 \text{ Å} + 0.4r(C^{+4})] + 0.16 \text{ Å} + 0.41 \text{ Å} = 1.85 \text{ Å}$$

Internuclear distances are, accordingly, consistent with the following bond diagram.

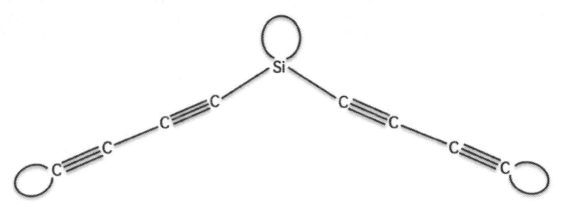

The bond diagram is the result of beginning with terminal octets and then completing other octets for the remaining carbon atoms. Terminal carbon atoms have formal charges of -1. The silicon atom has an incomplete octet.

Two features of the calculated structure are, however, at first sight, perhaps surprising: two CCSi bond angles of 168.1°; and the CSiC bond angle of 105.5°.

The usual triple-bond/single-bond angle, unstrained, is 180°.

And the usual bond angle at a second-row element of the *p*-block, such as P or S, that has in its valence shell one or two lone pairs and bonds to "innocent" ligands, such as hydrogen, or carbon, is, as, e.g., in H₂S, 92°. Examination of a valence sphere model of the ion Si(C₄)4⁻² suggests an explanation for why its CSiC bond angle is larger than 92° and why the adjacent SiCC bonds angles are smaller than 180°.

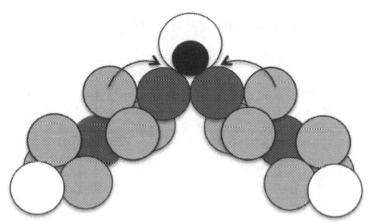

Valence sphere model of the ion $Si(C_4)_2^{-2}$. White spheres: domains of lone pairs of the terminal carbon atoms and the central silicon atom, with its lone pair dispersed about the large $Si^{+4}$ core; light gray: domains of triple bonds; dark gray: domains of single bonds; black: silicon's atomic core $Si^{+4}$. Not shown: carbon atoms' atomic cores, $C^{+4}$, in the model's tetrahedral interstices.

Arrows point from nucleophilic sites of the two interior triple bonds toward the vacant silicon atom valence shell domain, accessed by a collective "sliding" motion on the outer "surface" of a Si—C domain of an interior triple bonds' three domains toward the vacant silicon site, with the remaining five domains of that arm of $Si(C_4)_4^2$ following suit. Produced *simultaneously*, albeit not necessarily to equal extents, is an increase in the CSiC angle and a decrease in the SCC angles, as illustrated schematically below.

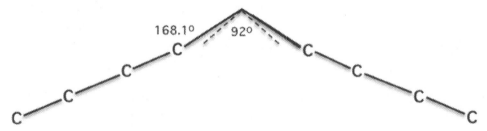

Changes in bond angles owing to the donor-acceptor interaction described above are:

$$\Delta(CSiC) = 105.5° - 92° = 13.5°$$
$$\Delta(SiCC) = 180° - 168.1° = 11.9°$$

Consistent with the outward tilt of silicon's two CCCC arms postulated above is the fact that the calculated silicon-carbon distance (1.816 Å) for what is deemed to be a slightly bent single bond is slightly less than the estimated length (1.85 Å) for a linear silicon-carbon single bond.

# Non-Planar Si₂H₄ and Non-Linear Si₂H₂

Unlike $C_2H_4$, famous for its planarity, and $C_2H_2$, famous for its linearity, *the molecule Si₂H₄ is non-planar and the molecule Si₂H₂ is non-linear.* Exclusive orbital models of the molecules suggest a physical reason for their shapes. The usual spherical domains for the multiple bonds' electrons (below left) do not utilize fully the low potential energy space for electrons about the large $Si^{+4}$ cores.

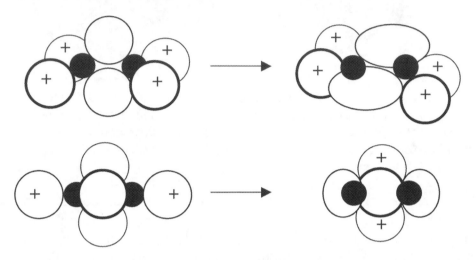

Exclusive Orbital Models of (top right) Non-Planar $Si_2H_4$ and (bottom right) Non-Linear $Si_2H_2$.

The model for non-linear $Si_2H_2$ contains a doubly protonated triple bond. That arrangement of its hydrogen atoms' protons frees up the localized electron pairs of Si—H bonds of linear $Si_2H_2$ for "solvation", as angularly dispersed lone pairs, of the large $Si^{+4}$ cores. In the model for non-planar $Si_2H_4$, silicon core solvation occurs via distortion of the model's double bond domains.

Illustrated is a domestication, so to speak, of the unusual structures of the first two hydrides of silicon through recognition of the leading role of atomic-core/valence-electron attraction in theories of the formation and shapes of molecules according to a Doctrine of Coordination by atomic cores of electron domains, to the point, in the case of $Si_2H_2$, of distortion of a pair of domains' normal shapes in valence shells toward the shapes of high s-character, "inert pairs" commonly exhibited by silicon's congeners tin and lead and as expressed in the phrase "delocalization of lone pairs about large atomic cores".

Nonlinear $Si_2H_2$ exhibits in its structure distinctive features characteristic of elements adjacent to silicon in periodic tables: namely boron (diagonally upward to its left), in the molecule $B_2H_6$ (a protonated multiple bond); carbon (directly above it), in the molecule $C_2H_2$ (a triple bond); and phosphorus (directly to its right), in the molecule $PH_3$ (a dispersed lone pair, present twice in $Si_2H_2$).

With its s-rich lone pairs in place of 2-center bonds to hydrogen, nonlinear $Si_2H_2$ may be viewed as an extreme instance of Bent's Rule.

# Bond Lengths of the Phosphorus Pentahalides

"Sometimes the hardest things to see," say artists, "are what stare us in the face." For fifty years a scientifically satisfying explanation, using valence sphere models of molecules, for why the two axial bonds of the phosphorus pentahalides are longer than their three equatorial bonds eluded the author.

True, if one extends the electron-pair-coordination-number-four model used with organic molecules to five electron pairs of a trigonal bipyramidal arrangement, one obtains immediately two axial bonds longer than three equatorial bonds.

### *Small-Core Valence Sphere Model for EPCN = 5*

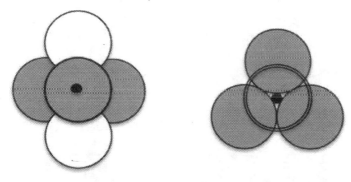

**Fig. 1. Left:** Side view of five spherical electron pair domains packed tightly about the site of an atomic core, indicated by the small black circle. Gray domains represent equatorial, white axial P—X bonds of $PX_5$. Not shown are X atoms' cores and unshared valence shell electrons. **Right:** Top view of the model at the left, for an atomic core sufficiently small to fit into the trigonal interstice formed by the three domains of the equatorial P—X bonds of $PX_5$.

The radius R of the domain of a P—X bond of $PX_5$, X = halogen, is determine chiefly by the more electronegative atom, the halogen, core charge +7, compared to +5 for phosphorus. For fluorine substituents, R ≈ 63 pm. To fit into a tetrahedral interstice formed by four electron pair domains of radius 63 pm, an atomic core must have, by the Radius Ratio Rules, a radius no larger than 0.225 R = 14 pm. Pauling's radii for $C^{+4}$, $N^{+5}$, $O^{+6}$, and $F^{+7}$ are, respectively, 15, 11, 9, and 7 pm. To fit into a trigonal interstice, the limiting size is 0.155 R = 9.8 pm. Pauling's radius for $P^{+5}$ is 34 pm.

Figure 1 presents, accordingly, an unrealistic picture of an exclusive orbital model of the phosphorus halides. The central $P^{+5}$ core should be shown to be about half the size of the valence shell electron pairs, Figure 2.

**Fig. 2. Left**: Model showing the axial/equatorial bond angle, $X_aPX_e = 90°$, supported by the large $P^{+5}$ core (black domain) of trigonal bipyramidal $PX_5$. **Right**: Model showing the equatorial/equatorial bond angle, $X_ePX_e = 120°$.

The two drawings in Figure 2 illustrate that the phosphorus core $P^{+5}$ in the phosphorus pentahalides $PX_5$ is not coordinatively saturated. Room exists in $P^{+5}$'s valence shell for a bonding pair of a sixth halide ion, yielding $PX_6^-$, all bond angles 90°, as at the left. The spherical large-core model predicts, however, that axial and equatorial P—X bonds of $PX_5$ are the same length. Conclusion:

### The $P^{+5}$ core of $PX_5$ is not spherical. It's ellipsoidal.

$P^{+5}$ in $PX_5$ can't be perfectly spherical, of course, as it's not in a spherically symmetrical environment. And powerful repulsions between electrons of opposite spin favor at any instant a spatially anticoincident arrangement of spins, such as have been used to account, e.g., for sudden changes in bond angles in the hydrides $H_3X$ and $H_2X$ on going from X = N and O, with their helium-like cores and nearly tetrahedral bond angles, to X = P and S, with their neon-like cores and nearly 90 degree bond angles.

*Different-Structures-for Different-Spin-Sets for $P^{+5}$*

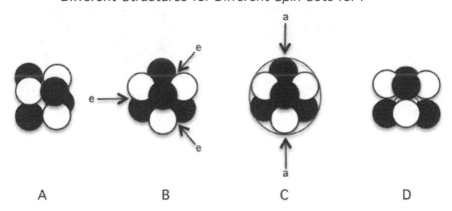

A          B          C          D

**Fig. 3. A**: Side view of a Lewis/Linnett configuration of maximum probability for the two spin sets of $P^{+5}$. **B**: View of **A** along a body diagonal. Arrows indicate sites of coordination of equatorial halogen atoms of $PX_5$. **C**: Relation of $P^{+5}$'s two spin sets to the core's presumed ellipsoidal character in $PX_5$. **D**: See text.

Left to be eplained is why the difference in axial and equatorial bond lengths in $PF_5$ (5 pm) is less than in $PCl_5$ (12 pm), with the latter figure slightly less than predicted by the model B/C. As mentioned, $P^{+5}$ in $PX_5$ is not coordinatively saturated. Bond-shortening dative bonding by the halogen's unshared electrons is expected to be greater for fluorine ligands than for chlorine ligands and greater from axial sites, with three electrophilic sites for each ligand to dative bond to (Fig. 3C), than from equatorial sites, with only two electrophilic sites to coordinate to (Fig. 3D).

# Fluxional Phosphorus Pentafluoride

*Valence-Stroke Diagram and Valence-Sphere Model of the Interchange*
*of Axial and Equatorial Positions in Trigonal Bipyramidal PF$_5$*

Axial positions 1 and 2 (**a** in the valence-sphere model) become equatorial positions (**e**) as, simultaneously, equatorial positions 4 and 5 become axial positions.

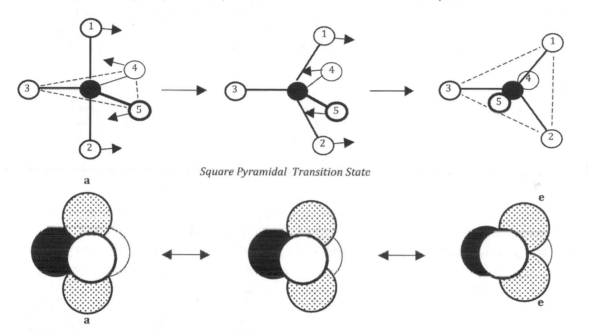

*Square Pyramidal Transition State*

Equatorial position 3 (black domain in the VSM), called the "fixed position" or "pivot point", does not move. The transformation is sometimes called a "pseudorotation" inasmuch as a rotation of the figure on the left about the site of the phosphorus nucleus 90 degrees in a plane perpendicular to the plane of the page yields the structure on the right, if one disregards domain's labels.

It's easy to exhibit the transformation pictured above in a kinesthetically pleasing fashion with a model constructed from smooth Styrofoam spheres connected to each other by rubber bands that pass through the spheres' centers along channels created by passage of a warm rod through the spheres, and that are held in place at the spheres' outer edges by brass paper fasteners bent into the shape of a "J". Twisting a digonal set inserted into a trigonal set crosses the rubber bands at the site of the phosphorus nucleus, thereby simulating nuclear-electron attraction. Pulling apart two equatorial domains, e.g. 4 and 5, is easy to do, for as 4 and 5 move outward, further stretching their rubber bands, domains 1 and 2 move inward. The model passes easily from the configuration on the left through the one pictured in the middle to the configuration on the right.

# The Double Bond of OPF$_3$

How to represent bonds between second and later row elements of periodic tables' p-blocks and terminal oxygen atoms has long been a moot question in structural inorganic chemistry. In organic chemistry terminal oxygen atoms of zero formal charge are bound by double bonds. That arrangement in inorganic chemistry yields controversial "expanded octets".

In the phosphorus oxides P$_4$O$_{6+n}$ (n = 1 – 4), the difference in lengths of the PO(bridging) bonds (ca. 162 pm) and the PO(terminal) bonds (ca. 142 pm) of ca. 20 pm is essentially the same as the difference of 20 pm in lengths of carbon-carbon single bonds (154 pm) and carbon-carbon double bonds (134 pm). It seems reasonable, therefore, to represent the phosphorus-oxygen bond of OPF$_3$ as a four-electron bond, usually written as -

$$
\begin{array}{c}
O \\
\parallel \\
P \\
F \quad\diagup \quad\diagdown \quad F \\
F
\end{array}
$$

Begged is the question: What is the most probable arrangement of electron domains about the phosphorus core? Neither a trigonal bipyramidal nor a square planar domain arrangement accounts for the molecule's shape. That shape is consistent with a resonant hybrid of tetrahedral and octahedral spin quartets and sextets about P$^{+5}$.

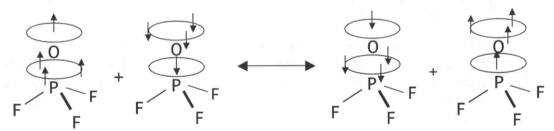

Existence of octahedral PCl$_6^-$ with normal P—Cl single bond lengths supports the assignment of spin-set structures that place six electrons of the same spin about P$^{+5}$: three from the phosphorus-oxygen bond and three from the three phosphorus-fluorine bonds.

The tetrahedral arrangement of spins about P$^{+5}$ favors FPF bond angles of 109.5 degrees. The octahedral arrangement favors bond angles of 90 degrees. The average, 99.8 degrees, is close to the observed value of 101 degrees.

# Tetrasulfur Tetranitride

I enthusiastically await your understanding of $S_4N_4$, a long-known but
poorly understood nonmetal species.   JOEL LIEBMAN, March 12, 2012

$S_4N_4$ has a number of "normal valent" structures, in which sulfur has a valence of 2,
nitrogen 3, and the molecule as a whole has an excess connective of 3, Figure 1.

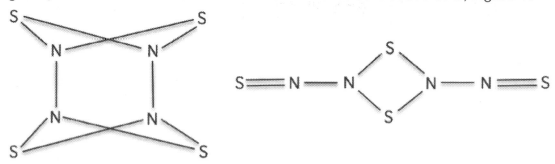

Fig. 1. Two "normal valent" bond diagrams for $S_4N_4$.

The sulfur atoms of the observed structure occupy, however, the corners of a
tetrahedron and the nitrogen atoms the vertices of a square that intersects the
tetrahedron, Figure 2.

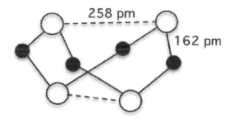

Fig. 2. Structure of $S_4N_4$. All sulfur-nitrogen bonds are the same length: 162.3 pm,
close to the average estimated for sulfur-nitrogen single and a double bonds, of 174 and
154 pm, respectively. Bond angles are NSN = 105.4°, SNS = 114.2°, and SSN = 88.4°.
The transannular sulfur-sulfur distance of 258 pm is intermediate between a bonding
S—S distance (208 pm) and a nonbonding van der Waals contact (ca. 340 pm).

To account for observed interatomic distances, investigators have proposed various
resonance structures, Figure 3.

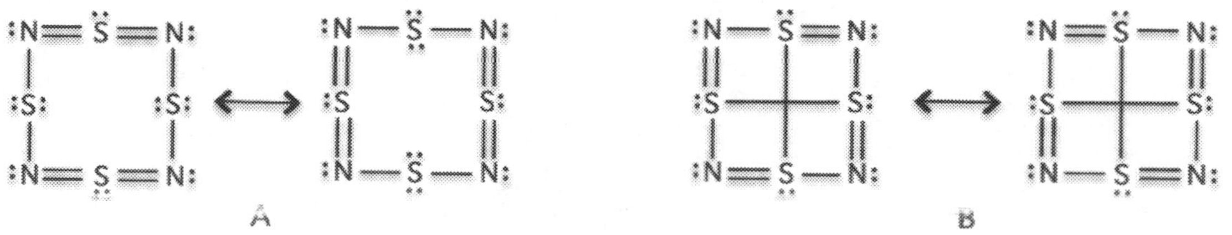

Fig. 3. Zero-formal-charge, expanded octet resonance structures for $S_4N_4$. A: 12
bonding pairs, 10 lone pairs, excess connectivity 5. B: 14 bonding pairs, 8 lone pairs,
excess connectivity 7.

Superficially, resonance structures B are attractive on three accounts: large numbers of bonding pairs; transannular sulfur-sulfur interactions; and sulfur-oxygen bond orders of 1.5. They violate, however, a cardinal tenant of valence bond theory. Structures B place two electron pairs at the same place at the same time. Structures A are satisfactory in that regard. How, on the other hand, does a valence sphere model of $S_4N_4$ account for the relatively short sulfur-sulfur distance? Start with a square pyramidal arrangement of electron pair domains about a $S^{+6}$ core, Figure 4.

**Fig. 4.** Valence shell of an atomic core $S^{+6}$ with an electron pair coordination number 5: 4 for pairs in bonds to double bonds to nitrogen and 1 pair as a lone pair domain.

Next, add at opposite edges digonal sets of pairs, in the form, at each edge, of a lone pair, on nitrogen, and a bonding pair, between nitrogen and a sulfur atom, Figure 5.

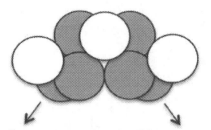

To the valence shells of $S^{+6}$ cores

**Fig. 5.** Complete valence shells for an N=S=N fragment (9 domains).

A duplicate set of domains nearly completes the model, Figure 6.

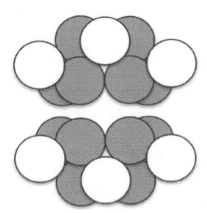

**Fig. 6.** Four dangling nitrogen-sulfur single bonds face each other across the gap in the model (as do nearly, also, four domains of sulfur-oxygen double bonds).

Closing up the model and finishing off with lone pairs the valence shells of the two bridging sulfur atoms on the bottom side of the figure completes the model, Figure 7.

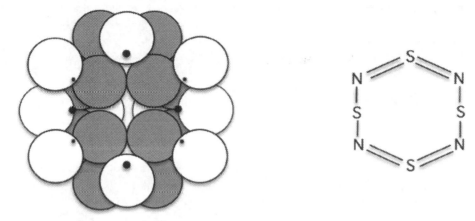

Fig. 7. Valence sphere model of one resonance structure of $S_4N_4$. Large solid circles: approximate locations of $S^{+6}$ cores. Small solid circles: approximate locations of $N^{+5}$ cores. Omitted at the right are lone pairs: one per nitrogen atom and quadrivalent sulfur atom and two per divalent sulfur atom.

The valence sphere model has three distinctive — and, on a first encounter with them — perhaps surprising, features.

- The model can be constructed! — from 22 electron pair domains, with provision for 8 chemically reasonable sites for atomic cores, in two sets, and with all nonbonding intramolecular interactions essentially normal, with one exception (see below).

- Resonance seems likely, since the two trans-annular sulfur-sulfur distances are nearly the same!

- In a particular resonance structure the valence shells of trans annular sulfur atoms bound to nitrogen atoms by double bonds are virtually in contact with each other!, consistent with the observation that "the transannular sulfur-sulfur distance of 258 pm is intermediate between a bonding S—S distance (208 pm) and a nonbonding van der Waals contact (ca. 340 pm)."

In summary: A packing model of 22 spherical valence shell electron pair domains for $S_4N_4$ fits the molecule's observed structure about as well as might be expected for an equal-sphere-size model, without fine tuning, by varying domains' sizes, and shapes, while retaining their exclusive orbital character.

# Orbital Descriptions of Bonding in SF$_6$

Pictured below at the left is the valence-sphere model of the valence shell of hexavalent sulfur's S$^{+6}$ core in SF$_6$. To its immediate right is the corresponding valence-stroke diagram. On the far right are "distinctive bond symbols" used by Weinhold and Landis (*Valence and Bonding*).

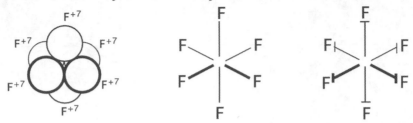

The valence-stroke diagram (center figure) may be viewed as a purely graphic expression — without reference to electrons or orbitals — of the atoms' "combining capacities" (6 for sulfur, 1 for fluorine), combined with the empirical rule that valence-strokes stay as far apart as possible while remaining attached to symbols of the chemical elements.

The valence-sphere model embodies Lewis' identification of valence-strokes as two electrons, and a strong form, so to speak, of an Exclusion Principle: namely, the hypothesis that two doubly occupied electron domains cannot be at the same place at the same time. The six domains that fill the S$^{+6}$ core's valence-shell of SF$_6$ correspond, approximately, to:

1.  The main lobes of sulfur sp$^3$d$^2$ hybrid orbitals.

2.  The main lobes of three pairs of equivalent bond orbitals (b$_1$ and b$_2$ below are one such pair) formed by taking sums and differences of three pairs of 3-center molecular orbitals (m$_1$ and m$_2$ below are one such pair) formed from linear combinations of sulfur 3p orbitals (p$_x$, p$_y$, and p$_z$) with pairs of fluorine orbitals (f$_1$ and f$_2$, below, directed toward S$^{+6}$). (Molecular orbitals m$_1$ and m$_2$ are formed in that manner in order to avoid use of sulfur 3d orbitals, deemed to be too diffuse to be significant in bonding in SF$_6$.) The coefficient N below is a normalizing constant (equal to $\sqrt{2}/\sqrt{3}$).

$$m_1 = (1/2)(f_1 + \sqrt{2}\, p_x + f_2) \qquad m_2 = (1/\sqrt{2})(f_1 - f_2)$$
$$b_1 = N[m_1 + (1/\sqrt{2})m_2] = N[f_1 + (1/\sqrt{2})p_x] \qquad b_2 = N[f_2 - (1/\sqrt{2})p_x]$$

Bond orbitals b$_1$ and b$_2$ describe polar-covalent bonds polarized toward fluorine atoms 1 and 2, represented by Weinhold and Landis by an annotated valence stroke: ⊢——.

3.  The main lobes of pure fluorine, equivalent orbitals (f$_{1,2,3,4,5,6}$) recovered from canonical MOs by taking linear combinations of six MOs formed from linear combinations of the fluorine orbitals (f$_{1,2,3,4,5,6}$), with symmetries of the atomic orbitals s (no nodes); p$_x$, p$_y$, and p$_z$ (1 node); and d$_{x2-y2}$, and d$_{z2}$ (2 nodes). The localized MOs f$_{1,2,3,4,5,6}$ correspond to a highly bond polarized, ionic model of SF$_6$: S$^{+6}$(F$^-$)$_6$.

The m$_1$/m$_2$ MO description in 2 allows one to say that sulfur in SF$_6$ does not exceed a formal, *Orbital* "Octet Rule" (not to be to be confused with Lewis' *Physical* Octet Rule regarding *actual numbers* of valence-shell electrons), in that in describing in orbital language SF$_6$'s electron cloud one does not use sulfur 3d orbitals. Paradoxically, however, one does not use, either, sulfur's *lowest lying valence orbital*: its 3s orbital! One might have thought that that would be the *first* orbital used to describe the occupancy of S$^{+6}$'s valence shell, in any species, in terms of spherical harmonics centered at S$^{+6}$.

Regarding "expansion of sulfur's octet" in SF$_6$, it should be noted that its S—F bond (156.4 pm in length) is slightly *shorter* than the S—F bond in SF$_2$ (159 pm), owing, presumably, to the core-enveloping, s-seeking, ligand-bond-elongating character of sulfur's 3s-rich, unshared electrons in SF$_2$ (F—S—F = 98°).

# Valence Sphere Model of a Metal

Research workers, in efforts to express fundamental laws of Nature in mathematical form [especially geometrically], should strive mainly for beauty. They should take simplicity into consideration in a subordinate way. . . It often happens [however] that the requirements of simplicity and beauty are the same. P. A. M. DIRAC

Several lines of evidence suggest for the electronic structure of calcium metal a beautifully simple exclusive orbital model.

1. **Calcium's Wavefunction.** Properly constructed wavefunctions for calcium metal are — as for all atomic and molecular systems — *antisymmetric*. Accordingly, the wavefunctions have, to some degree, exclusive orbital character.

2. **Metals' Structures and Salts' Cation Lattices.** Structures of some metals and cation lattices of some salts are *the same*, often that of face centered cubic packing of spheres. Replacement of the salts' anions by electron charge clouds yields electronic structures for the metals.

3. **Structural Equivalence of Oxide Ions and Electron Pairs.** Replacement of $O^{-2}$ in ROR', R and R' equal, say, to H, F, and/or $CH_3$, by electron pairs, indicated either by a valence stroke, —, or the symbol, $e_2^{-2}$, yields structures of the type R—R'. The same substitution transforms calcium oxide, $CaO(c) = Ca^{+2}O^{-2}(c)$, into calcium "electride", $Ca^{+2}(e_2^{-2})(c)$ and transforms $ClO_4^- = Cl^{+7}(O^{-2})_4$ into, successively, $ClO_3^-$, $ClO_2^-$, $ClO^-$, and $Cl^-$ [$= Cl^{+7}(e_2^{-2})_4$].

4. **Alchemical Transformation of Potassium Hydride into Calcium Metal.** Just as an alchemical transfer of a proton from a C—H bond of $H_3C$—H to the molecule's heavy atom nucleus yields $H_3N$:, with little change elsewhere in the specie's structure, so, similarly, one might expect, by that Isoelectronic Principle, little change in structure on transfers of hydride ions' protons of potassium hydride, $K^+H^-$ (with its rock salt structure, its cations and anions, separately, on sites of face centered cubic lattices), into the adjacent $K^+$ nuclei, converting them to $Ca^{+2}$ nuclei (on the same face centered cubic lattice the $K^+$ ions had in KH) and leaving behind electron pairs (on the same fcc lattice that the hydride ions, $H^-$, had in $K^+H^-$), yielding a model of "calcium electride", Figure 1 (following page).

5. **Interatomic Distances in KH(c) and Ca(c).** Molar volumes of the two isoelectronic "salts", $KH = K^+H^-$ and $Ca = Ca^{+2}(e_2^{-2})$, are nearly the same, 27.4 and 26.0 $cm^3$/mole, respectively. Their corresponding unit cells' $a_o$-values (Figure 1) are 5.7 and 5.6 Å. In the electride-ion/fcc model of Ca, $a_o = 2[r(Ca^{+2}) + r(\text{electride ion})]$. Taking r(electride ion in Ca) $\approx$ r(hydride ion in KH) $\approx$ 2.0 Å (Pauling) and (after Pauling) taking $r(Ca^{+2})$ = 1.0 Å yields $a_o$ = 6.0 Å, compared to the observed value of 5.6 Å. Alternatively, an atomic radius r(Ca) equal to half the Ca-Ca interatomic distance in Ca metal is, according to the model, given by the expression –

$$r(Ca) = \sqrt{2}[r(Ca^{+2}) + r(\text{electride ion})]/2 = 2.1 \text{Å (observed: 2.0 Å)}.$$

6. **Calcium's Reaction with Water.** A satisfactory model of calcium metal should account not only for its structure but also for it's leading chemical behavior: in particular, its reaction with water, Figure 1, far right.

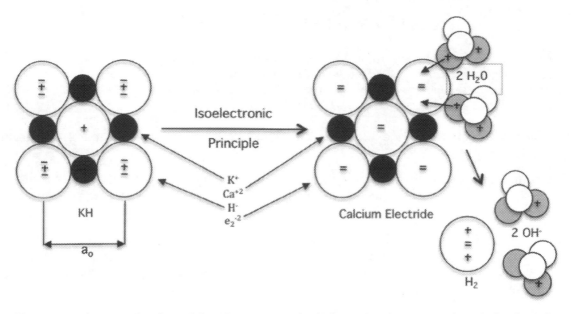

**Fig. 1.** Exclusive orbital models of potassium hydride and calcium metal and the latter's reaction with water, yielding dihydrogen and hydroxide ions

$$e_2^{-2} + 2\ H_2O(l) = 2\ OH^-(aq) + H_2(g)$$

followed by $\qquad 2\ OH^-(aq) + Ca^{+2}(aq) = Ca(OH)_2(c) + Heat!$

CAUTION! A few calcium turnings added to a test tube containing water may bring, after a brief induction period, the water to a boil.

7. **Trend in Bonding Across the Periodic Table.** The electride ion in the electride-ion/fcc model of calcium metal is a 6-center CaCaCaCaCaCa bond. The protonated electride ion of potassium hydride is a 7-center HKKKKKK bond. And the bonding in body centered cubic potassium may be viewed as body centered K atoms of one spin overlapping 8 K atoms of the opposite spin at the cube corners, yielding 9-center orbitals, in accordance with –

*A General Trend in Bonding across the Periodic Table*

| Element: | K | Ca | B | C | N | O | F | Ne |
|---|---|---|---|---|---|---|---|---|
| 1c "bonds" | 0 | 0 | 0 | 0 | 1 | 2 | 3 | 4 |
| 2c bonds | 0 | 0 | yes | 4 | 3 | 2 | 1 | 0 |
| 3c bonds | 0 | 0 | yes | 0 | 0 | 0 | 0 | 0 |
| 6c bonds | 0 | yes | 0 | 0 | 0 | 0 | 0 | 0 |
| 9c bonds | yes | 0 | 0 | 0 | 0 | 0 | 0 | 0 |

Integers are numbers of n-center bonds per atom.

8. **A Similar Model.** Another exclusive orbital model for metallic calcium places the element's two spin sets, as resonance-hybrids, in anticoincident, 4-center "plus" tetrahedral interstices (pointing one direction) and 4-center "minus" tetrahedral interstices (pointing the other direction) of a face centered cubic lattice of calcium cations. Yet another model depicts the two spin sets of a cation's outer electrons as partially anticoincident, Figure 2.

**Fig. 2** Drawing of a valence sphere model of one resonance structure of a "calcium electride" model of a unit cell of face centered cubic metallic calcium, $Ca^{+2}(e_2^{-2})$; and the rock salt structure of isoelectronic potassium hydride, $K^+H^-$. Black and white domains in Lewis/Linnett cubical arrangements represent the eight outer electrons of the atomic cores $Ca^{+2}$ and $K^+$ — presenting, for each cube, two tetrahedrally arranged domains of partially anticoincident spin sets. Resonance renders the two sets of domains, black and white, equivalent to each other. Large gray domains are occupied by spin-paired valence shell electron pairs, protonated in the case of potassium hydride.

Replacement of the domains of the electride ions of calcium electride by oxide ions yields the structure of calcium oxide. Replacement of the domains of the hydride ions of potassium hydride by fluoride ions yields the structure of potassium fluoride.

This situation with calcium is another instance where the isoelectronic principle helps reveal structural similarities in linguistic differences. Presented in each instance are -

- a pair of unrelated names:

  | methane | diborane | potassium hydride |
  |---------|----------|-------------------|
  | ammonia | ethylene | calcium metal |

- corresponding unrelated chemical formulas:

  | $CH_4$ | $B_2H_6$, | KH |
  |--------|-----------|-----|
  | $NH_3$ | $C_2H_4$ | Ca |

- and related ionic formulations:

  | $C^{+4}(H^-)_4$ | $(H^-)_2B^{+3}(H^-)_2B^{+3}(H^-)_2$ | $K^+(H^-)$ |
  |-----------------|-------------------------------------|------------|
  | $N^{+5}(H^-)_3(e_2^{-2})$ | $(H^-)_2C^{+4}(e_2^{-2})C^{+4}(H^-)_2$ | $Ca^{+2}(e_2^{-2})$ |

once it is understood that an electride ion, $e_2^{-2}$, is structurally equivalent to a protonated electride ion, a hydride ion, $H^-$, usually polarized, as a bond to hydrogen.

# The Alkaline Earth Metal Dihalides:
# Crystal and Gas Phase Structures

Although the dihalides of the alkaline earth metals, $MX_2$, have isoelectronic valence shells (14 electrons per 3 atoms), they have several crystal structures and two gas phase geometries: linear and bent. Coordination numbers (CN) cited below, after crystal structure types, are the cations' coordination numbers.

|    | Fluorides | Chlorides | Bromides | Iodides |
|----|-----------|-----------|----------|---------|
| Be | $BeF_2$<br>$SiS_2$, CN 4<br>linear(g) | $BeCl_2$<br>$SiS_2$, CN 4<br>linear(g) | $BeBr_2$<br>$SiS_2$, CN 4<br>linear(g) | $BeI_2$<br>$SiS_2$, CN 4<br>linear(g) |
| Mg | $MgF_2$<br>$TiO_2$, CN 6<br><u>bent</u>(g) | $MgCl_2$<br>$CdCl_2$, CN 6<br>linear(g) | $MgBr_2$<br>$CdCl_2$, CN 6<br>linear(g) | $MgI_2$<br>$CdI_2$, CN 6<br>linear(g) |
| Ca | $CaF_2$<br>$CaF_2$, CN 8<br><u>bent</u>(g) | $CaCl_2$<br>$CaCl_2$, CN 6<br>linear(g) | $CaBr_2$<br>$CaCl_2$, CN 6<br>linear(g) | $CaI_2$<br>$CdI_2$, CN 6<br>linear(g) |
| Sr | $SrF_2$<br>$CaF_2$, CN 8<br><u>bent</u>(g) | $SrCl_2$<br>$CaCl_2$, CN 6<br><u>bent</u>(g) | $SrBr_2$<br>$PbCl_2$, CN 9<br>linear(g) | $SrI_2$<br>$SrI_2$, CN 7<br>linear(g) |
| Ba | $BaF_2$<br>$CaF_2$, CN 8<br><u>bent</u>(g) | $BaCl_2$<br>$PbCl_2$, CN 9<br><u>bent</u>(g) | $BaBr_2$<br>$PbCl_2$, CN 9<br><u>bent</u>(g) | $BaI_2$<br>$PbCl_2$, CN 9<br><u>bent</u>(g) |

Average cation coordination numbers (CN) are: Be 4, Mg 6, Ca 6.5, Sr 7.5, and Ba 8.75

For the gaseous dihalides:
- all difluorides are bent, except $BeF_2$
- all barium dihalides are bent
- $SrCl_2$, with the smallest and most nucleophilic anion, after $F^-$, and the largest and most polarizable cation, after $Ba^{+2}$, is the only other bent gaseous dihalide.

Those facts are consistent with a model in which the electrostatic field of a relatively strong nucleophilic ligand (particularly $F^-$) forces the outer eight electrons of polarizable cations (particularly $Ba^{+2}$) of a Langmuir/Lewis/Linnett cubical arrangement into a spin-set coincident tetrahedral arrangement. Coordination off a pair of tetrahedron's faces yields bent gaseous molecules. Coordination off opposite faces of LLL-cubical cores yields linear molecules.

As is well known, crystal structures of ionic compounds illustrate operation of the nuclear-electron attraction term. The larger a cation (a metal atom's core), the larger tends to be the number of anions packed about it (with their outer electron's in the core's valence shell).

For cation coordination number 6, the heavier halides, particularly iodides, favor the $CdI_2/CdCl_2$ structures (they are essentially the same) over the $TiO_2$ and $CaCl_2$-distorted $TiO_2$ structures.

In the $CdI_2$ and $CdCl_2$ structures the halogen ions are arranged in approximately close-packed layers with the metal cations in half the octahedral interstices. Formed are infinite halogen-metal-halogen sandwiches stacked on top of each other through halogen-halogen contacts — often called (somewhat vaguely) "van der Waals' contacts".

In a halogen-metal-halogen sandwich, each cation is adjacent to 6 anions, in an octahedral arrangement, and each anion is adjacent to three cations, off to the inner side of its sandwich. Three of a halogen ion's four electron pairs are involved in inward-directed (covalent/dative) ionic bonds with those three metal ions. The halogen's fourth pair, a lone-pair, projects outward from the plane of the halogen-metal-halogen sandwich.

When sandwiches are stacked on top of each other, a halogen lone-pair of one sandwich nest between three lone-pairs of an adjacent sandwich. In $CdI_2$ the stacking of halogen layers of the sandwiches is ABABAB. In $CdCl_2$ it's ABCABC. The two structures have similar energies and give rise to dimorphism.

A virtue of the $CdI_2/CdCl_2$ 6,3 structures for the heavier halogens over the $TiO_2$ 6,3 structure favored by the fluorides resides in fuller use in the former instances of the potential energy space for electrons about halogen cores, particularly $I^{+7}$ ($r = 50$ pm) which, unlike small $F^{+7}$ ($r = 7$ pm), can expand its octet, as in $IF_7$. Occupancy of the valence shell of $I^{+7}$ is somewhat greater in the $CdI_2$ structure than it would be in the $TiO_2$ structure.

In summary: structures of crystalline and gaseous dihalides of the alkaline earth metals suggest that in minimizing energy by maximizing nuclear-electron attraction, it is useful to consider -

- anion interactions with metal atoms' atomic cores
- electron-pair secondary interactions with nonmetals' atomic cores
- forced spin-set coincidence of polarizable cations by strong ligand fields

# Valence Sphere Models of Gaseous Alkaline Earth Metal Dihalides

## Beryllium Dihalides

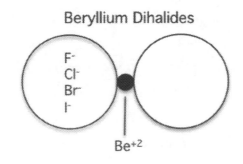

## Other Linear Dihalides

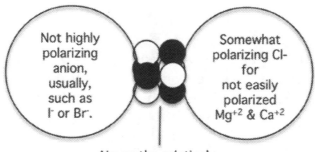

## Bent Dihalides

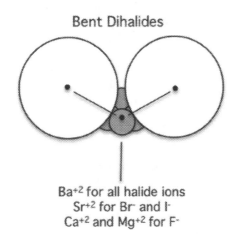

The gaseous dihalides tend to be linear for the soft, nonnpolarizing anions, such as $Br^-$ and $I^-$, coordinated by not easily polarized hard cations, such as $Mg^{+2}$ and $Ca^{+2}$ in Lewis/Linnett cubical configurations (center figure). They tend to be bent for the hard, polarizing anions, such as $F^-$ and $Cl^-$, coordinated by easily polarized soft cations, such as $Ba^{+2}$ (bent for all halide ions) and $Sr^{+2}$. All the difluorides are bent, except (of course) $BeF_2$ (whose little-polarisable $Be^{+2}$ $1s^2$ cation strongly retains a spherical shape).

# An Arithmetical Model of the Shapes of the Gaseous Alkaline Earth Metal Dihalides, $MX_2$

The larger the metal cation, $M^{+2}$, and the smaller the halogen anion, $X^-$, the greater the tendency for gaseous $MX_2$ to be bent. To model the gaseous alkaline earth metal dihalides, assign to the cations a size parameter M equal to 0, 1, 2, 3, and 4 for, respectively, Be, Mg, Ca, Sr, and Ba. And for the anions assign a size parameter X equal to 1, 2, 3, and 4 for, respectively, F, Cl, Br, and I. The larger M and the smaller X, the greater the tendency to be bent. Tabulated below for the 20 dihalides are values for the ratio R = M/X. One might expect large R-values to be associated with bent structures and small R-values to be associated with linear structures.

| M / X | | 1 | 2 | 3 | 4 |
|-------|-----|-----|-----|-----|-----|
| | | F | Cl | Br | I |
| 0 | Be | 0 | 0 | 0 | 0 |
| 1 | Mg | 1 | 1/2 | 1/3 | 1/4 |
| 2 | Ca | 2 | 1 | 2/3 | 1/2 |
| 3 | Sr | 3 | 3/2 | 1 | 3/4 |
| 4 | Ba | 4 | 2 | 4/3 | 1 |

Species with underlined R-values are linear. In every instance R ≤ 1. All species for which R > are bent. Bent $MgF_2$ and $BaI_2$ have R-values equal to 1. M-values for Mg and Ba of, say, 1.1 and 4.1, respectively, would allow one to say that all species with R ≤ 1 are linear and all species with R > 1 are bent.

The two species with R-values equal to 1, $SrBr_2$ and $CaCl_2$, are said to be "quasilinear" (Kelling K. Donald and Roald Hoffmann, *J. Am. Chem. Soc.* 2006, *128*, 11236-11249).

R-values for the barium halides track fairly well their calculated bond angles (loc. cit.).

| Halide | Calc.<XBaX | R(=M/X) |
|--------|-----------|---------|
| $BaF_2$ | 118 | 4 |
| $BaCl_2$ | 127 | 2 |
| $BaBr_2$ | 130 | 1.33 |
| $BaI_2$ | 134 | 1 |

The hexahedron/tetrahedron model of the shapes of the $MX_2$ cations predicts that the XMX bond angle will not be less than the tetrahedral angle, 109.5°. Angles greater than that, as above, might arise from anion-anion repulsion or, perhaps more likely?, from a quantum mechanical superposition of two extreme cation configurations: cubical and tetrahedral.

# Length of the BeF Bonds in Gaseous Beryllium Difluoride

An answer to the question What's the length of the bonds in gaseous $BeF_2$ illustrates Schrödinger's remark that we make calculations to see if our models are right.

A valence sphere model for a $BeF_2$ molecule that corresponds to a valence stroke diagram that pictures the BeF bond as a single bond, F—Be—F, yields an estimated bond length of 164 pm.

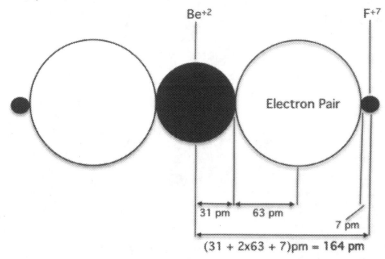

The observed bond length is much less: **137 pm**. The difference, 27 pm, lies midway between the difference between the lengths of carbon-carbon single and double bonds, 20 pm, and carbon-carbon single and triple bonds, 34 pm. That suggests — as does the exposure of the $Be^{+2}$ core in the figure above — that the molecule is a quantum mechanical superposition of a double-bonded structure, isoelectronic with $CO_2$ (with 50% dative bond character), and a triple-bonded structure, valence-shell isoelectronic with $SN_2$ (with 67% dative bond character). Pictured below are valence sphere models of those two structures.

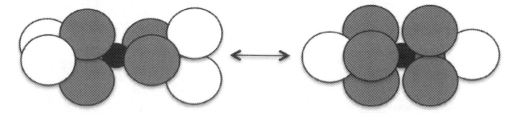

From the point of view of the bond diagram F—Be—F and its valence sphere model, the observed BeF bond length of 137 pm is *extraordinary*. It's even shorter than the CF bond of $CH_3F$, 138.5 pm, although the core $C^{+4}$ is half the size of $Be^{+2}$. Clearly –

*The BeF bonds of gaseous $BeF_2$ are not single bonds.*

The bonds' bond order (1 for single bonds, 2 for double bonds, 3 for triple bonds) appears to be about *2.5*.

$$Ta_6Cl_{12}{}^{+2}$$

# A Test of the Bond Number Equation

$$\sum(n-1)B_n = \sum(EPCN)_i - V$$

$B_n$ = number of n-center bonds
$(EPCN)_i$ = Electron Pair Coordination Number of atomic core i
$V$ = number of valence shell electron pairs = $(6\times5 + 12\times7 - 2)/2 = 56$

## Side View of a Valence Sphere Model for $Ta_6Cl_{12}{}^{+2}$

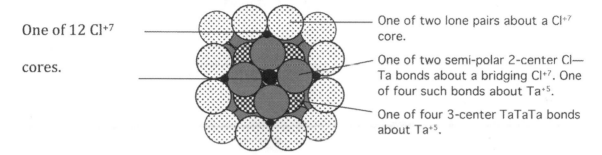

One of 12 $Cl^{+7}$ cores.

One of two lone pairs about a $Cl^{+7}$ core.

One of two semi-polar 2-center Cl—Ta bonds about a bridging $Cl^{+7}$. One of four such bonds about $Ta^{+5}$.

One of four 3-center TaTaTa bonds about $Ta^{+5}$.

## Building Outward

An inner cube of 8 3-center TaTaTa bonds
6 square-planer caps on each of the cube's six faces yielding 12 2-center Ta— Cl bonds
12 digonal sets completing as lone pairs valence shells of bridging $Cl^{+7}$ atomic cores
Total Number of Valence Shell Electron Pairs: $8 + 6\times4 + 12\times2 = 56$

## The Bond Number Equation

$$\sum(n-1)B_n = (3-1)8 + (2-1)24 = 16 + 24 = 40$$
$$\sum(EPCN)_i = 6\times8 + 12\times4 = 48 + 48 = 96$$

$$\sum(EPCN)_i - V = 96 - 56 = 40 = \sum(n-1)B_n$$

## Electronic Environments of Atomic Cores

$Ta^{+5}$: square antiprism of 8 electron pairs, as in $TaF_8{}^{-3}$
$Cl^{+7}$: tetrahedral arrangement of 4 pairs, 2 in 2-center bridging bonds, as in $Al_2Cl_6(g)$

## Oxidation Numbers

Cl: $+7 - 4\times2 = -1$
Ta: $+5 - 2(4)(1/3) = +2\ 1/3$
A Check: $12(-1) + 6(2\ 1/3) = +2$

On crystallization from aqueous solution coordinated to the ion's six faces with their somewhat exposed tantalum cores are two monovalent anions and four solvent molecules.

# Dihydrogen Complexes with Metal Coordination Compounds

Hydrogen gas is highly flammable, in oxygen, at flame temperatures. At room temperatures, however, dihydrogen is notably inert, easily demonstrated by squirting a jet of tank hydrogen at cold things. The colorless, odorless, cold gas doesn't react with the iron of its tank, the copper and zinc of the brass of its reducing valve, the glass of the glass wand it emerges from, the oxygen and nitrogen of the air it emerges into; or the skin of one's face, or one's hair, or the cotton or wool or other textiles of one's clothing, or a sheet of paper its squirted at; or water it's bubbled through. The H—H bond of $H_2$, is, in fact, one of the strongest single bonds in chemistry. And although, like HCl gas, the molecule has highly exposed electrophilic sites and, like $NH_3$ gas, it has highly exposed nucleophilic sites, hydrogen's mixture in a balloon with either gas — or with pure oxygen — yields no reaction whatsoever. Hydrogen's nucleophilic and electrophilic sites are weak, Figure 1.

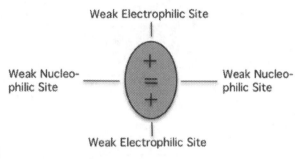

g

**Fig. 1.** Dihydrogen: H—H. The valence stroke "—" of H—H represents a shared electron pair ("=" in the figure). The symbol "H" represents the core of a hydrogen atom ("+" in the figure).

Intermolecular forces between $H_2$ molecules are weak. It's boiling point is only 21 K. Chemists were surprised, therefore, when it was discovered in 1984 that coordinatively unsaturated, d-electron-rich metal atoms, with adjacent electrophilic and nucleophilic sites, form (weak) molecular complex with dihydrogen, Figure 2.

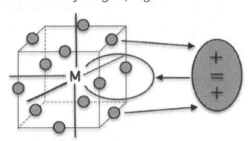

**Fig. 2.** Schematic drawing of coordination of $H_2$ by an initially pentacoordinate tungsten atom (M = W). [W's ligands (not shown) are 3 CO's and 2 P(i-propyl)$_3$]. Small circles represent lobes of three doubly occupied tungsten d-orbitals: $d_{xy}^2$ $d_{xz}^2$ $d_{yz}^2$. The "rabbit ear" represents a *vacant* coordination site.

Back donation of d-electron density from the metal atom to the dihydrogen ligand (indicated by the two long arrows) stretches the H—H bond, by about 0.2 Å, and decreases the coordinated molecule's $pK_a$, from 35 for pure $H_2$ to about 18 for coordinated $H_2$. Complete appropriation of the back-donated d-electron density by one proton of coordinated $H_2$ converts (after slight reorganization) the 3-center HMH bond of the hexacoordinate dihydrogen complex, M(H$_2$), to two 2-center M—H bonds of a heptacoordinate dihydride complex, M(H)$_2$, in a reaction called "oxidative addition", since hydrogen — a nonmetal — is more electronegative than metals.

230

# Geometries and Electronic Profiles of Halide Ion Monohydrates

Gaseous monohydrated halide ions, HOH·X⁻, have, by calculation (1), different structures, depending on whether the halide ion is the fluoride ion or one of its heavier congeners, Figure 1.

**Fig. 1.** Calculated geometries for gaseous HOH·F⁻ and HOH·I⁻.

For a single hydrogen bond (O—H·····X⁻) the linear geometry, shown for the fluoride ion at the left, Figure 1, is more stable than the bent geometry at the right. In the case of the iodide ion, however, evidently *two* bent O—H·····I⁻ hydrogen bonds are energetically superior to one linear hydrogen bond, for reasons suggested by the valence sphere models of Figure 2.

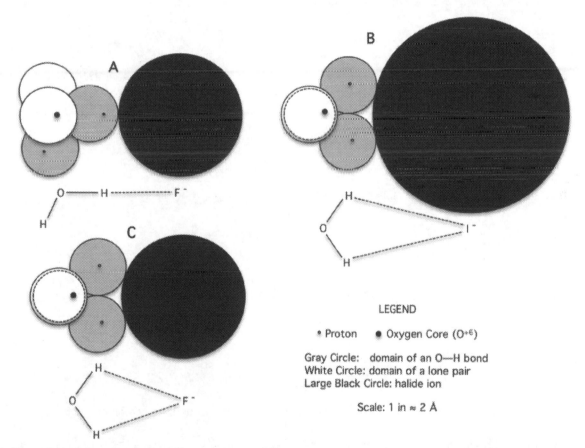

LEGEND

⁎ Proton    ● Oxygen Core (O⁺⁶)

Gray Circle: domain of an O—H bond
White Circle: domain of a lone pair
Large Black Circle: halide ion

Scale: 1 in ≈ 2 Å

**Fig. 2.** Valence sphere representations of approximate electron density profiles of, **A:** a monohydrated gaseous fluoride ion and, **B:** a monohydrated iodide ion. **C** is an isomer of **A**.

*For the chelating geometry B (and C) the larger the halide ion the less the bending of its hydrogen bonds.*

$$\text{angle } (O—H·····I^-)_B > \text{angle } (O—H·····F^-)_C$$

(1) Caldwell, G; Kebarle, P. *J. Am. Chem. Soc.* 1984, *63*, 967.

# Bonds to Hydrogen and Hydrogen Bonds

Because models, to be useful, must be wrong, in some respects, it behooves their users to be aware of their defects as well as their virtues.

*Leading Misleading Features of Ball-and-Stick Models and Valence Stroke Diagrams of Molecules*

- The models and the diagrams are poor representations of molecules' electron clouds. Skinny, one-dimensional sticks and strokes are far from being space-filling.

- The models' balls and the diagrams' chemical symbols exaggerate the sizes, relative to that of molecules' electron clouds, of the physical features that they represent: namely, atomic cores.

- Particularly misleading is location of a model's balls and a diagram's symbols "H" for hydrogen atom *cores*, on the *periphery* of a model or diagram, rather than being *embedded in a pair of electrons*, Figure 1.

Fig. 1. Valence stroke, valence stick, and valence sphere models of $CH_4$.

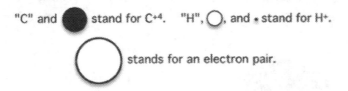

"C" and ● stand for $C^{+4}$.   "H", ○, and ∙ stand for $H^+$.

○ stands for an electron pair.

Hydrogen bonds and proton transfers are portrayed in the following fashion, Figure 2.

$$B: - - H — A \longrightarrow B — H — A \longrightarrow B — H - - - :A$$

Fig. 2. Valence stroke and valence sphere models of a proton transfer.

The valence sphere model of a proton transfer's transition state (the central figure in Figure 2) is unrealistic. The large circles represent electron pairs' profiles', with contours of about $0.032e$ (Weinhold and Landis, *Valency and Bonding*, p43, note 26), yielding a formal charge at the proton's site in the transition state of a proton transfer, as pictured, of nearly +1! Even allowing for the phenomenon of barrier penetration, existence of an electronically nearly bare proton seems unlikely.

Thus the question: Is it possible to depict proton transfers — the commonest transformations in chemistry — in a physically realistic manner using the logic of exclusive orbital models of molecules?

Strictly speaking, an electron pair's domains of exclusivity (one for each electron of the pair) is not, at any instant, fully represented, schematically, by a pair of *identical* domains. For already, in the 1920s, to obtain accurate calculated energies for the helium atom, Hylleraas was forced to employ in construction of his trial wave functions what has since been called the Method of DODS: Different Orbitals for Different Spins. Union of a DODS model with exclusivity for each spin set yields the following schematic representation of a bond to hydrogen.

**Fig. 3.** Valence stroke and valence-sphere/DODS model of a bond to hydrogen showing envelopes of domains of "alpha" and "beta" spins of different sizes to represent schematically radial "in-out" correlation.

Formation of a hydrogen bond between an electron pair donor B: and a proton donor HA involves partial overlap, as in a conventional covalent bond, of HA's alpha spin set (solid circle, say) with B's beta spin set (dashed circle), Figure 4.

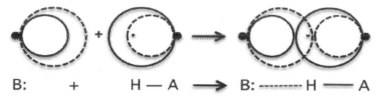

**Fig. 4.** Schematic valence-sphere/DODS model of formation of a hydrogen bond between a proton donor HA and a proton acceptor B:. Bond length H—A increases slightly (except in the case of $HCH_3$ and $H_2O$, next essay) as the internuclear distance B . . . H decreases significantly.

In a DODS model of bonds to hydrogen and hydrogen bonds, complete proton transfer can occur without passage of the proton through a region of exceedingly low electron density, at points of simultaneous tangency of four exclusive spin orbitals (two for the proton acceptor's lone pair and two for the proton donor's bond to hydrogen), because *orbitals for electrons of opposite spin in chemical bonds and lone pairs are not* — following Hylleraas (and subsequent investigators following in his footsteps, including Jack Linnett, with his "Double Quartet Hypothesis) — *completely spatially coincident*, owing to electron-electron repulsion between electrons of opposite spin.

The phenomenon of hydrogen bonding lends support — as usual, in the inferential sciences — for the inferences used in its explanation.

# Unusual Structural Changes on Formation of the Hydrogen Bond
## $H_2O \cdots H—CH_3$

> "I believe that as the methods of structural chemistry are further applied to physiological problems it will be found that the significance of the hydrogen bond for physiology is greater than that of any other single feature." LINUS PAULING

On formation of a hydrogen bond

$$B: + H—A \ = \ B: \cdots H—A$$

the distance $R_{H—A}$ usually *increases* and, correspondingly, the frequency $v_{HA}$ usually *decreases.*

However, according to calculations of Weinhold and Landis (*Valency and Bonding*, p609), the opposite occurs for $H_2O$ and $HCH_3$. Valence bond theory's primary and secondary principles suggest the following explanation for those counter-intuitive facts.

*Valence Stroke Representation of Electron Shifts in Formation of a Hydrogen Bond between Molecules of Water and Methane*

Curly arrows indicate that formation of a hydrogen bond is the first step of a proton transfer with formation, ultimately, in the present instance, of $H_3O^+$ and $CH_3^-$. Negative charge is transferred from oxygen (and, from the point of view of formal charges, its hydrogens) via hydrogen to carbon (and the hydrogens of its methyl goup).

By the s-Character Rule, carbon will therefore divert some of the s-character of its CH bonds of its methyl group to its bond to the hydrogen of the hydrogen bond, the initial receptor of negative charge from the water molecule's lone pair, thereby tending to *decrease* the length of that bond — and, also (a prediction of the model), tending to decrease the methyl group's HCH angles.

> Weinhold and Landis' natural carbon hybrid orbitals for carbon's CH bonds of its methyl group are carbon $sp^{3.04}$ hybrids, slightly depleted in s character and enriched in p character compared to tetrahedral $sp^3$ hybrids, whereas its orbital in its bond to the hydrogen of the hydrogen bond is an $sp^{2.87}$ hybrid, slightly enriched in s-character compared to tetrahedral $sp^3$ hybrids.

The postulated initial increase in electron density at the proton of the hydrogen atom of a hydrogen bond, indicated by the lower arrow in the figure above — which prompts, as postulated, a rehybridization of the carbon atom with, accordingly, a slight decrease in the distance between the proton and its covalently attached carbon atom — might occur in the *initial stages* of formation of all hydrogen bonds.

# Probing Molecules' Nucleophilic Sites with Brönsted Acids and a Lewis Acid

Probes of nucleophilic sites in the following discussion are the Brönsted acids H—X, X = F or Cl, and the Lewis acid diodine: I—I.

## *Electron Domain Models of HX and I₂*

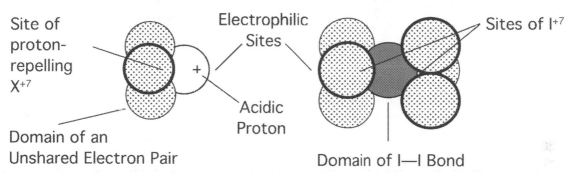

In acid-base adducts, geometries at the acidic sites, H or I, are linear.

$$B \cdots H - X \qquad B \cdots I - I$$

Intermolecular distances B $\cdots$ H and B $\cdots$ I are less than van der Waals contacts and greater than normal covalent bond lengths. Bonds H—X and I—I are stretched, slightly. If nucleophile B carries a substituent S, the angle SBH is a normal bond angle. The BHX adduct is the first step of a proton transfer. The BII adduct is the first step of an $S_N2$ reaction. The B $\cdots$ H interaction is called a hydrogen bond. The B $\cdots$ I interaction has been called a "pair-pocket interaction", a "face-centered bond", and a "halogen intermolecular bond".

## *Adducts of Ammines with HX and I₂*

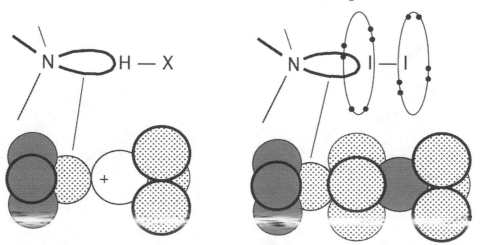

Both interactions are *electrostatic*: positive charges (H⁺ and I⁺⁷) attracting and attracted by negative charges (of lone pairs).

Some molecules, such as $H_2O$ and HCN, have both nucleophilic and electrophilic sites, N and E.

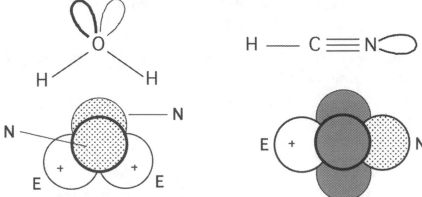

The water molecule — "tetrahedral" from the standpoint of its electron-pair domains — has with its two protonated O—H bonds two electrophilic proton donor sites and with its two lone pairs two nucleophilic proton acceptor sites. In the crystalline state, it behaves like a "tetrahedral carbon atom". Ice has the diamond structure.

Crystalline hydrogen cyanide consists of close packed, linear, hydrogen-bonded chains.

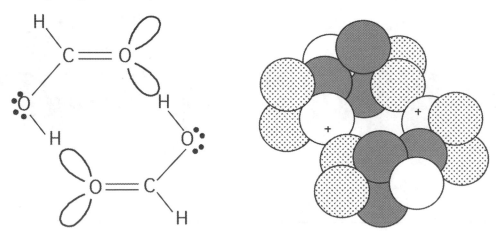

Notable instances of hydrogen bonding occur in the six-membered ring (not counting hydrogens of hydrogen bonds) of the dimer of formic acid.

Electron pairs of the 2-membered rings of multiple bonds are sufficiently exposed to serve as nucleophilic sites in formation of hydrogen bonds. The axis of an electrophilic hydrogen-bonding HX molecule is, as expected, perpendicular to the axis of the multiple bonds and for double bonds perpendicular to the molecular plane defined by the double-bonded atoms and adjacent atoms, illustrated below for ethylene.

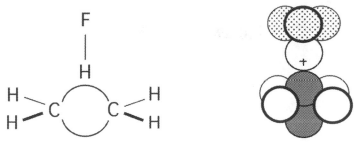

Carbon-carbon bonds of 3-membered rings are also sufficiently exposed to hydrogen bond to hydrogen halides, illustrated below for cyclopropane.

In the case of the allene/HF hydrogen-bonded adduct, the HF axis is displaced 0.127 Å from the midpoint of the C=C bond it's H-bonded to toward the central carbon atom, owing, in the present view, to core-core repulsions and consequent displacement of the terminal $C^{+4}$ cores from the centers of their tetrahedral interstices — with, accordingly, an opening up of the HCH bond angle from the tetrahedral value of 109.5 degrees to 116 degrees.

White circles represent the tetrahedral interstices formed by the carbon core's four pairs of valence shell electrons. Smaller black circles represent locations of carbon nuclei in allene.

Estimated below are the displacements in the model of the terminal $C^{+4}$ cores required to fit the observed HCH angle.

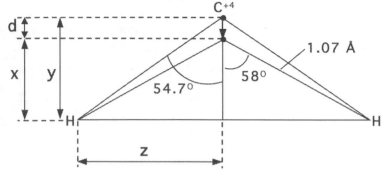

$x = 1.07 \cos 58^0 = 0.5670$

$z = 1.07 \sin 58^0 = 0.9074$

$C—H = z/\sin 54.7^0 = 1.112$

$y = CH \cos 54.7^0 = 0.6426$

$d = y - x = \underline{0.076}$

H-Bond Displacement = $\underline{0.127}$

PHILOSOPHICAL ASIDE: The figure illustrates the remarks that one makes calculations (as above at the right) to see if one's pictures (such as the one at the left) are plausible. And one makes pictures (as at the left) to make one's calculations (at the right) comprehensible.

The calculated terminal carbon core displacements outward from the centers of their tetrahedral interstice is comparable to but significantly less than the observed "displacement" of the hydrogen bond from the midpoint of the carbon-carbon double bond. The double bond's "midpoint" is not, however, the point of maximum electron density in that region, owing to the outward displacements of the terminal carbon cores from the centers of their interstices, which make their electrostatic hold on their double bonds' bonding electrons less than that of the central carbon core. As the terminal carbon cores move outward, double bond electron density moves inward and, with it, the hydrogen bond, thereby increasing its observed "displacement", from, in this account, 0.076 Å to 0.127 Å.

In orbital language, one says that the central carbon core uses $sp^3$ hybrid orbitals in its bent bonds, 25 percent s-character, whereas, since the terminal carbon cores use in their bonds to hydrogen s-enriched hybrids, more than 25 percent s-character, they use, accordingly, s-depleted hybrids, less than 25 percent s-character, in their hybrid orbital contributions to the double bonds' bent bonds. And with that decrease in s-character goes a decrease in electron attraction and, consequently, a shift in electron density toward the central carbon core.

The hydrogen-bonded complex of hydrogen chloride with but-3-en-1-yne raises several questions.

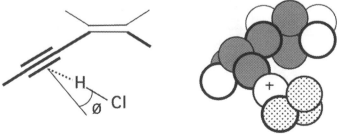

- *Why is the hydrogen bond to the triple bond rather than to the double bond?* An Ans.: Maximum donor-acceptor interactions across the carbon-carbon single bond staggers the three equivalent domains of the triple bond with respect to the three domains at the

238

other end of the single bond: two domains of the double bond and a C—H domain. Weakest of the six donor interactions is that of the triple bond domain trans to the C—H domain, making that triple bond domain the molecule's strongest nucleophilic site toward external electrophilic reagents.

- *Why is the hydrogen bond cis to the double bond, rather than trans, on the more exposed side of the triple bond?* An Ans.: Because, as mentioned, the triple bond's cis site is butyne's most nucleophilic site.

- *Why is the hydrogen bond's axis, perpendicular to the axis of the triple bond, displaced 0.04Å toward the vinyl group?* An Ans.: Because hydrogen is less electronegative than a carbon core of a vinyl group, the carbon cores of the triple bond are not equally electronegative toward the triple bond's electrons. By the s-Character Rule the interior carbon core of the triple bond devotes more s-character to the triple bond domains than does the terminal carbon core. Consequently, the triple bond's electron density, instead of being distributed equally between its two carbon cores, is shifted toward the interior carbon core and, with it, the axis of the hydrogen bond is shifted, in the same direction, toward the vinyl group.

- *Why is the hydrogen bond's axis rotated out of the plane of the molecule's nuclei by an angle Ø = 34 degrees?* A Tentative Ans.: A tendency for electron pairs of triple bonds to be angularly anticoincident moves one spin-set's electron density toward an eclipsed rather than a staggered configuration across the carbon-carbon single bond.

The hydrogen bond between molecules of water and hydrogen fluoride is another intermolecular interaction with interesting features. Both molecules have nucleophilic and electrophilic sites. The system's highest occupied localized molecular orbitals are the lone pairs of $H_2O$. Its lowest vacant localized molecular orbital is the electrophilic site off the proton of HF. Formed, accordingly, is the hydrogen bond $H_2O \cdots H—F$, represented below in two ways.

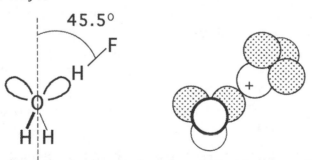

The angle between the axis of the hydrogen bond and the bisector of the HOH angle is, at first sight, perhaps surprising. Since the HOH bond angle in $H_2O$ is some 5 degrees less than the tetrahedral angle, the angle between the axes of the hybrid orbitals that describe equivalent lone pairs is some 5 degrees greater than the tetrahedral angle of 109.5°, i.e., about 114°, with a bisector angle of 57°. That would be the angle indicated above, rather than 45.5°, if the hydrogen bond indicated, correctly, the disposition of the lone pair.

$H_2O$ has, however, two adjacent nucleophilic sites. Tunneling of the OH protons, with the molecule's electrons following the nuclear geometry, flips the molecule so that the

HF molecule samples the other lone pair. At no time is hydrogen bonding completely broken, for the barrier to the tunneling is reported to be only 1.5 kcal/mole, about one-fifth the hydrogen bond energy. The flip may be pictured in the following manner.

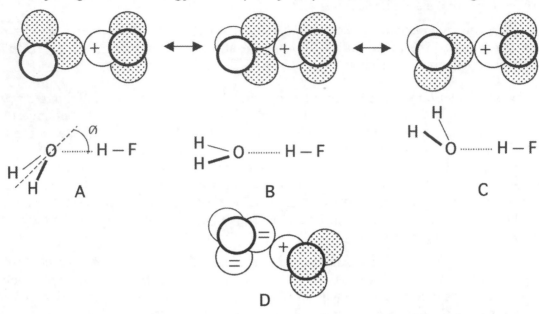

A  Hypothetical equilibrium configuration for the $H_2O$/HF hydrogen-bonded complex, FHO/HOH-bisector-angle $\emptyset \approx 57^\circ$.

B  Transition state: a bifurcated hydrogen bond, $\emptyset = 0^\circ$.

C  Second hypothetical equilibrium configuration. In the passage from A through B to C, the oxygen and fluorine nuclei remain essentially stationary.

D  Valence-sphere model of the observed equilibrium configuration that corresponds to hypothetical configuration C. Electrostatic attraction between the hydrogen-bonding proton and the oxygen lone-pair to which it is not intimately hydrogen bonded causes the proton to move toward that lone-pair, and, with it, the remainder of the HF molecule, thereby decreasing the FHO/HOH-bisector angle $\emptyset$ from approximately $57^\circ$ to the observed value of $45.5^\circ$.

In the valence sphere model of $H_2O$ above, all valence-shell domains of $O^{+6}$ have been taken to be the same size: $r/Å = 0.6 + 0.4 \times r(O^{+6}) = 0.6 + 0.04 \times 0.09 = 0.64$. One might wonder: Might the $\emptyset$-value of 45.5 degrees arise, in part, from occurrence of electron domains of different sizes? The model of one-size-fits-all-valence-shell-electron-pairs-about-$O^{+6}$-in-$H_2O$ yields for the hydrogen bond $O \cdots O$ distance in water and ice for r(electron pair domain) = 0.64 Å a value of $2[2r + r(O^{+6})] = 2[2 \times 0.64 + 0.09]$ Å = 2.74Å. The observed value is 2.76 Å.

Data cited in this essay are from A. C. Legon's Tilden Lecture on "The Properties of Hydrogen-bonded Dimers from Rotational Spectroscopy," *Chem. Soc. Rev.*, 1990, **19**, 197-237.

# SUMMARY
## Leading Accomplishments of Modern Conceptual Valence Bond Theory

"A theory of valency can only be justified," wrote Nevil Sidgwick, "by showing that it is applicable to chemistry as a whole." On the other hand, the opposite of a profound statement, Bohr liked to say, may be a profound statement. Thus, although "The object of theoretical physics is to calculate results that can be compared with experiment," wrote Dirac, "It is quite unnecessary," he added, "that any satisfactory description of the whole course of the phenomena should be given" — fortunately!, for for the most part science progresses in small steps. Limited accomplishments of Modern Conceptual Valence Bond Theory, sans a theory of compounds that contain $d$- and $f$-electrons, include, for compounds of $s$- and $p$-electrons, -

- "A wonderful heuristic scheme" (Roald Hoffmann)

- Leading properties of solutions to Schrödinger's equation without having to solve the equation

- Inexpensive models of many molecules' approximate electron density profiles

- Visual expression of wavefunctions' exclusive orbital character

- A simple explanation for the saturation and directional character of chemical affinity

- A student-friendly introduction to chemical bonding without reference to atomic orbitals, orbital mixing, or Schrödinger's equation

- When supplemented with a set of spheres and instructions for their assembly, a virtually fail-safe molecular analogue computer

- Simple explanations for existence of –

  o two types of elements: metals (large cores, L) and nonmetals (small cores, S)

  o three types of chemical bonds: covalent (SS), ionic (SL), and metallic (LL)

  o two leading branches of chemistry, featuring electron pair coordination numbers 4 and 6

  o the Octet Rule

  o the Tetrahedral Rule

  o the Bond Number Rule: $\sum(n-1)B_n = \sum(EPCN)_i - V$

  o the Valence Stroke Termination Rule

  o Bent's Rule: Electropositive substituents preempt atomic $s$ character

  o the stereochemistry of –

    ▪ single, double, and triple bonds' valence stroke environments

    ▪ "hypervalent" and "hypovalent" species

    ▪ multicenter bonding

  o dative bonding

  o inter- and intra-molecular electron-pair donor-acceptor interactions

  o the phenomenon of superposition ("resonance")

  o electronic structures of stable odd-electron molecules, such as nitric oxide

  o stable triplet molecules, such as dioxygen

- o nonlinear gaseous difluorides of Mg, Ca, Sr, and Ba
- o nonlinear, at carbon, $Ph_3P=C=CPh_3$; and other unusual molecular properties
- A natural sequel to Lewis's substitution of two dots for a valence stroke
- An explanation of the Valence Stroke Noncrossing Rule
- Generic models of isoelectronic species
- "Electride ion" models of metals
- Locations of molecules' nucleophilic and electrophilic sites
- Models of "curly arrow chemistry"
- Approximate models of molecules' configurations of maximum probability
- Concrete images of the terms in the expression $E_{total} = V_{ne} + V_{nn} + V_{ee} + T$
- Critiques of –
  - o VSEPR Theory
  - o Conceptual MO Theory
  - o Antiaromaticity
- A consilience between the principles of structural organic and inorganic chemistry, expressed by a *Generalized Doctrine of Coordination* and the phrases *"Ionic Models of Covalent Compounds"* and *"All compounds are ion compounds"*.
- A correspondence between a Valence Stroke Termination Rule of Valence Stroke Theory and the Hohenberg-Kohn Theorems of Density Functional Theory
- Provision of approximate molecular geometries for use in MO Theory's construction of molecular orbitals by the LCAO method

Those results arise from a union of chemistry and physics.

| From Chemistry: | Crum Brown's bond diagrams, and their back story |
| | van't Hoff's tetrahedral carbon atom |
| | Lewis's Inductions |
| |     Valence strokes = two electrons |
| |     Elements' symbols = atomic cores |
| |     Charge balance achieved with lone pairs |
| | Pauling's rules of crystal chemistry |
| | Ingold's physical organic chemistry |
| | Kimball's Discovery: valence strokes = valence spheres |
| From Physics: | J. J. Thomson's indistinguishable electrons |
| | Rutherford's nuclear model of the atom |
| | Moseley's atomic numbers |
| | Schrödinger's wavefunctions |
| | Heisenberg's *antisymmetric* wavefunctions |
| | Fermi holes |
| From Their Union: | Modern Conceptual Valence Bond Theory of Exclusive Orbital Models of Close Confederations of Electrically Charged Wave-Like Fermions |

# That's It

## *An Afterword*

That's it: the remarkable story of Conceptual Valence Bond Theory, comparable to the story of one's mother tongue.

The English language expresses every conceivable thought that one might have with merely 26 symbols and several punctuation marks (chiefly the simplest conceivable mark: a period), arranged as words and sentences, constructed according to grammatical rules.

Conceptual Valence Bond Theory is, similarly, a working language, for describing the structures of millions and millions of molecules, with the same 26 symbols and, so to speak, two "punctuation marks": the simplest conceivable one- and three-dimensional figures, the valence stroke and the valence sphere, arranged as bond diagrams and molecular models, according to a small number of structural principles, listed below.

### *Conceptual Valence Bond Theory's Leading Principles*

- close-packing about atomic cores of exclusive electron domains
- a bond number equation
- a valence stroke termination rule
- electron pair donor-acceptor interactions
- multicenter bonding
- dative bonding
- the isoelectronic principle
- core-core repulsion
- resonance
- different structures for different spin sets
- dispersal of lone pairs about large atomic cores

The Principles express chemists' efforts to submit to reality by way of observations and inductions. Jointly the Principles obey a Law of Poverty, being sufficiently poor in number to allow the same ones to be used frequently, over and over again, always with the same, fixed meaning.

Both the English language and Conceptual Valence Theory rely heavily on positional notation, in, respectively, rules of spelling and stereochemistry. Both satisfy a Law of Manageability, with easily manipulated symbols. And both satisfy a Law of Comprehension, generating images comprehended at a glance. Both create, consequently, among users, a Phenomenon of Fluency. Both are major achievements of human thought, often undervalued, however, owing to ease of use, once one has become fluent, after, perhaps, for Valence Theory, a year or two of organic and inorganic chemistry.

# APPENDICES
## *Mistakes Happen*

"I guess I appreciate the valence sphere model less than you do because
I don't want the physical (cork, Styrofoam, wood) models as much as you do."

A CORRESPONDENT

## Introduction

The correspondent may speak for many chemists, at the present time (2014).

How can cork, Styrofoam, or wood models of **electrons in molecules**, *for heaven's sake!,* possibly be taken seriously? For according to the dominant theory of the electronic structure of matter, electrons in molecules are pictured as being *delocalized* in orbitals that embrace *entire* molecules, in a theory called "Molecular Orbital Theory". Each electron's orbital shares, it's supposed, the same regions of space as all the other orbitals: namely, the entire space occupied by a molecule's electron cloud. The individual orbitals, albeit orthogonal to each other, owing to changes of sign, overlap each other extensively. The idea of representing them by mutually exclusive, *physically impenetrable spheres made of cork, Styrofoam, or wood* is preposterous! Molecules' electron clouds are soft and "squishy". Modeling them with hard spheres is ridiculous! Nothing could be further from the truth — including, perhaps, that "truth"?

*Mistakes happen.* Seventeenth century chemistry had its Phlogiston Theory. At one time in the eighteenth century Sir Humphrey Davy was the only person on the planet who believed that the pale green gas from sea salt, known to give an acid with hydrogen, an element, was itself an element, devoid of Lavoisier's acid-generating oxygen. Today chemists and chemistry teachers still have no universally recognized symbol for the smallest unit of "amount" (from a pedagogical point of view, a mistake) — say "e", for entity (and, hence, cannot write, e.g., that Avogadro's Constant, $N_A$, the number of entities per unit amount, $N/n$, is equal to $1/e \approx 6 \times 10^{23}$/mole, where mole = mol e, if one defines "mol" to be a pure number equal to the number of atoms in 12 grams of carbon-12). And for over a century, to the present time, in periodic tables on walls of chemistry buildings throughout the world helium resides above neon!

If such a whopper can exist so openly for so long, perhaps it's not altogether implausible to suppose that valence theory, too, has its helium whopper, stemming from Mulliken's rejection of "chemical ideology", and its localized valence strokes, for, instead, orbitals that sprawl over one another almost everywhere, even in molecules' ground states, in violation of Heisenberg's Principle of Spatial Exclusion for Fermions.

The purpose of the following three essays is to lend credence to the phrase "helium whopper", viewed in the present context as precedent for existence of a corresponding whopper in valence theory, in the form of ground state delocalized molecular orbitals.

# Regularities in Periodic Tables Contingent on Location of Hydrogen above Lithium and Helium above Beryllium

**Triad Locations.** If hydrogen is located above lithium and helium above beryllium in periodic tables, then *Groups' first triads ALWAYS begin with their SECOND elements.* <u>Never is a Group's *first* element a member of a vertical triad of atomic numbers</u> (in which the middle atomic number is the average of the other two). Locating He above Ne creates, however, two exceptions to the Triad Rule: the triad Be Mg Ca [Z's = 4 12 20, with 12 = (4 + 20)/2] begins (absent He above Be) with its Groups' first element (Be); and He, always a first element, becomes a member of a triad: He Ne Ar (Z's = 2 10 18).

**Groups' Sizes.** For H/Li and He/Be, and for atomic numbers running through 120, all of a block's Groups are the same size, with 8 − 2 $\ell$ members.

**Row Occupancy Rule.** Let R = ordinal number of a block's row within its block, beginning at 1. Let B = the ordinal number of a block when blocks are arranged by size, beginning at 0 for the 2-column block. Set P = R + 2B. Then in Bohr's Aufbau Process, the order in which blocks' rows are occupied is given by the rule: *Row with the smallest P first and, for a given P, largest B first.* There are NO EXCEPTIONS — in the d- and f-blocks, e.g., or elsewhere, unless, for instance, helium is located in the p-block above neon.

**Ordinal-Number/Quantum-Number Correspondence.** Let r and $\ell$ be, respectively, the radial and angular quantum numbers of the predominant type of orbital occupied by electrons in Bohr's Aufbau Buildup of the atoms of row R of block B. If H is located above Li and He above Be, then always, without exception, r = R and $\ell$ = B.

**Congeners' Number of Outer Electrons and Core Charges.** Universal validity of the rule that congeners have the same number of outer electrons and the same core charges requires location of hydrogen above lithium and helium above beryllium.

**Electronegativity Rule.** Groups' first elements always have their groups' largest electronegativities, with one exception, when helium is located above neon, since helium's electronegativity, on Allen's scale, is less than neon's electronegativity. The Electronegativity Rule is a special instance of —

**Block-to-Block Trends in First-Element Distinctiveness.** With H/Li and He/Be, the distinctiveness of blocks' first-row elements with respect to their congeners and their first-row neighbors increases, block-to-block, in the order: f < d << p <<< s.

**Block-to-Block Trend in Onset of Metallic Character within Groups.** With H/Li and He/Be, *suddenness* of the onset of metallic character within groups with increasing atomic number increases, block-to-block, in the above order: f < d << p <<< s.

**Block-to-Block Trend in $\ell$-Nobility.** For He above Be, difficulty of oxidation of a block's predominant type of differentiating electrons increases block-to-block for the last elements of blocks' first rows (He, Ne, Zn, Yb) in the order: f < d < p < s.

**Periodic Tables of Perfect Regularity.** The left-step, right-step, front-step, and other periodic tables of perfect regularity (regarding lengths of blocks' rows and columns and arrangements of gaps, if any, within periods and columns) require location of helium above beryllium.

*Helium-above-beryllium brings out the best in periodic tables!*

# A Striking Atomanalogy Involving Periodicity's First Four Elements

In a series of articles regarding classification of atoms according to the Periodic Law, Mendeleev introduced "*atomanalogies*". A striking atomanalogy is suggested by the shape of the left step form of the periodic table.

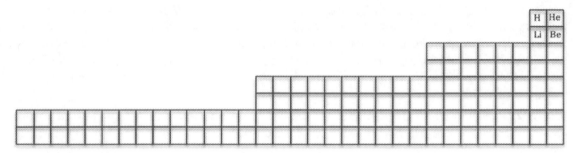

Atomic hydrogen stands to atomic lithium, suggests the table, as atomic helium stands to atomic beryllium.

$$H : Li :: He : Be$$

Stated algebraically,

$$H/Li = He/Be$$

The expression is obtained directly from the left step periodic table by placing horizontal vinicula between H & Li and He & Be, and adding an equals sign.

Along with atomic numbers, and atomic weights, one of the most atomic of atomic properties is atoms' first stage ionization energies. Letting elements' symbols stand for those energies (in eV) yields the expression -

$$H/Li = 13.6/5.6 = \mathbf{2.5} \approx \mathbf{2.6} = 24.6/9.32 = He/Be$$

The analogy is 96% accurate. It is one of the reasons for suggesting that location of hydrogen and helium at the top of the s-block is a *natural location* for those atoms in the Periodic System. The assignment is in complete agreement with the atoms' electronic structures, and with a number of recently recognized regularities in the Periodic System, including the Laws of Triads, Group Sizes, and a Block-to-Block Trend in First Element Distinctiveness.

Since quantum mechanical calculations yield with impressive accuracy the cited ionization energies, the numerical accuracy of the hydrogen-helium-lithium-beryllium atomanalogy might be viewed as quantum mechanical justification for location in periodic tables of hydrogen above lithium and helium above beryllium.

The assignments H/Li and He/Be agree with Mendeleev's assertion that classification of the chemical elements according to the Periodic Law is a classification of the elements as atoms [implied by their arrangement according to their *atomic numbers*] and not as simple substances.

The chief *chemical* justification for the helium-above-beryllium assignment is the block-to-block trend in First Element Distinctiveness: huge in the s-block (with H above Li and He above Be), smaller but still large in the p-block (with C above Si, N above P, and O above S), and least of all in the d-block (all of whose elements are metals).

The Helium Whopper and the MO Whopper are similar in their durability: well over a century for the Helium Whopper, well over half a century for the MO Whopper. A corrective stands in the wings for each one: the Left Step Periodic Table for the Helium Whopper, the Exclusive Orbital Models for the MO Whopper.

# Two Heliums

*ATOMIC HELIUM:* a $1s^2$ system
*SIMPLE-SUBSTANCE HELIUM:* an inert gas

Mendeleev was acutely aware of the immense significance for the Periodic System of the Elements of the distinction between *atoms* and *simple substances*. In an essay on "How I Discovered the Periodic System of Elements" (reprinted in William Jensen's book *Mendeleev on the Periodic Law)*, he wrote in note 3:

> "In the particular case of carbon, chemical nomenclature clearly expresses the difference between carbon as a simple body (charcoal) and carbon as an *atom* (carbon). For many other elements, indeed, for the majority, this distinction of terms does not exist. Thus one designates by the name oxygen both a gaseous body and the same element as a component of water and many other liquid and solid bodies. One would hope that this inadequate terminology will be perfected in time." MENDELEEV, 1899.

Owing to existence of the Periodic System's "problem elements" (especially hydrogen and heoium), natural philosophers' multi-millennial effort to define one word, the word "element", remains a work in progress.

In his famous work *An Essay Concerning Human Understanding,* John Locke, some two centuries before Mendeleev, devoted an entire chapter to remarkably prescient remarks regarding the type of "inadequate terminology" noted by Mendeleev.

> "Because simple ideas that coexist and are united in the same subject [a substance], being very numerous, and having all an equal right to go into the complex specific idea which the specific name is to stand for, men, though they propose to themselves the very same subject to consider [e.g., "helium"], yet frame very different ideas about it; and so *the name they use for it unavoidably comes to have, in several men, very different significations* [emphasis added]... For, though in the substance of gold one satisfies himself with colour and weight, yet another thinks solubility *in aqua regia* as necessary to be joined with that colour and weight; others put into it ductility or fixedness, &c., as they have been taught by tradition or experience. Who of all these has established the right signification of the word, gold?"

> > "There is no infallible authority for determining the connotation of names which signify sorts of substances," adds an editor. "'Gold' suggests one connotation to the banker, another to the mineralogist, another to the artist {and another to the bench chemist; and yet another to a Mendeleev}".

> "All [properties] together, seldom or never fail to produce that various and doubtful signification in the names of substances, which causes such uncertainty, disputes, or mistakes, when we come to a philosophical use of them." JOHN LOCKE (1632-1704), *Essay,* Book III, Chapter IX: "Of the Imperfection of Words" [slightly augmented].

Unfamiliarity with mankind's mistakes of "doubtful signification" owing to "inadequate terminology" owing to "the imperfection of words" has fostered a repetition of such mistakes regarding a central feature of the Central Science's central icon. Obviously the Periodic Classification of the Chemical Elements According to the Periodic Law is not about a classification of simple substances, such as graphite or diamond, white or red phosphorus, dioxygen or ozone, or metals and inert gases. Carbon, a light nonmetal, and lead, a heavy metal, are in the same Group, as are neon, an inert gas, and xenon, a chemically reactive gas. One might hope, with Mendeleev, that chemists will perfect their terminology, especially when speaking of element number 2 and its location in the Periodic System, through use of such phrases as "atomic helium", "atomic beryllium", and "atomic neon".

# Criticisms and Refutations

## A Dialogue Concerning Two Valence Systems

HAB  Author's Criticisms of MO Theory
*SKP  A skeptic's responses*
HAB  The author's rejoinders

The following dialogue is not made up. It actually occurred, between the author and a noted physical chemist, not identified here, to avoid possible embarrassment.

HAB  **Conceptual MO Theory is incomplete.** It offers in and of itself no recipe for deciding where the atoms of its LCAO approximations to molecular orbitals are.

*SKP  In principle MOs can be generated for a structure by the LCAO method regardless of where the nuclei are located.*

HAB  Exactly! Precisely my point! The fact that MOs can be generated <u>no matter where the atoms *are*</u> means that <u>Conceptual MO Theory, in and of itself, does not tell one where the atoms are</u>! For that information MO theorists must turn elsewhere: to classical conceptual valence bond theory!

HAB  **Writing down MOs for atoms that may be located anywhere is like <u>a game with</u>** <u>no rules</u>. It's too easy! No pain, no gain. Needed, to make an orbital-location game scientifically significant, are rules, such as those of classical structural theory, for handling valence strokes.

*SKP  Yes. If one is looking for the most stable structure, one can use some of the same guiding principles as conceptual VB theory.*

HAB  Conceptual VB Theory is, in other words, the ultimate oracle regarding stable (ground state) structures?

*SKP  Or one may use some other sources of intuition and insight. Sometimes the intuition is correct, sometimes not. For example, the most stable structure of a species with one Cl and two O is not O~Cl~O but Cl~O~O.*

HAB  Your implication seems to be this: If CVBT cannot account for the alleged OClO/ClOO fact, it's suspect? Well, then, let's see what CVBT has to say about OClO and ClOO.

OClO and ClOO have 19 valence shell electrons split, presumably, 9 of one spin and 10 of the other. For quartets of spins about each atomic core, the 9-membered spin set has in bonds $B_9 = 3 \times 4 - 9 = 3$ electrons. $B_{10} = 3 \times 4 - 10 = 2$. Formal charges for the O's and Cl in the OClO structure are, respectively, -3/4 and +3/2. For the ClOO structure formal charges are, respectively, +1/2, +1/2, and -1. Slightly better? Neither set takes into account the fact that $Cl^{+7}$, some three times the size of $O^{+6}$, can expand its quartets, and presumably does so when bound to oxygen atoms, with their lone pairs.

Suppose, accordingly, that in OClO and ClOO the electron coordination number for $Cl^{+7}$ for the 10-member spin set is 5 (instead of 4). Then $B_{10} = 5 + 2 \times 4 - 10 = 3$ (instead of, as previously, 2). Now formal charges for the structures are somewhat better, being for OClO, O -1/2 and Cl +1; and for ClOO, -1/2, +1, and -1/2 — still somewhat unsatisfactory for both spin sets. The compound is, in fact, explosive.

Tabulated below for the two structures, OClO and ClOO, are formal charges for the octet and expanded octet structures and their numbers of unshared or lone electrons (le).

| | O | Cl | O | Cl le | O le | | Cl | O | O | Cl le | O le |
|---|---|---|---|---|---|---|---|---|---|---|---|
| Octet | -3/4 | +3/2 | -3/4 | 3 | 11 | | +1/2 | +1/2 | -1 | 5 | 9 |
| Expnd Octet | -1/2 | +1 | -1/2 | 3 | 10 | | -1/2 | +1 | -1/2 | 6 | 7 |

To judge by formal charges, for octet structures ClOO is better than OClO. For expanded octet structures OClO is a shade better than ClOO. And for a given structure the expanded octet structure is better than the octet structure.

In terms of bascicity and stability of lone electrons, Cl lone electrons are less basic and, accordingly, more stable than O lone electrons, tending to make octet ClOO more stable than octet OClO and, also, expanded octet ClOO more stable than expanded octet OClO.

All in all, Conceptual VB Theory favors ClOO over OClO.

SKP  *To continue: If we have one H, one N, and two O's the most stable structure is H~O-N~O and not H~N(~O)2 but if we have one methyl (viewed here as an atom), one N and two O's the most stable structure is CH3~N(~O)2 and not CH3~O-N~O.*

HAB  Favoring the nitro-structure $RNO_2$ over the nitrite structure RONO is resonance, i.e. partial anticoincidence, for spin sets of the nitro group: thus the greater stability of the nitro-structure for R = $CH_3$.

For R = H, however, one needs to consider that anticoincidence for the two spin sets of the nitro-group leads to what I called years ago a "splayed single bond", to account for the planarity of $O_2N$—$NO_2$ and, in spite of its long NN bond, its relatively large barrier to internal rotation. To achieve a strong H—N bond, however, the two spin sets of H—$NO_2$ must become more nearly coincident than is normally the case for nitro groups.

HAB  **Conceptual MO Theory usually assumes as given, for aromatic systems, a sigma-bonded network.**

SKP  *If there are enough electrons for this network to be generated. If not, other insight is needed.*

HAB  Such as what? Hybridization?

SKP  *What's so bad about that?*

HAB  Hybrid orbitals are merely a *description* of chemical bonding, not an explanation.

"The starting point in the theory of hybridization is the experimentally determined geometry of a molecule. Methane, for example, is a tetrahedral molecule with each

H—C—H bond angle being 109° 28'" (Philip Matthews, *Quantum Chemistry of Atoms and Molecules*, page 71).

HAB  Also: **CMOT is incomplete.** To initiate applications of the Variation Theorem, it needs a "Z-Matrix", dependent on classical valence bond theory, and empirical data.

SKP  *My understanding is that the Z matrix is used to generate the coordinates of the nuclei. This is then used as first input for a "quantitative" calculation of the molecular energy in calculational MO theory . . .*

HAB  Precisely. Its use requires use of Conceptual Valence Bond Theory.

SKP  *. . . but [is] unnecessary for qualitative understanding.*

HAB    How, however, is "qualitative understanding" achieved in Conceptual Molecular Orbital Theory, without use, somewhere along the line, of Conceptual Valence Bond Theory?

SKP    *I have never done a VB calculation – what information is needed. How does one distinguish isomers or enter a plausible initial structure. Also, given that one is doing a calculation, doesn't any trial wavefunction (MO or VB) give an energy higher than the correct one (this is the Variation theorem) for any Hamiltonian we choos?. Now, if a different Hamiltonian is employed (as in DFT), then this theorem doesn't apply when comparing the energy from the two different Hamiltonians. Also, what empirical data is absolutely needed – in principle, one can calculate all of the energy minima and look at the one (ones) one cares about. The empirical data just helps one get closer to a given minimum of interest, if it be a minimum in fact at all.*

HAB    The point of <u>conceptual</u> theories lies in avoiding calculations and, accordingly, in the case of valence theory, in avoiding issues regarding wavefunctions, the Variation Theorem, Density Functional Theory, Hamiltonians, energies, etc.

       One is reminded of Gibb's statement. If I have had success in theoretical physics, he said, it has been by avoiding mathematical difficulties.

       Conceptual theories offer ways of figuring out the characteristics of an equation's solutions without having to actually solve the equation. It's what Conceptual Valence Bond Theory does for Schrödinger's equation for molecular systems.

HAB    And also: **CMOT is overwhelming**, for newcomers to chemical thought, in its use of atomic orbitals, whose only source is Schrödinger's equation.

SKP    *I think overwhelming is subjective and how overwhelming individual.*

       *Also, one can make pretty models of AO's and MO's, e.g. a sphere for an s orbital, a figure 8 or infinity symbol or dumbbell for a p, etc.*

HAB    Yet, where do the "pretty models" come from? What's the evidence for them? Upon what inductions are they based? And how are they generated by Schrödinger's equation? In fact, isn't it the case that the solutions require multiple modifications before they are useful in chemical situations? And, speaking of "pretty models" -

       Aren't valence sphere models even prettier, to the inner — if not (at first) to the outer — eye?

HAB    In addition: **CMOT is unnecessary.** Dioxygen's paramagnetism, e.g., is simply explained with Lewis's theory, used twice, once for each spin set.

SKP    *When do I know to use Lewis' theory twice?*

HAB    When the number of electrons of one spin is not equal to the number of electrons of the other spin. See Linnett's papers on the subject; or his last book, on a new approach to valence theory; or, e.g., *MCB*.

SKP    *Why is dioxygen paramagnetic? Isoelectronic formaldehyde is diamagnetic.*

HAB    Electron-electron repulsion between electrons of opposite spin is minimized for dioxygen if its 12 valence shell electrons are split 5 of one spin, arranged as for a triple bond, and 7 electrons of the opposite spin, arranged as for a single bond, so that where one spin set has a relatively high electron density the other spin set has a relatively low electron density.

       For good bond formation to hydrogen in nonlinear formaldehyde, its two spin sets must be essentially coinciden, as set forth clearly some fifty years ago by Jack Linnett.

SKP    *Why is triplet $CH_2$ nonlinear?*

HAB    Its 6 valence shell electrons are split 2 and 4. The 2-membered spin set favors a linear geometry. The 4-membered spin set favors a tetrahedral arrangement of spins with a bond angle of ca. 110°. Jointly the two spin sets produce a bond angle predicted to be ca. $(2 \times 180° + 4 \times 110°)/6 = 133°$.

SKP    *Why is ground state of $SiH_2$, valence-shell isoelectronic with $CH_2$, a singlet?*

HAB    Owing to nuclear-electron attraction, unshared electrons tend to solvate large atomic cores, such as $Si^{+4}$, some three times larger than $C^{+4}$. Solvation by one spin set is absent, however, if $SiH_2$ is a triplet, with only 2 electrons in one spin set, both in bonds to hydrogen, with none left over to "solvate" $Si^{+4}$.

HAB    **Bond angles opposite double bonds are generally greater than the tetrahedral angle, owing to core-core repulsion (and not to an unchemical sigma-pi formalism).**

SKP    *This is a quite subtle geometry effect. And, if one computes the core-core repulsion (unshielded cores, real interatomic distances), this term and its differences are much larger than chemical energies such as the difference of isomer stabilities.*

HAB    All the better, from the standpoint of explanatory power, than if differences are much smaller than chemical energy differences. Along with increases in core-core repulsion in going from single to double bond geometries are, of course, increases in core/electron attraction.

HAB    Furthermore: **CMOT is unnecessary.** The saturation and directional character of primary and secondary chemical affinities are easily accounted for with localized exclusive orbital models of molecules.

SKP    *"Easily" is like "overwhelming" – for whom?*

HAB    Newcomers to chemical thought.

HAB    Additionally: **Conceptual Molecular Orbital Theory is misguided, in use of atomic orbitals.** Needed in interpretative chemistry are electron density *profiles*, not electron densities near nuclei.

SKP    *What do you mean by profiles? And how "near" is "near"?*

HAB    Profiles are the outer electron density contours of Natural Bond Orbitals as depicted by Weinhold and others. "Near" generally means within half an angstrom or so.

HAB    What's more: **CMOT is mistaken**, in application of delocalization, a property of excited states, to <u>ground states</u>.

SKP    *The delocalized picture is often an approximate unitary transformation of the localized picture. The "true" MO description is such a unitary transformation of the "true" VB description, and the other way around.*

HAB    Granted. So, what's the point? A unitary transformation indicates a <u>mathematical</u> equivalence, not an <u>interpretative</u> equivalence.

HAB    And besides: **Conceptual MO Theory is counter-factual**, in ignoring in formation of molecular orbitals the indistinguishability of electrons and, thus, the fact that $\Psi(x, x, \ldots) = 0$.

SKP    *I put 2, never any more than 2, electrons in an orbital. I can ascribe this to the Pauli principle or indistinguishability of electrons in that I will say that the 2 electrons are one apiece of spin up and spin down -- I can't have 2 electrons in the same orbital with the same spin. Admittedly, this is an ad hoc constraint in that the Schrödinger equation alone doesn't demand this or even build it into any mathematical or pictorial search for a solution of understanding.*

HAB    The "Pauli principle" concerns <u>orbital populations</u>. The "indistinguishability of electrons" concerns <u>wavefunctions' character</u>. They're not the same thing!

        The Pauli principle, alone, allows two electrons of the same spin to be at the same place at the same time. The indistinguishability of electrons does not allow that configuration. It's a "strong" form of a Principle of Spatial Exclusion.

HAB    Finally: **CMOT is misleading,** in suggesting that electrons occupy orbitals that share the same regions of space. For then one may suppose that two electrons of parallel spin may occupy the same region regions of space at the same time.

SKP    *Why can't two orbitals occupy the same region of space?*

HAB    They can if one uses properly antisymmetrizied wave functions, which, however, so scramble electrons' coordinates as to render the phrase "occupy the same region of space" meaningless. In the words of Frank Weinhold (personal communication, July 3, 2011) to which I keep returning:

        ***"The MO imagery of orbitals sprawling over one another 'almost everywhere' is profoundly illusory and physically meaningless."***

SKP    *Frank agrees with you. But that a famous scientist agrees with you is not a proof of veracity of a statement.*

HAB    True. Mistakes happen. Many famous scientists still locate helium above neon in periodic tables and describe molecular electronic structure in terms of delocalized, nonexclusive orbitals. In the end, however, agreement is what science seeks. It may occur by way of a path mentioned on page 38 and described more fullly for a different situation by Planck in his *Scientific Autobiography* (p38), as -

### "An Odd Jest of Fate"

"It was an odd jest of fate," wrote Planck, "that a circumstance which on former occasions I had found unpleasant, namely, the lack of interest of my colleagues in the direction taken by my investigation, now turned out to be an outright boon. While a host of outstanding physicists worked on the problem of the spectral energy distribution, both from the experimental and theoretical aspect, every one of them directed his efforts solely toward exhibiting the intensity of the radiation on the temperature. On the other hand, I suspected that the fundamental connection lies on the dependence of entropy upon energy. As the significance of the concept of entropy had not yet come to be fully appreciated, nobody paid any attention to the method adopted by me, and I could work out my calculations completely at my leisure, with absolute thoroughness, without fear of interference or competition."

It is a mark of a significant scientific advance that its full significance may not be recognized at first, and that by the time it is deemed worthy of a Nobel Prize, its innovator has died, as happened in the case of van't Hoff's tetrahedral atom, Lewis's electron pair hypothesis, Boltzmann's use of atomic theory to account for Nature's Second-Law-like behavior, and Huggins' hydrogen bond.

"I am conscious of being only an individual struggling weakly against the stream of time," wrote Boltzmann, eight years before he committed suicide, suffering from severe headaches and acutely aware of growing hostility to his work by Ostwald, Duhem, Mach, and other members of the establishment, soon converted to Boltzmann's point of view, however, owing especially to Einstein's explanation of (i) Brownian motion, using atomic theory; (ii) the photoelectric effect, using Bohr's photon hypothesis, and (iii) the anomalous heat capacity of diamond, using Planck's quantum hypothesis.

# FULL DISCLOSURE

"I was away on a family vacation," writes a famous physical chemist, "and found *Molecules and the Chemical Bond* on my arrival [home]. I am working (with pleasure) through it. It has many, goodies in it, interesting chemical systems explained." However,-

"I would prefer not to write a blurb for the book. I think it has fascinating things in it but is unfair to Mulliken and molecular orbital theory."

Indeed, the entire book has turned out to be, to the author's surprise, a critique, in one way or another, of the theory of delocalized molecular orbitals, for molecules in their ground states. The author did not set out with that intention. His initial goal, in 1962, and for many years thereafter, was merely to investigate stereochemical implications of "Tangent Sphere Models" of molecules. Only half a century later, while preparing essays for this book, did the logic of conceptual valence bond theories lead, step by step, unexpectedly, to an "unfair [treatment] of Mulliken and molecular orbital theory."

"The strength of the book," adds its perceptive reader, in a remark paraphrased at the bottom of this volume's front cover, "is that it shows how far one can get with a localized orbital perspective."

The local orbital perspective leads to valence sphere models of molecules. Like all models, they are wrong, of course, in some respects (too large, for instance!), yet, nonetheless, useful in rationalizing molecular shapes, such as, e.g., that of sulfuric acid molecules, $(HO)_2SO_2$. The zero-formal-charge assumptions that the terminal oxygen cores are bound to the sulfur core by double bonds and its OH groups by single bonds yields an electron pair coordination number for $S^{+6}$ of 6. A trigonal prismatic arrangement of 6 domains (large black domains below) with $O^{+6}$ cores (small black domains) coordinated off two edges and two corners of the prism in the manner indicated below

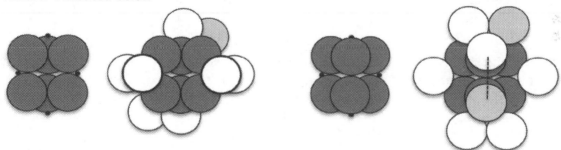

yields immediately the molecule's observed overall tetrahedral shape, two sets of sulfur-oxygen bond lengths, and a set of bond angles in accordance with the Bond Angle Theorem:

$$O=S=O \approx 120° > O=S-O > HO-S-OH$$

The corresponding bond angles in $O_2SF_2$ and $OSF_2$ are 124°, 106.8°, and 92.6-96°.

The dashed line on the right indicates an intramolecular hydrogen bond, which renders the molecule unsymmetrical with respect to locations of its hydrogen atoms.

# DISCLOSURES CONTINUED

## Evidence for Existence in Western Civilization of "Two Cultures"

Each surprise in the evolution of *MCB* has arrived in its own way. Payment for a pre-publication review produced this result:

### MOLECULES AND THE CHEMICAL BOND
*An Introduction to Conceptual Valence Bond Theory*

A dense, chaotically presented treatise on what holds small things together. Readers may wonder who the target audience is for this highly academic discussion of the valence bond theory, which uses notions of quantum mechanics to explain chemical bonding.

The book is filled with complex diagrams, but has no discernible narrative thread, so, as a result, casual readers may find themselves lost. However, even devoted academics and science buffs may have some difficulty appreciating this desultory discussion, and even those with an abiding interest in the inner workings of the natural world may find it nearly impenetrable on a sentence-by-sentence level:

> "A hybrid model with one P+5 core coordinated off a face of C+4's tetrahedron (second figure above) and one off an opposite edge (first figure), plus its mirror image, to make, by resonance, both PC bonds equivalent to each other, yields a PCP bond angle of 144.7O, compared to an observed angle of 143.8O," for example, describes the compound Bis(triphenylphosphoranylidene)methane.

> [Successful theories, it should be said, generate distinctive vocabularies — another example of "Hund's Rule", that fleas (technical terms) come with the dog (successful theories).]

Chemists and other readers familiar with such terms as "icosahedron" and an "electrophilic pocket" may be able to follow along, but even they may still find this dissertation on chemical combination to be an insurmountable challenge. Much of the work refers directly to, and therefore hinges upon, highly complex molecular diagrams; however, the renderings of these multidimensional objects on a two-dimensional surface may create more problems for readers than they solve. Ultimately, the book shows that an inherently complicated subject, such as this one, not only requires the intellect to tease out its mysteries—it also demands an uncommon facility to communicate these secrets to the masses, which this book doesn't provide.

A highly complex academic text that's not for the molecularly challenged.

— *Kirkus Review*

The hostile review brings to mind remarks regarding modern art by Braque, Klee, Picasso, and two art critics (H. Rosenberg and J. Russell), cited below, word-for-word, except for one change: substitution of the word "science" for the word "art" (1).

(1) "A Dialogue Concerning the Two Chief World Systems: Art and Science," Henry A. Bent, *Journal of Chemical Education*, Vol. 58, Number 4, 1981, pages 331-333.

# Impatience/Indignation/Exasperation (1)

For every acquisition there is an equivalent loss. The more comprehensive a work of science the more it loses in power and significance.

Modern science addresses itself to the elevated faculties of the mind. It reshapes the ordeal by initiation to which we are subjected before we can understand it. Spectators must acquire a special lore or be guided by professional critics. No more amateur gazing at science.

There's no shortcut to the enjoyment of science. Deciphering science requires industry and patience. The beholder, of course, all too often spends only a single moment coping with a work of science. A scientific theory cannot be appreciated without a chair.

Indignation at all this masks feelings to which we dare not give their true names. We feel personally affronted. Our identity as alert human beings has been called into question.

It is a great exasperation to come face to face with a new science and not make anything of it. We ought to be having a good time, and we aren't.

Reasoning is a path for the mind, said Braque, and a tumult for the soul — beginning with arithmetic and continuing with algebra, trigonometry, differential and integral calculus, and differential equations: $H\Psi = E\Psi$.


Ambition, distraction, uglification, and derision were Lewis Carroll's names for the four operations of arithmetic. Most people know when to add, subtract, and multiply. Division is the problem. When to do it? And which way?

Ratios permeate the exact sciences — moles per liter, grams per cubic centimeter, meters per second per second — and perplex nonscientists. Therein lies a pedagogical virtue of Conceptual Valence Bond Theory.

Yes, ratios are present in CVBT in, for instance, the Theory's Radius-Ratio Rules. Even there, however, as for the most part elsewhere in the Theory, geometry rules, in uses of valence sphere models of molecules.

The models are sights for outer eyes, sources of insights for inner eyes, and useful pedagogical props when teaching chemistry from demonstration-experiments.

# Suggestions for Teaching General Chemistry
## from
## *Demonstration-Experiments, Bond Diagrams, and Molecular Models*

You don't really understand something until you can explain it to the man on the street.

Peter Debye

LAVOISIER: Introduce no term or concept unless there's a need
for it based on an experiment or an observation.

WHITEHEAD: Exhibit yourself in your own true trade, *as a chemist*,
say, mixing and heating pure substances.

### *Teach from demonstration-experiments*!

### *SHOW and TELL.*

*"Let's see what happens when . . ."*

**Put chemistry's best foot forward.** Feature the BIG FOUR: *Flammable Gases, Liquid Nitrogen, Dry Ice*, and -

**Chemistry's Leading Induction**: *The Kinetic-Molecular Model of Matter.*

**Be relevant, here and now.** Discuss fires of industry and commerce, transportation and home heating, and *life*.

**Follow in Faraday's footsteps.** Use fire to fire up enthusiasm for chemistry!

**Tell a story.** Have each experiment follow in some fashion from the previous experiment and lead to the next one, as in research.

**Remind audiences of the Chemical — and kitchen chemists' — Imperative (a.k.a. "Collision Theory").** To react chemically molecules must collide with each other with bond-breaking violence.

### *Mix and Heat!*

*Safety First.* Emphasize the Hexagon of Safety: Observation + Knowledge + Memory + Patience + Logic (a.k.a. Common Sense) + Imagination (regarding the worse things that might happen) = Safe Passages through Life.

**Play around with the Principles of Fire-Extinction.** *Nothing can live on its own wastes!* (That would be perpetual motion.)

### *Have fun*!

**Engage students in the fun.** Mentor student-teams learning chemistry in order to execute safely and to explain correctly in terms of the kinetic-molecular model of matter striking demonstration-experiments, for peers, younger students, and the general public. It's a winner for all lives it touches.

**Establish a Trickle-Down Enterprise:** mentored college students mentoring high school students mentoring middle school students mentoring elementary school students working with still younger students to increase in each instance the educational content of "show and tell" sessions (a.k.a. teaching from demonstration-experiments).

**Use chemistry as a vehicle for students to acquire a liberal education.** Make "The Central Science" The *Central Discipline* that it can be in high school and college, by featuring uses in chemistry of reading, writing, and mathematics, inductive and deductive reasoning, laboratory and computer skills, interpersonal skills (in working with laboratory partners and teammates in programs of chemical demonstrations), and by fostering skill in public speaking.

**Introduce writing assignments** [possibly "life-transforming" (William Zinsser *On Writing Well*, Ch. 14: "Science")]. Describe for a demonstration-experiment in simple, short, declarative sentences *that follow each other logically* what was used, done, seen, said, imagined, drawn, written, recalled, concluded, and done next.

**Remember:** Programs of demonstration-experiments are no better than the preparation for them *at both ends.* Offer teachers workshops on, e.g., drawing bond diagrams — 1 "valence stroke" to "H", for starters; 2 to "O", because of the formula HOH; and 4 to "C", because of the formula OCO; with no dangling valence strokes — in order to prepare teachers for supervision of student-construction of posters that display bond diagrams of chemical species to be used in impending "Van Visits". Students love to see visiting scientists refer in van visits to students' bond diagrams.

**Truly believe that there are no such things as "failed experiments".** Nature always does her thing! There are only unimaginative responses to unexpected events. Those events provide golden opportunities to demonstrate problem-solving strategies, in real time. *Audiences of all ages eat it up!* Homo *sapiens* loves to see *minds in action.*

**Introduce entropy and the Entropy Ethic:** *Live leanly. Do not create entropy unnecessarily. Conserve transformable forms of energy.*

CONSIDER development of a departmental option for a degree in — or, perhaps better put, *through* — chemistry that features development of a "Van Outreach Initiative", designed to educate future chemical educators; and for liberal arts students, generally, who enjoy chemistry, public speaking, and public service (through interactions with students and their teachers, principles, and parents), thereby harnessing the enthusiasm, enhancing the self-respect, and, generally, bringing out the best in undergraduates who may not be gifted course-passers but who may be potentially highly talented in comparably significant ways.

*ADDENDUM*
*Simple, Short, Safe, Striking, Inexpensive Demonstration-Experiments*
*Presented as a Challenge, to Be Explain in Terms of the Kinetic-Molecular Model of Matter*
### What's Going on Here?

1. A coke can containing a little water, boiled, collapses when inverted over cold water.

   Boiling purges the can of air, replacing it with water vapor ("steam"), which, in contact with cold water, condenses, back to liquid water, creating, thereby, a partial vacuum, which allows the weight of the atmosphere to crush the can. Repeated with a can that has a screw cap screwed in place before cooling yields a collapsed can, which, returned to the source of heat, expands to approximately its initial volume; etc. Illustrated is the principle of the "Atmospheric [steam] Engine", precursor to modern steam powered generation of electricity, and modern civilization.

2. A candle burning in a large flask burns continuously (until all its wax is consumed). But when the apparatus is dropped and its free fall, of several feet, arrested *suddenly* (rather than slowly, say by extension of a slinky), the candle *suddenly goes out.*

   Convection, driven by gravity, forces relatively dense, fresh air into the stationary flask with expulsion through the central part of its opening of less dense hot combustion products. In free fall, however, every thing — flask, candle, candle flame, hot combustion products, and colder fresh air — falls (according to Galileo) at the same accelerating rate (some 32 feet per second per second at the earth's surface). Fresh air feeds the falling flame by diffusion (not by convection). The flame becomes smaller and nearly spherical in shape. When the flask is suddenly caught, its free fall is *suddenly* arrested, gravity is suddenly turned back on, so to speak, and cold air surrounding the flame rushes inward, pushes hotter gases upward, and blows out the flame, from all directions, without a flicker. The experiment might have appealed to Einstein, who, in one of his popular essays, asks the reader to imagine what happens when a gentleman in an elevator in free fall takes out a pocket watch and lets go of it.

3. A metallic strip ignited in a burner's flame burns brilliantly with a bushy flame that when brushed against the sides of a beaker produces black streaks that dissolve in hydrochloric acid and when heated turn white.

   $Mg(s) + 1/2 \, O_2(g) = MgO$(white solid) + heat. The bushy flame is a "diffusion flame". It obtains its oxygen from the surrounding air. The flame's bushy interior is filled with vaporized magnesium. (In his Periodic System, Mendeleev located magnesium with zinc, with cadmium and mercury, one of the "volatile metals".)  When brushed against a cold surface, the hot magnesium vapor suddenly condenses to finely divided, light-absorbing, black-looking powder, which dissolves hydrochloric acid (with evolution of little bubbles of hydrogen gas) and, when heated, in air, oxidizes to $MgO(s)$, a National Bureau of Standards' standard for whiteness.

4. Metal turnings ignited in a cavity in a slab of dry ice covered with a second slab produce a glow, eject a white cloud, and leave in the cavity a black solid.

   Since magnesium burns with a white-hot flame, whereas a candle's flame from combustion of candle wax, composed of carbon, hydrogen, and oxygen, is only yellow-hot, one might suppose that magnesium has a greater affinity for oxygen than do carbon and hydrogen and that, given a choice, oxygen unites with magnesium rather than with carbon or hydrogen. That is to say: Perhaps magnesium will *burn* in carbon dioxide and steam: $2Mg(s) + CO_2(g) = 2MgO(s) + C(s)$ and $Mg(s) + H_2O(g) = MgO(s) + H_2(g)$. Indeed, in the battle of the Falkland Islands an Argentinean-fired French Exocet missile ignited a British cruiser's magnesium-containing superstructure, which burned to the deck, despite efforts to extinguish the flames with water and carbon dioxide.

5. Water squirted into a beaker of dry ice and acetone produces a fizzing sound.

   Dry ice is cold, but not sufficiently cold to freeze acetone, in which, when cold, carbon dioxide is readily soluble. (Gas solubility increases with decreasing temperature and decreases with increasing temperature.) Liquid water squirted into cold, $CO_2$-saturated acetone freezes, liberates its heat of fusion (80 cal/g), and warms the surrounding acetone, which degasses, with a fizzing sound.

6. Dry ice dropped into a beaker of limewater yields a white suspension that subsequently clears up.

   $CO_2(g) + 2OH^-$(aq, from lime water) $= CO_3^{-2}(aq) + H_2O(aq)$

   $CO_3^{-2}(aq) + Ca^{+2}$(aq, from lime water) $= CaCO_3$(s, white; a.k.a. "limestone");

   $CO_2$(g, in excess) $+ H_2O(aq) = H_2CO_3(aq)$

   $H_2CO_3(aq) + CaCO_3(s) = Ca^{+2}(aq) + 2HCO_3^-(aq)$

   Summarized by the last two equations is the formation of limestone caves and hard water, by the first two equations the hardening of mortar made from slaked lime.

7. A metal wastepaper basket inverted at the top of a candle staircase, sided by Plexiglas sheets, causes the candles to go out, one by one.

8. A waste paper basket inverted at the top of a candle staircase with a single burning candle at the bottom yields after a few moments a large, luminous flame. (Young students often say: "Do it again!" Differently? "With *two* candles at the bottom." Done. One can almost feel their disappointment. But, hey! Perhaps they've lear something about "limiting reagents".)

9. An inverted waste paper basket righted at the bottom of an inverted candle staircase with a candle perched at its "top" yields after a few moments a descending flame, with, thereafter, extinction of the candle and formation of dew on the insides of the Plexiglas sides.

7, 8, 9: The wastepaper baskets contain, respectively, carbon dioxide, propane, and methane.

10. An inflated balloon cooled with liquid nitrogen and cut over a beaker yields a liquid that yields a vapor that initially extinguishes a burning splint and later causes a glowing splint to burn brilliantly.

    The balloon contained *air*. Distilled off first from liquid air is nitrogen-rich air, followed by oxygen-rich air. (Nitrogen boils at -195.8°C, oxygen at -183°C.)

11. An inflated balloon cooled with liquid nitrogen collapses and when cut over a beaker of water yields a colorless, water-insoluble, less-dense-than-liquid-water source of a flammable vapor, that, ignited, burns with a bushy yellow flame above a (vapor filled) dark space, and creates a small, floating, white solid, soon gone. [CAUTION: the cold liquid's flammable vapor, because cold, is denser than air (as can easily be shown, given the vapor's temperature), and, accordingly, pools *downward*. Ignite it ASAP!]

    The balloon was inflated with methane.

## Faraday's Experiments with a Candle

### THE TRIANGLE OF FIRE:

Fuel + Oxidizer + Heat, all at the same place at same time, = Fire

a. A candle in a room represents two corners of the "Triangle of Fire". What's missing, for a flame?

b. Light a candle and wait for it to reach a steady state. What shape is its wick?

c. What colors is the wick? Is it flammable? Why doesn't it burn along its *entire* exposed length?

d. Place a spatula in the flame's tip. What's the black stuff? High-melting? Flammable? A combustion intermediate?

e. Hold a cold spatula momentarily above the flame, blade horizontal. What's on its surface? Where did its hydrogen and oxygen come from?

f. Hold an inverted small Erlenmeyer flask above the flame for a few moments, then stopper it, right it, and, after a bit, add limewater, re-stopper, and shake. What's the white stuff? A confirmatory test?

g. Hold a spatula blade, horizontal, just above the wick for a few moments. What's in the black ring's center? ROY G BIV colors? Seen elsewhere?

h. Hold, horizontal, a wire screen (i) at the flame's tip; (ii) just above the wick. What are the smokes' colors? What might they be?

i. Blow out a candle's flame. What's the rising smoke's color? Is it flammable?

j. Hold a burning match in an extinguished candle's rising smoke. How far can you get the flame to strike back?

k. To simulate a burning candle flame's wick, soak a lab towel in a 50-50 alcohol-water mixture, wring it out, and, holding it with tongs, ignite it at the bottom. Why doesn't the towel burn?

N.B. Because energy is always conserved in demonstration-experiments and the entropy of the universe always increases, demonstration-experiments are excellent opportunities to illustrate the First and Second Laws of Thermodynamics — and an ecological point of view, owing to the necessity in bookkeeping net changes in energy and entropy of looking at the *whole works:* not only a particular system of interest, but also its *environment*.

# Thermodynamics

*Thermodynamics is not difficult if you can just keep track of what you are talking about.*
WILLIAM F. GIAUQUE

What are usually talked about in chemical thermodynamics are changes in energy E and entropy S of a chemical system σ, its thermal surroundings θ, and/or its mechanical surroundings wt.

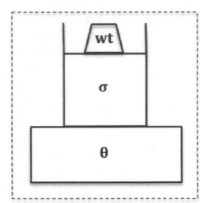

θ is often the surrounding air or a water bath.

In chemical thermodynamics the only thing that is important about θ is its temperature and about wt its mass m, its altitude h in a gravitational field, and its mechanical motion.

If the mechanical surroundings is the atmosphere, wt = atm, thought of as a mass m resting on the system σ confined to a cylinder beneath a piston of cross-sectional area A and exerting a pressure on σ of P = mg/A, then

$$\Delta E_{wt} = \Delta E_{atm}$$
$$=$$
$$mg\Delta h_{atm} = mg(\Delta V_\sigma/A) = P\Delta V_\sigma$$
$$\Delta E_\sigma + \Delta E_{atm} = \Delta E_\sigma + P\Delta V_\sigma = \Delta H_\sigma$$
if
$$H = E + PV$$
and if
$$P(= mg/A) = constant$$

Cartoon of the usual universe of discourse in chemical thermodynamics

Always
$$\Delta E_{universe} = \Delta E_\sigma + \Delta E_\theta + \Delta E_{wt} = 0^1$$
$$\Delta S_{universe} = \Delta S_\sigma + \Delta S_\theta + \Delta S_{wt} \geq 0^2$$

where, by the following definitions (framed in strict accordance with Nature's nature)[3],

$$\Delta E_{wt} = \Delta(PE) + \Delta(KE) = \sum mg\Delta h + \sum(mv^2/2)$$
$$\Delta E_\theta = (mc\Delta t)_\theta \qquad c = \text{"specific heat" of } \theta$$
$$\Delta E_\sigma = -(\Delta E_\theta + \Delta E_{wt})^4$$

$$\Delta S_{wt} = 0^5$$
$$\Delta S_\theta = \Delta E_\theta/T^6$$
$$\Delta S_\sigma = -(\Delta_{rev}S_\theta)^{7,8,9}$$

1 Often written $\Delta E = q + w$, where q = heat absorbed by σ from θ = $-\Delta E_\theta$ and where w = work done on σ by wt = $-\Delta E_{wt}$.
2 The "=" sign holds for reversible events.
3 Explained in *MOLECULES and the Chemical Bond*, Volume I, beginning on page 147.
4 This definition of $\Delta E_\sigma$ insures that for all events $\Delta E_{universe} = 0$.
5 Purely mechanical, friction-free events are reversible, non-entropy-producing events.
6 Definition of $\Delta S_\theta$, given $\Delta E_\theta$ and T; or definition of T, given $\Delta E_\theta$ and $\Delta S_\theta$.
7 The subscript "rev" indicates that the change "Δ" in σ has been executed as part of a larger reversible event, rev: e.g., a slow, fully harnessed expansion of a gas, rather than a free expansion.
8 Often written $\Delta S_\sigma = q_{rev}/T$.
9 This definition of $\Delta S_\sigma$ insures that for all reversible events $\Delta S_{universe} = 0$ ($\rightarrow \Delta S_\sigma = -\Delta S_\theta$).

Leading applications of the above relations are to the free and reversible expansions of ideal gases (PV = nRT). In a *free* expansion ($\Delta E_{wt} = 0$), Joule observed that $\Delta t_\theta = 0 \rightarrow \Delta E_\theta = 0 \rightarrow$ the energy of an idea gas does not depend on its volume. In a reversible ($\Delta S_{universe} = 0 \rightarrow \Delta S_{gas} = -\Delta S_\theta$) *isothermal* expansion ($\Delta t_{gas} = 0 \rightarrow \Delta E_{gas} = 0$) from $V_1$ to $V_2$, $\Delta E_{gas} = 0 \rightarrow dE_\theta = -dE_{wt} = -PdV = (nRT/V)dV \rightarrow \Delta E_\theta = -nRT\ln(V_2/V_1) \rightarrow \Delta S_\theta(= \Delta E_\theta/T) = -nR\ln(V_2/V_1) \rightarrow \Delta S_{gas}(-\Delta_{rev}S_\theta) = nR\ln(V_2/V_1) = -nR\ln(P_2/P_1)$. From there it is a few short steps to one of the leading relations of chemical thermodynamics: $\Delta G° = -RT\ln K$.

# ADDITIONAL ESSAYS

## A Thesis, Antithesis, and Synthesis

*Hegel's account of the evolution of understanding describes the transition from Bohr's dynamic model of the hydrogen atom and Lewis's static models of highly localized electronic charges to Kimball's static domains of dynamic electrons.*

The old saying in biology that ontogeny recapitulates phylogeny describes a situation in chemistry that sometimes troubles students who've been introduced to models of the electronic structure of matter by way of Bohr's *orbits* for the hydrogen atom (a seemingly logical way to begin: consider the simplest system first) and who then wonder: How in Lewis's model of chemical bonds (as *shared* electron pairs) does an electron pair reside *simultaneously* in the valence shells of *different* atoms, and count, often, toward an octet for *both* atoms simultaneously?* Pictured below for a hydrogen molecule are two responses to that question by Bohr and Lewis's contemporaries.

A dynamic model, after Bohr
Physics

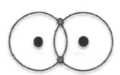

A static model, after Lewis
Chemistry

In the Bohr-like, dynamic model, the electrons move in figure-8 orbits, thereby residing, effectively, in both atoms. In Lewis's static model, the atoms' valence shells overlap each other, thereby allowing the electrons to reside in both atoms, simultaneously.

The dynamical model from physics is physically unrealistic, in that the "bonding" electrons spend much of their time off the *backsides* of the "bond", in anti-bonding regions. Lewis's static model from chemistry is close to valence sphere models of chemical bonds.

Highly localized, static electrons
After Lewis's electron dot diagrams

Dynamic, delocalized electrons
After Kimball's charge clouds

Pictured above in are a physical thesis (after Bohr, upper left), a chemical antithesis (after Lewis, upper right), and a Hegelian synthesis (after Kimball, lower right).

A chemical bond results from internuclear-distance-diminishing attraction of two atomic cores for, and by, the same portions of an electron cloud, a.k.a. an exclusive localized bonding molecular *orbital*.

The chemical bond's evolution in physical thought has been, briefly, from zero-dimensional Lewis dots, representing one-dimensional valence strokes, to three-dimensional Kimball domains.

* A valence sphere model of ethane is a good answer to that question.

# Induction of Wave Functions' Antisymmetric Property
## A Response to the Question: *Where Are Your Predictions?*

Scientifically sound theories explain and predict. Predictions are of two types: numerical and conceptual. Numerical predictions are the specialty of Computational Chemistry. Conceptual predictions are the specialty of Conceptual Theories.

Inductions of the principles of Exclusive Orbital Theory (this volume's first part) are *conceptual predictions*. So, also, are novel explanations of known facts using those principles, a.k.a. "post-dictions" (this volume's second part).

A leading post-diction of Exclusive Orbital Theory is the stereochemistry of Odd–Hassel-type, inter-molecular electron-pair donor/acceptor interactions, anticipated by the author prior to his knowledge of Hassel's experimental investigations. [H. Bent, "Structural Chemistry of Donor-Acceptor Interactions," *Chem. Rev.*, **68**, 587-648, (1968)]. Exclusive Orbital Theory's most significant physical post-diction may be the conclusion, reached below in five simple steps, that electronic wave functions are antisymmetric.

1. According to Born, an electronic configuration's probability is proportional to

$$\Psi^2$$

2. According to the indistinguishability of electrons,

$$\Psi^2(1, 2, \ldots) = \Psi^2(2, 1, \ldots)$$

    "1" and "2" represent space and spin coordinates of the first two labeled electrons.

3. Taking the square root yields

$$\Psi(1, 2, \ldots) = \pm\, \Psi(2, 1, \ldots)$$

4. *Finite molar volumes of dihydrogen and helium, however great the pressure, imply* — following the work of, among others, Thomson (on electrons), Moseley (on atomic numbers), and Lewis (on electron pairs) — *that two electrons of the same spin cannot be at the same place at the same time*. I.e. -

$$\Psi(1, 1, \ldots) = 0$$

    Electronic wave functions have — as mentioned several times — exclusive orbital character.

5. Choosing the minus sign in 3 and setting space and spin coordinates "2" equal to "1" yields the mathematical expression in step 4. For self-consistency regarding theory and observation one must evidently suppose that the electronic wave function $\Psi$ is antisymmetric:

$$\Psi(1, 2, \ldots) = -\Psi(2, 1, \ldots)$$

Computational Quantum Chemistry focuses attention on solutions of Schrödinger's equation, subject to the condition that $\Psi(1, 2, \ldots) = -\Psi(2, 1, \ldots)$.

**Conceptual Valence Bond Theory focuses attention *at the outset* on the importance of *both* (i) the antisymmetric condition *and* (ii) Schrödinger's equation, through use of, respectively, (i) *exclusive orbitals* of (ii) *finite size*. Early introduction in Conceptual Valence Theory of those two approximations greatly simplifies creation of approximate molecular electron density profiles.**

A Summary and Review

# Leading Evidence for Exclusive Localized Orbital Models of Electron Density Profiles of Molecular Ground States

Six disparate lines of evidence support the supposition that approximate practical electron density profiles of molecules in their ground states can be created by simply replacing valence strokes of classical valence stroke diagrams by valence spheres.

1. **The molar volume of dihydrogen is finite,** however high the pressure and however low the temperature. It appears that -

   *Two but no more than two electrons may be in the same region of space at the same time.*

2. Electrons are indistinguishable. Accordingly, electronic wave functions are antisymmetric: $\Psi(1, 2, \ldots) = -\Psi(2, 1, \ldots)$. Hence $\Psi(1, 1, \ldots) = 0$.

   *The probability that two electrons of the same spin are at the same place is zero.*

   That principle of spatial exclusion (after Heisenberg) is a stronger statement than the statement (after Pauli) that two electrons of the same spin cannot be in the same orbital at the same time — inasmuch as the delocalized, *non-exclusive* orbitals of canonical MO theory occupy *the same regions of space*, namely the entire space occupied by molecules' electron clouds.

3. **Lewis's interpretation of valence stroke diagrams** yields a principle of spatial exclusion. For since valence strokes never cross each other, it follows that -

   *Valence shell electron pairs are never at the same place at the same time.*

4. **Valence stroke and valence sphere models of molecules are Isomorphic.** For every scientifically sound valence stroke diagram there exists — as indicated below — a corresponding valence sphere model.

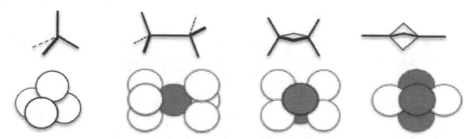

Valence strokes and valence spheres represent *exclusive localized molecular orbitals.*

*"The MO imagery of orbitals sprawling over one another 'almost everywhere' is profoundly illusory and physical meaningless".*
FRANK WEINHOLD, personal communication, July 3, 2011

5. **A deep consilience exists between the principles of structural organic and inorganic chemistry.** Cations and anions of ionic compounds correspond, respectively, to atomic cores and electron pairs of covalent compounds.

6. **The Hohenberg-Kohn Theorem of Density Functional Theory corresponds to the Valence Stroke Termination Rule of Conceptual Valence Bond Theory.** Just as electron densities in Density Functional Theory determine by the Hohenberg-Kohn theorem locations of atomic nuclei, so, too, in VB Theory bond diagrams sans symbols of the elements determine by the Valence Stroke Termination Rule locations of atomic cores.

# Electron Localization
## *By Induction, from Chemical Evidence, and by Deduction, from HΨ = EΨ*

Electron localization is what Conceptual Valence Bond Theory has been about, *unwittingly*, at first, with its symbols of the chemical elements connected by "valence strokes" *wholly unrelated to physical concepts*, until Lewis suggested that the diagrams' two types of components — chemical symbols and valence strokes — represent, respectfully, atomic nuclei plus inner-shell electrons (jointly: "atomic cores") and valence shell electron pairs, described later as residing in hybrid atomic orbitals whose main lobes Kimball modeled with exclusive spherical charge cloud domains that represent, variously, depending on their environments in bond diagrams, –

- single covalent bonds
- bent-bond components of multiple bonds
- lone pairs
- multi-center bonds
- dative bonds

Created by models of semi-localized exclusive electron domains have been, also, the phrases –

- Electron Pair Coordination Number
- Octet Rule
- Expanded Octet
- Double Quartet
- Formal Charges
- Valence Stroke Termination Rule
- Electron Pair Donor-Acceptor Interactions
- Lone Pairs Dispersal about Large Atomic Cores
- Anticoincident Spin Sets
- Resonance

Numerous attempts have been made to capture the concepts "chemical bonds", "lone pairs", and "atomic cores" *deductively*, through imposition of various physically plausible — if otherwise arbitrary — criteria on solutions of Schrödinger's equation.

From an historical point of view, those Johnny-come-lately mathematical deductions of the central concepts of a Conceptual Valence Bond Theory of Semi-Localized Electrons may be viewed as a kind of *imitation*, "the sincerest form of flattery".

Electron localization by deduction from Schrödinger's equation lends importantly (as said) an air of mathematical plausibility to what might otherwise be deemed to be a "bald and unconvincing narrative"—in the words of W. S. Gilbert—regarding electron localizations the old-fashioned way, by *inductions based on chemical and physical eviden*ce. Inductions are the only routes, said Einstein (among others) to truly *new ideas*. Later the ideas may be dressed up in sophisticated deductive garb to satisfy requirements of "rigor" in mopping up operations following introductions into science of major inductions. Computational scientists have been mopping up, so to speak, after Lewis, since 1916.

Often chemical inductions aren't firmly believed by chemists until they've been certified physically, by physicists (in the case of atoms, e.g., by Einstein and his interpretation of Brownian motion). "HΨ = EΨ is the ultimate oracle of chemical knowledge," write two chemists (Weinhold and Landis).

# Organic Stereochemistry Briefly Stated

Consider Nature's simplest, electrically uncharged molecule, dihydrogen, $H_2$. It's two protons embedded in the electron cloud of two electrons.

The circle on the left represents the approximate *profile* (or van der Waals domain) of an electron pair, symbolized on the right by a *valence stroke*.

In its condensed states hydrogen has a *finite molar volume*. Implied is the principal principle of Conceptual Valence Bond Theory:

*Two electrons can be in the same region of space at the same time but not three.*

Owing to electrostatic attraction of positively charged atomic cores for negatively charged electron domains of finite size, the italicized statement plays out in the following fashion for a molecule of Nature's simplest hydrocarbon, $CH_4$, with a total of eight valence shell electrons: four from its carbon atom and four from its four hydrogen atoms.

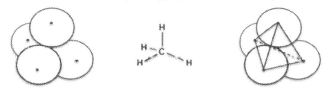

Each sphere and stroke represents two electrons. "C" stands for a carbon nucleus, $C^{+6}$, plus two tightly held inner shell electrons, yielding, jointly, a carbon core, $C^{+4}$, not shown in the nearly completely concealed "tetrahedral interstice" of the model at the far left. The figure at the far right shows why the arrangement of electron pair domains at the far left is called a "tetrahedral arrangement". The inscribed figure has four faces. (A cube, in that terminology, is a "hexahedron".)

The corresponding models of the two-carbon-core molecules of ethane, ethylene, and acetylene ($C_2H_6$, $C_2H_4$, and $C_2H_2$) continue the theme of a tetrahedral arrangement of electron pair domains about a carbon core (hence the Octet Rule). The tetrahedral theme (and Octet Rule) applies, also, to the electronic environments in stable species of the even smaller atomic cores $N^{+5}$, $O^{+6}$, and $F^{+7}$. Electronic environments of all compound-forming elements of the first row of periodic tables' *p*-blocks are isoelectronic: more specifically, tetrahedral.

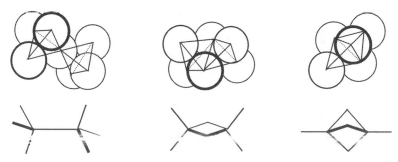

Valence sphere and valence stroke models of single, double, and triple bonds are based on a tetrahedral arrangement of electron pair domains about atomic cores (not shown).

The remainder of organic stereochemistry is chiefly repeated uses of the tetrahedral arrangemt.

# Exclusive Orbital and Molecular Orbital Models of the Isoelectronic Species -

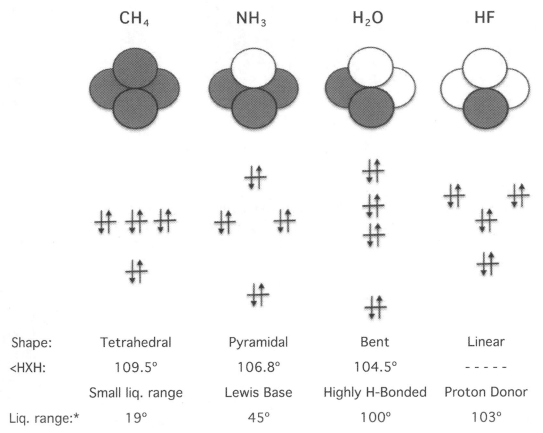

| Shape: | Tetrahedral | Pyramidal | Bent | Linear |
|---|---|---|---|---|
| <HXH: | 109.5° | 106.8° | 104.5° | - - - - - |
| | Small liq. range | Lewis Base | Highly H-Bonded | Proton Donor |
| Liq. range:* | 19° | 45° | 100° | 103° |

* With rising temperature molecules such as $CH_4$ that have nearly spherical electron density profiles begin to rotate in the solid state, thereby: removing some of the driving force for melting; thus raising the melting point, $T_{mp}$; and, accordingly, diminishing the liquid range, $T_{bp}$ – $T_{mp}$. Noble gases have liquid ranges of 3-5°, dihydrogen 7°, and neopentane [$(CH_3)_4C$] 21° — compared to 156° for its isomer n-pentane.

The four valence sphere models above have similar tetrahedral arrangements of electron pair domains. The corresponding molecules are said to be "isoelectronic". They differ in locations of their protons [in the shaded electron pair domains or in the heavy atoms' nuclei (not shown)].

The exclusive orbital models render the cited molecular shapes self-evident. Not immediately obvious from the pattern of molecular orbital energies, however, is what the shapes of the corresponding molecules are; or even that they are "isoelectronic".

The phenomenon of isoelectronicity is powerful support for the concept of exclusive orbital models of molecules. It extends the stereochemistry of compounds of carbon and hydrogen to the stereochemistry of compounds of nitrogen, oxygen, and fluorine. It led the author to a study of "tangent sphere models of molecules" (examined, independently, earlier — as "charge cloud models" — by George Kimball and graduate students at Columbia University).

Isoelectronic molecules have the same tangent sphere models, but not — as illustrated above — the same canonical molecular orbitals.

# Geometrical Models of Primary and Secondary Chemical Affinities

Easily overlooked when using valence sphere models of molecules is the ease with which they represent chemical affinities' leading features: *saturation* and *directional character*. The classical tetrahedral arrangement of valence strokes

handles with ease one set of leading facts of organic stereochemistry: the *directionality* of *primary* chemical affinities. Not accounted for, however, by valence stroke diagrams and valence stick models of molecules, are the phenomena of (i) *saturation* of primary affinities and (ii) *directionality* and (iii) *saturation* of *secondary, electrophilic affinities*. The latter three phenomena emerge immediately on replacing valence strokes of valence stroke diagrams by valence-shell-filling valence spheres.

The arrow points to an electrophilic site. It may be described for atoms that satisfy the Octet Rule (EPCN = 4) as the external lobe of a sigma anti-bonding orbital [H. Bent, "Structural Chemistry of Donor-Acceptor Interactions," *Chem. Rev.*, **68**, 587-648 (1968)], called of late a "σ hole" (J. Kemsley, "Defining a new Carbon Bond," C&EN, Jan. 6, 2014, p25). Exclusive Orbital Theory's electron domain molecular models are to the author's knowledge the only molecular models of the electrophilic dimples in electron densities' profiles.

Similar atomic-core/electron-domain packing models hold for cores that have electron-pair-coordination-numbers larger than 4 — e.g., 5 and 6.

| Trigonal Pyramid Tetrahedron EPCN 4 | Trigonal Bipyramid EPCN 5 | Square Pyramid EPCN 5 | Square Bipyramid Octahedron EPCN 6 |

By generating directly from classical bond diagrams approximate electron density profiles, Atomic-Core/Electron-Domain Attraction Theory accounts at a glance for *both* the directionality and saturation of *both* primary and secondary chemical affinities.

Seldom in valence theory has so much been expressed so simply.

# BEYOND HYDROGEN
## An Explanatory Note

It's joined in progress and runs in circles.
JAMES JOYCE

This book's introduction to Conceptual Valence Bond Theory begins, in a way, counter-intuitively, with bond diagrams and molecular models (page 1) for species with—good heavens! —4, 6, and 8 atoms and, respectively, 10, 12, and 14 valence shell electrons ($C_2H_2$, $C_2H_4$, and $C_2H_6$). A truly *fundamental* discussion of the electronic structure of matter would begin, one might have thought, with Nature's *simplest* molecule. Indeed, most modern textbooks books on molecular structure do begin with discussions of $H_2^+$ and/or $H_2$. Their results are of limited interest, however, for a truly *comprehensive* account of valence theory, for several reasons.

- Dihydrogen is merely a *diatomic* molecule. It has, accordingly, *no bond angles*, hence no stereochemistry (except in the case of weak coordination of hydrogen molecules by some coordinatively unsaturated transition metal ions). Absent, accordingly, in a mathematical analysis of dihydrogen, however accurate, is a leading feature of the structure of molecules that have at least three atoms and, accordingly, a nontrivial molecular *structure*, with *bond angles*. Also -

- Dihydrogen molecules have merely *one electron pair*. Absent, therefore, in a mathematical analysis of dihydrogen — again, however accurate it may be — is any consideration whatsoever of the *Exclusion Principle*, which, with Schrödinger's equation, is a leading physical principle of the physics of molecular electrons. Too -

- Dihydrogen molecules have *no inner shell electrons*. Absent, consequently, from a mathematical analysis of dihydrogen, is any consideration of the role in valence theory of *atomic cores*, of different charges, sizes, and, accordingly, different chemistries. And -

- Totally absent from a hydrogen-first, anti-historical introduction to valence theory by way of rigorous mathematical deductions based on Schrödinger's equation for dihydrogen is any indication of the nature of an *inductive* science.

Truth be told, valence theory was joined in progress, from inductions based on observations, and runs in circles, by way of inductions accepted as established principles used to account for new observations by deductions.

In summary: Because dihydrogen molecules have merely *two* atoms, *one* electron pair, and *no* inner shell electrons, missing from introductions to valence theory by way of dihydrogen are: the Octet Rule, the Valence Stroke Termination Rule, the *s*-Character Rule, expanded octets, multicenter bonds, and, indeed, most of the concepts associated with the technical terms of Conceptual Valence Bond Theory. Illustrated are limitations encountered when an inductive science is presented solely from a deductive point of view.

PERSONAL NOTE. When James completed with Coolidge the first successful quantum mechanical calculation of the bond length and strength of the dihydrogen molecule and left Harvard University with a Ph.D., he bequeathed his mechanical calculator to his neighbor in Harvard's Mallinckrodt Laboratory, the author's father, whose son later used the calculator to analyze for his father data collected from the faculty at the University of Missouri, Columbia, regarding the content of a general chemistry course taught by the University's graduate dean, Henry E. Bent, from demonstration-experiments featuring, often, dihydrogen and, especially in his famous Christmas Lectures for students and staff, flames and explosions.

# "Electrocyclic Reactions"

"A theory of valency can only be justified," Nevil Sigwick has been quoted as saying (p241), "by showing that it is applicable to chemistry as a whole." Accordingly, absence in Exclusive Orbital Theory (EOT) of models of mechanisms of "electrocyclic reactions" has been, for nearly fifty years, a source of unease for the author. Here's the problem.

In chemical reactions, some changes occur *simultaneously*. An $S_N2$ reaction is a prototypical example. As an interatomic distance between a pair of atoms of a pair of reactant species decreases, from the distance of a nonbonded interaction to the distance of a chemical bond, an adjacent distance between a pair of atoms in one of the reactants increases, from the distance of a chemical bond to the distance of a nonbonded interaction (p14). Another instance of simultaneous changes in molecular structure during a chemical reaction occurs in the mechanism suggested for formation of cyclopropane from ethylene and methylene (pp98-101).

For "electrocyclic reactions", all changes in interatomic distances and in atomic-core/electron-domain affiliations may seem to occur at once: hence the phrase "no mechanism reactions". The problem for Exclusive Orbital Theory in such cases stems from the fact that modern theories of "electrocyclic reactions" are generally explained in terms of positive and negative phases of p-orbitals' lobes. Those algebraic descriptors are absent, however, in EOT's equivalent orbital description of double bonds! Corresponding to the lobes' algebraic signs, it's finally been realized, are a pair of *geometrical descriptors* associated with an equivalent orbital description of a double bond.

EO Theory

+ and - p-orbital lobes --------------> EO domains *above* and *below* a double bond's plane

In describing mechanisms of "electrocyclic reactions" in terms of exclusive orbitals, one may say, accordingly: "See Woodward and Hoffmann (e.g.); and the change in terminology cited immediately above."

Owing to changes in formal charges in bare-bones' expressions of Walden inversions

$$A^- + B{-}C = A{-}B + C^-$$

the inversions are often executed in catalyzing, protonic solvents, such as water. In the gas phase an inversion may involve, correspondingly, several hydrogen-bonding water molecules. Shifting affiliations of the hydrogen bonds' mobile protons during an inversion diminish formal charges and yield, when represented by curly arrows [together with an arrow (next essay) for an inversion's primary changes in electron-domain/atomic-core affiliations] an electrocyclic circuit. Also, some Walden-type inversions are catalyzed on surfaces of metals, whereby formal charges are moderated by shifts of affiliations of mobile electrons, accompanied by changes in sub-surface interatomic distances. Representation of those shifts by curly arrows yields, again, electrocyclic circuits. "Electrocyclic reactions" may be more common than commonly realized.

The simplest "electrocyclic reaction" is homolytic scission of a covalent bond. Representation of the altered affiliations of its electrons by a pair of curly barbs, one for each spin set, anchored at opposite ends of parallel, one-electron valence strokes for the bond being broken, and pointing in opposite directions, yields a *short circuit*.

# Catalysis of a Walden Inversion by Proton Donors and Acceptors

*Curly Arrow Circuit-Completion by Way of Proton Transfers*

Nature resists separation of unlike charges. Puzzling, in that regard, is the following graphic representation of the mechanism of a Walden inversion (between two neutral species): namely, a lonely pair of curly arrows pointing in the same direction!

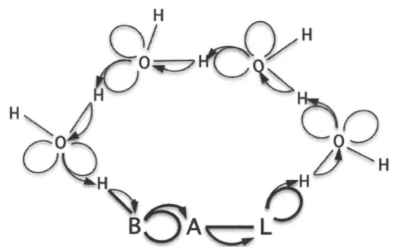

**A Walden inversion. A:** Lewis Acid, an electrophilic electron pair acceptor.
**B:** Lewis Base, a nucleophilic electron pair donor.  **L:** Leaving Group.

Such reactions are, in fact, usually executed (as noted in the previous essay) in proton donor-acceptor solvents, such as water, or alcohols, that, by proton transfers, complete — or partially complete — otherwise incomplete curly arrow circuits.  In the gas phase the rate law for a Walden inversion may include a factor for the concentration of water molecules to something like the fourth power, corresponding to the hydrogen-bonded reaction intermediate, or transition state, pictured below.

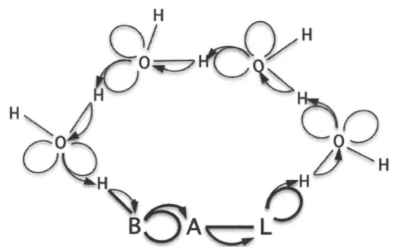

Shematic representation of the gas phase aquation of the participants in a Walden Inversion, by a chain of four hydrogen bonded water molecules. In the curly arrow circuit B, A, L, and four hydrogen-bonded water molecules, each atomic site is involved with two arrows: one in, one out. Hydrogen bonds, O—H : O, are approximately linear.

The four hydrogen-bonded water molecules act, jointly, as a catalyst. They participate in the reaction, but, in the end, are unchanged, except for their orientations. Each of the hydrogen bonds, O—H : O, becomes the related hydrogen bond O : H—O.

Nature has two ways of maintaining approximate local electrical neutrality during chemical reactions: by motions of protons, in protonic solvents; and by motion of electrons, for reactions catalyzed by surfaces of metals.

# As Bohr Liked to Say . . .

*The opposite of a profound statement may be a profound statement.*

### Example A
### Two Reviews of *MCB* II

Readers may wonder who the target audience is.
The desultory discussion has no discernable narrative thread.
Highly complex molecular diagrams may create more problems than they solve.
Not for the molecularly challenged!

—KIRKUS

Fascinating. VERY readable. There is almost a narrative feel to it.
Interested readers will be enthralled by its short paragraphs and diagrams.
A great supplement for college students going through their chemistry courses.
Anyone with an ounce of interest in valence theory will find this a must have book.

– THE US REVIEW OF BOOKS

### Example B
### Localized and Delocalized Orbitals

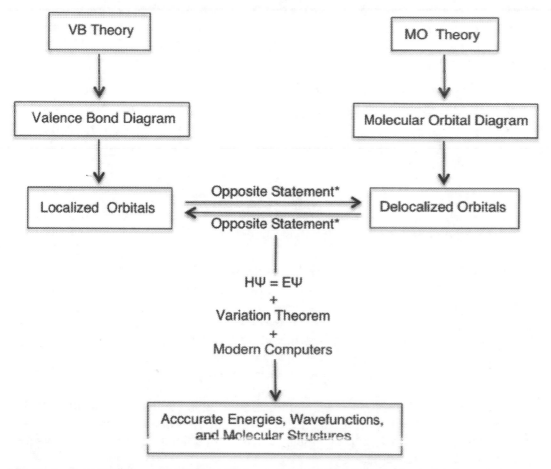

* By algebraic manipulations delocalized orbitals can be transformed into localized orbitals, and vice-versa.

The difference between localized and delocalized orbitals has been likened, as said, to the difference between night and day. Which is correct? For what purposes? For calculation of energies and numerical values of parameters of molecular structure, delocalized orbitals are usually used. For theorems regarding *bond* orders, locations of *bond* terminations, and other *chemical concepts*, localized orbitals are used.

Not shown in the previous diagram are one-way links between Valence Bond Theory and Molecular Orbital Theory.

Indispensable for determining where the atoms of MO Theory's atomic orbitals are, and for initiating applications of the Variation Theorem in calculations for molecules of moderate sizes, and larger, are approximate molecular gemetries, and corresponding "Z-Matrices", constructed with the aid of Conceptual Valence Bond Theory.

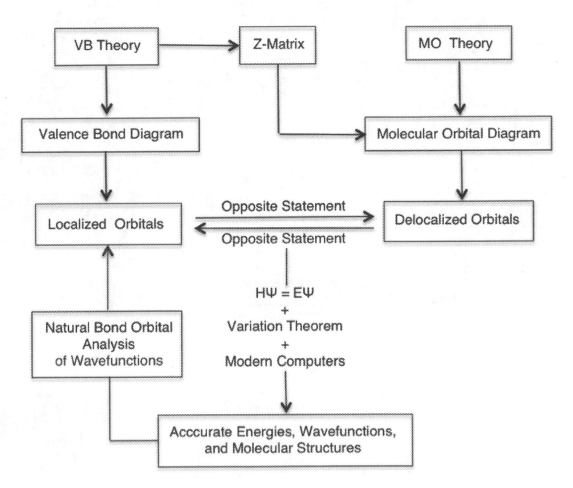

Electron localization procedures (such as Natural Bond Orbital Analyses) are indispensable in interpreting molecular orbital wavefunctions in terms of chemical concepts, such as core electrons, bonding pairs, and lone pairs. Accurate wavefunctions so analyzed serve to refine Valence Bond Theory's structures.

Determination and interpretation of molecular wavefunctions is, as said, in the words of James Joyce, *joined in progress and runs in circles.*

# Letter to Hoffmann Regarding Critiques of Valence Theories

08.15.13

Dear Roald,

Thanks for the reprint "Niels Bohr: between physics and chemistry". Bridging the gap between Bohr's dynamic model of the hydrogen atom and Lewis's static model of molecules eluded the physics and chemistry communities for quite some time, but turned out to be a simple thing to do.

*Use **static** domains populated by **dynamic** electrons.*

Your remarks regarding *MCB* are a good and fair description of it. I've used one of them on the book's front cover.

"Unfair"ness to Mulliken and his school is one of "many many" "fascinating things" that emerged *unexpectedly* from investigations of "how far one can get with a localized orbital perspective".

From that perspective, Conceptual MO Theory is not an *alternative* to Conceptual VB Theory, even though their orbitals may be mathematically equivalent to each other, for there's more to Conceptual Valence Bond Theory than construction of a set of orbitals. There are, also, the Theory's "Primary" and "Secondary Principles". In the case of Exclusive Orbital Theory, orbital construction is a (usually) trivial — albeit important first step.

The two theories, VB and MO, are complementary accounts of molecular electron density distributions: one for their *profiles*, for ground states; one for their *numerical values* particularly near nuclei, and especially for excited states.

Mulliken's induction, from his extensive work on excited states, of delocalized orbitals, applied to ground states is, from the point of view of Conceptual Valence Bond Theory, and its "many many goodies", a mistake.

What allows one to go directly from excited states to ground states in one's method of orbital construction?

My critiques of the MO Theory of Mulliken and his school are gentle, it seems to me, compared to some things said by advocates of MO Theory about Pauling and Valence Bond Theory — that, e.g., by popularizing Valence Bond Theory so successfully (for a time), Pauling set back valence theory by several decades. If there is truth — i.e., usefulness — to Exclusive Orbital Theory, the same thing might be said of Mulliken and Canonical MO Theory, applied to ground states, with regard to Exclusive Orbital Theory. The establishment's silence regarding "tangent sphere models of molecules" set back, in the author's experience, Exclusive Orbital Theory's development by several decades.

Enclosed is an expanded critique of MO Theory, when it is applied to ground states. Excited states are another matter.

Best regards,

Henry

# Scientific Phrases Related to the Concept of a Chemical Bond

Molecular Orbital Theory maintains that molecules' valence electrons are delocalized over entire molecules. The concept of a localized "chemical bond" has, accordingly, no physical significance in MO Theory. Valence Bond Theory maintains, on the other hand, that valence electrons are semi-localized in domains of chemical bonds and lone pairs — with a special kind of delocalization present in instances of "resonance" (between — or among — semi-localized structures). Even for aromatic systems — the prototypical examples in MO Theory of "electron delocalization" — modern Valence Bond Theory pictures valence electrons, after Linnett (1), as present in resonance hybrids, of partially anti-coincident, Kekule-type, semi-localized bond structures.

Modern Conceptual Valence Bond Theory associates with the term "bond" numerous phrases, including:

- valence bond theory
- conceptual valence bond theory
- computational valence bond theory
- single, double, and triple bonds
- ionic, covalent, and metallic bonds
- polar bonds
- dative bonds
- bent bonds
- banana bonds
- exposed bonds
- 2-center bonds
- 3-center bonds
- multi-center bonds
- protonated bonds
- large C—H bonds
- bond diagrams
- bond angles
- bond lengths
- bond multiplicities
- bond core coordination numbers
- bond nucleophilicity
- Bond Number Equation
- Bond Termination Rule
- Lewis' Bond Rule
- Bent's Bond Rule

Banishing, after Mulliken, "chemical ideology", and concepts associated with the word "bond", impoverishes the language of chemistry.

(1) J. W. Linnet, *"The Electronic Structure of Molecules: A New Approach,"* Wiley, 1964.

# Once More: MO Theory's Orbital Placement Problem
## *Why is methane tetrahedral?*

VB and *MO* below are advocates of two different qualitative theories of valence.

Science lives dangerously. It makes statements that can be falsified. E.g. -

VB  Conceptual Valence Bond Theory is, in and of itself, chemistry's only complete qualitative theory of valence that, e.g., explains, from scratch, why methane is tetrahedral.

*MO  Not so. See Gimarc: "Applications of Qualitative Molecular Orbital Theory" (1).*

> *"The tetrahedral structure of methane can be explained* [by Qualitative Molecular Orbital Theory] *without assuming* [after Pauling] *tetrahedral hybrid orbitals."*

VB  Or their equivalent?

*MO  Judge for yourself. Consider carbon's three p orbitals and, to overlap with them in formation of LCAO molecular orbitals, two arrangements for hydrogen's 1s orbitals: square planar and tetrahedral.*

VB  Aren't you assuming, here and now, at the outset, what you intend to explain?

*MO  Let me continue. The tetrahedrally located hydrogen 1s orbitals overlap constructively with carbon's p orbitals. Also, the square planar arrangement of 1s orbitals can be oriented so that they overlap even better with two of carbon's p orbitals. In that case, however, the third carbon p orbital is orthogonal to the hydrogen 1s orbitals.*

> *"[The] high energy* [of the third molecular orbital, a pure carbon p orbital without any hydrogen 1s character] *prohibits square planar geometry and makes [$CH_4$] tetrahedral."*

Q. E. D.

VB  Hold on. Gimarc merely shows, it would seem, that the assumption of three carbon p orbitals plus the assumption of a tetrahedral arrangement of hydrogen 1s orbitals are, jointly, equivalent, in discussing methane's electronic structure, to the use of four tetrahedral hybrid orbitals.

*MO  But not necessarily for carbon.*

VB  Be that as it may, students are still faced with the issue of carbon's p orbitals. Where do they come from? For a *complete* explanation of methane's shape one is confronted in Gimarc's Qualitative Molecular Orbital procedure with the mathematical complexities of solutions of Schrödinger's equation for the hydrogen atom.

Called to mind is a statement by Gibbs: If I have had any success in theoretical physics it has been by avoiding mathematical difficulties.

*MO  So, how do you account for methane's shape, nonmathematically?!*

VB  By inductions. Take hydrogen to be monovalent. Then oxygen is divalent, owing to the formula HOH; carbon is tetravalent, owing to the formula OCO, and tetrahedral, owing to the existence of only one compound with the formula $CH_2Cl_2$.

VB is indebted to professor Joel Liebman for calling his attention to Gimarc's article.

(1) B. M. Gimarc, "Applications of Qualitative Molecular Orbital Theory," *Accounts Chem. Res.*, **7**(11), 384-392 (1974).

# Unexpected Critiques of Conceptual MO Theory

Said the Bellman, What I tell you three times is true.
LEWIS CARROLL, "Hunting of the Snark"

Actually, there are four (not three) critiques of Conceptual MO Theory in this volume:

1. "Grounds for X-Rating MO Theory in General Chemistry", p54

2. "Why are Methane Molecules Tetrahedral?: An Appraisal of Conceptual MO Theory, p64

3. "Criticisms and Refutations: A Dialogue Concerning Two Valence Systems", p247

4. "Once More: MO Theory's Orbital Placement Problem, p275

The critiques were surprises. Studies of "Tangent Sphere Models of Molecules" began with the sole intention of investigating the models' stereochemical implications. Later a consilience between the structural principles of organic and inorganic chemistry emerged, along with exclusive orbital models of metals and theorems regarding bond numbers, bond angles, and valence stroke terminations.

The idea of criticizing Conceptual MO Theory was not on the author's agenda, at the outset. It emerged, slowly and unexpectedly, following a growing list of applications of Exclusive Orbital Theory, sometimes to puzzling chemical structures. Each successful application of the Theory increased the Theory's credibility, for the author, leading him to believe, eventually, with Weinhold, that –

> "The MO imagery of orbitals sprawling over one another
> 'almost everywhere' is profoundly illusory and physically
> meaningless."

Several statements summarize the case for Conceptual Valence Bond Theory (CVBT) vis-à-vis Conceptual MO Theory (CMOT).

1. For simplicity, CMOT is no match for CVBT.

2. CVBT's Valence Sphere Models fit like a glove the phenomenon of isoelectronicity, unaccounted for, so simply, by CMOT. Also,-

3. CVBT's Valence Sphere Models account for the consilience between organic and inorganic stereochemistry, unaccounted for by CMOT. Finally,-

4. CVBT is more fundamental than MO Theory, in the sense that computational MO Theory depends on CVBT twice over: once for locations of atoms, in formation of molecular orbitals from linear combinations of atomic orbitals; and once for Z-matrices, in initiating applications of the Variation Theorem.

One is led, finally, to this claim: *Conceptual Valence Bond Theory stands alone as the only stand-alone qualitative theory of valence.*

# An Explanation of Bent's Rule

*Use of the Isoelectronic Principle and the Hellman-Feynman Theorem*

The Isoelectronic Principle states that –

> *The overall arrangement of molecules' heavy (non-hydrogenic) atomic cores and electron domains is independent of the locations of the molecules' protons.*

Transformation, e.g., of a bond to hydrogen to a lone pair, with the bond's proton deposited alchemically in an adjacent atomic nucleus (as in the alchemical transformation of methane into ammonia) leaves the overall articulation of the electron cloud unchanged.

The Hellman-Feynman Theorem states that –

> *For molecules in stationary states, net forces on nuclei, calculated by Coulomb's Law, for nuclear-nuclear repulsions and for nuclear-electron attractions, for charge clouds treated as classical charge distributions, vanish —*

for otherwise nuclear motions in directions of non-vanishing forces would yield decreases in energy.

Relevance of the Principle and Theorem for Bent's Rule is indicated by the following two-dimensional valence circle models of methyl-methane and fluoro-methane.

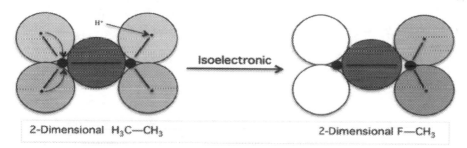

2-Dimensional $H_3C$—$CH_3$          Isoelectronic          2-Dimensional F—$CH_3$

Alchemical transformation of a "methyl" group of "methyl-methane" on the left by migration of its hydrogenic protons to the right into the adjacent "carbon" nucleus transforms the 2-dimensional "methyl" substituent into the more electronegative "fluoro" substituent, with an increase in coulombic repulsion between the two rightward-migrating protons and the right-most "carbon core", thrusting it further rightward and, thereby, opening up the "HCH" angle and shortening the "C—H" bonds, corresponding to an increase in carbon s-character in its "C—H" bonds, in accordance with Bent's Rule, that –

> *Atomic s-character tends to concentrates in orbitals directed toward electropositive substituents.*

Bent's Rule was based on accurate post-WWII determinations of molecular structure, especially by means of the spectroscopy of microwaves, based on development during WWII of radar (followed by television). Obtained were molecular moments of inertia, which depend on atomic masses (known) and bond angles and bond lengths (selected to fit observed moments of inertia, multiplied in number by isotopic substitutions), combined with the — at the time heretical — induction that, e.g., the short central carbon-carbon single bond of 1,3-butadiene, $H_2C=CH$—$CH=CH_2$, of only 1.46 Å compared to 1.53 Å for $H_3C$—$CH_3$ occurs chiefly because of a change in hybridization of the carbon atoms, from $sp^3$ to $sp^2$, rather than from the notion from MO Theory (in accordancy at the time) that the bond-length shortening occurs chiefly because of conjugation across the single bond (present, but less important than the change in hybridization). The hybridization model was rejected repeatedly by journal editors of the American Chemical Society, but eventually became, when finally published, a Citation Classic — and a significant step toward exclusive orbital models of molecules.

# Tetrahedrane

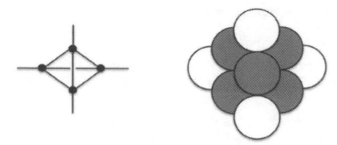

The valence sphere model of hypothetical tetrahedrane is the epitome of compactness: three cubic close-packed layers of, looking downward, 1, 3, and 6 electron-pair domains. The structure corresponds, accordingly, to unusually large — for a structure of its size — core/core and electron-pair/electron-pair repulsion. It would be, in a word, if synthesized, *spring-loaded*, so to speak, prone to fly apart by some such mechanism as the following:

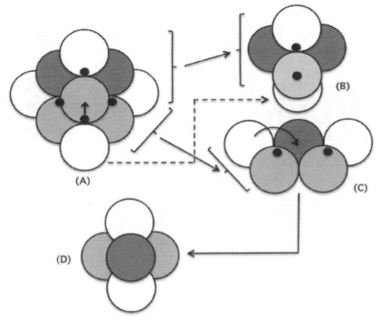

(A) Small black circles represent carbon cores, $C^{+4}$, in tetrahedral interstices. The short upward-pointing arrow represents migration of a carbon core through an adjacent trigonal interstice, created by the three light grey carbon-carbon bond domains, upward into the trigonal dimple created by the two dark grey carbon-carbon domains and the uppermost of the previous three domains. Separation of the top four domains together with a tag-along by the front-most white, carbon-hydrogen domain yields a molecule of acetylene, (B). Left behind is the five-domain fragment (C). Its curly arrow indicates a roll-up of the carbon-hydrogen domain into the dimple defined by the three grey domains, accompanied by the carbon core on the left. Similar motion downward on the right completes a second molecule of acetylene, (D).

Stabilizing the products with respect to the reactant is emergence of energy-lowering, partial spatial anticoincidence in the triple bonds of acetylene, absent in tetrahedrane.

# The Methyl Radical: Planar or Pyramidal?

MO theory's prediction that the methyl radial is planar with 120° HCH bond angles and an unshared electron in a *pure p orbital* [sic!] contradicts Bent's Rule that atomic s-character tends to concentrates in orbitals directed toward electropositive substituents, where, so to speak, "it does the most good". Unshared electrons are deemed to be in orbitals to substituents of zero electronegativity. (Bond angles in, e.g., molecules of ammonia and water — 107° and 104.5°, respectively — are, accordingly, less than tetrahedral.)

Some workers have carefully stated, however, that a small deviation from planarity, perhaps 10-20°, cannot be excluded. Sometimes the molecule has been said to be "quasi-planar", with an inversion barrier, if present, less than half the zero point energy.

What conclusions, if any, does Conceptual Valence Bond Theory add to those remarks?

CVBT begins with the knowledge that $CH_3$ has 7 valence shell electrons: 4 of one spin, 3 of the opposite spin. It assumes that the 4-member spin set in its configuration of maximum probability is arranged tetrahedrally about the carbon $C^{+4}$ core and that, similarly, the 3-member spin set is arranged in a planar trigonal configuration. A weighted average of those configurations yields an HCH angle of **112.6°** and a deviation from planarity of **14°**, pretty much in agreement with some of the views cited above, if, however, contrary to the most commonly held view regarding the methyl radical's geometry: namely, that it is planar.

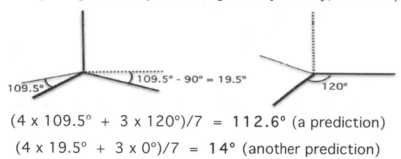

$$(4 \times 109.5° + 3 \times 120°)/7 = 112.6° \text{ (a prediction)}$$

$$(4 \times 19.5° + 3 \times 0°)/7 = 14° \text{ (another prediction)}$$

The barrier height for inversion of the radical's single unshared electron is expected to be less than one-half the barrier height for ammonia.

The orbital occupied by the unshared electron has, in the 112.6° HCH model, some carbon s-character. It is not — in accordance with Bent's Rule — in a pure *p* orbital.

To judge from HCH bond angles, $CH_3$'s C—H bonds are more s-rich than those of methane and, accordingly, shorter: 1.079 Å for $CH_3$ compared to 1.094 Å for methane.

A CAVEAT? For ethylene, whose HCH bond angle is 116°, the C—H bond length is not still shorter than that of $CH_3$ (with its smaller HCH angle) but, rather, longer: 1.085 Å. However, the reason why ethylene has a large HCH angle is different from the reasons for the bond angles of $CH_3$ and $CH_4$. From the standpoint of valence sphere models, ethylene's large HCH angle arises from $C^{+4}/C^{+4}$ repulsion, whose outward thrust, not present in single-carbon-core $CH_3$ and $CH_4$, thrusts the protons of its C—H bonds outward (also), thereby rendering ethylene's C—H bonds slightly longer than they would otherwise be.

In acetylene corresponding outward thrusts render its protons significantly acidic. Also, "outward thrusts" of dinitrogen's cores *directly into lone pairs* render $N_2$ molecules unusually stable, for ones having triple bonds. No other molecule has the same structural features (with the exception, to some extent, of HCN, also formed in fiery rearrangements of atoms) as $N_2$ — with its harsh consequences regarding man(un)kind's uses of high-nitrogen substances that decompose explosively to $N_2$.

# Small Molecules with Incomplete Octets
## *More Challenges for Exclusive Orbital Theory*

Exclusive orbital theory was, at the outset, in the form of Lewis's electron dot diagrams, a theory of octets. One might wonder: Can the Theory account for the shapes of molecules that have *incomplete octets*, such as those of the type AH₂ with 2 to 7 valence shell electrons? They've been discussed by Gimarc from the point of view of the "basic assumption" of MO theory, that "[e]lectrons in molecules are completely delocalized and move in molecular orbitals which extend over the entire molecular framework" (1).

### Two-Electron Species: Bent $H_3^+$ and Bent $LiH_2^+$

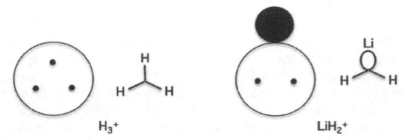

Valence sphere models and valence stroke diagrams for a pair of 2-electron species. **Large circle:** profile of an electro pair. **Smallest black circles:** H⁺. **Intermediate black circle:** Li⁺. **$H_3^+$:** A triply protonated electron pair; i.e., a 2-electron 3-center bond. The H atoms have formal charges of +1/3. **$LiH_2^+$:** Another 3-center bond, with a dative bond component directed toward Li⁺. Formal charges of H are 0 and of more electropositive Li +1.

### Three-Electron Species: Linear $H_3$ and $BeH_2^+$

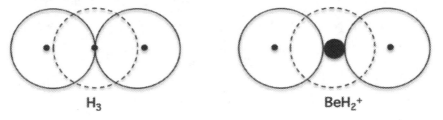

Electronic profiles are those for one, not two (spin-paired) electrons.

### Four-Electron Species: Linear $BeH_2$ and Isoelectronic $BH_2^+$

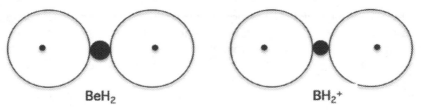

(1)   B. M. Gimark, "Applications of Qualitative MO Theory," *Accounts Chem. Res.,* Volume 7, Number 11, November, 1972, 384-392.

## A Five-Electron Species: BH₂

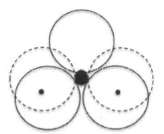

The 2-member spin set favors a linear geometry: <HBH = 180°. The 3-member spin set favors a bond angle of 120°, without allowance for operation of the s-character rule, which, through mutual repulsion of the two protons for the $B^{+3}$ core, thrust it, as shown, *directly* into the domain of the unshared electron, thereby decreasing the HBH angle, say to ca. 105°? The weighted averages of 180 and 120 and of 180 and 105 are, respectively, 144 and 135. The observed HBH angle is reported by Gimarc to be 131°.

## Six-Electron Species: Triplet and Singlet CH₂ and NH₂⁺

|  | Bond Angles | |
|---|---|---|
|  | $CH_2$ | $NH_2^+$ |
| Triplet | 136° | 140-150° |
| Singlet | 105° | 115-120° |

In the triplet states the species' six valence shell electrons are split 4 of one spin and 2 of the opposite spin. The weighted average of a bond angle of 109.5° (the tetrahedral angle) for the 4-member spin set and 180° for the 2-member spin set is (4x109.5° + 2x180°)/6 = 133°, close to the observed HCH angle for triplet $CH_2$. Bond diagrams for the singlet species are -

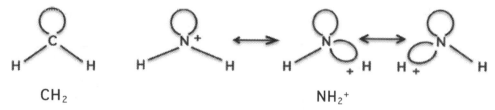

CH₂                    NH₂⁺

In accordance with Bent's s-character rule, the HCH angle for the singlet state is less than 120°, by 15° (as assumed above in a slightly different context for one of BH₂'s spin sets). For both $NH_2^+$ species, triplet and singlet, HNH angles are, however, some 10 to 15 degrees larger than the corresponding bond angles for $CH_2$. Those facts may be accounted for in the following fashion:

- Nitrogen is more electronegative than hydrogen. Therefore, –
- $NH_2^+$'s formal charge of +1 resides chiefly on its hydrogen atoms. That is to say, –
- $NH_2^+$'s NH bonds have dative bond character, in the sense shown at the right in the figure immediately above. In other words –
- $NH_2^+$'s H atoms act as highly electropositive substituents. Accordingly, -
- By Bent's Rule, nitrogen's bonding orbitals in $NH_2^+$ are relatively rich in s-character.
- Hence $NH_2^+$'s relatively large HNH bond angles.

In Summary: Exclusive Orbital Theory accounts for the shapes of the AH₂ species cited by Gimarc, without use of atomic orbitals, through use of different orbital structures for different spin sets, Bent's Rule, and the trio of interrelated concepts: electronegativities, formal charges, and dative bonds.

# Qualitative Valence Bond Theory of Small Hydrocarbon Dications

## *A Comparison with Quantitative Molecular Orbital Theory*

Modern quantitative Molecular Orbital Theory often yields molecular structures explicable in terms of the principles of a qualitative Valence Bond Theory that features: exclusive localized electron pair domains; an Octet Rule and, when the Rule is obeyed, tetrahedrally arranged spin sets about heavy atom (non-hydrogenic) atomic cores, with generally zero formal charges, in accordance with a Principle of Local Electrical Neutrality; and a Valence Stroke Termination Rule. For electron deficient dications, however, not all formal charges can vanish. The Octet Rule is not obeyed, nor, accordingly, can a fully tetrahedral arrangement of spins be present, at least not for both spin sets, simultaneously. One might wonder then: Is what remains of Conceptual Valence Bond Theory — chiefly arrangements of exclusive electron domains of minimum electrostatic energy — sufficient to account for Molecular Orbital Theory's structures for the three dications: $CH_2^{+2}$, $CH_3^{+2}$, and $CH_4^{+2}$ (1)?

### Legends

| Profiles, ± Spins | 2c/1e Bonds | Dative Bonds | 3c/1e Bond | ± Spins | $C^{+4}$ | $H^+$ |

$CH_2^{+2}$. The species has 4 electrons, sufficient for two 2-center/2-electron bonds.

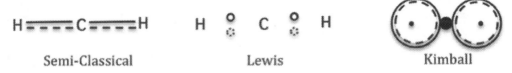

Semi-Classical            Lewis            Kimball

Formal charges, however, are poor: 0 for hydrogen, +2 for carbon. That can be rectified by introduction of dative bond character, in several ways, among them:

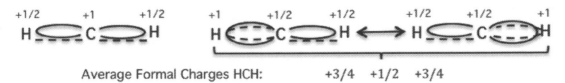

Average Formal Charges HCH:          +3/4   +1/2   +3/4

As carbon is generally assigned an electronegativity (2.5) slightly greater than that of hydrogen (2.2), the "Average Formal Charges" of +1/2 for carbon and +3/4 for hydrogen seem about right. They correspond to a structure in which the carbon-hydrogen bonds have a high degree of dative bond character, perhaps about 75%. Its calculated length is 1.150 Å (1). In covalently-bonded acetylene, in which the carbon atom, as in $CH_2^{+2}$, is hybridized *sp*, a CH bond's length, as expected, is significantly shorter: 1.059 Å.

(1) "Organic Dications: Gas Phase Experiments and Theory in Concert," K. Lammertsma, P. Schleyer, and H. Schwarz, *Angew. Chem. Int. Ed. Engl.* **28** (1989) 1321-1341.

$CH_3^{+2}$. This species has five electrons: three in one spin set, two in the other spin set. The cation has, by calculation (1), one long CH bond and opposite it a large HCH bond angle.

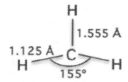

Calculated structure of $CH_3^{+2}$ (1).

A valence sphere model and the corresponding valence stroke diagram fit the calculated structure fairly well.

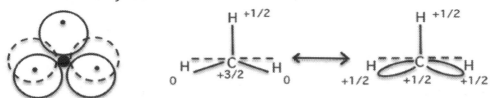

**Left:** Valence sphere model of $CH_3^{+2}$. The top-most, longest CH bond is a 1-electron 2-center bond. **Center:** Corresponding valence stroke diagram. Predicted for the large HCH angle: $(3 \times 120° + 2 \times 180°)/5 = 144°$. Carbon's formal charge $(+3/2)$ is, however, unrealistic. **Right:** Introduction of dative bond character into the 3-membered spin set increases the electro-positive character of the bottom two hydrogen atoms and, by Bent's Rule, increases carbon's s-character in its dative bond orbitals and, accordingly, increases the corresponding inter-orbital angle, yielding a value closer than $144°$ to the calculated value of $155°$.

$CH_4^{+2}$. The methane dication has six electrons, three in each of two spin sets, which, if coincident, yield a planar arrangement of electron domains.

**A.** Calculated strucure of $CH_4^{+2}$ (1). **B.** Exclusive orbital model of $CH_4^{+2}$. **C.** Valence stroke diagram corresponding to B, showing two conventional covalent 2c/2e CH bonds and one 3-center HCH bond, whose calculated HH distance (1) is about 0.3 Å greater than that of dihydrogen. The formal charge for carbon, $+4/3$, compared to those for the hydrogen atoms, 0 and $+1/3$, is poor. **D.** Creation of better formal charges through introduction of 50% dative bond character for the 2-center CH bonds. Implied once again, through use of Bent's Rule, is an HCH angle for the 2-center bonds that, as calculated (1), is greater than $120°$.

This essay illustrates the last procedure of a trio of sequential procedures: (i) use of Conceptual Valence Bond Theory in creation of a Z-Matrix (p55) for initiating quantum mechanical calculations; (ii) execution of quantum mechanical calculations, often through use of Molecular Orbital Theory; and (iii) interpretation of numerical results of quantum mechanical calculations through use, once again, of Conceptual Valence Bond Theory. Collectively the trio of procedures constitute a computationally and conceptually useful physico-chemical theory of valence.

# Conceptual VB Theory of Boron-Boron Bond Lengths in $B_2Cl_4$ and $H_2B_2O$

The theory begins with bond diagrams of zero formal charges. By the Valence Stroke Termination Rule, the number of valence strokes for the bond diagram for $B_2Cl_4$ is $(2\times3 + 4\times7)/2 = 17$. For $H_2B_2O$ it is $(2\times1 + 2\times3 + 6)/2 = 7$. Subtracting from 17 and 7 the number of lone pairs, $4\times3 = 12$, and $1\times2$, yields 5 for the number of bonding valence strokes for $B_2Cl_4$ and, also, 5 for $H_2B_2O$. Excess connectivities are, accordingly, $5 - 5 = 0$ and $5 - 4 = 1$, shown below as a 3-membered ring.

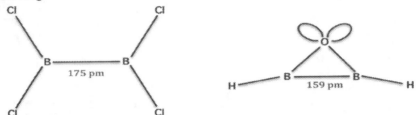

By the "R Equation" -

$$R(\text{radius of electron pair domain}) = 60 \text{ pm} + 0.4r(\text{radius of atomic core}).$$

With $r = 20$ pm (1), the model's BB distance in $B_2Cl_4$ is -

$$2(R + r) = 2[60 + 1.4(20)] \text{ pm} = 176 \text{ pm}.$$

The calculated BB distance for $H_2B_2O$ of 159 pm (2) is considered to be remarkably short (3), owing, presumably, to an oxygen-boron electron pair donor-acceptor interaction, with formation of a 3-center BOB bond.

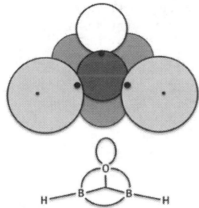

Valence sphere model and valence stroke diagram for a $H_2B_2O$ structure that satisfies the Octet Rule with, accordingly, $B_2 + 2B_3 = 3\times4 - 7 = 5 \rightarrow B_2 = 3$ and $B_3 = 1 \rightarrow B_1 [= V - (B_2 + B_3)] = 7 - (3 + 1) = 3$ (= 2 BH bonds and 1 oxygen lone pair).

The bond length difference 175 pm – 159 pm of 16 pm is approximately the difference in lengths of carbon-carbon single and double bonds (154 pm – 134 pm = 20 pm). And, indeed, the arrangement of $H_2B_2O$'s six valence shell electron pair domains, sans that of the oxygen lone pair, is, very approximately, that of a double bond. The H-B-B-H grouping is seen to be, as calculated, approximately linear.

(1)   Linus Pauling, *Nature of the Chemical Bond*, 3rd Edition, Cornell University Press, 1960, p514.
(2)   C. Laing & L. C. Allen, *J. Am. Chem. Soc.* **1991**, *113*, 1878.
(3)   H. Grutzmacher, *Angew. Chem. Int. Ed. Engl.* **1992**, *31*, 1329.

# $NO_3F$

## Valence Sphere Model and Valence Stroke Diagrams

Number of heavy atoms, N = 5. Number of valence shell electron pairs, V = 15.
Number of pairs in bonds, B (= 4N − V) = 5. Excess Connectivity = 1.

The molecule is isoelectronic with 1,1-difluoro- and 1,1-dimethyl-cyclopropane.

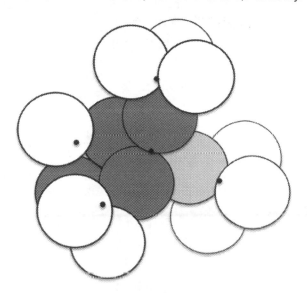

**Dark Grey:** Domains of NF, ring NO, and OO single bonds.
**Light Grey:** Domain of dative NO bond.
**White:** Domains of lone pairs of O and F.
• Locations of tetrahedral interstices occupied by atomic cores.

## A Proposed Instance of the Quantum Mechanical Principle of Superposition

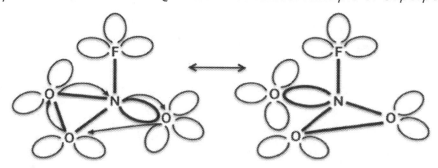

Bond diagrams for $NO_3F$ showing (by way of a Gauss circuit) resonance between, on the left, covalent ON and OO bonds and a NO dative bond and, on the right, different covalent NO and OO bonds and a different dative NO bond.

The linear structure O=N—O—O—F has, with no dative bonds, no formal charges. Absent, also, however, is "resonance" and, accordingly, diminished electron-electron repulsion between electrons of opposite spin, owing to occupancy by the two spin-sets of partially anticoincident spin-set structures, such as the two structures pictured immediately above.

The representations of $NO_3F$ illustrate the isomorphism that exists between a valence stroke drawing of a molecule and a valence sphere model of the molecule. Strokes in the former correspond to spheres in the latter, symbols of the elements in the former to locations of tetrahedral interstices in the latter.

# s-trans-Nitrosyl O-Hydroxide: HO—ON

## *The Longest Known Oxygen-Oxygen Bond*

HOON, an isomer of nitrous acid, HONO, isoelectronic with nitrosyl fluoride, FNO, and propylene, $H_2CH=CH_2$, has 9 valence shell electrons, V, 3 non-hydrogenic heavy atoms, N, and, consequently, if its bond diagram satisfies the Octet Rule with 2-center bonds, $4N - V = 3$ bonds, B, in its heavy-atom network, for an excess connectivity, E.C., of $3 - 2 = 1$, corresponding to a 3-member ring or a double bond, which, for overall local electrical neutrality (no formal charges), has 50% dative bond character.

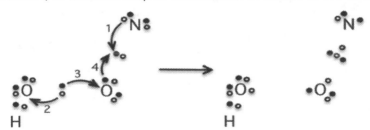

**Left:** Convention bond diagram with rabbit-ear lone pairs and unsatisfactory formal charges. **Middle:** Zero-formal-charge structure, with dative bonding shown for one component of the NO double bond. **Right:** Corresponding Lewis electron-dot structure. Dots represent schematically centroids of charge of exclusive localized molecular orbitals of HOON.

The s-trans configuration staggers the OH bonding pair and the two lone pairs domains of the OH group with respect to the other oxygen's lone pair and the two domains of the double bond.

A donor-acceptor interaction between the nitrogen lone pair trans to the OH bond and the oxygen-oxygen sigma antibonding orbital lengthens the ON bond, from 145 pm in HOOH to 191 pm in HOON, in the first step in dissociation of HOON to HO and ON.

**1** An unshared electron of the trans lone pair occupies the dimple in a valence sphere model opposite the OO bond, on its way to becoming a bonding electron. **2** An OO bonding electron becomes an unshared electron about the OH oxygen core. **3** The other OO bonding electron becomes an unshared electron about the other oxygen core. **4** One electron of the dative bond becomes a covalently bonding electron of the NO double bond..

The driving force for dissociation of HOON, and for its incipient dissociation, as a molecule with a long OO bond, arises, in part, from growth in passage from HOON to HO + ON of anticoincidence between the system's two spin sets, particularly in its ON moiety.

(O=N—N=O has the longest known NN bond.) Nitric oxide's low dipole moment implies that its 5-electron bond has, as shown above, about 20 percent dative bond character.

# The Enigma of the Nonexistence of Pentazole

The cyclic nitrogenous bases pyrrole and tetrazole, the latter isoelectronic with cyclopentadiene, exist, but not the last member of the series, pentazole, $HN_5$ (1).

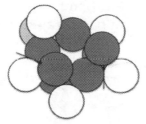

Valence sphere model of pentazole and species isoelectronic with it. Dark grey domains: heavy-atom/heavy-atom bonds. Light grey domain: hydrogen/heavy-atom domain. White domains: lone pairs for pentazole; domains of C—H bonds for cyclopentadiene. Arrows point to two of eight electrophilic dimples about hypothetical pentazole's two double bonds, a.k.a. lobes of $\pi^*$ orbitals.

Four cyclic electron-pair zero-formal-charge-maintaining donor-acceptor interactions yield from a hypothetical pentazole molecule molecules of dinitrogen and hydrazoic acid.

$$HN_3 + N_2 =$$

(A) A five-step electrocyclic circuit initiated by the NH lone pair. The third arrow around the circuit originates with the third lone pair. The circuit ends with formation of a sextet. (B) Transformation of the sextet back to an octet with a lone pair and concomitant formation of a dative-bond-component for the terminal NN double bond. (C) A four-step circuit initiated by a donor-acceptor interaction between a lone pair on the terminal nitrogen atom and a lobe of the NN $\pi^*$ orbital. The circuit is completed by transformation of a bonding pair to a lone pair and a dative bond to a covalent bond. Formed is a second sextet. (D) Transformation of the second sextet back to an octet and concomitant formation of a dative bond. Nitrogen lone pairs are used twice in the first step, (A), and once in subsequent steps, (B), (C), and (D). It seems likely that for a minimum-energy transformation of $HN_5$ to $HN_3$ and $N_2$ the four steps (A), (B), (C), and (D) would occur, in so far as possible, more or less simultaneously.

The complete mechanism uses in its first circuit a lone pair on the NH nitrogen and one other lone pair (bottom left). Pyrrole has the NH lone pair but not the other one. Tetrazole has the in-plane lone pairs but not the NH lone pair. Elusive pentazole, alone, has both types of domains.

(1) R. Janoschek, *Angew. Chem. Int. Ed. Engl.* 1993, *32. No. 2*, 230-232.

# $H_3B \cdot NH_3$

## Bond Diagrams for the Borane-Ammonia Complex

Before Lewis' electron-pair/valence-stroke hypothesis, the dot in the expression $H_3B \cdot NH_3$ was said to be "a full stop to thought." Later it became the central valence stroke of structure (A).

(A)　　　　　(B)　　　　　(C)

Etc.

Structure (B) has superior formal charges. Calculated "natural charges" of -0.84 for N and -0.17 for B (professor Frank Weinhold, private communication) suggest that the molecular complex is a resonance hybrid of structures (A), (B), and (C).

Because the electronegativities of boron and hydrogen are about the same, the BH bonds in structures (A), (B), and (C) are taken to be pure covalent bonds, indicated by a simple valence stroke, with, accordingly, formal charges on boron's hydrogen atoms of zero. To place a formal charge of -0.17 on boron, structure (A) must constitute a fraction 0.17 of the resonance hybrid. To make the formal charge for nitrogen -0.84, the contribution of each of the three structures (C) must be 0.84/3 + 0.17/3 = 0.34. Accordingly, structure (B) constitutes a fraction 1 – 0.17 – 0.34 = 0.49 of the resonance hybrid. Formal charges for nitrogen's hydrogen atoms are, accordingly, + 0.34.

The dominant structure is the zero-formal-charge-structure (B), fraction 0.49, which seems reasonable, since, by Coulomb's law, Nature abhors separation of unlike charges. The dative bond character of the BN bond is, by the present calculation, 0.49 + 0.34 = 0.83. The bond's corresponding polar-covalent character is, accordingly, 1 – 0.83 = 0.17.

According to an x-ray redetermination of the complex's structure, "[t]he B—N separation of 1.564 Å [in the crystalline phase] is deemed to be "surprisingly short" for such a dative complex. In contrast the B—N distance determined in the gas phase by microwave spectroscopy (1.672 Å) is more than 0.1 Å longer" (1). Crystal field effects presumably favor structure (A) with its polar covalent bond over structures (B) and (C) with their longer, non-polar dative BN bond.

The present application of Conceptual Valence Bond Theory illustrates two of the Theory's leading features, not cited, explicitly, previously.

1) The Theory expresses diverse facts about molecules with a small set of simple symbols, namely: those of the chemical elements; valence strokes (straight and rabbit eared); and the algebraic symbols + and –). And -

2) The Theory achieves its expressiveness with the aid of easily used guidelines regarding arrangements of its symbols into chemically significant forms.

(1)  M. Buhl, T. Steinke, von R. Schlerer, and R. Boese, *Angew. Chem. Int. Engl.* **30** (1991) No. 9, 1160-1161.

# Structure of the Donor-Acceptor Complex $C_2H_4 \cdots BrCl$

Structures of donor-acceptor complexes — reviewed in 1968 (1) — offer many instances of highly exposed lone pairs (1-member rings) serving as donors toward electron pair acceptors, such as BrCl, by way of BrCl's vacant $\sigma^*$ orbital.

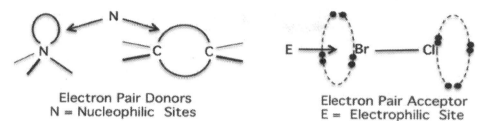

Electron Pair Donors
N = Nucleophilic Sites

Electron Pair Acceptor
E = Electrophilic Site

Twenty-six years later Legon and coworkers published the structure of the electron pair donor-acceptor complex formed by ethylene and the interhalogen BrCl (2). It has the structure expected from an examination of its electron density profile, based on its valence sphere model, based on valence stroke diagrams for $C_2H_4$ and BrCl.

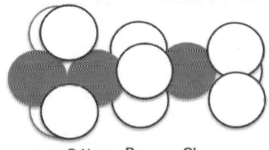

$C_2H_4 \cdots Br \text{——} Cl$
Electron Pair Donor-Acceptor Complex

The distance from the midpoint of the C=C double bond to the Br nucleus is reported to be approximately 2.98 Å. In terms of the parameters of the model pictured above, that distance corresponds to twice the radius of the shared double bond domain plus the radius of the bromine core, $Br^{+7}$, according to Pauling 0.39 Å, plus the relative short distance from the $Br^{+7}$ tetrahedral interstice to the tetrahedral interstice created by the electron pair donor-acceptor interaction. The apparent radius of a spherical C=C pair is accordingly slightly less than (2.98 Å – 0.39 Å)/2 = 1.3 Å. A double bond domain that size yields too large a double bond distance (by about 0.5 Å). Tentative conclusion: The cited distance of 2.98 Å is determined by "contact" between domains of the $Br^{+7}$ lone pairs and large C—H domains of $C_2H_4$ (cf. p29).

(1)  H. A. Bent, "Structural Chemistry of Donor-Acceptor Interactions," *Chem. Rev.,* **68**, 587-648, (1968).

(2)  H. I. Bloemink, K. Hinds, A. C. Legon, and J. C. Thorn, *Angew. Chem. Int. Engl.* **1994**, 33, No. 14, 1512-1513.

# Modern Structural Chemistry

[Explanatory Notes] and **Emphasis** Added
Highlighted: the inductive character of Pauling's studies of the chemical bond.

"I saw [Linus Pauling] as a brilliant lecturer and a man with a fantastic memory, and a great great showman. I think he was the century's greatest chemist. No doubt about it." MAX PERUTZ

"The best way to have a good idea is to have a lot of ideas." LINUS PAULING

A century ago the structural theory of organic chemistry was developed [by inductions]. Frankland in 1852 **suggested** that an atom of an element has a definite capacity for combining with atoms of other elements - a definite valence. [If 1 for hydrogen then, owing to the chemical formulas $H_2O$ and $CO2$, 2 for oxygen and 4 for carbon.] Six years later Kekulé and Couper, independently, **introduced the idea** of valence bonds between atoms, including bonds between two carbon atoms, and **suggested** that carbon is quadrivalent. In 1861 Butlerov, making use for the first time of the term "chemical structure", **stated** clearly that the properties of a compound are determined by its molecular structure, and reflect the way in which atoms are bonded to one another in the molecules of the compound. The development of the structure theory of organic chemistry [its valence stroke diagrams] then progressed rapidly, and this [empirical, pictorial, nonmathematical] theory has been of inestimable value in aiding organic chemists to interpret their experimental results and to plan new experiments.

A most important early addition to organic structure theory was made by the first Nobel Laureate in Chemistry, Van 't Hoff, who in 1874 **recognized** that the optical activity of carbon compounds [and the number of compounds with the formula $CH_2Cl_2$] can be explained by the **postulate** that the four-valence bonds of the carbon atom are directed in space toward the corners of a tetrahedron.

The structure theory of inorganic chemistry may be said to have been born only fifty years ago, when Werner, Nobel Laureate in Chemistry in 1913, **found** that the chemical composition and properties of complex inorganic substances could be explained by **assuming** that metal atoms often coordinate about [their atomic cores] a number of atoms different from their valence, usually four atoms at the corners either of a tetrahedron or of a square coplanar arrangement with the central atom, or six atoms at the corners of an octahedron. His **ideas** about the geometry of inorganic complexes were completely verified twenty years later, through the application of the technique of X-ray diffraction [the subject of Pauling's Ph.D. thesis at Cal Tech.]

After the **discovery** of the electron many efforts were made to develop an electronic theory of the chemical bond. A **great contribution** was made in 1916 by Gilbert Newton Lewis, who **proposed** that the chemical bond, such as the single bond between two carbon atoms or a carbon atom and a hydrogen atom represented by a line [a "valence stroke"] in the customary structural formula for ethane, consists of a pair of electrons held jointly by the [two atomic cores of the] two atoms that are bonded together. Lewis also **suggested** that atoms tend to assume the electronic configuration of a noble gas, through the sharing of electrons with other atoms or through electron transfer, and that the eight outermost electrons in an atom with a noble-gas electronic structure are arranged tetrahedrally in pairs about the atom['s atomic core].

After the discovery of quantum mechanics in 1925 it became evident that the quantum mechanical equations constitute a reliable basis for the theory of molecular structure. It also soon became evident that these equations, such as the Schrödinger wave equation, cannot be solved rigorously for any but the simplest molecules [containing one electron, such as the hydrogen molecule ion, $H_2^+$]. The development of the theory of molecular structure and the nature of the chemical bond during the past twenty-five years has been in considerable part **empirical** [i.e., by way of inductions] – based upon the facts of chemistry - but with the interpretation of these facts greatly influenced by quantum mechanical principles and concepts [and an Exclusion Principle: an extra-quantum mechanical principle].

The solution of the wave equation for the hydrogen molecule-ion by Ø. Burrau in 1927 completely clarified the question of the nature of the one-electron bond in this molecule-ion. Two illuminating quantum mechanical discussions of the shared-electron-pair bond in the hydrogen molecule were then simultaneously published, one by Heitler and London (Z.Physik, 44 (1927) 455), and the other by E. U. Condon (Proc. Natl. Acad. Sci. U.S., 13 (1927) 466).

In the approximate solution of the wave equation for the hydrogen molecule by Heitler and London a wave function is used that requires the two electrons to be separated, each being close to one of the two nuclei. The treatment by Condon permits the electrons to be distributed between the two nuclei independently of one another, each occupying a wave function similar to Burrau's function for the hydrogen molecule-ion. Condon's treatment is the prototype of the molecular-[delocalized]-orbital treatment that has been extensively applied in the discussion of aromatic and conjugated molecules, and Heitler and London's treatment is the prototype of the valence-bond [localized orbital] method [favored by Pauling]. When the effort is made to refine the two treatments they tend to become identical [in the numerical values that they yield for physical quantities, such as molecular energies and internuclear distances].

These early applications of quantum mechanics to the problem of the nature of the chemical bond made it evident that in general a covalent bond, involving the sharing of a pair of electrons between two atoms, can be formed if two electrons are available (their spins must be opposed, in order that the bond be formed), and if each atom has available [in its core's valence shell] a stable electronic orbital [i.e., an electron domain shared with the other atom] for occupancy by the [bonding] electrons.

The equivalence of the four bonds formed by a carbon atom, which had become a part of chemical theory, was not at first easily reconciled with the quantum mechanical description of the carbon atom as having one 2s orbital and three 2p orbitals in its outer shell. The solution to this difficulty was obtained when it was **recognized** [by Pauling and Slater] that as a result of the resonance phenomenon of quantum mechanics a tetrahedral arrangement of the four bonds of the carbon atom is achieved. The carbon atom can be **described** as having four equivalent tetrahedral bond orbitals, which are hybrids of the s and p orbitals. Further study of this problem [by Pauling] led to the **discovery** of many sets of hybrid bond orbitals, which could be **correlated** with bond angles, magnetic moments, and other molecular properties. In particular **it was found** [by Pauling] that $sp^3$, $dsp^2$, and $d^2sp^3$ hybrid orbitals **correspond** respectively to the tetrahedral, square planar, and octahedral configurations of inorganic complexes that had been **discovered** by Werner.

# Principal Take Away Messages

*Avoiding mathematical complexities is the key to capturing conceptual insights.*

*REMEMBER EINSTEIN'S ADVICE.*
*If you want to find out anything from theoretical physicists about the methods they use,*
*stick closely to one principle: don't listen to their words, fix your attention on their deeds.*

### In their informal day-to-day deeds chemists draw bond diagrams:
simple, abstract representations of
### Exclusive Orbital Models of Close Confederations of Semi-Localized Electrons.

### In formal calculations chemists use the Variation Theorem.
Two things should be said about its inputs and outputs.
1. *Poor conceptual inputs may lead, eventually, to excellent numerical outputs.*
On the other hand:
2. *Excellent numerical outputs do not mean necessarily excellent conceptual inputs.*
Indeed, according to the world's leading authority on Natural Bond Orbitals:
*"The MO imagery of orbitals sprawling over one another 'almost everywhere'*
*is profoundly illusory and physically meaningless."*

MO Theory predicted, e.g., that $CH_2$ is linear and $CH_3$ planar.
Both predictions violated Bent's Rule.
Both predictions were wrong.

Physical Theory states that $\Psi(1, 2, \ldots) = -\Psi(2, 1, \ldots) \rightarrow \Psi(1, 1, \ldots) = 0$.
*Two SPIN PARALLEL electrons cannot be at the same place at the same time.*
*<u>Electronic wave functions have to some degree exclusive orbital character</u>!*

However, in MO Theory construction of molecular orbitals is executed in the first instance
without giving any consideration whatsoever to a Principle of Electronic Spatial Exclusion.

Also: $H_2$, He, and LiH(c) have finite molar volumes, however great the pressure.
And valence strokes never cross each other.
<u>Two ELECTRON PAIRS cannot be at the same place at the same time!</u>

Packing of electron pair domains of finite size about smaller atomic cores
yields useful models of molecular electron density profiles.

Union of exclusive orbital models of molecules with supplementary rules and principles
> an s-character rule
> multicenter bonding
> a bond number equation
> a superposition principle
> an isoelectronic principle
> a valence stroke termination rule
> electronegativities and formal charges
> different orbitals for different spin sets
> lone pair dispersal about large atomic cores

yields a comprehensive qualitative account of valence of elements of the *s*- and *p*-blocks of
periodic tables without use of Schrödinger's intimidating equation, as one's sole source of
atomic orbitals, for use in MO theory's LCAO method of construction of molecular orbitals.

# Philosophical Perspectives

*MCB* follows in the footsteps of -

**The Philosophy of "What if . . . ?"** What if one replaces the two-dimensional valence strokes of valence stroke diagrams with three-dimensional valence spheres? Do the results make sense? Is it reasonable to view the valence strokes of organic chemistry's classical bond diagrams as shrewd (if crude) *schematic representations of localized exclusive molecular orbitals?*

**Heisenberg's Recommendation for Achieving Successful Improvements in Scientific Thought.**

*"Change as little as possible."*

Exclusive Orbital Theory is, ironically, less of a break with Mulliken's "chemical ideology" than is Mulliken's MO Theory.

**The Method of Trial, Error, and Improvement.** "Third time is a charm." With each trial — a fourth edition of a second volume of sequels to six essays about "Tangent Sphere Models of Molecules" — one tries to fail better.

**Hegel's Method of Thesis, Antithesis, and Synthesis.** An example is Bohr's dynamic model of a hydrogen atom, Lewis's static model of a dihydrogen molecule, and Kimball's models of static domains of dynamic electrons.

**Eclecticism.** "The Method of Physical Chemistry," said Latimer. Use what works!

**Pragmatism.** The meaning of a proposition lies in its observable consequences. Do semi-localized, exclusive orbital models of molecules correspond to observed facts?

**Operationalism.** Theoretical terms are defined by the procedures that lead to them: e.g., "valence", from molecular formulas; "bonds", from graphic formulas; "lone pairs", from electron counts; "resonance", from multiplicity of bond diagrams.

**Reductionism:** Explaination of complex phenomena (such as the saturation and directional character of chemical affinity) achieved with simply stated principles (close-packing of electron domains of *finite size* about smaller atomic cores).

**Whewell's Fundamental Antithesis of Science:** A philosophy of the inductive sciences that focuses attention on the differences between things and thoughts, facts and theories, evidence and inductions — exemplified, e.g., by the number of isomers of $CH_2Cl_2$ and the tetrahedral model of the carbon atom.

**Philosophical Acceptance of "Hund's Rule".** A model of some thing must be wrong in some respects, else it would be the thing itself, not a model of the thing. The fleas (negative analogies) come with the dog (the positive analogies).

With models one must learn, in words of a popular song of the 1940s. "to accentuate the positive and 'diminuate' the negative."

# A Simple Resolution of an Embarrassment of Riches

The two statements -

- "You have no exact knowledge unless you can express it in numbers." LORD KELVIN (defining "exact knowledge"); and -

- You have no *understanding* unless you can *visualize* what you are talking about.

reflect the fact that modern Valence Theory has a *dualistic* character. It has a quantitative aspect, in its *labeled numbers* for numerical values of physical quantities (such as coordinates of atomic nuclei in molecules). And it has a qualitative aspect, in its *named concepts* for non-numerical variables (such as "chemical bond"). Featured, accordingly, are two different styles of reasoning: the computer-facilitated deductive reasoning of Computational Valence Theory, using Schrödinger's equation, and the topological style of reasoning of Conceptual Valence Theory in back-of-the-envelope calculations using Langmuir's equation.

## VALENCE THEORY

| Computational Molecular Orbital Theory | Conceptual Valence Bond Theory |
|:---:|:---:|
| Use of a Variation Theorem | Resonance |
| Labeled Numbers (e.g.: "atomic coordinates") | Labeled Ideas (e.g.: "chemical bond") |
| Deductive Reasoning | Inductive Reasoning |
| Numerical Output | Topological Output |
| Schrödinger's Equation: $H\psi = E\psi$ | Langmuir's Equation: $B = 4N - V$ |
| $\psi$ is Antisymmetric | Exclusive Orbital Models |
| Delocalized Orbitals | Localized Orbitals |

Jointly the two versions comprise a history of Valence Theory expressed in the form of a –

thesis: <u>localized orbitals</u> (for conceptual convenience) and its –

antithesis: <u>delocalized orbitals</u> (for computational convenience).

The difference between the two types of orbitals has been likened to the difference between day and night. Which one is right? As impossible as unnecessary to say? For just as Conceptual Valence Bond Theory offers, in and of itself, no way to calculate Computational MO Theory's quantitative, numerical output, so, too, Computational MO Theory offers, in and of itself, no way to create Conceptual Valence Bond Theory's qualitative, non-numerical concepts, including a way to select from an infinite number of ways of expressing a Slater, antisymmetric determinantal wave function a single, distinctive, "right" way. Current chemical practice is a *synthesis.* It uses both qualitative and quantitative versions of Valence Theory. They're not redundant; nor contradictory. Molecular Science is, in fact, fortunate to have two fundamental, complementary expressions of a theory of molecular structure: one for its numerical character, one for its non-numerical character. The greater the difference between them, and their outputs, the greater Valence Theory's comprehensive character. Supplementary, extra-quantum mechanical electron-localization procedures permitted by a Slater determinant's indeterminancy reveal that Computational MO Theory and Conceptual Valence Bond Theory are not rivals. *They're teammates!*

# Complementary Features of Computational and Conceptual Valence Theory

CMOT: Computational MO Theory      VSD: Valence Stroke Diagrams
TMOT: Textbook MO Theory      EOM: Exclusive Orbital Models

| | CCVS | TMOT | VSD | EOM |
|---|---|---|---|---|
| It Requires Computers, Computer Software, and Computer Literacy. | Yes | No | No | No |
| It Makes Sense of Schrödinger's Equation without Having to Solve It. | No | No | Yes | Yes |
| Its Lends Itself to Back-of-the-Envelope Calculations. | No | Yes | Yes | Yes |
| It Requires Atomic Orbitals. | Yes | Yes | No | No |
| Its Molecular Obitals are Linear Combinations of Atomic Orbitals. | Yes | Yes | No | No |
| Its Orbitals are Delocalized. | Yes | Yes | No | No |
| Its Orbitals are Exclusive. | No | No | Yes | Yes |
| Its Orbitals are both Localized and Exclusive. | No | No | Yes | Yes |
| Its Wavefunction is formed from Hartree Products of Molecular Orbitals. | Yes | No | No | No |
| Its Wavefunction is an Antisymmetrzed Sum of Hartree Products. | Yes | No | No | No |
| Its Wavefunction is Subjected to the Operation of the Variation Theorem. | Yes | No | No | No |
| Its Wavefunction is an Approximate Solution of Schrödinger's Equation. | Yes | No | No | No |
| It Yields Electron Density Distributions. | Yes | No | No | No |
| It Yields Approximate Electron Density Profiles. | No(1) | No | No | Yes |
| Its Output is Numerical. | Yes | No | No | No |
| Its Output is Conceptual. | No(2) | No(3) | Yes | Yes |
| Its Output is Topological | No | No | Yes | Yes |
| Its Output Yields the Concepts *Chemical Bond* and *Bond Order*. | No | No | Yes | Yes |
| Its Output is Easily Visualized. | No | No | Yes(4) | Yes |
| Its Output Satisfies a Bond Number Relation. | No | No | Yes | Yes |
| Its Output Usually Satisfies a Valence Stroke Termination Rule. | No | No | Yes | Yes(5) |
| Its Output Yields Formal Charges. | No | No | Yes | Yes(5) |
| Its Output Mimics Lewis Structures. | No(6) | No | Yes | Yes |
| Its Output Corresponds to Classical Chemical Ideology. | No | No | Yes | Yes |

(1) Not prior to electron localization.

(2) In principle, Computational MO Theory is about numerical quantities, not conceptual qualities. In practice, however, delocalized orbitals that emerge from trials of the Variation Theorem are deemed to be models of electron density distributions, although in principle those emergent orbitals can be chosen in an infinite number of ways. Computational MO Theory, in and of itself, offers no way to choose among mathematically equivalent alternative expressions of a Slater determminantal wave function.

(3) In Textbook MO Theory electron density distributions are visualized, incorrectly, from the point of view of Exclusive Orbital Theory, in terms of the schemes' linear combinations of atomic orbitals.

(4) Especially in its valence-stick version.

(5) In its valence stroke precursor.

(6) Not in the absence of electron localization.

The Yes-No table's first and last columns are orthogonal to each other, in the sense that what one provides regarding Valence Theory's qualitative and quantitative aspects the other one lacks, and vice-versa. Valence Theory's two aspects — conceptual (VSD and EOM) and computational (CCVS); visual and numerical; classical (VSD) and modern (CCVS) — are mutually complementary. On the other hand, an Exclusive Orbital Model (EOM), with its Lewis-like localized orbitals, and Text Book MO Theory (TMOT), with its delocalized orbitals) are rivals, as different from each other as, as said, "day and night". It would seem that one or the other version of Valence Theory must be, from a conceptual point of view, physically meaningless.

# ACKNOWLEDGEMENTS

*MCB* II builds on work on the nature of the chemical bond by many investigators including a number of Nobel Laureates: van't Hoff (1901, Tetrahedral Atom), Rutherford (1912, Nuclear Model of the Atom), Werner (1913, Doctrine of Coordination), Haber (1918, Ionic Model), de Broglie (1929, Wave Nature of Electrons), Langmuir (1932, Bond Number Equation), Pauling (1954, Valence Bond Theory), Mulliken (1966, Charge Transfer Theory), Hassel (1969, Conformations of Cyclohexane and Molecular Complexes), Herzberg (1971, Electronic Structure and Molecular Geometry, particularly Free Radicals), Lipscomb (1976, 3-Center Bonds), Fukui (1981, Frontier Orbital Theory), Hoffmann (1981, Number of Inversions in Curly Arrow Chemistry), and Kohn (1998, Electron-Density Theorems). Notably absent from the list is G. N. Lewis (Electron Pair Bond, 1916; and Electron Pair Model of acids and bases); and Maurice Huggins (Hydrogen Bond, 1922).

Gratefully acknowledged, also, are contributions to the present study of Doyle Britton, for introducing the author to the merits of making molecular models; the National Science Foundation, for support during the author's first summer of work on molecular models, 1962; William Kieffer, editor of the *Journal of Chemical Education*, for going out on a limb and publishing the author's essays on "Tangent Sphere Models of Molecules" some fifty years before their time; William Jensen, for his early enthusiasm for the models; Jack Linnett, for his "Double Quartet Hypothesis"; Roald Hoffmann, for insightful responses to trial balloons; Joel Liebman, for several "yes but" challenges and "Hund's Rule"; Emil Slowinski, for an expression of interest in the Exclusive Orbital Model of a metal, featured on this volume's back cover; Professor Frank Weinhold, Theoretical Chemistry Institute and Department of Chemistry, University of Wisconsin, for permission to quote him, frequently, and for providing through his Natural Bond Orbital analyses of accurate molecular wave functions an air of mathematical and physical certitude — to paraphrase W. S. Gilbert (once again) — to an otherwise perhaps bald and unconvincing narrative concerning Exclusive Orbital Models; and, closer to home, his family: his father, Dean Henry E. Bent, for inspiring a son to follow in his footsteps as a chemist and educator; his own son, Brian E. Bent, for overtaking in his brief brilliant life both his father and grandfather, as a chemist and educator; his daughter, Libby Graves Weberg, for especially her foreword for this work; and especially his wife, Anne McKnight Bent, for attending to her family's domestic needs, again and again, year after year, for over fifty years, thereby allowing her husband to think and perhaps to dream — and lecture in his sleep, she says — about Exclusive Orbital Models of Molecules. Thank you! Thank you! Thank you, Anne!

And apologies to experimentalists, theoreticians, and other investigators for poaching on their preserves and arriving at conclusions that they may not agree with. An inductive science progresses by generation of general principles from particular facts, created in an open society by a vast cast of talented and dedicated investigators, gratefully thanked for their many trusted contributions to this book.

# GLOSSARY
## The Linguistic Side of Conceptual Valence Bond Theory
*A fruitful theory generates a useful terminology.*

**Absolute Valence.** The charge of an atom's atomic core. A constant, the same in all compounds. For sulfur in $H_2S$ and $SF_6$, 6. Essential information for assigning locations of atomic cores in valence stroke diagrams using the Valence Stroke Termination Rule.

**"Anion Lattices".** Valence stroke diagrams (or, more explicitly, valence sphere models) sans symbols of the elements (and domains of atomic cores).

**Anti-aromatic.** A name given, ad hoc, to unstable or nonexistent species that have 4n pi electrons. Should perhaps be retired, for specific reasons appear to exist for each instance of the cited phenomena.

**Anticoincident Spin Sets.** Different structures for electrons of different spins, owing to electron-electron repulsion between electrons of different spin. Introduced by Hyllerass in his study of helium's electron cloud. Used by Linnett to account for dioxygen's paramagnetism, structures of odd-electron species, and aromatic systems.

**Atomic Core.** An atom less its valence shell electrons. A nucleus plus its inner-shell electrons. What an element's symbol in a bond diagram stands for. Occupant of an interstice in an exclusive orbital model of matter. Characterized by two parameters: size and charge.

**Atomic-Core Coordination Number of Electron-Pair Domains.** One for lone pairs, two for 2-center bonds, three for 3-center bonds, etc.

**"Atomic Orbitals".** Solutions of Schrödinger's equation for the hydrogen atom, *modified* (hence the quotation marks) so as to point in bond directions. Basic ingredients of the LCAO Method of formation of molecular orbitals. Not needed in Conceptual Valence Bond Theory, concerned solely with electron density *profiles*, not densities near atomic nuclei. Their absence in CVBT is a major simplification of valence theory. Their presence in introductory chemistry courses, where, of necessity, students have no alternative but to accept them *on faith*, confers on such courses the character of faith-based enterprises.

**Back Story** (for the Introduction of the tetrahedron into chemical thought). Features the chemical formulas $H_2O$ and $CO_2$, graphic representations of the concept "valence" (or "combining capacity"), and the number of isomers of $CH_2Cl_2$.

**Banana Bond.** *See Bent Bond.*

**Bent Bond.** An electron domain of a 2-center bond whose two coordinated atomic cores are not on opposite sides of the domain. A bond in a small ring. More exposed than non-bent bonds, hence nucleophilic, especially for 2-member rings of multiple bonds, and to a lesser extent, for 3-member rings. Lone pairs may be viewed as limiting instances of small rings, and limiting instances of electron domain exposure.

**Bond Angle Theorem.** The more electron-pair domains two atoms A and B share with a third atom C, the larger tends to be the bond angle ACB. The theorem is captured most simply by construction of valence sphere models of molecules. (Indeed, there is no mathematically rigorous derivation of the Theorem, based on Schrödinger's equation — or, indeed, of any other theorem whose description uses the word "bond" — inasmuch as the concept of a "bond" is not apart of the oracular character of Schrödinger's equation.)

**Bond Number Equation.** The algebraic oracle of Conceptual Valence Bond Theory. Numbers of n-center bonds, $B_n$, are related to the number of valence shell electron pairs, V, and electron pair coordination numbers of atomic cores, $(EPCN)_i$, by the relation $\sum(n-1)B_n = \sum(EPCN)_i - V$. Reduces in many instances to the Langmuir expression $B_2 = 4N - V$.

**Born-Oppenheimer Approximation.** Locations of electrons and nuclei in molecules may be treated as separate problems. Calculated in Computational Valence Theory are electronic wave functions, from Schrödinger's Equation, $H\Psi = E\Psi$, for fixed nuclear positions, followed by determination of nuclear positions, as those that minimize $E = H\Psi/\Psi$. Calculated in Conceptual Valence Theory are numbers of n-center bonds, from the Bond Number Equation, $\sum(n-1)B_n = \sum(EPCN)_i - V$, followed by determination of positions of atomic cores, as those that minimize the energy, through creation of local electrical neutrality, through creation of zero formal charges, through use of the Valence Stroke Termination Rule.

**Boys' Orbital Localization Procedure.** Formation of localized molecular orbitals through minimization of orbitals' spatial extent.

**Cation.** Usually a large atomic core, such as $Na^+$ and $Ca^{+2}$. Called "atomic cores" if isoelectronic with helium or neon or its congeners.

**Charge Cloud Models.** The name used by Kimball and his group for valence sphere models of molecules. A.K.A. "Electron Domain Models" and "Tangent Sphere Models". The simplest known models of molecular electron density profiles and nucleophilic and electrophilic sites.

**Chemical Bonds.** Valence strokes (or valence spheres) of valence stroke diagrams (or valence sphere models), and the corresponding electronic charges, in the valence shells of two or more atomic cores attracted, accordingly, by the same portion of an electron cloud.

**"Chemical Ideology".** Mulliken's phrase. A.K.A. "Chemical Voodo". Physicists' view of chemical inductions, including over the years: atomic theory, the tetrahedral atom, bond diagrams, resonance, and valence sphere models of molecules.

**Conceptual Valence Bond Theory (CVBT).** What this book is about. A chemical theory of interatomic distances visualized by means of valence stroke diagrams and valence sphere models of molecules. Valence theory without use of Schrödinger's equation, or atomic orbitals. A theory of molecular electron density profiles and nucleophilic and electrophilic sites. A generalization of the classical structural theory of organic chemistry. The view that all compounds are ion compounds.

**Covalent Bonds.** Electron domains in the valence shells of atomic cores of the same or approximately the same size.

**Curly Arrows.** Exhibit changes in valence strokes' affiliations. Are always attached in this volume by their tails to a valence stroke (rather than left unattached to anything).

**Cycloethane.** Another name for ethylene (located, accordingly, in the class of small ring compounds).

**Dative Bonds.** Rabbit-ear valence strokes in bonding regions. Often a scheme for eliminating in bond diagrams unfavorable formal charges. Longer and weaker than covalent bonds.

**DODS.** *See Double Spin-Set Theory.*

**Density Functional Theory.** A widely used computational method for determining molecular electron density distributions. A basic lemma states that those distributions determine locations and charges of atomic nuclei.

**Double Bond.** A 4-electron bond. Two valence strokes shared by a pair of atomic cores. A 2-member ring. A pair of bent or banana bonds. ("Bent bonds are best," said Pauling. The popular sigma-pi description removes, improperly, double-bond-containing molecules from the class of small ring systems and places them in a class with aromatic molecules.) Site of two exposed (nucleophilic) electron pairs. Also, owing to core-core repulsion, a site of two somewhat exposed (electrophilic) atomic cores and, for the same reason, site of bond angles opposite a double bond that are usually greater than the tetrahedral angle. The bond is deemed to be in this study isoelectronic with the central, doubly protoated bond of $B_2H_6$.

**Double Spin-Set Theory.** A theory of spatially anticoincident spin sets in which Lewis' electron dot model is applied to each spin set separately. Leading uses include applications to: benzene and other aromatic systems, the carbonate and nitrate ions, and other systems that exhibit "resonance"; species that have two unequally populated spin-sets, such as dioxygen and the odd-electron species NO and $NO_2$; and to atomic cores that have eight outer electrons and in their valence shells lone pairs, as in $PH_3$ and $H_2S$, with their nearly 90° valence angles.

**Duet Rule.** Protons in stable chemical species have in their valence shells two electrons.

**Electride Ion.** A localized valence shell electron pair. An unprotonated valence shell domain of a valence sphere model. The anion of ionic models of covalent compounds.

**Electron Deficient.** Refers to species comprised of atomic cores — other than protons — whose charges are less than +4, such as boron hydrides.

**Electron Domain.** An exclusive semi-localized molecular orbital. What the valence strokes of valence stroke diagrams represent.

**Electron Pair Coordination Number (EPCN).** The number of electron pair domains packed about an atomic core. Four for cores that satisfy the Octet Rule. May exceed the number of low-lying atomic orbitals of a central atom, such as S of $SF_6$.

**Electrophilic Site.** Usually, for atoms that satisfy the Octet Rule, a "pocket" or "dimple" opposite a bond to an electronegative atom; or opposite a component of an equivalent orbital model of a multiple bond; or off the end of a bond to a protonic proton.

**EPCN.** Electron Pair Coordination Number (of an atomic core). Usually 4 (the Octet Rule).

**Excess Connectivity.** Number of bonding valence strokes in the bond diagram of an N-heavy-atom chemical species in excess of N − 1. Manifested in bond diagrams as rings and/or multiple bonds (2-member rings). Sites of unsaturation.

**Exclusion Principle.** Excludes configurations in which two spin-parallel electrons are at the same place at the same time (Heisenberg) or in the same orbital (Pauli). The first exclusion is the more fundamental one, in that it does not refer to orbitals, which are approximations.

**Exclusive Orbitals.** Non-spatially-overlapping orbitals. An induction based most directly, arguably, on matter's impenetrability. Generally localized orbitals for compounds of the *p*-block of periodic tables. Symbolized in bond diagrams by valence strokes, in Lewis dot diagrams by dots, and represented in Kimball structures by electron domains of finite size.

**Expanded Octets.** Electron Pair Coordination Numbers (EPCN) of atomic cores greater than four. For EPCN = 5, the electron pair arrangement is usually a trigonal bipyramid. For EPCN = 6, the arrangement is usually octahedral.

**Face Centered Cube.** Arrangement of atomic cores of many metals and cations of many salts, such as the sodium ions of sodium chloride and the potassium ions of potassium hydride, isoelectronic with calcium metal.

**Faraday-Gauss Lines of Force.** Reveal a test charge's direction of motion. Analogous to valence strokes of valence stroke diagrams, in never crossing each other; staying as far apart as possible, while remaining anchored at sites of electrical charges; and in having numbers of terminations proportional to magnitudes of anchoring electrical charges.

**Fermi Hole.** The immediate region about a fermion not penetrated by other fermions of the same spin. A linguistic expression of the mathematical statement $\Psi(X, X, \ldots) = 0$.

**Fermi Domain** (of finite size). An induction, based on Fermi Holes and the facts of sterochemistry. An exclusive molecular orbital.

**Fermions.** Elementary species with spin 1/2, such as electrons, protons, and neutrons.

**Formal Charge.** For an atom the difference: (core charge) – (number of valence stroke terminations at the core's symbol in a valence stroke diagram). If negative, usually associated with an electronegative element, if positive with an electropositive element. Can be diminished, for molecules with adjacent formal charges of opposite sign, by introduction of dative bonds. Seldom greater than +1 or smaller than -1.

**Frontier Orbital.** A nucleophilic or electrophilic site. Exposed electron domains, for nucleophiles. Exposed atomic cores, for electrophiles.

**Gauss Circuit.** Linked curly arrows in which the number of arrows that terminate at the site of an atomic core in a valence stroke diagram is equal to the number of curly arrows that originate at that site. Leaves formal charges unchanged. The reason why (i) water is a good medium for many reactions, owing to Gauss-Circuit-completing proton transfers between water molecules; and why (ii) metallic surfaces catalyze many reactions, owing to Gauss-Circuit-completing electron transfers. Presence in hypothetical chemical species of easily completed intramolecular Gauss circuits gives rise to nonexistent species, such as $(H_2N)CH_2Cl$ ($\rightarrow HN{=}CH_2 + HCl$).

**Gauss's Law.** Number of Faraday lines of force entering into or emerging from a region of space is proportional to the net charge within that region. Corresponds to chemistry's Valence Stroke Termination Rule and Density Functional Theory's Hohenberg-Kohn Theorem.

**George Kimball.** Coauthor of an important book, with Henry Eyring, on quantum chemistry and father, while a professor of chemistry at Columbia University, of "charge cloud models" of molecules. Focused attention on the models' energetics (not their forte) rather than (as here) their stereochemical implications (rooted in the Exclusion Principle), which may explain why he didn't pursue investigations of the models throughout his career in chemistry. He had hold of the right stick, it's believed, but, arguably, not its right end. Ended his career at A. D. Little Co., in operations research.

**Geometrical Methods.** A companion, in Conceptual Valence Bond Theory, to Computational Valence Theory's numerical methods.

**Gilbert N. Lewis.** Father of "the concept of the chemical bond comprising a pair of electrons shared between two atoms[,] the keystone of valence theory" (KENNETH S. PITZER). Identified, also, the physical significance in bond diagrams of symbols of the chemical elements, as standing for atomic cores. And introduced a theory of acids and bases that, in modern terminology, identifies acids as nucleophiles and bases as electrophiles. Father, all told, of the modern electronic interpretation of chemistry.

**Heavy Atom.** Any atom other than a hydrogen atom.

**Hellman-Feynman Theorem.** For a molecule in a stationary state of a local energy minimum, forces on its nuclei owing to attraction of the electron cloud, calculated classically for a distributed charge distribution, and to repulsion of the other nuclei, vanish. Used by Bent to account for "Bent's Rule".

**Highly Electronegative.** Small, highly charged atomic cores, most notably $O^{+6}$ and $F^{+7}$.

**HLOMO.** Highest Localized Occupied Molecular Orbital. A nucleophilic site. An exposed electron pair. Often a lone pair (of a one-membered ring), or an electron pair of a two-membered ring of a double bond.

**Hohenberg-Kohn Theorem.** A molecule's electron density distribution determines locations and charges of its nuclei. Density Functional Theory's analogue for atomic nuclei of Conceptual Valence Bond Theory's Valence Stroke Termination Rule for atomic cores.

**Hund's Rule.** An atom in its lowest energy configuration has its greatest spin multiplicity (owing to correlation of motion of electrons of the same spin, which cannot be at the same place at the same time). Also: The rule, named by Joel Liebman, that for physical models the fleas (negative analogies) come with the dog (the positive analogies).

**Hydride Ion.** A protonted electride ion. Symbol: H⁻. Structurally comparable to F⁻.

**Hypervalent.** Adjective assigned to species such as $SF_6$ that appear to violate an orbital "Octet Rule". Always the central atom has a large core able to occupy an interstice created by more than four electron pair domains of coordinated ligands *without rattling*.

**Hypovalent.** Adjective that one might assign to, e.g., S of $SF_2$ if, following Mendeleev in his development of the Periodic System, one chose as a reference for sulfur's valence its *highest* state of oxidation.

**Interatomic Distances.** Determined by physical methods, including: x-ray and neutron diffraction, microwave spectroscopy, and infrared and Raman rotational spectroscopy. Interpreted by Conceptual Valence Bond Theory as, e.g., single, double, and triple bonds. Produced: "bond lengths", dependent on "bond orders" and sizes of bonded atomic cores.

**Ion Compound.** Anions packed about cations. Also: electron pairs packed about atomic cores. The same structural principles apply to both situations.

**Ionic Bonds.** Electron domains in the valence shells of both small and large atomic cores.

**Isoelectronic Species.** Molecules or ions that have the same valence sphere models.

**Langmuir Relation.** For species that satisfy the Octet Rule by means of lone pairs and 2-center bonds, the Bond Number Equation is $B(= B_2) = 4N - V$, where N is the number of (Octet-Rule-satisfying) heavy atoms.

**Large C—H Models.** Electron domains of carbon-hydrogen bonds are larger than those of carbon-carbon single bonds. Account for the inertness of the par-affins.

**LCAO Method.** Formation of molecular orbitals from Linear Combinations of Atomic Orbitals. Assumes at the outset what the Method seeks to account for, namely: locations of a system's atoms. Motivated by desire to compute accurate molecular energies, which requires accurate electron densities *near nuclei* — whereas models of electron pair donor-acceptor interactions (the essence of chemistry) require knowledge of electron density profiles.

**Lewis Structures.** The first successful physical interpretation of classical valence stroke diagrams. Replaces valence strokes by pairs of dots (for electron pairs), elements' symbols by symbols of elements' atomic cores (set in bold face type, initially), and introduces lone pairs (to complete cores' valence shells). Mimicked, in a manner of speaking, by modern electron localization procedures.

**LLUMO.** Lowest Localized Unoccupied Molecular Orbital. An electrophilic site. Includes a vacant coordination site; and a valence sphere model's dimple opposite a good leaving group.

**Local Electrical Neutrality.** Zero formal charge. No long valence strokes.

**Localized Frontier Orbitals.** Nucleophilic and electrophilic sites.

**Localized Molecular Orbitals.** Are generated by electron localization procedures of Boys, Rudenberg, Weinberg, and others. Are represented geometrically, in the limiting cases of exclusive orbitals, by 1-dimensional valence strokes and by 3-dimensional valence spheres.

**Loge.** A region of space where the probability is a maximum for finding one but no more than one electron of a given spin. Introduced by Daudel.

**Metallic Bonds.** Electron domains in the valence shells of only large atomic cores.

**"Missing in Action".** The Principle of Spatial Exclusion, in formation of Canonical Molecular Orbitals.

**"MO Theory".** A qualitative theory of molecular structure. Features delocalized "molecular orbitals" spread out over entire molecules! Stops short of creating antisymmetric wave functions subjected to the Variation Theorem. Absent, accordingly, is any hint of wave functions' exclusive orbital character. From the point of view of Conceptual Valence Bond theory, conceptual MO Theory is an incomplete and misleading theory of molecular structure; and unnecessary, as its leading "triumph" (an account of oxygen's paramagnetism, through use of one of Hund's empirical Rules) is handled in a more fundamental fashion by Conceptual Valence Bond Theory.

**Modern Conceptual Valence Bond Theory.** Classical Conceptual Valence Bond Theory plus new features, including: Valence Sphere Models of Molecular Electron Density Profiles; a Valence Stroke Termination Rule; a New Notation for Dative Bonds; a Bond Angle Theorem; a Generalized Bond Number Equation; Electron-Pair Donor-Acceptor Interactions; Bent's Rule; Different Structures for Different Spin Sets; and an extensive Consilience between Structural Organic and Inorganic Chemistry.

**Multicenter Bond.** An electron domain in the valence shells of three or more atomic cores. Easily represented by valence spheres, less easily represented by valence strokes.

**Noncrossing Rule.** An unstated, supremely important rule of structural organic chemistry: *Valence strokes of rational bond diagrams never cross each other!* It was an early manifestation of a Principle of Spatial Exclusion for electrons, required for (i) the analogy between valence strokes and Faraday-Gauss lines of force (*MCB*, Volume I) and in order for (ii) Lewis' Induction regarding valence strokes to be consistent with Heisenberg's statement regarding the indistinguishability of electrons. Conversely, given the Noncrossing Rule, and Lewis' Induction, it follows that two electron pairs cannot be at the same place at the same time.

**Nooks and Crannies.** Close-packing about atomic cores of individual electron pair domains of many-electron atoms create in the resulting electron clouds nooks and crannies that correspond to the lobes of chemists' approximately exclusive *d*- and *f*-orbitals. An aspect of Exclusive Orbital Theory that has not yet been examined carefully. The nooks and crannies correspond to the dictum that successful theories are *open-ended*.

**Nucleophilic Site.** Exposed, usually unprotonated, electron pair of a small ring. A lone pair (a 1-member ring) or an electron pair of a multiple bond (a 2-member ring). The carbon-carbon single bonds of a cyclopropane ring are slightly nucleophilic.

**Octet Rule.** In stable compounds the small atomic cores $B^{+3}$, $C^{+4}$, $N^{+5}$, $O^{+6}$, and $F^{+7}$ have in their valence shells 8 electrons.

**Octahedron.** A polyhedron of eight faces and six vertices. A bicapped square. Centers of three close-packed spheres nesting on top of three similarly close-packed spheres (rotated 60°) generate locations of a regular octahedron's vertices. Its dual (vertices and faces interchanged) is a cube. An octahedron's face does not, like that of a tetrahedron (its own dual), lie opposite an octahedron's vertex. Thus "back side" attack in an $S_N2$-type reaction is not possible for atomic cores surrounded by six electron pair domains in an octahedral arrangement. The kinetics in inorganic chemistry of subtitution at an octahedrally coordinated atomic core are, accordingly, different than those for a tetrahedrally coordinated atomic core. The interstice of an octahedral arrangement of close packed spheres is nearly twice the size of the interstice of a tetrahedral arrangement of similar-sized close packed spheres; hence the existence, without rattling, of sulfur hexafluoride but not of oxygen hexafluoride.

**Oracle** (of Conceptual Valence Bond Theory). The Bond Number Equation.

**Pauli "Forces".** Mutual spatial exclusion of electron domains owing to operation of the relation $\Psi(1, 2, \ldots) = -\Psi(2, 1, \ldots) \rightarrow \Psi(1, 1, \ldots) = 0$. More important in valence theory than electrostatic repulsions.

**Pauling's First Rule of Crystal Chemistry.** A polyhedron of anions is formed about each cation. Similarly: a polyhedron of electron pairs is formed about each atomic core.

**Physical Model.** A concrete object that exhibits positive analogies with some thing — along with, of course, negative analogies (else it would be the thing itself).

**Polar Covalent Bond.** A bond represented by covalent/ionic or covalent/dative bond resonance.

**Principle of Substitution.** Widely used by Mendeleev. His version of Valence Bond Theory. Entities at each end of a covalent bond between atoms of zero formal charge can substitute for each other in chemical compounds.

**Protonated Electron Pairs.** Protons in molecules are always embedded in electron domains. Single protonation: a hydride ion, or a heavy-atom/hydrogen-atom bond, or a protonated boron-boron single or double bond (as in $B_2H_6$); double protonation: a hydrogen molecule, H—H; and triple protonation: the species $H_3^+$ (the simplest instance of a 3-center bond).

**Protonic Protons.** Protons of bonds to hydrogen repelled toward the edges of their electron domains by small, highly charged adjacent atomic cores (such as $O^{+6}$ and $F^{+7}$). Electrophilicsites in hydrogen bonding.

**Quartet Rule.** For nonhydrogen atoms with small atomic cores, the number of valence strokes in valence stroke diagrams and the number of spheres in valence sphere models of stable molecules is four.

**Rabbit-Ear Valence Stroke.** A valence stroke that begins and ends at the same symbol for an atomic core. A 1-member ring. Used for lone pairs, dative bonds, and ionic bonds. A source of unsaturation for atomic cores that can expand their octets (e.g.: :$PCl_3$ + $Cl_2$ = $PCl_5$). Counts in the Valence Stroke Termination Rule as two terminations for the atomic core to which the rabbit-ear is attached, and zero terminations for the atomic core toward which the rabbit ear points. Usually indicated by an arrow: a notation that fails to satisfy, however, the Valence Stroke Termination Rule.

**Rattling.** Descriptive of the situation in which an atomic core is too small to fill the interstice created by its coordinated valence shell electron pair domains. Rattling is "bad". It's an unstable situation with respect to ejection from a core's valence shell of one or more coordinated electron pair domains. A case in point: hypothetical $OF_6$ decomposing to $OF_2$ (plus two $F_2$ molecules).

**Resonance.** A situation in which a chemical species has two or more plausible bond diagrams for similar locations of its atomic cores. The classic example is benzene's two Kekule structures. Resonance is useful in expressing with curly-arrows the phenomenon of *latency*. It's an energy-lowering, stabilizing phenomenon. (Other molecular properties are of intermediate character, with regard to those expected for individual resonance structures.)

> MO Theory attributes resonance's energy-lowering effect to electron delocalization, contrary to the implications the Virial Theorem (which states that a system's total energy is equal to the negative of its electron kinetic energy). Modern Conceptual Valence Bond Theory attributes resonance stabilization to the outcome of diminished electron-electron repulsion between electrons of opposite spin residing in different spin structures. Resonance's expression of latency is chemistry's analogue of the Superposition Principle of quantum physics, deemed to be one of that science's leading principles. Pauling, similarly, deemed his contributions to Resonance Theory to be his most important contribution to valence theory. In Pauling's view, formation of tetrahedral hybrid orbitals from atomic orbitals is an example of resonance.

**Ruedenberg's Orbital Localization Procedure.** Formation of localized molecular orbitals through maximization of orbitals' self-energy.

**Rule of Two.** Stable molecules of elements of Periodic Tables' *s*- and *p*-blocks generally have an even number of electrons. Lewis suggested, consequently (his famous induction), that valence strokes represent *two* electrons. Notable exceptions are NO and $NO_2$ (and many compounds of d-block elements). Physicists were skeptical. "If two electrons, then why not three?" Lewis could only say: "The facts of chemistry [an inductive science] require it [by induction]." Within a decade physicists had induced from physical evidence reasons for the number 2. The most important numbers in chemistry are 2 (for the electron pair), 4 (for the tetrahedron of electron pairs of organic chemistry), and 6 (for the octahedron of electron pairs of inorganic chemistry). Called to mind is the cheer at a Chemical Olympics: "Two, four, six, eight. Whom do we appreciate? The Octet Rule."

**s-Character Rule.** An atom's s-character tends to concentrate in bonds to electropositive substituents. Most electropositive substituent is no substituent at all; i.e., a highly s-seeking lone pair. The result of core-core repulsion, for small atomic cores.

**Screened Atomic Cores.** Atomic cores surrounded by tightly packed electron pair domains are "screened", from attack by nucleophilic reagents. With increasing electron pair coordination numbers, beginning at 2, first instances of particularly tightly packed domains about atomic cores are the tetrahedral and octahedral packing arrangements of organic and inorganic chemistry. Packing of impenetrable spheres about a central site accounts for the two leading branches of chemistry.

**Sextet.** The electrons of an unsaturated atomic core that contains in its valence shell only 6 electrons, of three pairs, in a triangular arrangement. Simple examples are the valence shell electrons of the isoelectronic species $BH_3$, $CH_2$, $NH$, $O$, and $CH_3^+$. The electrically neutral species easily dimerize.

**Small Atom Cores** (other than $H^+$): $B^{+3}$, $C^{+4}$, $N^{+5}$, $O^{+6}$, $F^{+7}$, and $Ne^{+8}$. Usually surrounded in compounds tetrahedrally by four electron pairs (the Octet Rule).

**$S_N2$ Reaction.** A bimolecular ("2") substitution ("S") of a nucleophilic reagent ("N:", the entering group) for a weaker nucleophile (say :L, a leaving group) by way of backside attack by N: on the attacked bond, from A to :L (A—L). Begins with formation of an electron pair donor-acceptor interaction (N $\cdots$ A—L). Ends with a similar interaction (N—A $\cdots$ L). Passes through a linear transition state (N — A — L) that has an electron pair coordination number at A, initially an Octet-Rule-satisfying atom, of 5. Inverts the configuration at A. Geometrically possible because a tetrahedron is its own dual, in which vertices (sites of nucleophilic electron pair domains) lie opposite faces (electrophilic sites). A leading reaction mechanism of organic chemistry. Often reactions are sequences of inter- and intra-molecular $S_N2$ rearrangements.

**Steric Hindrance.** Arises from *adjacency* of electron domains in the valence shells of *different atomic cores*. A manifestation of the fact that two electron pairs cannot be at the same place at the same time. Source of the electronic armor of paraffins, in the form of relatively large C—H domains about $C^{+4}$ cores. Accounts, also, for the inertness of $SF_6$ (inorganic chemistry's paraffin) and for why molecules have finite molar volumes, however high the pressure. Generalizing, –

> Two things (other than gases) cannot be at the same place at the same time because two molecules cannot be at the same place at the same time because two electron clouds cannot be at the same place at the same time because two electron pairs cannot be at the same place at the same time because two electrons of the same spin cannot be at the same place at the same time.

> The fundamental premise of Exclusive Orbital Theory — exclusivity of electron pairs — is a direct induction from a property of matter that stares one in the face (often the hardest thing to see): *two things* (other than gases) *cannot be at the same place at the same time.*

> "We have no other evidence of universal impenetrability," said Newton, "besides a large Experience without an experimental exception."

**Tangent Sphere Models (TSM).** Name used by the author in the 1960s for Valence Sphere Models (VSM), the phrase used in this book because it's linguistically analogous to the phrase "Valence Stroke Diagrams", which are isomorphic with Valence Sphere Models.

**Tetrahedral Bond Angle.** $109.5°$. Close to the bond angles of $NH_3$ and $H_2O$ and many other species that have bond angles at C, N, or O atoms that are defined by two single bonds.

**Tetrahedron.** A four-sided figure. A triangular pyramid. A mono-capped triangle. It's own dual. Each vertex is opposite a face, each face opposite a vertex — an important consideration in $S_N2$ reactions, in which entering groups enter opposite leaving groups. The leading geometrical figure of organic stereochemistry. Generates locations of substituents off single, double, and triple bonds, described as two tetrahedra sharing, respectively, a corner, an edge, and a face. Is the geometrical arrangement of electron pair domains about atomic cores that obey the Octet Rule. The fundamental basis of Exclusive Orbital Theory: centers of four close-packed spheres generate locations of the vertices of a regular tetrahedron.

**Trigonal Bipyramid.** A bicapped triangle. Usual arrangement of electron pair domains about an atomic core that has an electron pair coordination number of five. The electronic configuration about an atomic core in the transition state of an $S_U 2$ reaction. Its three equatorial bonds are shorter than its two polar bonds, suggesting an elliptically shaped atomic core (p214). Easily distorted to a tetragonal pyramid.

**Triple Bond.** Three valence strokes (electron pairs) shared by two atomic cores. Two adjacent 2-member rings. Three bent bonds. Energy-rich (owing to core-core repulsion) yet kinetically unusually inert (owing to anticoincidence of the bond's spin sets in the triple bond region). Protons of adjacent C—H bonds are notably protonic (HCN, e.g.; also HCCH). Bond angles that involve a triple bond and a single bond of an Octet-Rule-obeying atomic core are 180°.

**Valence Shell.** The space surrounding an atom's core occupied by an atom's outer electrons.

**Valence Stroke.** Graphic representation of the mutual saturation of two chemical affinities. A shared electron pair. A 1-dimensional model of an exclusive bonding molecular orbital.

**Valence Stroke Diagram (VSD).** An arrangement of valence strokes and atomic symbols that usually satisfies the Valence Stroke Termination Rule and the Quartet Rule for small atomic cores (other than hydrogen). A highly schematic diagram of a species' exclusive valence shell orbitals.

**Valence Bond Systematics.** Construction of bond diagrams beginning with a Bond Number Equation, continuing with a Valence Stroke Termination Rule, and concluding with consideration of the possibilities of donor-acceptor interactions, resonance, core-core repulsions, and different structures for different spin-sets.

**Valence Stroke Termination Rule (VSTR).** The number of terminations of valence strokes of a bond diagram at the symbol of an atom that has no formal charge is equal to the charge of the atom's core.

**Variation Theorem.** The story of the Variation Theorem in chemistry is the story of a hero and a villan. Just as the role of Conceptual Valence Bond Theory in interpretive chemistry is to fit bond diagrams to observed facts, so, too, the role of the Variation Theorem in computational chemistry is to fit trial wave functions to observed facts. The Theorem states that introduction of adjustable parameters into trial wave functions $\Psi$ always lowers calculated energies $E = H\Psi/\Psi$, on minimization of E with respect to the adjustible parameters of $\Psi$. The Theorem is computational chemistry's leading tool and, simultaneously, in interpretive chemistry, a leading source of misconceptions. For no matter how conceptually misleading a wave function may be from a physical point of view — perhaps through complete disregard of the Exclusion Principle in its initial formulation of molecular orbitals — its use with the Variation Theorem can lead, eventually, in principle, after perhaps millions of iterations, to excellent numerical results. Conceptual garbage in does not necessarily mean numerical garbage out: that's the essence of the Variation Theorem. Reciproally, however, excellence of numerical output does not mean excellence of conceptual input. Highly delocalized, nonexclusive orbitals may yield, eventually, after many iterations with the Variation Theorem, acceptable molecular structures and energies while, as Weinhold has written (private communication), "The [initial] MO imagery of orbitals sprawling over one another 'almost everywhere' is profoundly illusory and physically meaningless." Used systematically, the Variation Theorem is the hero of computational chemistry. Used uncritically, it is the villan of conceptual chemistry.

**VSEPR Theory** (Valence Shell Electron Pair Repulsion Theory): A popular theory, for its ease of application. It accounts for molecular shapes through explicit reference to the "Pauli Principle" and to electron-electron electrostatic repulsion. Only indirectly does it allude, however, to nuclear-electron attraction, through discussion, e.g., of "Points on a Sphere" (of, unrealistically, fixed radius). VSEPR Theory often gets right answers for wrong reasons. It gets wrong answers regarding, e.g., equilibrium confirmations of hydrogen peroxide and hydrazine.

**Virial Theorem.** For species in stationary states of local energy minima, total energy E is equal to the negative of the kinetic energy T: $E = -T$. Suggestions that resonance, in delocalizing electrons, lowers T and, hence E, are contrary to the Virial Theorem, illustrated most simply by a hydrogen atom in its compact, low-energy, high-T 1s state, compared to its more diffuse 2s state of lower T and higher (less negative) E.

**Wavicules.** Electrons behave as particles or waves, depending on the circumstances.

**Woodward-Hoffmann Rule.** For pericyclic reactions, the number of participating electron pairs plus the number of Walden inversions is an odd number.

**Yin-Yang Symbol:** Summarized — in its stepwise construction from two dots (for two electrons) to two distinguished dots (for electrons of opposite spin) to the sinusoidal curve (for electronic wave-like character) to the circumscribed circle (for expression of a Principle of Spatial Exclusion) — is the evolution of an Exclusive Orbital Theory of molecular structure.

**Z-Matrix:** Use of chemical knowledge to construct approximate internal molecular coordinates for use in applications of the Variation Theorem. It's use reveals that computational valence theory is not, in general, in and of itself, a complete, stand alone theory of molecular structure.

# Related Publications by Bent

Fools persisting in their folly find wisdom.
CHINESE PROVERB

Truth is the daughter of time.
ANOTHER PROVERB

Q: How can you tell if your research is successful? A: Are you encouraged to continue?
JOHN OVEREND

Tangent-Sphere Models of Molecules  (Initial Essays on Exclusive Orbital Theory)

  I. Theory and Construction, *J. Chem. Educ.,* **40**, 446-452 (1963).

  II. Uses in Teaching, *J. Chem. Educ.,* **40**, 523-530 (1963).

  III. Chemical Implications of Inner-Shell Electrons," *J. Chem. Educ.,* **42**, 302-308 (1965).

  IV. Estimation of Internuclear Distances; The Electronic Structure of Metals, *J. Chem. Educ.,* **42**, 348-355 (1965).

  V. Alfred Werner and the Doctrine of Coordination, *J. Chem. Educ.,* **44**, 512-514 (1967).

  VI. Ion-Packing Models of Covalent Compounds, *J. Chem. Educ.,* **45**, 768-778 (1968).

"The Tetrahedral Atom. I. Enter the Third Dimension," *Chemistry*, **39**, 8-13 (1966).

"The Tetrahedral Atom. II. Valence in Three Dimensions," *Chemistry*, **40**, 8-15 (1967).

"Isoelectronic Systems," *J. Chem. Educ.,* **43**, 170-186 (1966).

"An Appraisal of Valence-Bond Structures and Hybridization in Compounds of the First-Row Elements," *Chem. Rev.,* **61**, 275-311 (1961). (Origin of the *s*-Character Rule)

"Structural Chemistry of Donor-Acceptor Interactions," *Chem. Rev.,* **68**, 587-648, (1968). (An Early Account of Secondary Chemical Affinities' Pair-Pocket Bonds)

"Localized Molecular Orbitals and Bonding in Inorganic Compounds," *Topics in Current Chemistry*, Bd. 14/1, 1-48 (1970). (Overview of Essays I–VI on TSM)

"Chemical Bonding," *Encyclopedia of Physics*, Rita G. Lerner and George L. Trigg, editors, VCH Publishers, Inc., New York, 2nd ed., 1990, pp146-151.

*The Second Law: An Introduction to Classical and Statistical Thermodynamics* (Oxford, 1965). (The First of Four Volumes about General Chemistry in a New Key)

*New Ideas in Chemistry from Fresh Energy for the Periodic Law* (AuthorHouse, 2006).

*MOLECULES and the Chemical Bond* (Volume I: Trafford, 2011).

*FLAMES AND EXPLOSIONS: An Introduction to Teaching General Chemistry from Demonstrations-Experiments* (Trafford, 2014)

# The Author

Formerly professor of physical chemistry at the University of Connecticut and North Carolina State University, professor of inorganic chemistry at the University of Minnesota, and director of Pitt's Van Outreach Program for teaching chemistry for newcomers to chemical thought from demonstration-experiments, Henry Bent is currently a professor emeritus living in Pittsburgh. He is a recipient of several of his nation's leading awards in chemical education; has served as chair of the American Chemical Society's Division of Chemical Education, its Committee on Professional Training, and its Presidential ad hoc Committee on Column Labels for Periodic Tables; is a fellow of the American Association for the Advancement of Science; and author of a well-received book, on *The Second Law: an Introduction to Classical and Statistical Thermodynamics* (Oxford 1966), and approximately one hundred articles on chemistry and chemical education, including a citation classic on hybridization and valence bond structures, leading to "Bent's Rule", and "a breathtakingly clear analysis" (Roald Hoffmann) of inter- and intra-molecular electron pair donor-acceptor interactions.

His most popular public lectures have been on "Flames and Explosions", "Science and Abstract Art", "Einstein and Chemical Thought", "Quantum Theory in Historical Perspective", and, in the 1960s, "Haste Makes Waste, Pollution, and Entropy". He offered the first NSF-supported Chautauqua Short Course for College Teachers, on "Thermodynamics, Art, Poetry, and the Environment", in which he introduced the concept of a Personal Entropy Ethic, a companion to a National Energy Policy.

## THE ENTROPY ETHIC

*Live leanly!*
*Do not create entropy unnecessarily!*
*Conserve transformable forms of energy!*

The admonitions address most aspects of an environmental crisis.

Born in Cambridge, MA, in 1926 and educated at the University of Missouri, Oberlin College (A.B. 1949), and the University of California at Berkeley (Ph.D., physical chemistry, 1952), professor Bent is a member of a family of chemists (father, son, daughter, daughter-in-law, and son-in-law) who vacation at family-built log cabin constructed in the Scandinavian fitted-log style, without power tools, in the Gunflint Trail Corridor through the Boundary Water Canoe Area Wilderness of Northern Minnesota.

During WWII Bent served as a radar technician in the US Navy. For the US Coast Guard he studied the kinetics of the thermal and explosive decomposition of molten ammonium nitrate, for the US Air Force the permeability at elevated temperatures of polyethylene to organic solvents, and for the US Navy the combustion of Nike rockets' double-base nitroglycerin-nitrocellulose propellants and the infrared spectra at liquid helium temperatures of matrix isolated oxides of nitrogen, which led to his current interest in molecules and the chemical bond.

During the red scare in the late 1940s and early 1950s Bent declined to sign a loyalty oath created by the regents at Berkeley for all employees of the University of California: that he was not nor had he ever been a communist. It seemed to be an un-American imposition, especially imposed on an individual who had recently been honorably discharged from the US Navy, where he'd had top secret "Q Clearance". The chemistry department's sole nonsigner of the oath was dismissed from his teaching assistantship (grading papers for professor Giauque's thermo course) and informed by the Dean of the College of Chemistry, professor Joel Hildebrand (his father's research advisor when he was a graduate student at Berkeley in the 1920s), that "Bent, you'll never get ahead that way." Because the department had no immediate replacement for its loyalty-oath non-signer, he continued grading for professor Giauque. Several years later, in a suit brought by distinguished dismissed faculty members, including several famous physicists, the California State Supreme Court ruled that the regents' loyalty oath was unconstitutional, and that dismissed faculty should be reinstated. Pay not paid Bent for services rendered would be today, with interest, a tidy sum.

In his 9th decade Henry's hobbies have changed from reading, gardening, hiking, bicycling, jogging, and canoe camping to the more exciting activity, for him, of exploring the explanatory power of exclusive orbital models of molecules.

He and his wife, Anne, of fifty-five years, have four grandchildren: two granddaughters, one an honor student in animal science, a natural trumpet player, and a steeplechase conference champion, at the University of Vermont, and one a major in human biology and a published undergraduate, of research on hypercardiomyopathy (which killed her father), at Stanford University; and two grandsons, one a chemistry major, a distance runner, and an accomplished cellist, at Macalester College, and one an engineering/material science/computer science major at MIT.

Anne and Henry have enjoyed for many years the companionship of golden retrievers.

After their son Brian died, in 1996, Henry's brother Bob said to him: "Just do something Brian would be proud of." This book may not earn Henry a Nobel Prize. (That was his hope, and perhaps reasonable expectation, for Brian.) But it may come as close to doing so as Henry is able to do.

*MCB* illustrates uses of Exclusive Orbital Models of Molecules. Often that mission may be, in truth, unnecessary. For with ordinary valence stroke diagrams, one is already using schematic representations of packing models of exclusive orbitals. *MCB* merely adds a physical interpretation to those diagrams, in order to increase their usefulness, as approximate, practical representations of molecular electron density *profiles*.

Suggestions welcome. *MCB* is a work in progress. It can use all the help it can get in its engagements with Nature's nature.

Yet to be encoded: interatomic distances in compounds that contain *d*- and *f*-electrons; and also: other structures in which an Exclusion Principle reigns supreme, such as atomic nuclei, where it appears that two protons and two neutrons can be at the same place at the same time, as in an alpha particle, but not three.

Henry.ABent@gmail.com

*A Sketch of a Scientific Autobiography*
# Perceived Errors in Chemistry and Chemical Education

Errors are of two types: omissions and commissions.

Errors of omission include absence of –

- Valence sphere models of molecules.

- Interpretation of valence sphere models as approximate profiles of molecular electron density profiles.

- Systematic symbols for dative bonds.

- A Valence Stroke Termination Rule.

- A Valence Stroke Noncrossing Rule.

- A Generalized Bond Number Equation.

- A Theorem Regarding Bond Angles and Sums of Bond Orders.

- An induction regarding molecular orbitals from the fact that dihydrogen and atomic helium have finite molar volumes, however great the pressure.

- An induction regarding electron pairs based on Lewis' identification of valence strokes and the valence stroke noncrossing rule.

- An induction regarding a Principle of Spatial Exclusion based on first stage ionization energies of atomic hydrogen, helium, and lithium.

- The fact that ethylene is isoelectronic with diborane.

- Consideration of tne electronic structure of the protonated double bond of diborane in discussions of the electronic structure of the double bond of isoelectronic ethylene.

- A model of the electronic structure of calcium metal based on the structure of isoelectronic potassium hydride.

- Consideration of atomic cores' sizes in discussions of "hypervalent" compounds.

- An extensive consilience involving structures of ionic compounds and ionic models of covalent compounds.

- The backstory regarding creation of directional "atomic orbitals".

- A Faraday-Gauss-lines-of-force interpretation of valence stroke diagrams.

- Core-core repulsion model of the *s*-character rule.

- A short name for "electron pair donor-acceptor interactions."

- A pedagogical hierarchy for valence theory, K through graduate school, of progressively more advanced uses of the same fundamental concepts.

- A name for the physical quantity "n" (other than "amount"), such as "population" (of entities) that suggests for newcomers to chemical thought n's physical significance.

- A symbol for the smallest unit of the physical quantity "n" (such as "e").

- An algebraic symbol for the number of atoms in 12 grams of carbon-12, such as "mol" (and, hence, the expression: "mol e = mole").

- A calculus of SI prefixes.

- A systematic procedure for displaying pictorially and for calculating algebraically solutions' proton escaping tendencies.

- Construction of periodic tables from Dobereiner's first triad and its congeners, without use of atomic orbitals and a rule of orbital occupancy.

- A physical interpretation of Lagrange's Multipliers, as partial derivatives of an extremalized function (say S) with respect to constraints (E and n).

- Derivation of the leading equations of statistical thermodynamics without use of calculus or Stirling's approximation

- Bridgman's tables for calculating thermodynamic derivatives.

- A simple, algebraic method for creating Bridgman's tables.

- A set of simple rules for calculation of changes in entropy of purely mechanical systems, thermal reservoirs, and other parts of a universe of discourse.

- Commonplace quantum mechanical features of chemical thought.

- Chemical features of Einstein's thought.

- Teaching general chemistry in the grand inspirational manner, from demonstration-experiments.

- Faculty-mentored students team-teaching general chemistry from demonstration experiments.

Errors of commission include -

– Belief that Gay-Lussac (and Dalton) showed that gas volumes are approximately proportional to the absolute temperature, whereas, in fact, what they discovered was that gas volumes may be used to establish a rational temperature scale.

- Belief that electrons in molecular ground states occupy highly delocalized, mutually overlapping (if orthogonal) orbitals.

- Creation of molecular orbitals from linear combinations of atomic orbitals without taking into account the expression $\Psi(1, 2, \ldots) = -\Psi(2, 1, \ldots)$.

- Belief that molecules with expanded octets are "hypervalent".

- Belief that valence shell electron pair repulsion is the dominant determinate of molecular structure.

- The sigma-pi description of double bonds.

- Attribution of unusual stability of aromatic systems to unusual electron delocalization.

- Ad hoc attribution of instability of aromatic systems with 4n π-electrons to "antiaromaticity".

- Expression of the conservation of energy as $\Delta E = Q + W$, instead of, say -
$$\Delta E_1 + \Delta E_2 + \Delta E_3 = \Delta E(\text{total}) = 0$$
where 1 = a chemical system of particular interest, 2 = the system's thermal surroundings, and 3 = the system's mechanical surroundings.

- A focus on the expression $\Delta G(\text{system}) \leq 0$, which requires that T and P be constant, rather than on the expression $\Delta S(\text{total}) \geq 0$, which holds for any T and P.

- Location of He above Ne in periodic tables, as if the tables were tabulations of the elements as *simple substances*, rather than as *atoms*, arranged according to their *atomic* numbers.

- Use of atomic orbitals, accepted on faith, in explanations of the electronic structure of matter and chemical periodicity, giving, thereby, introductory chemistry courses the character of faith-based courses.

Shown, below, is a fresh connection, by way of the Isoelectronic Principle (IP) and the Superposition Principle (SP), between chemistry's one-dimensional valence stroke, in, e.g., the bond diagram for dihydrogen, and Bohr's two-dimensional, dynamic model of a hydrogen atom.

*From Classical Chemistry and G. N. Lewis to Bohr*

The diameter of a Bohr orbit is the approximate *length* of a carbon-hydrogen bond.
Its circumference represents the approximate *profile* of a carbon-hydrogen bond.

# 3-Electron and 5-Electron Bonds

Chemists have systematic representations for 2-, 4-, and 6-electron bonds: namely, the valence strokes — one, two, and three — of single, double, and triple bonds. Needed for odd-electron bonds are "half-valence strokes", so to speak. Used instead, usually, are three dots.

*Conventional, Unsystematic Dot-Diagrams for Odd-Electron Bonds*

A • • • B                A •••• B

3-Electron Bond          5-Electron Bond

Absent in those Lewis-type dot representations are any indications whatsoever of the bonds' stereochemistry: in particular, their associated nucleophilic bumps and electrophilic dimples. Present, instead, regarding, e.g., the sulfur-based radical cation pictured below, is the remark: *"three electrons are not a crowd"* (1). Implied is the operation of a revolutionary new physical principle.

One can construct a valence stroke diagram for the radical cation by starting with the valence stroke diagram for a well known molecule $F_2SO$, replacing the double bond to O by a double bond to the sulfur atom of the sulfur-containing fragment, and then removing an electron from the sulfur-sulfur double bond. Representing each step by an appropriate valence stroke diagram yields the following figure.

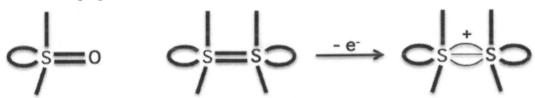

Thick valence strokes represent electron pairs.
Thin valence strokes represent single electrons.

A 3-electron bond is half a single bond superimposed on half a double bond:

$$(1/2)(2e) + (1/2)(4e) = 3e$$

In passing from a double bond to a 3-electron bond, the spin set from which an electron is removed suffers a reorganization.

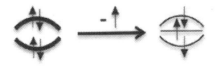

A 5-electron bond, such as occurs in nitric oxide, NO, is half a triple bond superimposed on half a double bond: $(1/2)(6e) + (1/2)(4e) = 5e$.

(1) *C&EN*, October 27, 2014, p25.

# Epilogue

The following remarks by Dirac and C. P. Snow describe *MCB's* principle scientific feature and its leading literary feature.

> *"The underlying physical laws necessary for the mathematical theory of a large part of physics and the whole of chemistry are thus* [with quantum mechanics] *completely known, and the difficulty is only that the exact application of these laws leads to equations much too complicated to be soluble. It therefore becomes desirable that approximate practical methods of applying quantum mechanics should be developed, which can lead to an explanation of the main features of complex atomic systems without too much computation."*
>
> P.A.M. DIRAC

Development of "approximate practical methods" of applying quantum mechanics to chemistry in order to lead to an explanation of the main features of Valence Theory without too much computation is precisely what Conceptual Valence Bond Theory is about. Its style mirrors, accordingly, what has been said of Einstein's style in his famous three papers of 1905, on relativity theory, the photoelectric effect, and Brownian motion.

> *"All of them are written in a style unlike any other theoretical physicist's. They contain very little mathematics. There is a good deal of verbal commentary. The conclusions, the bizarre conclusions, emerge as though with the greatest of ease: the reasoning is unbreakable. It looks as though he had reached the conclusions by pure thought, unaided, without listening to the opinions of others. To a surprisingly large extent, that is precisely what he had done."*
>
> C.P. SNOW

# Index

$Al_2(CH_3)_6$ 39
$Al_4^{-2}$ 207-209
"A fact is a familiar theory" 96
"A" or "the" MO theory? 62
Absolute valence = core charge 89
Accomplishments, of MCVBT 241-242
Acetylene's first excited state 109-110
"Acetylenes are the sweet spot for organic
    chemists" 108
Affinities, active and latent 26
Afterword: "That's it" 243
Alkali halide paradox 156
Alkali metals, proposed electronic structures for
    142-143
Alkaline earth metal gaseous dihalides 224-226
"All Henry has is pictures." 58
"All calculations need as input a molecular
    geometry" 55
"All compounds are ion compounds" 15-17
Allene-HF H-bonded complex 237
Aluminum trimethyl dimer 39
Ammine-$I_2$ charge transfer complex 11
Ammines probed with HX and $I_2$ 235
Ammonia,
    member of a famous isoelectronic family 1
    reason for bond angle 82
Annecdote, about a mathematician 74
Anion lattice,
    analogue of a bond diagram 17
    as a frame of reference 81
Anomalous properties:
    bond angle at C in $Ph_3P=C=Ph_3$ 177-178
    bond angle, $NH_2$ 179-180
    bond lengths, in general 50
    bond length, $NH_4^+$ 181
    $NO^+$ stretching frequency 191
    ring current, aromatic hydrocarbon 141
    structures of LiX(c), X = Cl, Br, I 157
    water-methane hydrogen bond 234
Antiaromaticity, alternative explanations:
    cyclobutadiene 41
    cycloheptatriene anion 133
    cyclopentadienyl cation 130, 132
    cyclopropene anion 129
    oxirene 123
Anticoincidence-assisted dissociation of
    hydrogen peroxide 51
Anticoincident spin sets, in explanation of:
    acetylene's unexpected kinetic stability 108
    alkaline earth metal gaseous dihalide bond
        angles 226
    $Al_4^{-2}$, structure of 207

Anticoincidence (cont.), in explanations of –
    benzene's thermodynamic stability 136
    calcium electride's structure 223
    formaldehydes low BDEs 105
    HOOH's relatively long weak OO bond 51
    Hund's Rule 61
    Hydrogen bonds 233
    LiO distance in $Li_2O$ 150
    naphthalene's bond lengths 139
    nitric oxide's bond length 182
    phosphorus pentahalides' bond lengths 214
    PO bond of $OPF_3$ 216
    structure of $H_3$, $BeH_2^+$, $BH_2$ & $CH_3^{+2}$ 280ff
    triple bonds' character 108
    triplet $O_2$ 59, 203
    unusual methane/water H-bond 234
    water's ionization energies 200-201
Antisymmetric property, of ψ, induction of 262
Appraisal of MO theory of methane 64
Arithmetical model of gaseous $MX_2$ 227
Atom analogy: H:Li::He:Be 246
Aromaticity's 4n + 2 rule 137
Atomic core 10
Atomic cores, p-block, charges and sizes 30
"Atomic helium" 247
Aomic orbitals chemically modified 75-76
Atomic models: 10
Newton, Rutherford-Bohr, Lewis, Linnett, Kimball
    10
Atomic number theorem 38
Atomic orbitals chemically modified 75-76
Atomic orbitals, irrelevance of 74
Atomic s-character, distribution of 277
Axial and equatorial bond length in $PX_5$ 213-214

$BH_2$ 281
$BH_2^+$ 280
$BH_3$ 33, 34, 35
$B_2CH_2$ 161
$B_2(CO)_2$ 165
$B_2H_6$ and the isoelectronic principle 78
$B_2H_6^{-2}$ 144-145
$B_2CH_2$ 161-162
$B_2Cl_4$ 284
$B_2H_2O$ 284
$B_3H_8^{-2}$ 144-145
$B_4H_4$ 43, 174, 175
$B_4H_4^{-2}$ 172-173
$B_4X_4$ structures, special features of 175-176
$B_4H_{10}$ 164
$B_5H_5^{-2}$ 172
$B_5H_9$ 164

317

$B_5H_{11}$  44, 164
$B_6H_6^{-2}$  168
$B_7H_7^{-2}$  170
$B_{12}H_{12}^{-2}$  171
$Be_2$, nonexistent, models of  159
$Be_4$  159
$BeH_2$  280
$BeH_2^+$  280
$Be_4B_4H_4$, proposed structure for  160
$BeF_2$  228
$BeH_2$  33
$B = 4N - V$  39
Back story, of the tetrahedral C atom  3
"Bald and unconvincing narrative"  264
Banana bonds  5
Beautiful color, of $I_2(g)$  12
BeF bonds in gaseous $BeF_2$  228
Bellman, and the truth  276
Bent, Brian E., and construction of VSM  87
"Bent bonds are best"  63, 79
Bent bonds' exposures  86
Bent gaseous alkaline earth dihalides  224
Bent, Henry E., Dennison story  63
Bent or banana bonds  5
Bent's Rule, and -
    ammonium ion's bond lengths  181
    atomic s-character  82, 105, 179, 234
    core-core repulsion  80, 194
    formaldehyde  105
    its history  277
    nn repulsion  80
    pyramidal methane  103
    VSEPR theory  73
Bent's Rule, explanation of  277
$B = 4N - V$  39
"Beware of tidings of delocalization"  136
"Beyond Hydrogen"  268
$BH_3$ dimerization  35
Bicapped polygons  20
Bicyclopentane  134
Bis(triphenylphosphoranylidene)methane  177
Block-to-block trends, in periodic tables  245
Bohr, on profound statements  271
Bohr's aufbau process  91
Bohr's dynamic model of the atom 261
Bond and lone pair numbers  47
Bond angle theorem  49
Bond angles in $H_2SO_4$  253
Bond angles opposite double bonds  82
Bond banishment in MO Theory  274
Bond diagram  18
Bond diagrams for HBCBH  161-162
Bonding across the periodic table  222

Bond lengths  50
Bond Number Equation  39, 47
Bond types, and core sizes  32
Bonds to hydrogen & hydrogen bonds  232-233
Borane-ammonia complex  288
Borane carbonyl: OCBBCO  165
Borazine, nonaromatic character of  166
Born-Oppenheimer Approximation  18
Boron hydrides, multicenter bonding in 163-164
Brief history of LMOs  83
Bump/dimple model of $I_2$-ammine complex  11
Butadiene,
    reduction of, with Na  120-122
    rotamers  116ff

Ca(c)  221-223
$CaB_6$  169
$CH_2$  97
$CH_3$  279
$CH_3^{+2}$  283
$CH_2Cl_2$, number of isomers  4
$CH_2O$ (oxirene)  123-125
$CH_4$  64, 102, 103
    estimated heat of heterolytic dissociation to
        $C^{+4}$ and $H^-$  66-69
    ionization potentials of  65
    Kimball's model vs. VSEPR theory  70
    why tetrahedral?, according to conventional
        wisdom  64-65
$CH_4^+$, electronic structures of  65
$CH_4^{+2}$  283
$CO_2$ dimer  13
$C_2$  106
$C_2H_2$  108
$C_2H_2^+$  109
$C_2H_4$  82, 87
$C_2H_4^{+2}$  111
$C_2O_2$  126-128
$C_3$, with 3-center bonds  107
$C_3H_3^+$  112, 137
$C_3H_4$  39, 129
$C_4H_4$  278
$C_4H_4^{+2}$  137
$C_4H_6$  116-118
$C_5H_6$, 130-132, 134
$C_5H_8$, bicyclopentane  134
$C_7H_8$, anion and cation, stabilities of  133
$C_8H_6$  135
Ca(c), exclusive orbital model of  223
$CaB_6$  169
Cadmium chloride structures  225
Calcium electride plus water  21, 222
Calcium electride, VSM for  221-223

Campbell, Norman: "a most beautiful theory"  3
Carbene ($CH_2$), mechanism of hydrogenation  97
Carbenoids $LiCH_2F$  146-148
Carbon dioxide's dimer, structure of  13
Cardinal rule of valence sphere models  41
Carroll, Lewis, Hunting the Snark  261
Catalogue of types of valence strokes  100
Catalysis, by metals  269
Catalysis, by mobile protons  269
Catalysis, of a Walden inversion  270
Cation, origin of term  95
Caveat, regarding physical models  94
"Change as little as possible"  94
Chain-like dianion $Si(C_4)_2^{-2}$  210-211
Charge cloud model of methane  66-69
Charge cloud models  92
Charge leakage, from anions  157, 158
Charges, of p-block atomic cores  30
Charge transfer complex  11
Chemical bond  24
"Chemical bonding is a highly localized
        phenomenon"  151
"Chemical ideology", Mulliken's turn from  63
"Chemical voodoo"  80
Chemically modified atomic orbitals  75-76
Chinese proverb, concerning fools  261
Christmas lecture, by H. E. Bent  268
Christmas toast, to J. J. Thomson  83
Close packing, of electron domains  22, 267
Closo-boranes $B_nH_n^{-2}$, n = 6-12  167-174
CO from HCO  104
Comparison of valence theories for $O_2$  57
Computational MO theory, steps in  53
"Conceptual garbage in does not necessarily
        mean numerical garbage out"  45
Conceptual Valence Bond Theory,  leading
        accomplishments of  241-242
Configurations of maximum probability  91
Conformers of 1,3-butadiene  119
Conservation of energy, statements of  260
Consilience between -
    bond diagrams and valence sphere models  1
    computational and conceptual valence
        theories  18-19
    structural organic & inorganic chemistry  15,
        274
    VSTR and the Hohenberg-Kohn Theorem  18
Construction of a bond diagram for NOF  10
Converging lines of evidence  90-94
Coordination compound  15
Core-core repulsion, effects of on bond angles
        and bond lengths  81

Core-core repulsion in -
    butadiene  116
    ethylene  82
    HOH, HOF, and FOF  202
Core sizes and bond types  32
Correspondence Principles  15, 89
Coulson, C. A., on –
    MO theory of $O_2$  57
    LCAO method  74
Covalent compound  15, 32
Cowan, R. D., on Hund's Rules  58
Craig, Norman, on $C_4H_6$ rotamers  116-118
Criticisms and refutations  248-252
Critiques, of conceptual MO theory  54, 64, 276
        MOs formulated w/o consideration of a
                Principle of Spatial Exclusion  53
        requirement of a "Z-Matrix"
        unnecessary, incomplete, and misleading  54
Crude theory, yet shrewd  94
Cube, and the tetrahedron  2
Cubical atoms, of Lewis and Linnett  10
Cyclobutadiene dianions, carbon group  113-115
Cyclobutadiene: VSD and VSM  41
Cycloheptatriene's ions, stabilities of  133
Cyclopentadienyl anion and cation  130-132
Cyclopropane, exposure of ring bonds  35
Cyclopropane-HCl H-bonded complex  237
Cyclopropane from ethylene + $CH_2$  98-101
Cyclopropene, unusual acidity of  129
Cyclopropenyl cation, with 3c/2e bond  112

d- and f-electrons in nooks and crannies  77
d-orbitals  22, 84-85
Dangling valence strokes, prohibition against  3
Dative bonding in –
    $B_2(CO)_2$  165
    $BeF_2(g)$  228
    borazine  166
    CO  104, 127
    $CdCl_2/CdI_2$ layer structures  225
    general  24 (Fig. 2), 100
    $H_3BNH_3$  34
    $NO^+$  183
    $NH_4^+$  181
    $N_2O$  194
Debye, Peter, and the man in the street  256
Deltahedral closo-boranes $B_nH_n^{-2}$  167
Dennison, David, on organic chemists  63
Density Functional Theory  23, 37, 38, 81
Departures from spherical electron domains  84
Dependent particle models of matter  91
Dialogue concerning art and science  254

Dialogue concerning two valence systems 248-252

Dications, of small hydrocarbons 282

Dichloromethane: only one isomer! 4

Dihydrogen and -
    absent features of 268
    oxidative addition 36
    transition metal complexes of 230

Dilithium methane 152

Dimer of $CO_2$ 13

Dimer of hypothetical $Be_2$ 159

Dimerization of $CH_2$, mechanism of,
    curly arrow representation 98
    valence sphere model of 98

Dimerization of NF 197

Dimples, hollows, and pockets 8

Dioxygen, in MO theory 57

Distances involving features of a regular
        tetrahedron 149

Divalent oxygen 4

Donor-acceptor interaction, intermolecular, in –
    $(CO_2)_2$ 13
    ethylene-BrCl complex 289
    $I_2/NMe_3$ 11
    $S_N2$ reaction 14

Donor-acceptor interactions, intramolecular, in –
    $C_2H_4^{+2}$ 111
    $C_3$ 107
    FNO 11
    $Si(C_4)_2^{-2}$ 210-211

Donor-acceptor model, of NaCl(c) 156

Double bond,
    bent or banana bond representation 5-7
    from $B_2H_6$ + Isoelectronic Principle 78
    from dimerization of :$CH_2$ 79
    from methane + atomic carbon 79
    four routes to (a summary) 79
    of $OPF_3$ 216

DSDSS: Different Structures for Different Spin
        Sets 19
    acetylenes' triple bonds 108
    alkaline earth metal dihalides 226
    $C_2O_2$ 126
    naphthalene 138-140
    NO 182
    $NO_2$ 192-193

Dynamic delocalized electrons 261


"E = - T" 136

Early math'l descriptions of valence strokes 83

Eclecticism 293

Editors, of bond diagrams and wavefuntions 42

Edmiston-Ruedenberg localization 83

Einstein,
    advice from 291
    and Brownian motion, and atoms 264
    on new ideas 264
    on the finest things in life 42

Electrical neutrality, methods of maintenance, in
        chemical reactions 270

Electride-ion/oxide-ion structural equivalence 15

Electrocyclic reactions 269

Electron cloud, as a frame of reference 14

Electron deficient species 39

Electron localization, by induction and deduction
        264

Electronic armor 29

Electronic kinetic energy 19

Electronic structure of $H_2O^+$ 200-201

Electron Pair Excusion Principle 90

Electrons, dynamic, in static domains 273

Elipsoidal atomic core of $P^{+5}$ of $PF_5$ 214

Emergence of Kimball-like structures 92

English language & VB theory compared 243

EPCN 5 and 6 267

Equatorial and axial bond length in $PX_5$ 213-214

Essence of natural philosophy 95

Essence of organic stereochemistry 1

Ethenedione 126-128

Ethylene-BrCl complex 289

Ethylene-HF H-bonded complex 237

E(total), expression for 71

Excess connectivity 97

Exclusive orbital models of molecules, evidence
        for, reviewed and extended 90-94

Exclusive orbital condition 135

Exclusive orbital model of $Al_4^{-2}$ 207

Exclusive orbitals, shapes of 84

Expanded octet(s) 16, 27, 28, 215, 216, 220

Explanation of Bent's rule 277

Exposure, of bent bonds of small rings 86

Exposure, early, to VSM, of Brian Bent 87

Extraordinary explanatory power 11

Extraordinary stability of $SF_6$ 31

Extra-quantum mechanical principle 60


Face centered cube, two views of 21

Face centered $I_2$/ammine bond 11

Facts, in natural philosophy of Whewell 95

Faraday, experiments with a candle 259

Faraday-Gauss diagram for $H_2CO$ 25

Faraday, lines of force, and valence strokes 24

Fermi holes 60

Fitting hybridization to the facts 75-76

Five-electron species 281

Flat-earthers 96

"Fleas" and flea powder  52
Fluxional phosphorus pentahalides  215
FNO, bond diagram for  40
Fools, follies, and wisdom  304
Formal charges in –
    ammonium ion  181
    borane-ammonia molecular complex 288
    dications  282
Formaldehyde, low BDEs  105
Foster-Boys orbital localization  83
Four-center bond, in $C_4H_4^{+2}$  137
Four-electron species  280
Franklin, Edward  26
From dots to domains  261
Frontier orbitals in conventional VB and MO
        theory  8
Frustrated acid-base pair's reaction with $H_2$  36
Full disclosure  253
Fundamental antithesis of science  95, 293
Fundamental physical forces and MCVBT  80

Gap, between Bohr and Lewis, resolved  273
Gaseous $MX_2$, structures of  224
Gauss' Law  24, 25
General remarks regarding valence theory  56
Generalized bond number equation  39
General principle of induction  84
Geometrical methods  1, 267, 269
Gilbert, W. S.  264
Gimarc, on MO theory  275
Gold, different significations of  247
"Goodies", in MCB  273
Graphic representation of properties of Ψ  46
Grounds for x-rating MO theory  54
Group sizes, in periodic tables, and helium's
        location in them  245

$H_2$  36, 230, 268
$H_3$  280
$H_3^+$  280
$H_4$  64
$H_3BNH_3$  288
HCN  236
HCO  104
HCOOH  236
$H_2B_2O$  284
$H_2CO$  25, 105
$H_2O^+$  200-201
$H_2SO_4$  253
HOF  202
HOON  286
Halide ion monohydrates  231
Hammett, L. P.  29

HBCBH structure  161-162
Hegelian synthesis  261
Heisenberg's recipe  94
Heisenberg's relation  53
Heitler-London  83
Helium above beryllium, in periodic tables  245
Helium whopper  244
Hellman-Feynman Theorem  19, 80, 81, 277
Herschel, William, on science and inductions  95
Heterpolar models of homopolar compounds  15
History of localized molecular orbitals  83
H-K Theorem and VSTR  23
H-K basic lemma, proof by contradiction  37
Hoffmann  144, 227, 241
    acetylene: energy rich, kinetically stable 108
    chemical bonding, measures of 106
    "goodies"  PREFACE
    Letter to  273
Hohenberg-Kohn Theorem  18, 23, 263
Homolytic bond scission  269
Hybrid p-orbitals, & methane's directionality  75
Hydrates of halide ions  231
Hund's Rule(s)  58, 61, 94, 293
Hydrogen bond, water-methane  234
Hydrogen bonds, anticoincidence in  233
Hybrid orbitals, composition and bond angles  6
Hydration of $NO^+$  183-191
Hydrogenation of $CH_2$  97
Hydrogen peroxide's long OO bond  51
Hylleraas' model of He  61, 233
Hypervalent XeNOF?  48

"If you can draw the molecule you can do the
        calculation"  55
$I_2(g)$, $I_2(c)$, and $I_2(soln)$  12
$I_2/NMe_3$ intermolecular complex  11
Imitation, of classical structural theory  264
Impatience/indignation/exasperation  255
Incomplete octets, in small molecules  280-281
Incomplete valence theory  54
Independent particle models of matter  91
Induction,
    general principle of  84
    in Pauling's Nobel Lecture  290-291
    of exclusive orbitals, leading evidence for
        263
Ingold and King, structure of $C_2H_2^+$  109-110
Inner shell  10
"Insertion reaction", of $CH_2$ into $C_2H_4$  98
Interatomic distances  50
Intramolecular donor-acceptor interaction  11
Iodine/ammine molecular complex  11
Iodine, color of, in various solvents  12

Iodine, crystal, bonding in 12
Ionic bond 32
Ionic models of covalent compounds 15
Ionization energies of H, He, and Li 91
Ionization energies of $H_2O^+$ 200-201
Inorganic benzene ($B_3C_3H_6$) 166
"Insertion reaction" 97
Irrelevance of atomic orbitals 74
Isoelectronic 15, 19, 23, 34, 78, 81, 92, 95,
     123, 126, 132, 144, 146, 160, 162, 165,
     166, 195, 199, 203, 221, 223, 224, 228,
     250
Isomers among sulfur species 28
Isomorphism between VSD and VSM 1, 17, 93

James' calculator, bequeathed to H. E. Bent 268
Jensen, Frank, and Z-matrices 55
Jensen, Wm., & chemical pedagogy, of VSM 88
"Joined in progress and runs in circles" 268
"Johnny-come-lately" deductions 264
Joyce, James 268

Kinetic energy, of electrons 19
Kinetic stability of sulfur hexafluoride 31
Kirkus, review of *MCB* 254
Kitchen chemistry 87
Klemperer, $CO_2$ dimer's structure 13
Kockelmans, Joseph, philosophy of science 95
Kohn's Nobel Lecture 37

$LiCH_2F$ 146-148
$LiCO^+$ and $LiOC^+$, structures of 151
$Li_2CH_2$ 152
$LiH_2^+$ 280
$Li_2O(s)$, estimated interatomic distances 150
Language, of valence bond theory 274
Large C—H models 29, 34
Large core species 207-209, 210, 212
Latent affinities 26
Latimer's Rule 16
Lavoisier, precept, on teaching 256
Leading chemical manifestations of fundamental
    physical forces 80
Leading accomplishments of MCVBT 241-242
Leading evidence, for exclusive orbitals 263
Leading induction of MCVBT 60
Letter to Hoffmann 273
Left step periodic table 246
Lewars, Errol, *Modeling Marvels* 125
Lewis dots to Kimball domains? 60
Lewis-like structures 53
Lewis-Linnett-Kimball atomic models 10
Lewis' conclusion, a different route to 25

Lewis' cubical atom 10
Lewis' electron dots: 0 dimensional MOs 83
Lewis's interpretation of bond diagrams 263,
    264
Lewis's static model of the atom 261
Liebman
    butadiene rotamers 118
    Hund's Rule (in jest) 94
    pyramidal methane 103
    "riveting" introduction xix
    $S_4N_4$: comment about its structure 217
Lines of Force 24
*Lingua franca*, of chemistry 93
Linnett's cubical atom 10
LiO distances in $Li_2O$ 150
Liquid ranges 266
Lithiated boron hydrides 144-145
Lithium methyl tetamer 154-155
Lobes of d-orbitals 22
Local electrical neutrality 17, 270
Localized and delocalized orbitals 271
Localized molecular orbitals 1
Locke, John, imperfection of words 247
Logic of induction and deduction 95
Logic, of rabbit-ears 26
Lone pair 17
Lone pairs, delocalized, about large cores, in
    $Al_4^{-2}$ 207-209
    $Si(C_4)_2^{-2}$ 210
    $Si_2H_4$ and $Si_2H_2$ 212
Longest known OO bond 286
"Long live the electron. May it never be of use to
    anyone." 83
"Low end, inexpensive models" 58
Lutidine 36

major simplification of chemical thought 74
Mathematician, anecdote about 74
Mendeleev, on atoms & simple substances 247
Mental images of atoms 10
Metal, electride ion model of 221-222
Metallic bond 32
Methane,
    and hybrid orbitals 75
    appraisal of MO theory of 64-65
    chemical origin of tetrahedral character 4
    dilithium derivative 152
    IPs, interpretations of 65
    pyramidal form 103
methane, viewed as an ion-compound 66-69
Methyl radical, planar or pyramidal? 279
Misleading notation for bonds to hydrogen 232
Misleading valence theory 54

Missing in action  53
Mistakes happen  244
Molar volumes, of $H_2$ & He, significance of  263
Molecular bond number equations  47
Molecular orbital whopper  244
Molecular orbitals for $O_2$  57
"Most beautiful color in chemistry"  12
Most important figures in chemistry  1
MOs for $CH_4$, $NH_3$, $H_2O$, and HF  266
Monohydrates of halide ions  231
Mopping up operations  264
Mulliken. R. S.  2, 11, 63, 253, 273
Multicenter bonds in –
    $Al_4^{-2}$  209
    boron hydrides  163-164
    $C_3H_3^+$ and $C_4H_4^+$  137
    $Ta_6Cl_2^{+2}$  229
"Murky chemical voodoo"  80

Na(c)  142-143
$Na_2$(g)  142-143
$NH_4^+$, dative bonding in  181
$NH_2^+$  281
$NH_n$, n = 1, 2, and 3  179-180
$Ni(CO)_4$  85
$N_2F_2$ properties, explanations of  196-199
$NF_4^+$  181
$N_2O$  194-195
$N_3F$, bond diagrams for  196
NO  182
$NO^+$  183
NOF  11, 40
$NO_2$  192
$NO_3F$, and bond-nobond resonance  285
Napthalene's bond lengths  138-140
Natural Bond Orbital Analysis  92, 272
Natural philosophy according to Herschel  95
Nature of the double bond  5
Neon, models of  10
New bottles, for old wine  1
New life for classical structural theory  85
Newton's atomic model  10
$NH_n$ species, structures of  179-180
Night and day difference between VB and MO
    pictures of a double bond  7
Nitric oxide, bond diagrams for  182
Nitrogen dioxide, large bent bond  192
Nitrosyl fluoride  11
Nitrosyl O-hydroxide  286
Nitrous oxide,
    structure and reactivity  194-195
    azide formation with alkali amides  195
    nn repulsion  80-81

$NO^+$(g) hydration, mechanism of  183-191
Nobel lecture, Kohn  37
Non-linear $Si_2H_2$  212
Non-planar $Si_2H_4$  212
Nuclear-nuclear repulsion and -
    Bent's rule  80, 277
    rotamers of butadiene  116-118
Nucleophilic sites probed with acids  235-240
Nucleus-electron attraction,
    and molecules  71
    and valence theory  80

OClO and ClOO  248-249
$O_2$  57-59
$O_2^-$  203-205
$O_2^+$  59
$O_3^-$  203-205
$O_4^-$  206
$OF_2$  202
$OPF_3$  216
Octahedron, two views of  20
Octet & corresponding non-octet structures  28
Octet rule  1, 16, 23, 39, 60, 92, 71, 92, 167
Octect-rule structures for sulfur  28
Old erroneous induction  152
Old wine, in new bottles  1
Once more: Why is $CH_4$ tetrahedral  275
OO bond lengths, in dioxygen systems  59
OO distances in $O_2$, $O_3$, $O_2^-$, $O_3^-$, and HOOH  204
Operationalism  293
Oracles and Editors  42
Oracle and chemical knowledge  264
Orbital octet rule  220
Organic stereochemistry, in a nutshell  1, 265
Overwhelming  54
Oxacyclopropene  123-125
Oxidative addition  3
Oxide-ion/electride-ion equivalence  92
Oxirene, it elusiveness  123-125

Packing models, of chemical affinity  1, 265, 267
$PCl_3$, unsaturation of  97
Par-affins  29, 34
Particle in a box model, criticism of  136
Particulate models of matter  91
Pauling,
    Nobel Lecture, 1954  290
    on cation-cation repulsion  81
    radii of p block atomic cores  30
    rules of Crystal Chemistry  15-17, 72
Pedagogical hierarchy  88
Pentazole, enigma of nonexistence  287

Periodic System,
   regularities contingent on He/Be 245
   two heliums 246
Periodic table whopper 244
Philosophy of "What if . . . ?" 293
$Ph_3P=C=Ph_3$ (bent at carbon) 177-178
Phosphorus pentahalide bond lengths 213-214
Planar methane 102
Pockets, hollows, and dimples 8
Post-dictions 262
Pragmatism 293
Primary Principles of MCVBT 77
Principal takeway messages 292
Principles of MCVBT 77
Probing nucleophilic sites, with acids 235-240
Problem, for EO Theory: p-orbitals' signs 269
Profound statements, Bohr's view of 271
Proof of H-K Atomic Number Theorem 38
Propane, valence sphere model for 29
Proton/electron-pair principle 78, 81
Protonated 3-center BBB bond? 44
Protonation/deprotonation of electron pairs 89
Pseudopotential 18
Pseudorotation, of $PX_5$ 215
$PX_5$ 213-215
Pyramidal methane 103

Quadrivalent carbon 3
Quartet Rule 58

Rabbit ear representation of lone pairs 23, 26
Radius-ratios for the alkali halides 156
Rattling 30, 67, 102, 145
Reductionism 293
Regions of zero electron density? 52
Regularities contingent on He/Be 245
Reorganization, in ionization of $H_2O$ 200-201
Replacement, of valence strokes, by spheres 8
Resonance, novel examples of
   $B_nH_n^{-2}$ 168
   Ca(c) 223
   cyclic conjugated hydrocarbon 141
   naphthalene 138-140
   $SOF_4$, $SO_3$, and NSN 49
Ring currents, calculated, for cyclic conjugated
   hydrocarbons 141
Ritz Variation Procedure 18
Rioux, Frank, on VSEPR theory 73
Row occupancy rule, in periodic tables 245
Rutherford, on "exact knowledge" 80
Rotamers of 1,3-butadiene 116 - 118
Rutherford-Bohr atomic model 10

$Si(C_4)_2^{-2}$ 210
$Si_2H_2$ 212
$Sl_2H_4$ 212
SNOF 49
$S_4N_4$ 217-219
$SF_6$ 26, 31, 220
$S^{+6}$ valence stroke environments 27
s-Character Rule. See Bent's rule
Schlick, Morritz, on nonvisualizable micro-
   processes 60
Screened and exposed reaction sites 33-36
Secondary affinities, stereochemistry of 267
Secondary principles of MCVBT 77
Self-saturating valence strokes 26
Semi-localized orbitals 85
SF bonds of $SF_6$ 220
$SF_6$, extraordinary kinetic stability of 31
Sharing, of a polyhedrons corners, edges, and
   faces 17
Shrewd theory 94
Sidgwick, Nevil, on valence theories 241, 269
Sincerest form of flattery, for classical valence
   theory 264
Six-electron species 281
"Size [of atomic cores] matters" 113
Sizes, of p-block atomic cores 30
Small- and large-core models of $PX_5$ 213-214
Small molecules, incomplete octets 280
Small-ring strain, and nn repulsion 80
Snark, hunting of 276
$S_N2$ reaction mechanism, model of 14
Somorjai, Gabor 87
Song of the toad xix, 274
s/p hybrid orbitals 6
Space-filling with orbitals' lobes 22
Stand alone valence theory 276
Static domains populated by dynamic electrons
   273
Sterically frustrated D/A interaction 36
Stereochemistry of secondary chemical affinities
   11-12, 93
Steric hindrance, in cyclobutadiene 41
Steric hindrance, inhibition of resonance by 141
Strategies used by e-deficient species 208
Strong form of the Exclusion Principle 59
Structural equivalence of lone pairs and
   protonated pairs 1, 89
structures of –
   FOF, HOF, and HOH 202
   $O_2$, $O_2^-$, $O_3^-$, $O_2M^+O_2^-$, $O_2^-M^+O_3^-$ 203-205
styx numbers for boron hydrides 163
Square planar methane 103

Subatituents, locations of, off single, double, and triple bonds  1
Suggestions for teaching general chemistry  256
Sulfur hexafluoride, extraordinary stability  31
Superposition principle  19
Support for the idea of exclusive orbitals  90-94
Synthesis, of Bohr and Lewis atomic models  261
Systematics, of bond diagram construction  40

$Ta_6Cl_{12}{}^{+2}$  229
Tangent sphere models  20
Test of the Bond Number Equation  229
Teachable topic  87
Teaching from demonstration-experiments  256
Terminal atoms, bonding of  48
Termination Rule, of valence strokes  23
Test, of bond number equation  229
Tetrahedral angle  2
Tetrahedral arrangement, widespread occurrence of  1, 23
Tetrahedral interstice  1, 265
Tetrahedral methane  275
Tetrahedral orbitals and antibonding orbitals  9
Tetrahedral species  1
Tetrahedrane, spring-loaded  278
Tetrahedron and circumscribed cube  2
Tetrahedron, distances between corners, edges, and faces  149
Tetrahedron's back story  3
Tetrahedron: corner-, edge-, & face-sharing  4
Tetrahedron, relation to a cube  2
Tetrasulfur tetranitride, VSM for  217-219
"That's it", an afterword  243
The chemical bond  261
"The cat [let] out of the bag"  55
THE induction of MCVBT  60
"The models work!"  263
"THE" MO theory?  62
"The most beautiful color in chemistry"  12
Theory and fact according to Whewell  96
Thermodynamics, in a nutshell  260
Thesis, Antithesis, and Synthesis  261
Third dimension, in structural chemistry  4
Thomson and Tait, on geometrical methods  1
Thomson, J. J., Christmas toast to  87
Thoreau, song of the toad  xix
Three-center AlCAl bonds  39
Three-electron species  280
Toad, song of  (See INTRODUCTION)
To be useful a model must be wrong in some respects  94
"To whom is a fact a fact?"  96
Transferability of bond properties  92

Trend in bonding across the periodic table  222
Triad locations in periodic tables  245
Trial, error, and improvement  293
Trial functions, numbers of  93
Tricyclopentane  134
Triple bonds: energy-rich, kinetically stable  108
Truncated MO theory  64
Two cultures, existence of  254
Two-electron species  280
Two familiar facts  3
Two heliums, and periodic tables  247
Tuition refund, request for  73

"Ultimate oracle of chemical knowledge"  42
Understanding, Wittgenstein on  15
Unexpected critiques, of MO theory  276
Unfairness, to Mulliken?  253
Universe of discourse, in thermodynamics  260
Unnecessary valence theory  54
Unsaturation and hydrogenation  97
US Review of Books, review of *MCB*  271

Valence bond systematics, illustrated with –
    $Al_2(CH_3)_2$  39
    $B_2CH_2$  161
    Boron hydrides  43, 44, 163
    NOF  40
    XeNOF  48
Valence of H, O, and C, origin of  3
Valence shell  10
Valence Shell Electron Pair Repulsion Theory (see VSEPR)
Valence-shell-filling strategies used by electron deficient species  208
Valence sphere existence theorem  135
Valence sphere model of a metal  221-223
Valence Stroke Exclusion Principle  90
Valence Stroke Termination Rule  17, 23, 263
Valence-Stroke-Diagram/Valence-Sphere-Model Isomorphism  1, 17
Valence stroke environments of $S^{+6}$  27
Valence strokes, different types of  100
Valence strokes, replacement of, by valence spheres  1, 267
Valence strokes, viewed as representations of localized MOs  1
Valence theories, computational and conceptual, compared  42
Valence theory and the exclusion principle  92
Valence theory and the word "bond"  274
van der Waals' dimer of $CO_2$  13
van't Hoff's induction  4
Variable valence, and Edward Franklin  26

Variation theorem  45, 93, 272

VB Theory, what it's been about  264

Virial Theorem  19, 80, 136

Visual puns with tangent sphere models  20

V(ne): the term responsible for molecules  71

VSEPR theory,
    appraisal of  71
    comparison with Kimball's model, for $CH_4$  70

VSTR and Hohenberg-Kohn Theorem  23


Walden Inversion,
    catalysis of  270
    valence sphere model of  14

Water molecules, catalysis by  270

Water: bond diagram for its ion $H_2O^+$  200-201

Water-HF H-bond  239

Wave functions and the Variation Theorem  45

Weinhold  11, 37, 76, 83, 151, 232, 234
    Bent's Rule/VSEPR Theory comparison  73
    charge leakage from anions  158
    Introductory remarks. *See* Foreword
    unusual water/methane H-Bond  234
    molecular orbitals, assessment of 54
    Natural Bond Orbitals  92
    Oracle of theoretical chemistry 42
    resonance for $B_{12}H_{12}^{-2}$  171

"What's going on here?"  257

"Where are your equations?"  46

"Where are your predictions?" 262

Whewell, William,
    advisor to Faraday regarding terminology  95
    brief biography of, by Kockelmans 95
    fundamental antithesis of science  95
    on theories and facts  96

Whitehead, A. N., & one's own true trade  256

Whoppers, in chemical thought  244

"Why are methane molecules tetrahedral?"  64, 275

Why does $B_4Cl_4$ exist but not $B_4H_4$?  175-176

Willful departure from "chemical ideology"  63

Wittgenstein, on understanding  15

Woodward and Hoffman  269

Wrong turn, by Mulliken?  63


XeNOF  48

X-rate MO theory, in general chemistry?  54


Yin Yang symbol and MCVBT  46


Zero electron density, regions of?  52

Z-matrices  55, 272

# Drawings of Approximate Molecular Electron Density Profiles
## Listed in Order of Appearance

Methane 1
Ethane, ethene, ethyne 1
Ammonia, water, HF 1, 266
Neon 10
Nitrosyl fluoride (FNO) 11
$I_2/N(Me)_3$ complex 11
Carbon dioxide dimer 13
$S_N2$ reaction 14
Ethane, ethene, ethyne 17
Octet 23
$C_2H_6$: large C—H model 29
A par-affin 29
$C_3H_8$: large C—H model 29
Sulfur hexafluoride 31
$BeH_2$ and $BH_3$ 33
$BH_3 + NH_3$ 34
$H_2$ and He 35
Cyclopropane 35
$2 CH_2 = C_2H_4$ 35, 98
t-butyl group 3
Cyclobutadiene 41
$B_6I_{11}$ isomers 44
$SOF_4$ 49
$SO_3$ 49
NSN 49
$SO_2F_2$ 49
SNOF 49
Triplet dioxygen 58
$CH_4$: Ionic models 70
$B_2H_6$ and $C_2H_4$ 78
$H_2CH_2 + :C: = H_2C=CH_2$ 79
$P^{+5}$ 84
$d^{10}$ ion 85
Cyclobutane 86
Cyclomethane 86
$:CH_2 + H—H = CH4$ 97
$C_2H_4 + :CH_2 = cyclo-C_3H_6$ 99
Planar methane 102-103
$C_2$ 106
CCC (& HBCBH) 107
Acetylene 108
Excited state of $C_2H_2$ 109
$C_2H_4^{+2}$ 111
$C_3H_3^+$ 112, 137
$R_4S_4^{-2}$ 113-115
$R_4Ge_2Si_2^{-2}$ 115
Butadiene conformers 119
Oxacyclopropene 123-125
OCCO = 2 CO 126-128

Cyclopropene 129
Cyclopentadiene 131
Tricyclopentane 134
Bicyclopentane 134
Bicyclopentalene 135
$C_4H_4^{+2}$ 137
Alkali metal dimers 142-143
Lithiated boron hydrides 145ff
$LiCH_2F$ isomers 146-148
$Li_2O$ 150
$LiCO^+$ and $LiOC^+$ 151
$Li_2CH_2$ 152-153
$(LiMe)_4$ 154-155
NaCl structure 156
LiX, charge leakage 158-159
$Be_4B_4H_8$ 160
$B_4H_{10}$ 164
$B_5H_9$ 164
$B_5H_{11}$ 164
$CaB_6$ 169
$B_7H_7^{-2}$ 170
$B_5H_5^{2}$ 172
$[B_4H_4]$ 172
$B_4H_4^{-2}$ 173
$B_4Cl_4$ 174, 175-176
$Ph_3P=C=PPh_3$ 177-178
$NO^+$ 183
$NO^+ + H_2O = HNO_2 + H^+$ 183
$NO_2$ 193
NNO 194
$2 NF = FNNF$ 197
$FNNF = FF + NN$ 198-199
FOF 202
OO 203
$O_2^{-1} + M^+ = MO_2$ 205
$Al_4^{-2}$ 207-209
$Si(C_4)^{-2}$ 211
$Si_2H_4$ 212
$Si_2H_2$ 212
$PX_5$ 213-215
$S_4N_4$ 218-219
$SF_6$ 220
$Ca+2H_2O = Ca(OH)_2+H_2$ 222
Ca 223
Bent gaseous dihalides 226
FBeF(g) 228
$Ta_6Cl_{12}^{+2}$ 229
Dihydrogen complexes 230
Halide ion monohydrates 231

Hydrogen bond 233
$H_3N: + HX$ 235
HCN 236
$(HCN)_n$ 236
$2 HOH = (HOH)_2$ 236
Cyclopropane + HCl 237
But-3-en-1-yne + HCl 238
HOH + HF 239-240
$H_2SO_4$ 253
EPCN 4, 5, 6 267
Tetrahedrane 278
$H_3^+$ 280
$LiH_2^+$ 280
$H_3$ 280
$BeH_2^+$ 280
$BeH_2$ 280
$BH_2^+$ 280
$BH_2$ 280
$CH_3^{+2}$ 283
$CH_4^{+2}$ 283
$H_2B_2O$ 284
$NO_3F$ 285
Pentazole 287
$ClBr/C_2H_2$ complex 289

# Bond Diagrams

Each bond diagram in *MCB* is an answer to a question: Given a molecule's *molecular formula*, what is its bond diagram? *MCB* may be viewed, accordingly, as a self-instruction manual for construction of bond diagrams.

Methane 1, 2, 66
Ethane, ethene, ethyne 1
Ammonia, water, HF 1, 266
Neon 10
Nitrosyl fluoride (FNO) 11
$I_2/N(Me)_3$ complex 11
Carbon dioxide dimer 13
Ethane, ethene, ethyne 17
$H_2CO$ 25, 104
$SF_6$, $SF_4$, and $SF_2$ 26
Octet & expanded octets 28
$BH_3 + NH_3$ 34
$H_2$ and He 35
Cyclopropane 35
$Al_2Me_6$ 39
FNO 40
Cyclobutadiene 41
$B_4H_4$ 43
$B_5H_{11}$ isomers 44
XeNOF 48
$H_2O_2$ 51
$O_2$ 54, 58
$B_2H_6$ and $C_2H_4$ 79
2 $CH_2 = H_2C{=}CH_2$ 98
$C_2H_4 + CH_2 = c{-}C_3H_6$ 99
Planar methane 103
HCO 104
CO 104
$C_2$ 106
CCC (& HBCBH) 107
Acetylene 109
Excited state of $C_2H_2$ 110
$C_2H_4^{+2}$ 111
$C_3H_3^{+}$ 112, 137
$R_4S_4^{-2}$ 113
$R_4Ge_2Si_2^{-2}$ 115
Butadiene conformers 116
Oxacyclopropene 123
OCCO = 2 126
OCCCNH 127
Cyclopropene 129
Cyclopentadiene 130
Cyclopentadiene anion 133
Cycloheptadiene anion 133
Tricyclopentane 134
Bicyclopentane 134

Bicyclopentalene 135
Napthalene 137-139
$C_4H_4^{+2}$ 137
$Li_2CH_2$ 152
HBCBH 161-162
$B_4H_{10}$ 164
$B_5H_9$ 164
$B_5H_{11}$ 164
Borazine 166
$B_5H_5^{-2}$ 172
$[B_4H_4]$ 172
$B_4H_4^{-2}$ 173
$Ph_3P{=}C{=}PPh_3$ 177
NH, $NH_2$, and $NH_3$ 180
$NH_4^{+}$ and $NF_4^{+}$ 181
$NO^{+}$ 183
HONO 188
NNO 194
NNNF 196
FNNF 197
NNF 199
$H_2O^{+}$ 201
FOF and HOF 202
$O_2$ and $O_2^{-}$ 203
$O_3$ and $O_3^{-}$ 303
$O_4^{-}$ 206
$Si(C_4)^{-2}$ 210
$PX_5$ 213, 215
$S_4N_4$ 217
$SF_6$ 220
FBeF(g) 228
$Ta_6Cl_{12}^{+2}$ 229
Halide ion monohydrates 231
$H_3N{:} + HX$ 235
HCN 236
$(HCN)_n$ 236
2 HOH = $(HOH)_2$ 236
Cyclopropane + HCl 237
$H_2C{=}C{=}CH_2 + HF$ 237
But-3-en-1-yne + HCl 238
HOH + HF 239-240
EPCN 4, 5, 6 267
Hydrated $S_N2$ reaction 270
Tetrahedrane 278
$H_3^{+}$ 280
$LiH_2^{+}$ 280

$BeH_2$ 280
$CH_2$ and $NH_2^{+}$ 281
$CH_2^{+2}$ 282
$CH_3^{+2}$ 283
$CH_4^{+2}$ 283
$H_2B_2O$ 284
$NO_3F$ 285
Pentazole 287
HOON 286
$H_3BNH_3$ 288
ClBr/$C_2H_2$ complex 289

# The Triangle of Valence Theory

Chemistry has three kinds of molecular icons:  Molecular Formulas
Valence Stroke Molecular Diagrams
Valence Sphere Molecular Models

They can be linked to each other by arrows in six ways.

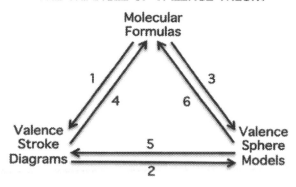

THE TRIANGLE OF VALENCE THEORY

Each arrow signifies an exercise.

### 1. Creation of Bond Diagrams from Molecular Formulas

Frequently executed by chemists and chemistry students. A leading feature of *MCB*. Systematized via use of Bond Number and Valence Stroke Termination Rules.

### 2. Production of Valence Sphere Models from Bond Diagrams

Executed by substitution of hard spheres for non-crossing valence strokes. Produced are approximate electron density profiles. A second major feature of *MCB*.

### 3. Creation of Valence Sphere Models from Molecular Formulas

Executed in *MCB* via arrows 1 and 2. Executed in computational chemistry by calculation of wavefunctions, followed by electron localization procedures.

### 4. Creation of Molecular Formulas from Bond Diagrams

By inspection. Simple when working from full bond diagrams. More challenging—yet suitable for newcomers to chemical thought—when working from abbreviated bond diagrams.

### 5. Creation of Bond Diagrams from Valence Sphere Models

Executed by replacing valence spheres by straight, bent, or rabbit-eared valence strokes, according to a few elementary conventions.

### 6. Creation of Molecular Formulas from Valence Sphere models

Requires use of a valence-sphere-analogue of the Valence Stroke Termination Rule. Yields chemical labels for Valence Sphere Models.

Exercises' Order of Difficulty

$$4 \ll 5 \approx 6 < 1 < 2 \ll 3$$

4: for beginners; 5 & 6: for high school chemistry students; 1 & 2: for college chemistry students; 3 for computer-and-chemical-savvy investigators, someday?